Global Corporations
and Sovereign Nations

Global Corporations and Sovereign Nations

Collision or Cooperation?

DAVID J. SAARI

QUORUM BOOKS
Westport, Connecticut • London

Library of Congress Cataloging-in-Publication Data

Saari, David J.
    Global corporations and sovereign nations : collision or
cooperation? / David J. Saari.
        p.   cm.
    Includes bibliographical references and indexes.
    ISBN 1–56720–205–5 (alk. paper)
    1. Investments, Foreign.   2. Investments.   3. Trade regulation.   4.
Democracy.   5. Representative government and representation.   6.
Competition, International.   I. Title.
HG4538.S16   1999
332.67'314—dc21   98–41036

British Library Cataloguing in Publication Data is available.

Library of Congress Catalog Card Number: 98–41036
ISBN: 1–56720–205–5

First published in 1999

Quorum Books, 88 Post Road West, Westport, CT 06881
An imprint of Greenwood Publishing Group, Inc.
www.quorumbooks.com

Printed in the United States of America

The paper used in this book complies with the
Permanent Paper Standard issued by the National
Information Standards Organization (Z39.48–1984).

10 9 8 7 6 5 4 3 2 1

To Martha, to many colleagues and
friends who helped, to the authors
whose work stimulated me, and to students,
colleagues and others at American University
and elsewhere over the last seven years.

The large corporation fits oddly into democratic theory and visions. Indeed, it does not fit. (Lindblom, 1977)

In truth, it [nationalism] flourishes as an expression of the antinomian passion which is the deepest drive of the age. (Barzun, 1989)

The global corporation, adrift from its national political moorings and roaming an increasingly borderless world market, is a myth. States charter MNCs and shape the operating environment in which they flourish. States retain the political authority to steer their activities. (Doremus, Keller, Pauly and Reich, 1998)

The barbarism implicit in the restless energies of big-time, global capitalism requires some sort of check or balance, if not by a spiritual doctrine or impulse, then by a lively interest in (or practice of) democratic government. (Lapham, 1997)

But perhaps the biggest challenge posed by globalization is the one facing national governments and regulators. "One of the big issues of government now, is to figure out what kind of cooperative legal regimes are needed to provide a stable foundation," said author Yergin. (Daniel Yergin, co-author of *The Commanding Heights* (1998) in an interview by Martha M. Hamilton, "Going Global: A World of Difference," *Washington Post*, May 10, 1998: H-1, H-5)

Contents

Preface and Acknowledgments

If you want to think of a recent real-world problem to which this book addresses itself, please consider, as one example, the U.S. labor fight of General Motors (GM) and the United Automobile Workers' (UAW) strike in 1998. Labor relations "on the rocks" was the situation in mid-1998. General Motors is one of the largest globalizing corporations in the world—inside and outside the United States. The union raised the basic question: Why not invest GM capital profits in Flint, Michigan plants?, as was apparently promised by GM. In a similar way, the present volume asks: *Who is to decide where to invest profits?* This book's inquiry raises nearly the identical question to the one raised by the unions with GM.

Answers to that question are offered in the nine chapters that follow. No matter how the GM–UAW strike was settled, that critical investment question will remain a matter for both labor relations and for domestic and global public policy. Workers in every nation should be concerned, including managers and shareholders of giant global companies. Hopefully, this book will contribute to a clarification of the policy debate and suggest ways to resolve what is essentially an *open* question: Who is to decide where to invest profits?

While brief, my acknowledgements express my deep gratitude to all who have helped me to design and shape this book over the last seven years. It is grounded upon the work of others and is intended as a tribute to those found in the bibliography—an intelligent, very thoughtful and hard-working group of writers grappling with the toughest issues of life. Some of them may agree or disagree with this book, and that reaction is to be expected.

Closer to home, I wish to acknowledge the support of American University, Michele Provost, Karen Woodcock, Peter Lepsch and many graduate students whose criticisms improved the book. Parts of it in draft form have been used in classes; and thanks are due Eric Valentine, publisher of Quorum Books, who did what authors like most—he offered suggestions in a writer-friendly manner. My wife, Martha, put up so gracefully with all that a writer's life dishes out that I owe her a special thanks with love for understanding and help in countless ways. For the shortcomings of the book, please look kindly to the author alone.

Acronyms

ABC	American Broadcasting Company
ADM	Archer Daniels Midland, Inc.
AT&T	Atlantic Telephone & Telegraph
BCCI	Bank of Credit and Commerce International
BEA	Bureau of Economic Analysis
BRT	Business Roundtable
CBS	Columbia Broadcasting System
CFC	Chlorofluorocarbon
CL	Credit Lyonnais (French bank)
CNN	Cable News Network
ESOP	Employee Stock Option Plan
EU	European Union
FBI	Federal Bureau of Investigation
FCPA	Foreign Corrupt Practices Act (1977)
FDI	Foreign Direct Investment
GAO	General Accounting Office
GM	General Motors
IBM	International Business Machines
ILO	International Labour Organization
IMF	International Monetary Fund
IRS	Internal Revenue Service
ITT	International Telephone & Telegraph

MAI	Multilateral Agreement on Investments
MFN	Most Favored Nation
MGM	Metro-Goldwyn Mayer
MIC	Methyl isocyanate (pesticide)
MLAT	Mutual Legal Assistance Treaty
MM	*Multinational Monitor*
MNC	Multinational Corporation
MNE	Multinational Enterprise
NAFTA	North American Free Trade Agreement
NBC	National Broadcasting Company
NGO	Non-Governmental Organization
NIJ	National Institute of Justice
NYT	*New York Times*
OAS	Organization of American States
OECD	Organization for Economic Cooperation and Development
OTA	Office of Technology Assessment
PAC	Political Action Committee
PBS	Public Broadcasting System
RCA	Radio Corporation of America
RICO	Racketeering Influenced and Corrupt Organizations Act
SEC	Securities and Exchange Commission
TIAA-CREF	Teachers Insurance and Annuity Association—College Retirement Equities Fund
TNC	Transnational Corporation
TNEC	Temporary National Economic Commission
UAW	United Auto Workers
UCIL	Union Carbide (India) Ltd.
UN	United Nations
UNCTAD	UN Conference on Trade and Development
UNCTC	UN Center on Transnational Corporations
USTR	United States Trade Representative
WP	*Washington Post*
WSJ	*Wall Street Journal*
WTO	World Trade Organization

Chapter 1

Introduction:
An Eye on the Ball—*Fortune* 500
Globalizing Corporations

CONNECTING THE DOTS: DEMOCRATIC GLOBALISM'S BIG JOB

> [It is] . . . very, very empowering to realize that so many of the crises we see around us are related, are connected. [This realization is] . . . one of the most empowering things that can happen to us.
>
> Helena Norberg-Hodge, Third International Forum on
> Globalization, Berkeley, California, April 1997

These words of deep insight are from the Swedish philosopher, teacher, linguist, author and activist Helena Norberg-Hodge, who has been a warrior for the last three decades fighting for cultural diversity on three continents. Why war? Cultural monocultures being designed and pushed by corporate globalizers are literally tearing apart local communities; thus her noble goal is to reweave our spiritual healing connection to the natural world so that we will reconnect to place and to nature once again. This book, too, as one of many efforts to get at the truth of the human global condition, addresses itself to citizens of the world's democracies to help them empower themselves as sovereign citizens. Once empowered, citizens may begin to reweave the fabric of community, and by so doing, reassert the paramount power of the people in a democracy (Resnick, 1997). "We need to start addressing questions of governance at the global level" (Resnick, 1997: 5).

The argument is that each citizen must begin to connect the dots to see clearly the genuinely big picture of reality found in the relationships of 750 giant corporations operating in 185 nations. This is empowering in itself. Virtually no help is given to us by the mass media, by higher education and by many other sources to connect the dots. Each citizen must decide to become a generalist in order to understand this big picture. That means one must abandon an easier, but ultimately more dangerous, course that could be described by words such as tunnel vision, cubicle vision, mental slavery, or specialist's mentality—all of which attempt to dominate our thinking in the world today. We must insist that each of us attain "the knowing of things together," as William James, one of America's great psychologists and philosophers, described it in his essay (James, 1992). We know the constellation Orion, the taste of lemonade and the sight of a friend. This is knowing things together.

By knowing things together or knowing the big picture, we find a direct path to empowering ourselves to become better sovereign citizens who, after all, are the underlying premise of a democracy. However, there is a constant threat. Five hundred years of disempowerment found in the goals of colonialism, found in the current efforts to recolonize the world and found in specialism require fitting one's life into someone else's world view and plan. That must now be rejected (Raghavan, 1990).

As will be illustrated throughout this book, we are now discovering, especially in the last 15 to 20 years, that much of corporate globalization is merely modern colonialism refashioned as a form of capitalism that opts for centralization of command in giant corporations just as communism did in government, and both are headed for the trash heap of history. "Imperialism (colonialism) has no proponents left; racism as an official policy is restricted to the southern tip of Africa; and capitalism has been so modified that it is at many points indistinguishable from communism, itself also hybridized" (Barzun, 1989: 169). The World Trade Organization (WTO) is a prime example of senseless centralization that even one of its creators, Mickey Kantor, found worrisome:

"This is about sovereignty, multinational corporations, the new post-cold-war world, global standards and international harmonization," said Mickey Kantor, chief trade negotiator and Commerce Secretary for President Clinton during his first term. "These are very important issues. But it is like they are being dealt with in a closet somewhere and no one's watching." (Jeff Gerth, "Where Business Rules," *New York Times*, January 9, 1998)

Who should be watching the WTO? If they become empowered again, citizens of nations, the great middle classes of all societies, will begin to connect the dots and then take practical steps to reassert their individual political sovereignty against all usurpers.

The dots to be connected will illustrate clearly the utopia offered by corporate globalizers, but the dots the utopians deliberately omit are included in this book because they are so significant.

Here are some of the omitted dots to be connected, through this book, in your thinking:

- Environmental destruction
- Business corruption, fraud and crimes
- Excessive financial speculation in money and the global social instability created by it
- The exploitation of labor and abandonment by downsizing and outsourcing of labor and their desperate search for work and its connection to migration
- Potential food shortages caused by failures of monoculture crops
- Debasing of all professions by commercial market norms
- Striking workers across the globe
- Disease outbreaks related to global transport of food and people
- Loss of indigenous tribes
- Thoughtless and wasteful international trade
- Useless global homogeneity and deadening, stifling growth
- Needless and excessive patenting of seeds and other life forms
- Dangerous global warming
- An end to oil in 40 years

Many people, including those in the media, do not begin to see the big picture because they fail to grasp the brazen political implications of the corporate ideology of restructuring, privatization, deregulation and dismantling of democratic rule. Many fail to see that such an ideology is not inevitable, but rather, it is merely centralized and utopian in the same way as communism. Corporate globalizers spread the model of *inevitable, even imperative undemocratic globalization* and they look back over the last 500 years of colonization and say that it was good work. But who benefitted? And who will benefit in the future (Sakamoto, 1994)?

By contrast, spreading the model of democratic globalization, as this book does, will mean abandonment of colonial mentality, and it will mean getting rid of those in power in government and in business whose views are destructive to labor, to the environment and to democracy. It will mean pressing forward with a new moral force to reconnect the right dots to form a new paradigm of the people in power in a democracy. These informed citizens will serve their own ends, not the corporate global ends of wasteful consumption and consumerism that merely make the rich even more wealthy. Furthermore, many believe that both left and right no longer mean much politically, since both would further centralize global authority, both would rape the natural world, and both would destroy the local community. Some of the finest politicians on earth have been seduced and duped into supporting undemocratic globalization. As Jim Hightower noted in his recent book, "Some say we need a third party. I say we need a second one" (Hightower, 1997).

The truth is that the political parties today do mask a single party in the United States. It's the Corporate Party; and we are on the way to the corporate planet. Joshua Karliner, in his book *The Corporate Planet*, outlined what such a world is like in reality from the corporate perspectives of Chevron and Mitsubishi (Karliner, 1997).

Drawing these initial arguments together suggests that empowering the people, the ordinary people, in a democracy is still regarded as a work of political subversion, just as it seemed long ago to the kings and queens of Europe. The current plutocratic, corporate order resents the intrusion of the people into business affairs and such plutocrats are even more resentful if the people want a powerful voice in international trade rules, practices and regulations. "What do *they* know" is often what you hear behind the scenes. But the people do not need corporate fronts masquerading as political interest groups; the people do not need corporate mucking around in the initiative and referendum process. Corporate treasuries should not be spent on campaigns of politicians; those dollars should be declared to be dividends and sent to the shareholders, the owners. These topics get more attention later on in this book, but they evoke a feeling of an immense agenda that will take forever to accomplish. As Maude Barlow, a Canadian activist, said, "What else have we got to do?" And as William Greider, an American journalist and author, asked in 1992, *Who Will Tell the People*? The work on this book was undertaken with that same spirit. The second major theme must be stated at the outset and it is equally important.

PERPETUAL SEPARATION FROM AND SUBORDINATION OF CORPORATIONS TO THE PEOPLE AND TO THEIR STATE

Ralph Nader and Wesley Smith, in their book *No Contest* (1996), referred to the stretching of corporate sovereignty and the shrinking of public places:

Few ambitions were greater than those of the corporate trade attorneys who conceptualized the charter of the World Trade Organization (WTO) within the General Agreement on Tariffs and Trade (GATT). . . . Even more creative corporate legal strategies are being designed to help companies escape national jurisdictions, allowing them to choose the most favorable rules, including those of brutal or corrupt regimes, under which to operate. (Nader and Smith, 1996: xxv, xxvi)

Few statesmen would be happy with this state of world affairs. Escaping state jurisdictions in the United States has now escalated to the international level for American corporations, but the reality is that this has always been the case, as you will see later on in this book, especially in Chapter 8. Recognizing that there is the escapist mentality, a major theme of this book is to search for new ways to separate corporations from public authority and to subordinate corporations, once again, to the democratic will of the people and their state. There should be no escape.

The idea of separation of power is designed to allow democracy to thrive in a society. There are two areas that deserve to be mentioned: one is church and state separation and the other is separation of the powers of governments into three branches, a clear anti-monarchical tool of the people. Churches are not states and states are not churches, but this was not always so, and many who left England where the two were blended in the 1600s were persecuted for their ideas about religion. Those who left England envisioned a world where church and state were kept separate. The outcome was long experience in separation and its daily significance. When the Catholic Church and Protestant sects were finally separated from the state, religious war was reduced. The executive branch is not the legislature, nor is the judicial branch. This, too, is part of the American experiment. The rationale for keeping three branches of one government is to avoid tyranny. The rationale for separation of corporations and subordinating them to the nation-state is exactly the same justification—to halt corporate tyranny. People learned the wisdom of keeping the church and state apart, and anyone who hates tyranny must love separation of powers of government so that it cannot gang up on the people.

Just as the people learned to accept the two separations just mentioned, they must learn again the wisdom of separation of corporations from the public affairs of the people and their government. This basic principle of democratic governance is explored in some depth later on. However, as Nader and Smith noted, the separation of corporation and state is breaking down under the pressure of clever international schemes (like the WTO) to evade public order and public control of the people in a national society. The goal is to substitute corporate order and control of the people. The argument is that clear public order must prevail by subordinating all corporations to the state in every way possible. Separation of corporations is vital to preserve the power of the people to govern themselves. Corporate governance that is clearly subordinated and separated from the state should remain the constitutional norm for all democratic nations where popular sovereignty reigns.

The nature of this inquiry into the relationship of 185 nations to 750 giant corporations is a trip into a rather mysterious world of economic, social, political and legal power spread out among the elite inside nations and corporations that globalize. It will be important not to lose sight of the central inquiry point of the book—*can 185 nations allow 750 giant corporations to invest the profits of the corporations solely in a way that they see fit—or must public authority of 185 nations be used to check, structure and confine investment decisions by 750 giant corporations as they move about the globe?* It is clear that capitalism in its wildest free-enterprise form yearns for no restraint by nations. But there are many forms of capitalism and not all are wild. There are many ways to restrain and guide investment decisions. This requires a deeper analysis in subsequent chapters.

In Part I, we shall examine the meaning of globalizing corporations and popular national sovereignty, then move to capitalism and political characteristics of corporations. Appendix B examines more in depth the corporate data. In Part

Figure 1-1
Mankoff Cartoon

"And, in a move sure to attract the attention of regulators, the private sector made a bid to acquire the public sector."

II, Chapters 6 and 7 focus on the trade and investment practices and policies of giant corporations. Regulation, taxation and finance are significant crosscutting themes. Chapter 7 studies the human side of the millions of people who work for the giant globalizers and then get downsized in the effort to be lean and mean, or, as the late David Gordon put it, becoming fat and mean as the century closes. In Part III, Chapter 8 reveals the troubled civil legal personality of a giant multinational corporation and all of its family of subordinate subsidiary corporations, joint ventures, alliances and other ties across the world. Chapter 9 explores the negative side of the globalizing corporation, perhaps best characterized as the dark side of transnational crimes emerging from globalizing corporations. The ethical and moral issues rise with great force. We do need to be aware of different perceptions of business success not merely as a simple, single measure of 20% profitability rising year after year—forever, or being number one or two in any line of business (a goal of General Electric in the United States).

Finally, in Part IV, Chapter 10, the chickens come home to roost for casino capitalism. In the era of the last 100 years of astounding material growth, only a handful of the extremely prosperous nations (no more than 20 by most measures), with only 1.5 to 2 billion people compared with the rest of the world's people, have struck it rich. Since few, if any, of the remaining nations could ever hope to achieve the material wealth of the United States or Switzerland, what will be the future of the relationship of 185 nations to 750 globalizing corporations? Can the last 100 years of material growth be repeated in the future during the next 100 years? Are there no limits to material growth and material prosperity for 3 to 4 billion other people on earth who are not highly wealthy? By 2039—in 40 years, when oil runs out—what then? It is in this context that the key issue for regulated capitalism will be reached. *Who is to decide where to invest profits? That issue will become the paramount issue of the next century to be battled out on many fronts.* The issues flowing from that single investment issue will suggest rapid expansion of regulatory capitalism that seems to want to emerge now from place to place on earth. The struggle will be epic in nature between contending centers of power.

The following important themes are reflected in this book about globalizing corporations in democratic nations:

1. The way the Western corporate vision of trade and investment impacts on nations and societies of people trying to sustain themselves for generations to come in a finite environment on earth.

2. The reawakening of national governments to their public responsibilities to regulate and tax business corporations for the public interest to support the societies of the world. Corporate camouflage is seen often for what it is: to evade responsibility to people.

3. The recognition in most fields of work of the global implications of everything we do to and for one another—a heightened sensitivity to the interconnectedness of the people and their profound tie to the land, water and air across the globe. Global damage reports from terrorism, organized crime and business corruption in white collar crime are now as common as global damage reports from hurricanes, floods and fires. Everyone has heard of the Chernobyl nuclear disaster, the failure of a global Pakistani bank called BCCI and the infamous 1984 Bhopal, India chemical-plant killing and injuring of thousands of Indian people by an American company—Union Carbide and its subsidiary corporation in India.

4. The central issue of corporate investment and disinvestment that crosses national borders; and who is in charge of making such decisions, why do they decide the way they do and what can nations do about these businesses' decisions to guide them or stop them? Plant closings are an example of deep stress on a community.

5. The harms caused to national sovereignty by globalizing corporations that work across national boundaries and what has been done to relieve and eliminate such public injuries over the last 100 years of commerce.

6. The growing recognition that more complete national governance of the corporations operating across national boundaries is good in order to create more local, national and international understanding of business and its strengths and weaknesses. Concomitantly, cross-border intergovernmental cooperation is growing rapidly in many

fields to enhance control by nations—coordinated global control over all corporations is growing in interest.

The six themes are not exhaustive, but merely illustrative of the significant implications of this inquiry into globalizing corporations in democratic nations. No other inquiry exceeds this one in public importance across the globe in all nations.

What about the globalizing corporations in non-democratic nations? This circumstance carries with it high political corporate risk, for example, in Sudan, Cuba, Libya, Iran and Iraq in 1999. With such nations, investment is subject to the high political risk of loss and may be lost through expropriation, or profits may not be allowed to be expatriated to the parent corporation or home base. The popular sovereignty of the people in democratic nations is not at stake, nor is it threatened by actions of non-democratic political leaders and business operations in non-democratic nations in a direct manner, although state-owned multinational corporations may impact people in other nations. One takes a risk of loss of investment and insures against it, if possible. Otherwise, it is money potentially to lose in high-risk, non-democratic nations.

In closing Chapter 1, we look ahead to the next part. Modern corporations of the *Fortune* 500 type are central to the American society and other societies, to law and to public policy and public affairs. For this reason they deserve exceptional attention by everyone. Everyone includes those who work in them (about 20 million plus people) as well as those who may be customers, shareholders, suppliers, directors, regulators, competitors and many others. But, because of their great size and complexity and because of their growing globalization in many locations across the world, it is virtually impossible for the ordinary business person, investor, citizen, governmental official or student to grasp the important dimensions of such corporations: social, political, economic, legal and business dimensions. For all of these reasons, any analysis of the *Fortune* 500 corporations requires a full explanation, description and exposition appropriate to the focus and emphasis of this work. How big are these institutions? Compared to what? Can we grasp size easily? What are the practical consequences of size in prices, quality, jobs and availability of goods and services? How is competition affected? What is the state-corporation relationship? What of their globalization?

The target of Part I and its chapters is the globalizing giant corporation inside democratic nations. The inquiry presented in this book is just that—exploration into a connected set of mysteries involving these immense institutions, all connected to their investment practices.

Part I

Foundations of Corporate Order: Popular National Sovereignty and Regulatory Capitalism

Chapter 2

Corporations and Nations

WHERE TO START? GLOBALIZING CORPORATIONS

Among the most important set of relationships on earth are those between the people living in 185 nations and their relations with 750 globalizing corporations scattered among the nations on earth, but principally corporate emanations from Europe, the United States and Japan. Global trade and wide regional trade as a human activity is ancient in origin—from the famous traders of Phoenicia, to the traders in Marco Polo's time, to the traders across the colonies set up by European powers and then to the modern traders of the last 100 years—starting with global traders in commodities—principally oil. In the last 50 years of global trade since World War II, trade has dominated Western civilization and spread its character deeply across the globe into other civilizations and most of the 185 nations. Aided by oil, modern Boeing 747 jets and other similar planes, Internet, television and corporate finance trading across the globe, satellites, low-wage assembly platforms in various nations with easy in or out of nation movement and transactions not taxed by international subsidiaries and alliances, joint ventures and other arrangements—the growing global monopoly tendency for goods, services and markets has tended toward larger and larger global monopolistic businesses. For example, being highly competitive in making cars for a market the size of the United States soon failed to present a sufficient challenge to auto manufacturers. Today, many view the global auto market as their place of business. The Chrysler and Daimler-Benz merger announced in 1998 illustrates most perfectly what's happening.

From all of the business perspectives outlined above, there are further major reasons to believe in the astounding importance of the relationship between 185 nations and 750 giant corporations. The most significant reason is peace—during conditions of peace, trade thrives; during war, trade is severely constrained. Peace has been a fortunate by-product of the global nuclear superpower stalemate of the last 50 years. The major recent transformation of the cold war—its demise, to a great extent, is another significant reason for putting trade at the top of important international relationships; and trade is three fields: in goods, in services and in investment of capital. From cars to bananas, to accounting and computer services, to mutual funds—the spread of the global market is well-known to everyone—particularly residents of the United States who buy globally—New Zealand apples, Chinese-made clothing, Latin American products and oranges from Israel, Volvos from Sweden, oil from Venezuela, timber from Canada. On the outgoing side, American goods and services that are exported are jet aircraft, apples, wheat, timber, electronics and much more.

So we know that daily national life today is deeply affected by the global market; we know, also, that peace has helped trade flourish. But we are often misled into believing that trade creates and brings peace. This is an 1850s Cobdenite view (Bowman, 1996: 293–296). However, it is argued here that trade does not and cannot bring peace. It often brings disharmony. Peace is first achieved among nations for other reasons than trade—then trade may flourish if encouraged by government policies and by people who want to buy goods and services from people of other nations. Quickly, all of this global trade can be turned on a dime and stopped in its tracks to prevent import or export of anything in times of civil unrest and war. As a consequence of this belief, the foundation of this book is that nations are the foundations for world order within which reasonable global trade exists, not the reverse. Part I should demonstrate the truth of this assertion of the paramount significance of nation-states.

So the most important set of relationships between 185 nations and 750 global corporations is very significant in (1) north–south global relationships, (2) the maintenance of a flourishing trading world, and (3) warding off extreme isolation—a normal condition in the recent past—say, from 1850, when basic populations had much less international traffic of any kind. Importance does center in the desire for world peace so strongly that global trade, it is hoped, will never get in its way or be a threat to peace. Trade is just not more important in the scale of human values than peace for 5.6 billion people—an unprecedented number of people on earth.

Where to start analyzing the relationships between nations and globalizing corporations is a major question of this chapter. It is precisely here, in the very beginning of inquiry of a relationship, that we must step back to grasp exactly and in detail the meaning of 185 nations and the meaning of 750 corporations. Failing to step back at the beginning will cloud up and confuse any further understanding of the relationship between the nations of the earth and the principal business corporations on earth. This chapter's major burden is to define the paths to the relationships, to note major characteristics of 185 nations that more or less represent 5.5 billion people.

A profile of 185 nations is a must to understand the relationship, but equally one must understand the composite profile of the 750 corporations. The number 750 is used as if it were an absolute, but it is an approximation for the late 1990 decade. In the list of corporations in Appendix A, there are precise corporate names included. Some are no doubt missed. Even though there is so much known about each of these corporations, it will become obvious—there is much that is not known because there is so much secret proprietary data never released to anyone about some businesses, as public as they may be. Non-public giant companies remain hidden from public view. The Japanese kieretzu is not a corporation, but is very important; and types of giant corporations such as multinational companies may be consortiums of governments (e.g., Airbus) or may be wholly owned by a government.

One thing is clear: giant major corporations from two nations—the United States and Japan—dominate in numbers of corporations (300) alone, if not in many other characteristics, the total of companies thought to be the major globalizing international players. That fact is the principal justification for examining the contributions and characteristics of U.S. corporations that we would safely judge to be globalizing American corporations. Furthermore, most of the giant corporations of the United States are now (or have recently become) involved in the globalizing process. A few of the giants are mostly domestic in nature—but they are the exception. If one wanted to assert that big business is largely international, many could agree in general. But the giant globalizing companies are not identical in structure or operations or international focus.

Where to start this inquiry is, then, in gaining a contemporary knowledge of the condition of 185 nations and gaining insight into the kind and character of 750 corporations and asking pertinent questions. What do we mean when we ask: What is globalization of a business? Does it mean sales in one home country and one foreign nation? Must a corporation have more than 25% of its sales from outside its home base nation to qualify as a globalizer? When does a company become so global it no longer is tied in any significant manner to a home country for profit? And when this globalized existence arises, is the corporation then stateless? Does it exist somewhere in space and should nobody ask where or why or how come?

There is an interesting and important parallel that has received very little attention. The parallel is between giant corporations in the United States and their love of the state of Delaware. Many giant corporations in the global trade world (United States corporations included) find no other place like the state of Delaware on earth—that is, no nations on earth like the state of Delaware. There may be one or two tax haven nations that act somewhat like the state of Delaware and its incorporation or chartering relationship to American giant globalizing corporations. The tax havens are few in number among the nations and they are becoming more transparent—Switzerland in particular. The absence of an international site like the state of Delaware is reflected in the yearning of some corporate officials for a private island that would be the home country that would never bother a multinational corporation—just like Delaware in the

United States rarely bothers the U.S. giant globalizing corporations. We will explore throughout this book the peculiar corporate chartering attractiveness of Delaware as a magnet for globalizing U.S. corporations and the implications of such a status inside the United States and throughout the world.

First, let's use an illustration at the outset to explain what is meant by investment decisions. When Ford Motor Company has profits of $200 million or when it has retained earnings or if it has a depreciation account or a goodwill figure on its books—any of the above, and its CEO yearns to use the $200 million to invest in building a car assembly plant in Vietnam, or Korea, or to invest more in a Japanese auto company (Ford partly owns Mazda)—who is to say to Ford Motor Company, just a minute. By what authority do you decide to move sizable wealth from nation to nation without first obtaining approval of the home nation and recipient nation? This type of decision may have CEO approval, Board of Directors approval and maybe even union approval—but where is public approval? There are no cross-border police to examine such a decision and the real question for the people is—Should there be cross-border investment police? This question is not often on the horizon in the United States.

Some capitalists argue that this type of decision is a private decision and then the old outworn public-private distinction is thrown up as a false dichotomy to foreclose public review and scrutiny of major investment decisions by giant corporations made on a global scale. The excesses of wild or casino capitalism are not tempered by the more cautious regulatory capitalism that is the dominant mode of thinking in the United States. In great contrast, we publicly castigate wealthy citizens who make a bundle of money in the United States, but who are making themselves non-citizens to escape taxation in the United States. Various proposals are considered necessary to curb such wealth transfers without taxation consequences. How could corporations do the same thing as "citizens" and not even be significantly challenged by 185 nations? It is both a paradox and a double standard.

It should be obvious that this book deals with a potentially explosive political and economic topic—the structuring, checking and confining of the global investment decisions of major American and all other major corporations. The topic ultimately is vast, but not so vast that it cannot be tackled in some reasonable manner. This inquiry is of central concern to all 185 nations and all 750 giant corporations. Everyone on earth has a stake in this investment issue. The investment question is one that recently was approached courageously in South Africa and across the globe when people questioned and then stopped South African investments of global business. The disinvestment decisions were made in an apartheid South Africa. This single example suggests that we have, speaking as a global people in an emerging world society, just begun to ask about investment decisions harmful to people or helpful to them. And who gets harmed or helped by such decisions? Or, are these mostly private businesses decisions, not public business? That is the ultimate question. Richard Falk, an international affairs expert, refers to the metaphor of apartheid extended to the world when he considers these issues (Falk, 1997: 480 in Sakamoto, 1994).

THE TAILS WAGGED THE DOGS

The hidden truth is that corporations, for much of their existence on earth, have been the tails that wagged the dogs or the nations. They did not at first. Some call this a myth but they are in error. Most people, especially citizens of democratic nations, initially thought the reverse would naturally be true—that dogs wag tails or nations create and control corporations, especially democratic nations where the people are supposedly in charge of the society and they, the people, via their constitutions "regulate domestic and foreign commerce." This paradox generates an inquiry—why so? Because corporations generate a lot of income (cash flow is enormous every hour and minute of the day, particularly in the domestic and foreign giant corporations) there is an obvious extraordinary interest in corporations by nations—for several valid reasons. The main reason is taxation, but health, safety, regulations and other reasons such as security create national public interest. Exceptional multimillion dollar salaries and benefits are laid on the men and women in some nations who are responsible for guiding and operating the corporation. This attracts people who want the money and careers managing corporations.

No one can doubt the universal growth of business or commerce in the world almost everywhere. Business corporations are nearly everywhere in most nations on earth; and, most importantly, who studies these phenomena? Schools of business have much to say about operating business. Economists continually express interest in business activity of markets and many claim to know a lot about it. Legal scholars and politicians are working constantly on business issues and problems. Journalists and other media experts usually spend great resources following and reporting on Wall Street and Main Street businesses. International relations experts are increasingly aware of the globalizing corporations as significant non-governmental entities on the global scene impacting upon relations among nations for good or ill. While of some interest to them, most of the natural scientists, political activists, historians and sociologists have, perhaps, the least interest in corporations and what they do in a society. However, even their contributions are growing in significance to this inquiry.

The common ignorance about the facts of giant corporations is that they are in reality large families of corporations or combinations of corporations scattered across the globe. This fact is perhaps one of the most significant troublesome features of this inquiry. The invisibility of corporations is a function of the abstract legal, accounting and economic nature of corporations. Common ignorance can be attributed partly to abstraction. But there is "purposeful invisibility" (submarining) that makes this inquiry much more difficult, as it has in fact turned out to be. The torrents of data about corporations, both their domestic

and foreign parts, are often incomprehensible, not comparable, delightfully incomplete or missing critical data sets, inevitably changing, and so it goes. Invisibility can be caused by torrents of raw data from thousands of subsidiary
corporations. Invisibility can be caused by being too big to audit for a government tax department. And invisibility is needed legitimately to protect trade
secrets of commercial value and patented processes protected by law as part of
intellectual property rights in most nations. The result is a mess for investors,
regulators, citizens and their legislators, judges and governors.

Invisibility in corporate operations means secondhand information for others,
filtered data and unauditable data. Not keeping information needed for regulation, say, of toxicity of plant waste water, is another form of invisibility. Invisibility and transparency fight one another in the most peculiar ways; for
example, the freedom of information act applies to the United States federal
government. That is good transparency. Generally, freedom of information is
not readily available from giant domestic and foreign corporations. Sunshine
laws, however, do not shine on corporations. There will be many examples of
artful business evasion scattered throughout this book. Invisibility is part of
corporate strategy in many ways that many have never begun to realize. Also,
invisibility is linked to deception, fraud and corporate crime in some cases.
Sometimes the dog wags and its tail is invisible. This could be frightening for
some, like an earthquake that can be felt but cannot be seen.

THE GOVERNING PARADOX

The central paradox is this: democracy is the public order chosen to run our
governments in the United States. By great contrast, autocracy—one-man rule—
is the private order chosen to run most giant corporations. Autocracy is akin to
tyranny as a form of ruling. Why the deep chasm of difference between democratic public order for governments and the private order of autocrats or tyrants
for giant corporations? Is the difference of public versus private order justifiable
on some important and permanent grounds? Must we listen only to those who
support and argue for a difference between public order and private order—the
apologists for some brands of capitalism? Or, are we justified now in ignoring
completely the public-private distinction in our lives, and saying that those business people, economists, lawyers, politicians and political scientists who argue
for such a distinction are just trying to support some form of parochial capitalism? And if we ignore public-private distinctions, are we really communists
who would argue that all private property is ultimately public in nature, especially the means of production like factories? Then how do we account for the
public constitutional government power of eminent domain (the power to take
any private property for public purposes if money is paid to the owners)? How
then do we account for all of your private property or wealth becoming magi-
cally transformed into public property if you leave neither a written will nor
have living relatives? The result is ultimate escheat or transfer of your wealth

to the state—the government triumphs in the end. What happens to the public-private distinction in these two examples? And what of the conscription by government during war of all resources—public or private?

The paradox of accountable public order and the anguish over unaccountable private order in giant corporations suggests to me that we may be arriving at some new way stations in our thinking about both political and economic power in the United States. Let me explain what I mean. Let us compress the American experience of the last 350 years into a compact understanding with all of its inherent weaknesses and lack of nuance. Let us start with the big picture. Not all of the issues of power were settled by American colonists who eventually, after several generations, rudely pitched out the Indians and then kicked out foreign rule by European powers in 1776 with a clear Declaration of Independence. Yet, in settling their constitutional public order in 1787 and 1791, the founding fathers never settled all of the constitutional issues of power (although they settled many issues), and certainly not those of slavery or states' rights. It was the ominous Civil War in 1865 that did begin to settle some of the issues of private order (no ownership of slaves) and public order (states are part of the union). But, the growing industrial revolution that followed the Civil War gave rise to new corporate and trust institutions for ordering industry and ultimately society—there arose the giant corporations, trusts and combines (alliances today) of the Robber Barons who developed excessive wealth in an earlier, supposedly egalitarian society. Then, over a 100 years ago, President Theodore Roosevelt, the first significant trust-buster, challenged this emerging corporate industrial order with antitrust laws and logic. Over a 100 years ago the public order of democracy prevailed for a time over the autocratic, private industrialized order of giant corporations. But the seeds of autocracy were sown then for giant corporate empires to emerge, and emerge they did. From 1900 to almost 2000, the world has experienced, and will experience again, the power of the corporate autocratic rule coming from a supposedly "private sector." World Wars I and II plus the Korean, Vietnam and Desert Storm wars, among other cold war scares, nurtured and reinforced the deliberate creation of the military-industrial complex that President Eisenhower carefully labeled the *Fortune* 500 and the federal government, especially the Defense Department. This compact view of our history of power is the foundation upon which we can next begin a more thorough analysis of public and private domains.

Hopefully, many questions of a profound political nature are raised, not settled, and this is no search for utopia (More, 1997; Scott, 1998). No argument is made that all of life is public or communitarian, nor is the opposite argument made—that all of life is private and we merely tolerate a little government or public order as much as we can stand at any particular moment in our history, always ready to revolt in Jeffersonian heritage. Neither do I think we are savages in primal existence ready to push our evolutionary power as a species to the limits against other species on the planet, even though there are 4 billion more of us since 1950. Nor are we angels in a heaven of private existence, never exploiting one another for personal gain—unjustly enriching ourselves at the expense of others with no redeeming return, grace or generosity to other people. Utopia lies in our dreams, not in the real world.

One item of devastating significance is my growing belief that among the citizens of the United States there are many who, in positions of great power, are bringing daily destruction to public order in the name of increasing the size and scope of "private order" of giant corporations. As one Canadian management expert, Henry Mintzberg, saw it: "And no nation today can afford anything but strong government. Isn't it time that all the knee-jerking condemnation of government in the United States stopped?" (Mintzberg, 1996: 83). There is a powerful tension at work in America, now only dimly sensed, that is stretching public credulity and warping public trust in democracy. Giant corporations and their officers are at the heart of this tension and trouble. Evidence of this tension will surface again and again in this book. And, as with plate tectonics of Mother Earth—when the plates rub together and jostle one another—will we witness another Mount St. Helen's volcanic eruption or earthquake of the Oakland, California variety in our distribution of political power? At the hottest spot of volcanic political explosions in the future of the United States are the extraordinary concentrations of wealth of the largest American corporations—the *Fortune* 500 and a few others plus their sister corporations across the globe; and within the hottest spot of all rest the chief executive officers (CEOs) of the *Fortune* 500 corporations. These are the autocrats—the Jack Welches of the world, the CEO of General Electric, who rest at the core of all the power. Many bow and scrape to the CEO who wields such great powers, and it is no Dilbert-like joke that great incompetence has been promoted to the all-powerful top position of CEO. These are competent men, most of them. Their power is both private and public with virtually no justifiable or intelligent distinctions left between what is Caesar's and what is not. If the public-private distinction ever had any utility for mankind, it no longer has any rationale for "private corporations" of the size of General Electric, and all of the other giant corporations across the globe. For every conceivable purpose, these corporations that number about 750 in the world appear to be public institutions owned by public shareholders. That argument seems to me to be unassailable as a fact of life.

Another wrinkle is of some significance. As we shall see, the Business Roundtable (in the United States some 200 CEOs of the largest corporations) phenomenon has spread from the United States to much of the Northern Hemisphere of the earth. This particular political phenomenon—business political autocracy—stamps an indelible mark on witnessing the end of the public-private distinction in giant corporate life across the world, and these organizations are at most only about 25 years old. Business is politics and politics is business— this is what the CEOs argue today.

From my study of the issues and facts there emerges a truism or maxim that could be stated like this: no giant corporation is a private institution for any purpose, so deeply does it affect the public interest of the community, state, nation or among nations. This may make "small is beautiful" more interesting in the corporate world. Both ITT and AT&T are now broken up voluntarily. Is this a trend? It reminds one of the Japanese saying—the nail that stands up above the others will get pounded down first. The pounding may become a volcanic public smoldering rage at decisions made by these CEOs to downsize manufacturing in the United States (Buchanan, 1998). Downsizing has been simmering politically since the 1970s. The decisions made by corporate CEOs clearly cumulate over time into the terrible loss of at least 4.6 million manufacturing jobs—that is, good-paying and supposedly secure jobs in the heartland of American industry (the *Fortune* 500) from 1980 to 1994, just fourteen years, are gone—vanished as if by magic. A nation that grows by 2 million people a year does not reduce its need for manufactured goods or for jobs making the goods. But we know there is no magic, that responsibility rests with someone for this tragedy, and that it is with the cadre of CEOs over the years just past and no one else. This job loss is the outstanding late-twentieth-century fact of corporate oligarchic rule in the United States; and much of the same is going on continually today in the United States and Germany and Japan. Job loss is a fact of life wherever giant corporations rule in fact and not just in some theoretical sense. The global search for markets and cheap labor is now all consuming. Jobs do not disappear without a conscious and deliberate decision made by one of the autocratic business men who would make such a decision—regardless of the turmoil of downsizing or plant closings. This eventually leads into the key bias in the public-private distinction: to close a plant is a private decision, to open a plant is a private decision. Who said the action is private? Why it is so obvious? The leaders of the *Fortune* 500, who make such choices, say that all decisions to open or close plants are private. And capitalism is defined as private control over investment decisions. However, this limited logic of capitalism offers no room for the broad public powers vested by the people in their sovereign capacity to authorize the government to keep peace, establish justice, fight wars and tax and regulate in the public interest both interstate and international commerce on behalf of all the people. The people offer through corporate law an opportunity for citizens to create corporations. This downsizing and plant closing tension is built into the fabric of a democratic American society and it remains so to this day. The opposites are clear enough in the example of plant closings—business people brook as little as possible interference by government in their choices to open or close plants. And both the public and the government strangely remain puzzled in a capitalist order by the sustained assault for the last two decades resulting in the open public destruction of over 4.6 million manufacturing jobs. Whose order is it anyway? Is it the order of General Motors or DuPont—Is that the will to follow, or is it the will of the people that eventually triumphs? The paradox is found in this question: Will investment decisions of any corporation above a certain size emerge as publicly made decisions in some modified form of regulated capitalism—decisions suitable to the demos and suitably in the public interest? During war there is little room for public-private nicety; in peace the question remains open. This is where we are today (Silk and Silk, 1996: 189–205).

A paradox is a puzzle—a statement or proposition seemingly self-contradictory or even absurd, but in reality expressing a possible truth. The contradictory nature of capitalism in a democracy is nothing new and the truth of the public nature of investment decisions by giant corporations is obvious once the decisions reach a certain level in dollars, a certain number of people are affected and commitment to a way of life is thrust upon the public who must consider public infrastructure issues—roads, sewers, schools, housing, water supply, and hospitals—among a legion of other important decisions that make for a sound choice to invest or not to invest. Let us explore this just a bit more.

A clear example is this: take the decision *not* to invest in rail and bus transportation. The United States contrasts with Europe and Japan and most people know it. Private auto and truck transport is the most dangerous, complex, polluting and expensive, and it dominates the United States. Why? Private decisions still trump public decisions but with what result and for how much longer? Private auto, airplane and truck transportation systems suck up most of the world's oil supply every day; they create the politically unstable inner cities and crime-ridden rot and the affluent suburban places and malls, they pollute the air and water beyond understanding, they foster freeway systems of exceptionally costly and wasteful design and add the biggest insult to our intelligence—they hurt the public with thousands of deaths and millions of injuries a year and property damage beyond calculation. Such a bloody transport system is coming to an end sooner than we may think, because the Chinese and Indians want more steel and oil and rubber and so do millions of others. The markets in just those two nations with half the people of the globe will put enormous strains on available resources. Very expensive is the only way to describe the future of auto and truck transport systems. What then becomes of the "private decision" to buy an automobile? When private becomes public in such consumer choices then industrial planning logically raises its head. At what price—$5.00 to $10.00 a gallon (Europe today) or $25.00 a gallon—will gas become rare like perfume? The chaos of markets like the long waiting lines of the 1973 era at gas stations is a politician's nightmare. Saudi Arabia and Kuwait look more and more like just another possession of the United States. What has this world become just to drive a car? Or a truck? One may ask: must the United States seize the oil-rich nations? Why should they get $20.00 a barrel? Where does all of this logic lead 260 million people on a globe living peacefully with 5.24 billion others? America is but a small part of the world population (under 5%)—should its soul be wedded to commercial interests or is there something of a higher purpose to life as we know it? Better yet, how rapidly could America change its ways if it developed the powerful public will to do so? Recall the transformation of America as it started to fight Germany, Japan and Italy—it took a very short time (months) to change into a fighting machine for World War II, or later to dismantle. This may be just the type of transformation needed before the year 2005 to assure the sane growth of the United States in a sustainable manner. This book is deeply concerned about the fitness of America for the future. Our own house needs to be put into better order now, but not in a trivial manner. Most of the public now sense the same looming chaos and they yearn for statesman-like decisions to guide the nation–corporate relationship.

MORE COWBOY CAPITALISM

Another important thesis is that industrial giant corporations in America (that account for 75% of all U.S. sales of goods and services—the *Fortune* 500 corporations) consciously and deliberately began to hollow out the American manufacturing base starting in the late 1970s, by shifting production outside of the United States more and more. A major reason for the start of the drop in late 1970s of the number employed by the *Fortune* 500 industrial base in America is the shift to foreign investment and production. *The Deindustrialization of America* (1982) by Barry Bluestone and Bennett Harrison was based on late 1979 data. Their work was some of the initial recognition of this hollowing phenomenon (Bluestone and Harrison, 1982). Many others have taken increasing recognition of the phenomenon; add computers as a minor factor for labor reduction to this mix as well.

But this is 1999, some 20 years later, and where has the hollowing-out process taken us? (A new Japanese word, *kudoka*, means the same as "hollowing out" according to William Greider [Greider, 1997: 15].) First, notice how *Fortune* 500 data (in Figure 2-1 and Table 2-1) from its start in 1954 to 1994 reveals growth, peak and significant decline. The years are important—the start in 1954 is merely *Fortune*'s attempt to explore large corporations. The peak is just before 1980—the decline lasts right up to 1993 data; then, in 1994 the data for both industrial and service and other corporations came together in May 1995.

Wisely, *Fortune* expressed the reality of adding service company employment to industrial employment showing in a most revealing chart how the concept of the *Fortune* 500 employment from 1993 to 1994 rose from 11.6 million to 20.2 million just by adding service and other companies to the list. No secrets here at all. Industrial policy is vivid.

In other words, the hollowing out of the manufacturing base of America is done at its significant core—*Fortune* 500 industrial corporations—not at the periphery of the American economy in agriculture or the giant service sector. If the industrial base of America is being swept away by "visible hands" (according to Chandler)—who are these "visible hands" hollowing out the American industrial base so that manufacturing jobs in America go from over 16 million in about 1979 to 11.6 million in 1994. How does a nation growing by 2.5 million a year or 20 million people a decade for four decades do this? It is

Figure 2-1
Hollowing Out or *Kudoka* (U.S. *Fortune* 500—Total Employment 1954–1993)

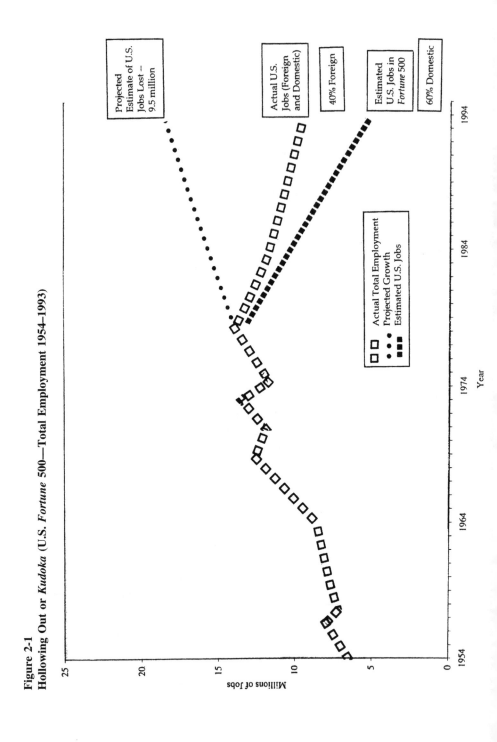

Table 2-1

Fortune **500 Corporations—Total Employment by Year, Manufacturing Industrial Core of the United States**

	Decade 1950		Decade 1960		Decade 1970		Decade 1980		Decade 1990
1950	a	1960	9,178,511	1970	14,607,581	1980	15,909,985	1990	12,400,000
1951	a	1961	9,266,928	1971	14,324,890	1981	15,635,041	1991	11,973,236
1952	a	1962	9,652,050	1972	14,676,849	1982	14,362,190	1992	11,811,792
1953	a	1963	9,966,488	1973	15,531,683	1983	14,052,735	1993	11,546,647
1954	7,857,483	1964	10,464,383	1974	15,255,946	1984	14,195,792	1994	b
1955	8,604,531	1965	11,279,085	1975	14,412,992	1985	14,034,477	1995	b
1956	8,793,347	1966	12,307,222	1976	14,836,136	1986	13,400,000	1996	b
1957	9,078,606	1967	13,097,938	1977	15,298,292	1987	13,143,948	1997	a
1958	8,523,611	1968	13,987,217	1978	15,785,439	1988	12,707,979	1998	a
1959	9,052,009	1969	14,813,809	1979	16,193,344	1989	12,539,817	1999	a

a -- Data not collected.
b -- Data not comparable.

Source: Fortune Magazine, Annual Reports.

23

certainly not mysterious forces of technology or fierce competition or invisible hands of the market; it is deliberate corporate planning to weaken America and the other industrial nations.

For argument's sake, say 4.6 million solid manufacturing jobs in the *Fortune* 500 sector were lost to America from 1980 to 1994—and many more followed in 1995 through 1999. Is there anything else done by the managerial "visible hands" of the *Fortune* 500? The answer is most clearly seen in the gigantic dollar asset shift *out* of the United States of productive American investment dollars into other nations on the globe by American corporations. Outbound foreign direct investment by CEOs of giant American corporations increased by a trillion dollars outside the United States in the same period.

The U.S. Department of Commerce has established the "debtor nation" status of the United States by watching two fund flows—U.S. assets directly invested abroad and assets from outside the United States invested here. The U.S. debtor state condition began in 1988. More was invested here by foreign multinational corporations (MNCs) than American MNCs invested abroad. Ours became a negative net investment position technically—not a debtor position like that of Brazil. But the evidence of foreign direct investment is strikingly related to hollowing out the manufacturing base of America. Some may call it, from an economist's perspective, "outsourcing," a wise practice to them, but clearly it is union-busting. Or Paul Krugman, who is a noted economist, may say of *Fortune* 500 manufacturers, they are dinosaurs and who cares about manufacturing anyway? But these observations by a well-informed economist tell just part of the picture of a long-term strategy by the visible hands of American industry—the CEOs of the *Fortune* 500 large corporations. Gut American industry and invest elsewhere is the industrial policy. Is this wise? From 1980 to 1994 a conscious policy had been followed by giant American business to invest overseas—as of 1994 either $761 billion dollars at current cost or $1,049.4 billion (over a trillion dollars) at market value. This is the clearest evidence of such a policy, while foreign interests at $580 billion (current cost) or $771 billion (market value) invest in the United States. The hollowing-out process began with the investment decisions of the CEOs of giant corporations like General Electric, General Motors, IBM, Coca-Cola, DuPont and Exxon. The decisions are followed by creations of new manufacturing jobs in the places outside the United States—in Canada, Mexico and elsewhere. The logical consequence is a drop of 4.6 million jobs at a minimum in the core industrial base in America. To sum up, the visible hands of American giant corporations—the CEOs—decided to invest a trillion American dollars outside of the United States, chop off 4.6 million jobs plus more in 1995 through 1999, in the United States, and simultaneously downsize—fire people at the rate of 400,000 a year for 15 years and more. Where will this leave the United States of America in 2000 and beyond? And what of the long-range future? And why is no clear responsibility placed upon the CEOs? After all, who is in charge of the autocratic empires? We must move to the crucial question of popular national sovereignty.

Chapter 3

Popular National Sovereignty in America and Corporate Size

"WE, THE PEOPLE OF THE UNITED STATES..."

The first line of the Constitution of the United States starts with the idea of popular national sovereignty—the declaration of 13 million people in 1787; the comparable continuing declaration of 260 million people in 1999. With a 550-year lineage, the Founding Fathers of America, particularly Thomas Jefferson, the author of the Declaration of Independence (in which the serious accusations against King George were laid down in writing) adopted the view that the voice of the people was a sovereign voice. This voice is the paramount and supreme voice under the Supremacy Clause of the Constitution and all of the amendments. And this voice is not to be superseded by the voice of the president of the United States nor the voice of Congress—both of whom are mere agents of the people. The Supreme Court of the United States is a powerful agent of the people, but it is nonetheless an agent of the people, subject to the constitutional limitations of its power.

The people of the United States are not just the people of any single state or group of states unless the constitutional amending provisions of the Constitution are considered. To change the voice of the people of the United States in its written constitutional form requires three-fourths (75%) of the states to agree to such a change. To withdraw from the Union is not possible for subgroups unless the Constitution is itself amended through the normal amending process exercised less than 30 times successfully in the last 200 years with over 11,000 tries attempted so far (Vile, 1997). The Union in the Civil War was the central focus of attention. Disunion brought on the Civil War and the death and ravishment followed. These beliefs about popular national sovereignty are not a trifling matter in American society and they are a central core of common understanding that Americans depend upon for the solid and secure notion expressed in the idea of *a* United States of America.

The idea of national popular sovereignty is misunderstood and confused— even by presidents of the United States. This being so, it seems advisable to take care to examine the idea of national popular sovereignty with some patient, caring attention rather than slipping by the essential idea of American government. This review deserves a central place in our consideration of sovereignty because it is the basic premise of the American society as it persists into the twenty-first century. Two centuries of American logic and experience must be joined with five and a half centuries of European developments. As Samuel Beer so brilliantly expounded—only by the long view do we overcome the historical parochialism that plagues us in America from understanding ourselves better. This we shall get to in more depth later in this chapter.

TWO SPECIFIC CASES OF FOREIGN DIRECT INVESTMENT—FORD AND HANOI, AND BOEING AND CHINA

You may ask, Of what possible relevance is a decision by a Ford Motor Company executive relevant to the preceding and later more full review of national popular sovereignty in this chapter? Let me try to explain this by starting with former Ford CEO Alex Trotman's decision to build an automobile manufacturing plant in Hanoi—with a capacity of 25,000 to 50,000 cars a year, a "minor" facility in his estimation. He mentioned this choice casually in a speech to the Washington Press Club in 1995. From the perspective of American, European and Japanese auto production (15 million units a year), the Hanoi idea of Ford seems small enough to be considered in an offhand manner. But that is the first mistake.

It is a mistake to think that the wealth of the United States may be deployed in any manner that a giant corporation thinks appropriate. Whether from debt or retained profits, the decision—each single decision by each giant corporation—is a decision about the appropriate use of wealth generated on behalf of, or in the United States by a corporation with its home base in the United States. Grossly mistaken is the notion widely accepted today that Ford's decision is its own to make unilaterally. That simply cannot be the case, if national popular sovereignty is to have any practical meaning in the regular day-to-day affairs of giant corporations as they roam the global landscape looking for profitable investments. The question never settled in the industrialization of America is this: Who may direct the wealth of the nation found in its giant corporations like Ford Motor Company? Who may decide what to do with the enormous wealth generated by giant corporations every day? The annual profit from the *Fortune* 500 was $325 billion in 1997. I know that giant corporations are arguably private institutions and thus not subject to careful public oversight in every action they take, but that is not the position of anyone who grasps the significance of national popular sovereignty. Export controls are one way a people would protect itself. Nuclear weapons are the best example of the need of the 260 million Americans to assert export controls and many other controls over an industry that is arguably a "private industry." Nuclear non-proliferation is the goal of the American public—and it is not to be ignored by American corporations or their foreign subsidiaries. If ignored, there would be public retribution and, perhaps, even a cry for seizure and dissolution of such a corporation by the U.S. government. Dissolution would follow a serious enough violation of public policy in the nuclear field, as would criminal convictions of executives and directors. This is national popular sovereignty at work in American business—a good example.

Alex Trotman's casual reference about building a plant in Hanoi is just a typical example of the mistaken idea CEOs have of their own power in the United States. One can understand his basic fear that one of the world's giant corporations must compete in the "hottest" car market in the future—the Asian market. China makes several hundred thousand cars for 1.5 billion people. The market is obvious if we want the Chinese to be "like us." But that may be an unrealistic and never-tested assumption made by all the giant automobile manufacturers in the world. Do the sovereign powers of the United States, people of this nation, want other people to be like us—the most wasteful, excessively consuming nation on earth? I am certain Trotman and others at Ford, even the Ford family itself, are oblivious to serious ramifications flowing from a decision to build one small automobile manufacturing plant in Hanoi. There are some who would use the power to tax corporations to stop such unilateral decision making and make it highly unprofitable to build a plant in Hanoi.

The basic fact is that the sovereign power of this nation is never even consulted by giant corporations in their decisions to invest outside of the United States. The tail wags the dog. This may have been good in public policy, to encourage overseas investment after World War II in 1945 to repair ravaged economies in Japan, Germany and Europe, but this is nearly 2000 A.D. Since the 50-year repair job is over and it ought to be so understood, this is a new world we are entering. The old formula of the giant corporations spreading their investments across the globe may need to be tested in every such instance— Hanoi, for example. Why not build a bicycle factory in Hanoi? Or build some electric facility for production of non-polluting cars? The image of self, in all its ancient glory, is too much for some people to grasp. To be like us may be the very worst thing one could wish on another people. Pushing the auto at the very clear end of the auto age (the auto century from 1900 to 2000 is *not* a boon to the Vietnamese in the twenty-first century) it is a self-congratulatory wish—it is a self-fulfilling prophecy—but it is not good sense for the people of Hanoi to ape Americans ways by driving automobiles. Maybe Hanoi could be spared the urban spread, the deaths caused by autos, the exhaust fumes of Los Angeles or Mexico City or Tokyo; maybe people in Hanoi want clean things and fresh air and no accidents for their children. And maybe Hanoi does not want to be hooked into the unstable and ever more costly oil market where it is subject to the powers of other giant corporations. Maybe the best course for Hanoi is to say to Ford Motor Company—thanks, but no thanks for the ''great'' opportunity to build a little auto factory. My guess is that Alex Trotman could never think this way and the Board of Directors of Ford Motor Company are so self-absorbed, the folly of their ways for an entire people thousands of miles from Detroit eludes them completely. Their eyes glaze over at the profit margins and well they should, but only if and when the American public approves of such obvious auto colonization. Most Americans would be so appalled by the decision of Ford Motor Company, they would wonder where Ford acquired the right to place its profits anywhere that pleased it. Ford got the right from the sovereign people of the United States, who allow it to exist as an organization and who have the right to abolish Ford Motor Company if they see it doing things destructive of the American sovereign people. Political dominance is just that clear if popular national sovereignty is grasped fully.

Now, sovereignty is not a pleasant subject to those who believe in a stateless world or a borderless world. This includes most of the CEOs of globalizing giant corporations. A superior political force lies within the sovereign people of the United States. That is the clearly argued position of this book. Also, it is clear that corporations have done everything they could to try to release themselves from public authority. The globalization game is played with just such a goal by major corporations who are globalizing. Not all corporations globalize, but those who do are determined not to be restrained by any political authority; and just as vigorously the public authority, the sovereign people of the United States, resist these incursions on their authority to govern themselves. The storm over the behavior of the CEOs of multinational corporations is gathering in the distance and the clouds pile on top of one another. The storm over the multinationals, seen so clearly by Raymond Vernon in the early 1970s (who is a significant twentieth-century expert on globalization), is gathering again (Vernon, 1971 and 1977). There is little doubt that every decision to globalize in any irresponsible way will increasingly come under review by the American people who have little interest in subjecting national wealth to loss by political risk, currency risk, and other risks associated with foreign investment. The world envisaged by Alex Trotman may not be the world envisaged by the sovereign popular power of the people of the United States. Trotman and the Board of Directors of Ford may just be badly misunderstanding their role in the world economy. Aggressive Asian expansion of Ford, General Motors and others as well as the oil companies, may be the *lowest* item on the agenda of important things Americans want to be done on their behalf by giant globalizing corporations. There is lack of concordance between what major corporations want to do and what the sovereign power of the people want the corporations to do. Conflict is certainly going to ensue if the giant corporations start to act in a unilateral manner as they have in the past. Past behavior is no guide to what is acceptable for the future.

Boeing's Dilemma: Public or Private?

I don't think you can ever separate politics from business.
Philip M. Condit, Chief Executive Officer, Boeing Company,
July 11, 1996, in Sandra Sugawara, "With Billions in Sales at
Stake, Boeing Goes to Bat for China," *Washington Post*: H-1, H-6

Perhaps no American CEO has ever been so honest publicly than was Philip M. Condit. I agree with him and disagree with him. Condit's statement was quoted as part of the saga of Boeing's involvement with China in the last few decades, since the 1972 visit of President Nixon. According to this story by Sandra Sugawara, Boeing has 70 percent of the Chinese market for Western-made planes—$5.3 billion in sales from 1992 to 1994. From Condit's perspective, we should all be cheering the sales.

Boeing's involvement in China is so great that its officers think that they must now act in America in favor of Chinese policy or lose sales, as they did in April of 1996 when China agreed to buy 33 airplanes for $1.89 million from Europe's Airbus Industrie—a company owned by several nations in Europe. That stung Boeing. Boeing and China "stand shoulder to shoulder" on lobbying to preserve trade privileges (most favored nation status) and on aid to China's burgeoning aerospace industry. And Motorola, Inc. and Caterpillar, Inc. joined Boeing, Inc. in their joint pursuit to shape American foreign policy attitude toward China. They see their job as "normalizing relations with China." This they think is nothing more or less significant than trading with China, regardless of the fact that what China did in saber-rattling toward neighbors, in human rights abuses and in other ways to shake up others is certainly just as significant and question-raising. Condit asked: "The question is, do you believe in isolation or constructive engagement?" (*Washington Post*, Sugawara, July 11, 1996, H-6; Jingsheng, 1997). This reminds one of gunboat diplomacy and opening up China to foreign trade. This question of Condit from a business perspective of a false dichotomy is borne of the long effort to sell aircraft to China that are made in the United States and now, increasingly, parts of the aircraft are being made in China for sale there and elsewhere.

Boeing has committed $100 million to help China develop its aviation industry. (One wonders whether the U.S. State Department approved.) It set up a spare parts center in Beijing Capital Airport like the centers it has in London and Singapore. Boeing trained 1,000 Chinese pilots and others in Seattle, and it gave two Boeing 737 jets to help China train pilots and crew. Boeing buys vertical fins, horizontal stabilizers, forward access doors and trailing edge ribs from Chinese Xian Aircraft Co. and cargo doors from Shenyang Aircraft Co. This is indeed deep involvement in aircraft construction in China, even though a large jet may have a million parts.

Characterized as "technology transfer," Representative Christopher H. Smith (R, NJ) wanted to stop this Boeing type of transfer and to deny most favored nation (MFN) status to China. But President Clinton approved MFN status anyway. Christopher believed that Boeing activity would build up both the Chinese military as well as civilian authority and strength; and it is all dominated by a Chinese government that is rather authoritarian to its own people and neighbors. Furthermore, the number of Boeing employees dropped in the United States from 155,000 to 106,000, a 31% drop from 1991 to 1996. Outsourcing by Boeing to Chinese manufacturers and others was the subject of a recent strike in 1995–1996 at Boeing, and downsizing of Boeing American workers is most clearly linked in this Boeing example to outsource. Both techniques (downsizing and outsourcing) contribute to killing American industrial manufacturing strength in one of its key export areas: aircraft. One would think this story is about people consciously desiring to hurt and seriously injure the economy of their home nation and its people. Yet, it is a story of ''well-intentioned'' people who run Boeing Corporation the way they see fit into their own corporate globalization future, regardless of local wishes in a place like the United States.

Perhaps more important than the false dichotomy—''isolation or constructive engagement''—offered by Condit, Boeing's CEO, it would be better to see the Boeing decisions as part of global geopolitical strategy by the United States of America where democratically and constitutionally elected presidents and Congresses establish and execute foreign policy for the entire nation—not just a narrow CEO who happens to run Boeing Corporation for a few years. Boeing may claim to be a private corporation, but that may be a fictional screen; it earned its wings with billions of tax dollars during the cold war during this century and it is part of the military-industrial complex still thriving as such with military contracts. And, as such—it is not a very ''private'' corporation; even more shockingly, its aim—open and public—is to interfere in American foreign policy to suit its own narrow corporate interests in aircraft sales to China. Here is another example of the globalization process by multinational American corporations in its rawest political form. Corporate officers of three ''private'' corporations—Boeing, Motorola and Caterpillar—are injecting their views, according to the *Washington Post*, into American foreign policy questions as if corporations had some God-given right to do so. If they have such a right to interfere in public policy, who elected them to their offices in their corporations? Who is the authority behind these three corporations reputed to be so private? Weren't these corporations established to manufacture goods and provide services rather than to establish American foreign policy? Where did the CEOs of these corporations even get the idea that private corporations were supposed to be mucking around so deeply with private money or public money in public policy issues? Do the charters of these corporations from public authority authorize their boards of directors and officers to influence American foreign policy? Do the shareholders approve of these explicitly political actions by such business people? Where is the documentation?

Mr. Condit hit the nail on the head for the entire Business Roundtable of

CEOs of the *Fortune* 500 when he said you cannot separate business and politics. The trouble with Boeing or Caterpillar or Motorola or any other corporate giant being in politics as deeply as they are is simply this: none of the CEOs or boards of directors can claim to represent the interests of 260 million Americans in a highly loyal manner. Remember to ask: Who elected them to public office? It's China first, not the United States, to put it in the bluntest language possible, if the companies want to sell to the Chinese markets. This conflict is daily, powerful and political in nature. The political sovereignty of 260 million Americans would rest in the hands of three CEOs, not elected by the people of the United States. And, who authorized this corporate usurpation of the authority of the people? To challenge usurpers, the U.S. Constitution contains a few well-chosen words about treason, and it is simple to understand: it is a constitutional level of criminality. One must realize that the phrase, "We the people of the United States" in the U.S. Constitution does not authorize any private corporation or its CEOs or boards of directors to make public policy for the 260 million people of the nation. That job is explicitly given to *elected* public officials of the U.S. government.

What we can see very clearly in the worlds of Philip M. Condit, the CEO of Boeing, and hundreds like him is a terribly misguided understanding of constitutional order in the United States. Their lack of understanding is so shocking that one wonders why they have not been told long ago to drop back into their role of private business person if that is what they claim to be—not emperors of commerce of the world. It strikes me as a preposterous stance for executives like Mr. Condit to interfere even a little in public affairs of this nation until they are elected to a public office. Then they may argue and use public office to pursue public ends. But now such CEOs are using their high offices and vast financial resources to pursue private ends, or so they must logically claim if they are "private" corporations. Thus, the CEO is caught in his own inconsistent and illogical reasoning. If the CEO is a public official in reality, then he should be elected by the public or appointed in some open and contested manner. CEOs are not so elected or appointed. If the CEO is not a public official, then he or she ought to keep his or her nose out of public business and acknowledge the narrow source of authority—the board of directors (20 or so people anonymous to the public) of that specific corporation. The "high falutin" view that a CEO represents more than his private corporate interests is pure nonsense and quite fallacious. But, the bill of goods sold to the American people is that these CEOs are an omniscient bunch of fellows—quite capable of guiding a nation without being elected to office. They may guide their own corporations in an autocratic manner, but the CEOs have no authority to guide or even shape the public opinion of the United States. They neither speak for it nor are they knowledgeable enough to speak for America, nor are they elected to office to set policy for the public. All that they do is run a corporation. The mixture of CEO roles at this moment is both foolish and potentially dangerous. What happens if war with China arises? Will Mr. Condit be held publicly accountable and responsible? Does Condit know the limits of his authority? We should know, as Americans.

TRANSFER PRICING SURPRISES

In 1993, U.S. Senator Byron L. Dorgan of North Dakota stated:

The tax avoidance by multinational firms, and especially foreign-based firms, is epidemic. As the GAO (United States Governmental Accounting Office) will testify today, some 72 percent of foreign based corporations that do business here *pay no federal income taxes.* ... We are talking about some of the largest corporations in the world, including foreign auto and electronic makers that are household names. *They do business in our country, earn money in our country; but pay no federal income taxes in our country.* (United States Senate Committee on Governmental Affairs, 1993: 2) (emphasis added)

Not a penny in federal income taxes was paid by one foreign automaker that sold $3.4 billion worth of cars in two years in the United States, Senator Dorgan stressed during Senate hearings.

You may ask, But how is this possible? You may credit deliberate transfer price schemes between foreign parent corporations and the U.S. corporate subsidiary selling goods here. The subsidiary must play by the tune of the parent corporation pricing scheme to shift profits from a U.S. corporation subsidiary to the home country parent. It is an old game of deception of nations in international trade. The problem is more complex than presented here—much more complex—but the heart of it all is that U.S. taxpayers—individual and corporate—are paying the full tax bill for hundreds of Japanese, British, German, French, Korean and other companies to do business here on the streets of America without being taxed fairly. Is this just further evidence of the art of deception played on Americans who are led to believe that foreign trade is such a great boon to the nation? There are billions of dollars of taxes at stake here. Every citizen has a right to get at the truth which is slowly coming to light. Many transfer pricing schemes are part of white collar crime—evasion of taxes, federal, state and local.

CORPORATE SIZE

Never Too Big for America: Normlessness

Normlessness—socio-anomie—is the distinguishing character of giant corporate size in America, maybe in the world. No American corporation can ever be too big for America. There are no limits upon the scope of corporation powers and activities in most state laws of incorporation and none in Delaware. In the late 1800s and early 1900s all of the limits in the state laws were repealed mainly to attract tax revenues—the race to the bottom was to laxity in the corporation-state relationship. As a result, there is no determining principle for size of American business—anything is proper. The dead hand and dead head of Western corporate imperialism is based upon the premise of normlessness in size. Bigness or giantism is equated with goodness. Cultural myopia is widespread on this issue. The standard paradigm of corporate size amounts to nothing. No one wants to face the truth of these issues. However, a "native suspicion of bigness of all kinds in America" is what President Clinton saw in 1998 towards mergers and alliances growing in America (Phillips, 1998: A-1).

A Scenario of the Future: A Corporate Size Deemed Excessive

Let us use our imagination to think of a time some years ahead. By the year 2050, America was blessed with larger numbers of moderate and small-sized businesses than ever before. The *Fortune* 500 industrial corporations were gone—the dinosaurs died and everyone cheered in great relief that names such as these were never to be mentioned in business news again:

General Motors	Ford	General Electric
Johnson & Johnson	DuPont	IBM
General Dynamics	Dow	Union Carbide

The generals died in battles of competition and downsizing. There was a Saturn Corporation; it produced Saturn cars and was owned by some investors and mostly by employees. By 2050, the biggest corporations in the United States, and there were thousands, had a maximum of $1 billion in annual sales. For some peculiar reason, the billion dollar annual sales figure was the biggest that a large corporation ever got in size. As recently as 1993, there was a dominant clique of giant corporations in service and industry—some 1,000 to 2,000 companies ran American business life. They were even trying to run the federal government and the 50 states as well as the rest of the world. They were threatening to close plants, and they did, to scare the people into giving tax concessions. They threatened the United States by closing plants in the United States and moving them to low-wage assembly platforms in Mexico, Honduras, Haiti, Jamaica, Hong Kong, Bangladesh and South Africa—anywhere the population was young, numerous and desperate for jobs at under $1 per hour with no other responsibilities or benefits. These companies manufacturing offshore were declared persona non grata and banned from doing business in the United States by Congress. This changed business decisions overnight, and size of corporation revenues was limited to $1 billion a year.

Furthermore, the bar in size led to rapid changes in corporate philosophies of size. Congress passed the Corporate Size Bill in 2005 A.D., limiting corporate organizations and all other business forms to no more than $1 billion in annual sales in *total* worldwide. This new public policy then set up the wildest scramble of change ever seen in the United States. Shareholders were given vast new sources of money as retained earnings were paid in dividends and stopped in all of corporate finance. Dividends soared beyond anyone's expectations. Spin-offs of new, separate corporations created more employment and more stockholder opportunities in new, smaller ventures. More employment in manufacturing expanded rapidly. No more mergers or acquisitions occurred. It was a sure sign that Congress was on the right path. No more antitrust decision work meant a small place for such fears of monopoly and cartels. Corporate funds never went to support advertising or charities—the advertising industries withered. Corporate funds were turned to profits and dividends and turned back to stockholders who then gave to the charity of their choice on their own. No more generous posturing by giant corporations and their CEOs with other people's money. Congress required every expense of corporations on politics to be approved by every shareholder in writing in advance—it was called the Dividend Paycheck Protection Act.

Unless we were fighting global wars, it was widely believed giant global corporations were not necessary in America. A legitimate corporation in America was moderate in size or small. Most of the upper ends of *Fortune* 500 industrial and service corporations were no longer legitimate business in the United States The source of illegitimacy stemmed from their excessive pressure and the needless interference in the government and political life of the nation. People had enough corporate interference in their lives. Congress ended giant-ism. Corporate PACs died. The people took over Washington again.

From 2000 to 2050, America weaned itself from oil and autos. This was a world where many of the *Fortune* 500 had no place. Without oil and auto companies, where did America grow? Rail lines, canals and ships were reborn. Horses came back and so did bicycles. Small and medium-sized businesses flourished. The center of the continent filled with people again. In the year 2050, a slower pace of life, more local in nature, was reborn. The philosophy seemed to be seeping around the globe. A life of the people sustained for centuries into the future was the goal of the sovereign people of America. Nothing could interfere with it. Other nations cheered the anti-colonial policies of America in a trimmed down global economy of fewer trades and traders.

The Love of Giantism

The madness of America is seen in its love of giant things. Consider the giantism of Mount Rushmore, the vastness of the Grand Coulee Dam and the reach of the Sears Towers in Chicago. The identical pattern of worship is found in the adulation of General Motors, in the fixation on General Electric and Coca Cola and the strangeness of the RJR Nabisco corporate giant sizes in the American economy. One would wonder just what drives the American people to love the curse of bigness that Justice Brandeis saw in the American law at the turn of the last century and the beginning of the twentieth century. The curse is getting worse; it is so bad that it may result in the demise of America as it is currently known. Is this potential disaster a real thing in our future? I think such a disaster may be a high probability series of events unless the nation soon recognizes just exactly what is at stake.

So who was Brandeis? It may just be that a knowledge of this man and his continued great importance to America would make a significant difference to a lot of people. I will attempt to explain him to you later. At least you would know of a man in American history who loved his country and who knew of its self-destructive commercial tendencies better than most of his contemporaries and perhaps better than most of our contemporary colleagues. We have not heard the end of Brandeis yet. The real difficulty is to capture one's imagination about such a judicial character so that the American economy through his eyes is not just some jumble of incoherent numbers. It is instead, real choices made by real people with real consequences for the future of the American society. This is where I shall try to start.

Another thesis of this book is simple—America already has chosen for the last 100 years a basic policy of regulation toward corporations. It did not take the course of destroying corporations. It did not take the course of nationalizing them. Each of these courses plainly was open to anyone who looked at this society and the relationship of the state to the corporation in the formative stages of the industrial revolution after the Civil War. Since the course of public policy toward corporations is so very clear from the 1890 Antitrust era to the present notification of plant closing law recently passed by Congress near the end of the twentieth century—a policy of regulation—there honestly is little else for us to speculate about in the American state-corporate relationship.

A policy of trade regulation clearly must have a coherent set of policies toward giant corporations and their regulation. There is little doubt, again, that when the evidence presented here is reviewed with an unbiased mind, the regulatory aims of American society have been thwarted almost completely. Reality is different. It is tails wagging dogs. The giant corporations decided to regulate America to suit themselves rather than letting the people have any say in the matter. William Greider's powerful observations that American democracy is on the ropes and that no one will tell the people just how bad things have become—unless, perhaps, you read Greider's *Who Will Tell the People?* I think the opening has now arrived to begin the truth-telling process so that the American people are no longer left in the dark. The ultimate reality is that corporations govern and regulate American society—contrary to what television, newspapers and textbooks would tell you. Trade regulation by more than 20 federal agencies is a cruel joke on the American public who believe in the silly fiction of Ross Perot, that this is your country—you are the owners. What a bunch of hogwash and malarkey it is to think of the people as owners in this way. Ask any CEO.

The consequences of this reality are so profound and have been developing for such a long period that most people have not the slightest inkling of how far we have gone to become the corporate-dominated state that we have surely become. President Dwight Eisenhower warned us of the dangers of the military-industrial complex that is now unwinding its intertwined love affair. Downsizing is one consequence felt widely. What are the consequences of this social-business transformation? Who exactly is in control of what? What are the practical and real dangers to the American society from the inverted dominance of corporate culture? One vivid example, among others, is white collar crime of the upper class. It is a powerful example of the very real danger of corporate domination to America. Chapter 9 of this book offers vivid details of this corporate world.

Not every consequence can be understood at this time nor every implication grasped, but what is abundantly plain to the most disinterested observer of America is that the corporations—the giant corporations—the *Fortune* 500 and particularly the first 100 of the giants, burst forth into public consciousness with an obtrusive behavior of advertising excessively, making people suffer every day by taking time every few minutes to tell people about things they have heard too many times before and have not the slightest interest in hearing again. How many times have you taken your remote control device and shut off the corporate intruder into your home spreading commercialized nonsense? My guess is that the managers of American corporations who authorize and pay for all of the advertising ($180 billion a year) spend little time watching it. The humane question is: Why must others be besieged with it? Why must the cost of products and services bear the $180 billion expense of costly advertising at the level it has assumed? Why do the supposed owners of America allow giant corporations to use such public media? The inverted world of corporate control is a world we understand very completely. The aim of this book is to tell the people the truth about corporate perversion of the corporate-state relationship in America.

Giant Corporations—the 1990s

Americans ought to stop kidding themselves. It is true that the Curse of Bigness is upon us with a massive, forceful and ominous power. Here is a case in point: IBM shares dropped from nearly $100 to less than $50 in the 12 months preceding mid-1995. That is shocking; just as shocking—they have risen again. Peak IBM employment was in the mid-1980s about 400,000 but it fell to 300,000 and was falling further with an estimated 50,000 to 70,000 more "buy-outs" of IBM personnel in 1993. Losses of $5 billion in 1992 faced this giant corporation even with sales of $65 billion in 1992. The blood was draining out of IBM, America's fourth largest industrial giant. Steel and auto industries were in similar difficulty. By 1999, IBM under new management bounced back to vigorous life.

What to do about it? Downsizing seemed logical, but so did splitting up the IBM company:

Many shareholders would like to see the company split up, according to Ralph Whitworth, president of United Shareholders of America. There are two or three $10 billion or $12 billion companies slopping around in there that don't necessarily have to be under one tent, Whitworth said. (*Washington Post*, July 3, 1993: F-7)

The new CEO of IBM, Louis Gerstner, does not want radical dismembering of IBM; he likened it to ''atomizing'' of a company as if it would disappear if split. That viewpoint seems odd indeed, given all of the very recent changes—corporate spin-offs arising in the defense industry.

The blues were being sung at Big Blue, as IBM is called. The blues of such giant businesses are a direct result of growing too big for their own health. Optimum size has been exceeded by a large margin. The *Fortune* 500 have dropped employment from over 16 million to 11.6 million in the last few years. This fact may not be a good sign or it may be a very healthy sign. So it seems the future of American industrial manufacturing growth lies not in bigger companies on the *Fortune* 500 list, but in the medium- and smaller-sized companies. The AT&T break-up of the last decade into Baby Bells is beginning to sound like good business for other giants. Recognition of the truth about the curse of bigness was obvious to an American leader whose collection of writings is titled: *The Curse of Bigness* (1934). A Justice of the Supreme Court of the United States, Louis D. Brandeis (1852–1941) was just that type of man who could see far, maybe 100 years or more into the future of America. Another leading business thinker, Adoph A. Berle, Jr. (1895–1971), a student of Justice Brandeis and himself a noted co-author (in 1932) of the ground-breaking *The Modern Corporation and Private Property* wrote, looking back in time in 1959:

Perhaps the last great opponent of the large corporation as we know it today was my old master, Louis D. Brandeis, famous as a reformer-lawyer, and later as Justice of the Supreme Court. But he wanted, not socialized business, but good private business. The American corporations of his time exhibited a tendency to grow to dimensions of unforeseeable size, and he wanted to put limits upon them. His fear was that big business could never be good—and that its power, if allowed unrestrained expansion, could not be prevented from over setting the principles of free democracy. *He may well have been right: time only will tell.* (Mason, 1959: x) (emphasis added)

Considering the exceptional stature of A. A. Berle, Jr., his observation, made eighteen years after Brandeis died in 1941, shows us just how much the threat of bigness is a perpetual curse—a Damocles sword hanging for 100 years over the American economy. It was an unending battle for the best of America's thinkers. As if to reinforce this point, Berle went on to write, in the same book:

Since his (Brandeis) era, great corporations have grown even twenty times bigger than the size he thought impossible of efficient organizations or effective restraint, yet the American political state still seems capable of coping with corporate power. The ''curse of bigness'' is still with us. But we see it now as a congeries of personal and philosophical problems rather than as an insoluble political dilemma. (Mason, 1959: Foreword, x and xi)

To the contrary, time is now telling us that Justice Brandeis was right, just as Berle hinted in 1959. There is an insoluble political dilemma in giant corporations in modern America and the dilemma will force all of us to make both political and economic choices as citizens, consumers and stockholders about the future of these giant companies. For example, Ralph Nader et al. publicly made their choice for federal corporate chartering when they argued for *Taming the Giant Corporation* in the 1976 book of that title. More recently, the noted American economists, the late Walter Adams and James W. Brock, in their *The Bigness Complex* (1986), confronted the myth of America's corporate culture: that industrial giantism and organizational bigness are the handmaidens of economic efficiency. They brilliantly argued instead that bigness is at the heart of American economic decline—especially in the *Fortune* 500.

It was 1992 when William Greider finally asked the key question in his book on betrayal of American democracy by big business: *Who Will Tell the People?* As a nation, we have not been completely aware of the reality of bigness of corporations, nor have we been honest with ourselves.

The meaning of the words *giant corporation* was transformed to some extent over the last 100 years. Thus, Brandeis saw bigness from before 1900 to 1941 and never liked what he saw in giant companies. A. A. Berle, Jr. saw bigness from the late 1920s to 1971, and in 1959 he still wondered about it. Nader et al. and Adams and Brock viewed the last few decades with some dismay on the subject of bigness in corporations. Given the transnational character of most of the giant corporations in global business, the idea of giant has evolved further beyond giant or big or huge or galactic. We do not have a word for it—transnational is too tame. Such economic units are now beyond anything in size imaginable to our most thoughtful predecessors who themselves gave the subject a lot of thought. Where does all of this concern get us? In the last 100 years, the fears of bigness surfaced just before World War II in the famous hearings on the economy—the Temporary National Economic Commission (TNEC). Senator Estes Kefauver deeply probed administered pricing from 1957 to 1963. Monopoly power was feared. In 1972, Congress again had hearings on the role of giant corporations—a third major expression of fear of their global reach. In 1998, President Clinton was reviewing public policy on bigness once again.

Is giantism of America's corporations a menace to the health of the nation? The problem is narrower than the *Fortune* 500 because a look at the data about the large companies reveals an empirical breakpoint between the first or top 100 companies and the rest of the 400 companies. The focus of concern is narrower if the data is sensibly interpreted. Furthermore, there are many ways to answer the question of menace from a utopian, a socialist, a communist to a liberal or conservative, to a pro-business or anti-business view and even other dimensions of comparison. But the size of the largest 100 industrial companies is unprecedented in the history of business in the world. The corporate practices, apart from making things to sell to consumers or others, have another dimension from patent licensing to political bribery to self-adulatory advertising to improve the corporate image. The most damaging actions of the corporate giants is their criminal *repeat* behavior and their violations of all of the laws and regulations that the public wants enforced against them. Concentration of economic wealth has bought a new form of corporate immunity. So far, only William Greider in *Who Will Tell the People?* has asked: How can giant corporations, like General Electric, repeatedly be charged with crimes, be convicted, pay fines and then carry on their business as if nothing happened? Ordinary people cannot do this. Career criminals are prosecuted to the hilt. This corruption and abuse of power is the focus of the new federal sentencing guidelines, but since 1949, a noted scholar, Edwin Sutherland, who authored *White Collar Crime* (1949), and again Marshall Clinard, in *Corporate Corruption* (1990), have quietly probed the meaning of corporate crime in this nation. Rarely is such data brought to bear in the discussion of bigness and its dysfunctions in American business. Finally, the *Economist*, in April of 1993, predicted editorially that big business is going to fall across the globe. They argued that both downsizing and break-up are in the cards. Consumers, the editors explained, will benefit from this rather than the cartels, keiretsus, monopolies and oligopolies of massive firms towering over world markets. They say: "The era of corporate empire-building is over. An age of broader, fiercer global competition, with all of its risks and uncertainties has begun" (*Economist*, April 1993: 13–14).

The *Economist* market vision is tough, but the corporate vision proposed here is even tougher. The top 100 of the *Fortune* 500 could be transformed to create a vast new manufacturing base if we just went about it in an intelligent manner. Just as there may be two or three good-sized companies slopping around in IBM, there may be dozens more slopping around and languishing in General Electric, Mobil, Philip Morris, E. I. DuPont de Nemours, Chevron, Texaco, Chrysler, Boeing, Procter and Gamble, Amoco, PepsiCo, United Technologies, Shell Oil, ConAgra, Eastman Kodak, Dow Chemical, Xerox, Atlantic Richfield, McDonnell Douglas, Hewlett-Packard and USX, to name just the top 25. We must examine this option with a clear-eyed vision, and we must ask: When was the last time the business broke into smaller parts? The logic of smaller business is not lost on the growing list of micro-breweries, nor is it lost on the mini-steel mills, nor are the smaller airlines, Southwestern, for example, letting the corporate airline giants run over them in competition. No one could argue sensibly for a return to the Mom and Pop store on the corner as the only answer, but the upper limits to Wal-Mart stores are being tested today in various places where such chain bigness is not wanted. Fights have begun in new locations for them. Somewhere in the middle, not too big and not too small, there seems to be a growing light ahead to resolve the curse of giantism so that it can be put to rest forever. The curse may be solved in the not too distant future if public policy toward the political economy is focused on the important question. That is one of the precise aims of this book. We must sharpen and clarify the consequences of corporate bigness and its inevitable curse, exacerbated by globalization.

An Optimum Size for a Business Corporation: How Big Is Too Big?

Is there an optimum size of corporations—neither too small nor too big—that should be the norm for all American business? A central question of this book is more of a philosophical question than a question that could be settled only by empirical research. Even so, empirical research must underlie any question of corporate size no matter how many data sets it takes to understand size of a corporation. The essential premise is one nurtured by Justice Brandeis, that bigness is a curse, not a blessing in organizational life. This premise is open to question itself, and it will be examined in some depth. But as a central focus, this book does not start out neutral about giant corporations. Bigness comes with too much baggage of needless trusts and domination, unfair and ruthless competition, cartel creation, needless mystery and secret operation, offshore behaviors that cannot be traced, anti-unionism, strikebreakers, excess wartime profits, gobbling up the little businesses by mergers, buyouts and forced bankruptcies, and even patent theft and exploitation. The corruption, fraud and criminal behaviors are piled on top of all of the other negative connotations of big business. Three industries—oil, auto and pharmaceuticals—are illustrations of giantism and trouble. They pour their advertising treasuries into a concerted effort to *image* away the stark reality of economic power that has grown astronomically in the last 100 years. One could logically ask: In the next 60 years or so, by 2050, what if rail transportation improved so much that autos and trucks were dropped by the world markets? Who would need such giant operations or need the Middle East or other oil or need American, German or Japanese automobiles?

The giant corporations of today are creatures of many decades of development and retained earnings, many decades of assets acquisition, of elaborate growth inside and outside of the United States and many decades of minimal dividends and wealth creation. People who were associated with General Motors when it started are gone, just as they are in any of the major corporations. New faces took over the seats of power. Shares of stock have gone through several estates. We should grasp that some giant corporations are *stayers*—they last in perpetuity as their corporate charters suggest they should. Some giant corporations are *leavers*. They leave the scene of business to be absorbed into another business or fold. There are even *returnees* to prominent corporate size in a decades-long perspective. The relative fluidity of giant corporations is a subject of some complexity, but it has definite outlines of truth about it (Fligstein, 1990: 314). Finally, the giant corporation takes many forms—the conglomerate form is represented by General Electric (GE). Other forms include the divisional form of

General Motors (GM); the vertically integrated form of Exxon Corporation—from oil well to gas tank—is another type. There is not one type of giant company in America or even globally. This adds to difficulty in understanding corporate giants.

The distinguished American educator and writer Peter R. Drucker, in his *Post-Capitalist Society* (1993) mused about governing corporations and, in his characteristically straightforward way, said:

Any Government, whether that of a company or a nation, degenerates into mediocrity and malperformance if it is not clearly accountable to someone for results. This is what happened to the big American corporation in the thirty years between 1950 and 1980. (p. 80)

If you trace the evolution of corporate powers, the managers emerged the winners in that period. Without so much as raising a question about size of big corporations, Drucker seems to think that a public audit of the big company will emerge to set things right. Chandler reinforces the dominance of the management revolution in large corporations and the advent and development of managerial capitalism (Chandler, 1977).

The rightness in Drucker's view is a balance of management for all of the "stakeholders" in the corporations—management, workers, creditors, shareholders, suppliers, bondholders, directors and others. But something is missing, seriously absent in this viewpoint. If Drucker can miss the obvious, so can everyone else miss the most obvious thing about American big business corporations. The size of big business is not understood by the ordinary investor, the ordinary citizen, the tax people, the legislator, the judge or the governor. Drucker has lost touch with this reality as well. Most media cannot begin to convey the reality of the size of the corporation giants because there is not only too much to comprehend that changes so fast, but the question of size is no longer discussed to any extent. Size is given—a ridiculous position.

For example, are we to worry about who runs or controls the information society and who makes money from the estimated 3 trillion dollar business that is supposed to evolve from the transformation of the television broadcasting companies, telephone companies, cable television companies and computer firms? That question is already settled; the people of the sovereign nation of the United States are in a paramount position on all of these issues. Or is it merely a hope that Congress and the president actually protected the public interest in the new legislation? Time may reveal the truth.

What is the relationship of 185 nations to 750 giant globalizing corporations? Do transnational corporations need more public accountability to the people? We have opened inquiry into these questions, keeping an "eye on the ball"—the *Fortune* 500 and global 500 corporations. Themes opened here will be developed in the chapters that follow. Let us now focus some further attention on the nations of the earth, in the next chapter.

Chapter 4

The Nation-State and Sovereignty

"IN DEMOCRATIC NATIONS"

In a world of somewhat united nations where the earth is almost completely divided among them, what is international trade? Is it the people, goods, services and money moving across national borders, counted differently, legally different? To look at nations we focus first on philosophy—what should guide this inquiry in terms of values? The basic values of nations are not simply trading or free trade. That view is too simple-minded. There are more profound considerations than those expressed in material goods, money or consulting services. This leads to a study of sovereignty—its modern relevancy in public discourse.

PHILOSOPHY

In *Beyond Growth* (1996), Herman E. Daly offers a coherent and valuable foundation for a philosophy that is valid, truthful and lasting to anyone who questions the status quo in economics and particularly those who question the wisdom of the free trade ideology that is commonplace today. His views began in the early 1970s and will be explained shortly. Beside Daly's philosophy, others have a point of view, such as John Cavanagh, a global policy analyst and activist. There must be a "third way," as John Cavanagh called it at the International Forum on Globalization in 1995. The "third way" as he defined it rejects the absolutes of wide open free trade with no national regulation or control and the "third way" also rejects the selfish position of no trade—each nation for itself, the rest of the world be damned. The "third way" is primarily local, intranational, intrastate and intracity, self-sufficient trade first, and international trade (probably regional) only at the very last. Now we know that this is probably not a definition of a "third way" that interests Japan or England, which as island economies are eager to maximize trade of all kinds for their people. Nor would tobacco companies like the "third way." But in larger, continental-sized economies (United States, Australia, Brazil, China, India, Russia), there is a different outlook, and it is reflected here by this author—the "third way" makes a lot of sense in trading goods, especially cross-border services and particularly capital investment. This is one philosophical stance taken explicitly.

From 1945 to 1995, a 50-year period of unquestioned open international trading was dominant in the West. The United States helped both Europe and Asia, especially conquered Germany and Japan, to recover from their war devastation, humanely integrating three economies—Europe, the United States and Japan. Open trading was a good public policy for those times. That recovery task is now over—in fact, it has been over for some time. America's trade policy in the office of the United States Trade Representative (USTR) over the past half century was an American "crusade" for free trade (Dryden, 1995). It is appropriate to stress "crusade" because it was an ideology in the form of a public policy, supported by most economists, politicians and business men, and it reflected American views of "growth" of that era. But some economists recently thought of "free trade" as a myth and said so (Batra, 1993). Their arguments and evidence were dismissed summarily, especially by supporters of big globalizing corporations. A former chairman and commissioner of the United States International Trade Commission, Alfred E. Eckes, Jr., is another myth-buster. Not only did he attack the disinformation spread about the Smoot-Hawley Tariff Act of 1930, putting that issue into a larger historical perspective where it needed to be, but he, in a very scholarly fashion, examined U.S. foreign trade policy since 1776 (Eckes, 1995). Eckes wrote, "In the public mind Smoot-Hawley, like Munich, became an indelible metaphor for public policy failures" (Eckes, 1995: 281). So much was the ideology of free trade used in the NAFTA and GATT debates in 1993–1994 that President Bush argued, "I think protectionism is just 180 degrees wrong . . . We're in a global economy. It's no longer just the United States. We can't live behind those borders" (Eckes, 1995: 280). Not everyone agrees—especially downsized workers in the millions who have little choice but to live behind borders. And Eckes questioned free trade ideology in his broad review of trade over an exceptionally long period of time.

Also, new voices emerged to explain what a third way of global trade and local trade might look like. Paul Hawken, a businessman, in *The Ecology of Commerce* (1993), stated, "There is no polite way to say that business is destroying the world" (Hawken, 1993: 3). We do not know how to answer the question of the maximum population of human beings that can live decently on earth. This is called earth's "carrying capacity." We are typically not aware that industrialization is over, he argued.

Daly's *Beyond Growth* (1996) is a basic effort to define what is meant by sustainability in development of the earth and human societies. Daly thinks a good, ethical steward of the earth could not hand the world to the next generation in bad shape and would think a "degraded state capable of supporting less life, less abundantly, and for a shorter future, is surely a sin" (Daly, 1996: 222). The sin is the current generation's sin.

The phrase in economics and business literature that justified big plants for manufacturing is "economies of scale." There is some truth and a lot of silly cant about this concept in the minds of some that is often nothing more elaborate for monopolists than bigger is better and monopoly is best. Business scholar Alfred Chandler noted limits to economies of scale and scope in 1990 (Chandler, 1990: 621). By contrast, Daly strikes clearly at scale—optimal scale cannot be avoided. Nothing on earth grows unlimitedly forever among the living. An idolatry of unlimited growth, of bigger is better and of faster growth must be confronted by limits—"*limits* to growth in per capita resource use, *limits* to population growth, *limits* to the growth of inequality" (Daly, 1996: 224) (emphasis added). The earth itself has limits to how many people it can carry through space. Such limits used to be called "conservation" in the 1930s. Conserving the earth and its animals, fishes and resources was the generous impulse of prior and current generations toward current and future generations expressed by national parks, national forests, game and fish limits, commercial fishing limits and many other limits. Human beings must be obsessed with the welfare of the next generation and their children's welfare on earth (Weiss, 1989). The philosophy of this book is that St. Francis of Assisi offered a way to view the excessively material world of globalizing corporations in democratic nations. Poverty, few material possessions, piety, a belief in Christ and his life as a model, a Mother Teresa lifestyle—all of these ways of living are messages to the Western material world to check and confine its appetite for material wealth. There is no future for them, their children or the South in it. Wealth and its accumulation is a source of grave social strife. Think of St. Francis and his life as a revolt to what greed brought to the world then and what the fighting over material goods brought to the castle-built medieval world St. Francis inhabited. There is too clear a parallel between the world St. Francis rebelled against in 1200 and the world of 2000 globalizing, free trading, predatory capitalism in the Western corporate visions spawned by globalizing giant corporation executives today. The philosophical lesson is clear: stop growth and greed—start thinking intergenerationally and be fair to the future, unborn generations. After all, who has a voice to speak for them? Surely not just the Catholic Church. This book attempts to ground itself in intergenerational philosophy and concerns for the future. It fights avarice, or pleonexia, as the Ancient Greeks called it.

Let us turn next to a more complete study of sovereignty as a way to understand nations and what they are really all about. The literature about globalization, globalizing corporations and nations as objects of study is voluminous. What follows is a carefully selected examination of the key topic—popular sovereignty, the core of modern nations, most of them that claim honestly a democratic foundation of legitimacy where the people vote, the people govern themselves, the people make their own laws and obey their own constitutions. The limits on the economy mentioned by Daly are parallel to the limits on governments and corporations expressed in the idea of sovereignty—popular sovereignty.

POPULAR SOVEREIGNTY: THE WILL TO AUTONOMY IN MAKING ONE'S OWN LAWS

Importance of Sovereignty

We must assess how important the idea of sovereignty in nations is to this inquiry. The best answer is this one:

This approach has underscored for us the fact that sovereignty is a practical concept as well as an abstract one. It is derived from the practice of states. As practices change, so too have the uses of the term. The "skin of the living thought" of sovereignty is likely to continue to adapt to future circumstances within international society. (Fowler and Bunck, 1995: 163)

The work by Michael Fowler and Julie Bunck (1995) is a major synthesis of more than 370 books and articles, over 40 legal cases and 35 statutes and treaties and diplomatic correspondence on the subject of sovereignty. The authors asked why the idea of sovereignty is ambiguous, why the idea is important, what is a sovereign state, how is the idea applied in theory and practice and why the idea of sovereignty is useful. They asked the key question—will sovereignty prosper or decline? And the answer was offered just above in the quoted material. To summarize their reasons for seeing a future in the theory and practices associated with sovereignty, the authors offered the following. The idea of sovereignty will:

1. Help to organize the "cluttered roster" of modern political entities (Andorra to Outer Mongolia to the Vatican).
2. Remain the "rallying cry" for issues of secession and self-determination.
3. Help sort out the new Balkanization now underway after the cold war ended. Nations are splintering, disintegrating much more rapidly than integrating into larger nations and groups of nations.
4. Help to shape responses of "humanitarian intervention" such as Somalia, Haiti and other nations.
5. Counterbalance the inherently revolutionary nature of nationalism with the devotion to "sovereignty-ism" meaning the stability of a satisfied nationalism.
6. Aid cross-border policing by law enforcement to obtain witnesses and to gather evidence in cooperation with other sovereign police departments and law enforcement agencies across the globe.
7. Help finish off environmental disputes to the mutual satisfaction of different nations.

8. Guide the uses of national natural resources (e.g., the laws of the seas).

9. Shape national responses to violations of human rights.

10. Shape the future of regional and multinational organizations of which the state is a member like the European Union or GATT.

Fowler and Bunck conclude that "Reports of its demise notwithstanding, sovereignty appears to us to be prospering, not declining, as the 20th century draws to a close" (Fowler and Bunck, 1995: 163). This very significant conclusion based upon the comprehensive research and writing and the thorough analyses by these authors suggests that anyone who seems to believe the nation-state is finished is in error—as wrong as thinking the earth is flat. Why would anyone write and publish a book extolling the flatness of the earth with what we know? This is the mystery of this inquiry that certainly deserves more attention, which we will get to shortly.

The lineage of the idea of sovereignty is long and complex—from classic times through medieval development to Bodin, Althusius, Grotius, Hobbes, Pufendorf, Locke and Rousseau (Merriam, Jr., 1968; Bodin, 1992). The common literature in sovereignty is well over 600 items today. For example, Bertrand deJouvenel, a French scholar, wrote *Sovereignty: An Inquiry into the Political Good* in 1957. This illustrates the endless general fascination for the topic. Before there was a United States of America, there were changing perceptions of popular sovereignty. In 1780, Thomas Paine said about sovereignty, "there could be no such thing . . . as power of any kind, independent of the people (Kammen, 1988: 15). Many seem to have forgotten this elemental idea.

Despisers of Sovereignty

As suggested above, there must be people who despise the idea of sovereignty for many reasons. Who dislikes sovereignty and what could be their possible motives? Two groups come to mind—sea pirates and their modern counterparts, terrorists and air pirates. Janice Thomson focused upon privateers—the pirates— the mercenaries and upon mercantile companies acting as an arm of the state (Thomson, 1994). In her view, during nation-state-building before 1900, extra-territorial violence was pervasive in early modern Europe and it needed a response, a violent response, to address non-state actors beyond the state borders. Sovereignty was the result of disarming insiders and eventually outsiders. Thus, the nation-state grew stronger and sovereignty became the international institution that organized global politics as we know it today. And modern terrorists did not want to be brought to justice any more than pirates did. There is a natural antipathy to the state and its power in these groups. Yet, aircraft high-jacking today is down and sea pirates roam remote stretches of the China Sea— not at all a major world problem.

What are the possible motives behind those who see an end or twilight to independent sovereignty of nations? Let us examine some more of them.

The basest motives of non-loyalty to any nation may be with those who pursue international crime—creating fraudulent international banks such as BCCI, or wanting to move the cash made from illicit drug sales out of one nation into other nations without being held responsible for illegal profits, or moving immigrants for $30,000 a head across seas and land borders illegally, or having other illegal criminal enterprises in prostitution, goods, services, and so on. Intellectual piracy is a stunning example of global theft by many.

Another set of motives to discredit the nation-state are with those who do *not* wish to pay taxes on income or property inside a nation (Davidson and Rees-Mogg, 1997). This group includes many individuals and multinational corporations across the globe who transfer assets with great and somewhat unaccountable ease across national borders. National and state taxing authorities are well aware of transfer pricing. But the evasion also includes nationals bent on earning wealth but skimming cash to evade detection and taxes and spiriting the cash assets overseas across national boundaries into no- or low-tax locations or Caribbean hideaways for pleasure, or Swiss bank accounts.

Another set of detractors to the idea of sovereignty wish to weaken the regulatory reach of nation-states in those economic and social policies that demand for workers minimum wages, health insurance, pension protection and labor union safeguards. Other regulatory fields—safety, clean water and air, food and drugs, safe workplaces, all the financial truth-in-lending and security and credit protection regulations—are the target of those who wish to evade such regulations by moving out of one nation into another with lower or absent regulatory standards for business. The famous "rush to the bottom"—the Mexican maquiladora—is the motive here for these people. Some of these well-motivated actors are in giant corporations.

But the motives to denigrate the nation-state do not end here, with criminal motives and business motives to evade taxes and regulation and to create low-wage secret sweatshops inside the United States and assembly platforms outside the United States. There are many other motives that on their faces seem harmless, but nonetheless give one the impression that the nation-state is doomed.

Those who are creating the European Union must, by necessity, find fault and weakness with the nations of Europe to justify their own supranational regional authority. This means that books by European scholars and officials who support a European Union may take a decided twist toward finding that, globally, the nation-state is about to end and that the terrible nation-state is the source of much European grief since its inception. The nation-state is a more modern form of governance started after 1648 in the Treaty of Westphalia. Nearly three and a half centuries of national fighting—much of it on the European continent with the two world wars and Bosnia in this century alone—leave these detractors of European nations highly motivated to pursue their unique viewpoint about the inherent waning sovereignty of nations. The idea of detraction of sovereignty is pursued as an unqualified good for Europe.

There are world federalists and "one worlders" who understandably are bent on the creation of a single, supranationalist government of the world and who find no interest in the idea of national sovereignty. There are a wide range of scholars who study economics, business and international relations who find sovereignty on its last legs at the end of the twentieth century (Camilleri and Falk, 1992). Human rights activists have trouble with national sovereignty which may act to shield violators inside nations. It would appear that the unruly and unholy alliance of international criminal enterprises, multinational corporations, international regionists, human rights activists, world federalists plus many scholars would just about spell doom for any rational belief that sovereignty could exist for very long in the twenty-first century. We hear, "The end is near"—sovereignty was good for 350 years as a notion among nations—its time for burial is now. This sounds quite religious in motive, or it has the sound of ideological fervor (almost Marxist in nature)—a passionate belief in the rightness of a position. It has a flavor of the cosmopolitan telling the nativist his position is all wet—there is nothing to a love of country, a love of place. The Italian city republic strong *companilismo* emotion of parochialism has no place in the modern global society. Italy, now in its umpteenth national government, borders on predictable anarchy. It is as if the sound of the local church bell in the bell tower, or the campanile at the University of California in Berkeley, has not one bit of romantic influence over the life of the campus, or that the bells in Assisi, Italy, home of St. Francis, have no influence locally among Franciscans. This may be doubted as the globe turns from global cold war toward the potential for a warm hearth at home in the community anywhere on earth.

Lovers of National Sovereignty

President Theodore Roosevelt—one of the four great American presidents carved on Mount Rushmore in South Dakota—expressed a vigorous view of the "True American" in a brief essay in April 1894 in the *Forum*. This essay found its way into his many writings, one in 1900 called *American Ideals*. The view of President Roosevelt was this:

The stoutest and truest Americans are the very men who have the least sympathy with the people who invoke the spirit of Americanism to aid what is vicious in our government or to throw obstacles in the way of those who strive to reform it. (Roosevelt, 1901: 47–48)

His view of Americanism is not simple in nature. The breadth of Americanism he appreciated is this:

There are two or three sides to the question of Americanism, and two or three senses in which the word ''Americanism'' can be used to express the antithesis of what is un-wholesome and undesirable. In the first place we wish to be broadly American and national, as opposed to being local or sectional. We do not wish, in politics, in literature, or in art, to develop that unwholesome parochial spirit, that over-exaltation of the little community at the expense of the great nation which produces what has been described as the patriotism of the village, the patriotism of the belfry. (Roosevelt, 1901: 51–52)

President Roosevelt had thought through his reasons for such concerns and they lay in the fear of provincial patriotism and its tendency toward anarchy. In a large, continental-sized America it was and still is no easy matter to keep a center alive and thriving if it must compete with hundreds and thousands of other sources of loyalty. Thus, Roosevelt's view of true Americanism insisted upon a national perspective: ''Politically, the indulgence of this spirit (of the belfry) was the chief cause of the calamities which befell the ancient republics of Greece, the medieval republics of Italy, and the petty states of Germany as it was in the last century'' (Roosevelt, 1901: 52). Roosevelt looked then, in 1894, at South America to illustrate his point of the lack of a broad continental perspective on that continent. Nor have 100 years changed South America that much.

As a nation-builder in America filled with vast numbers of newly arrived immigrants, President Theodore Roosevelt's negative attitude toward a parochial interior attitude is very clear. But just as clear was a powerful need he expressed to assimilate immigrants and to be vigorous about it to achieve the broad national outlook he thought was important for each citizen. That Roosevelt attitude led toward a loyalty to a large nation which was much more important than *no* loyalty to any nation or any place, which he abhorred. The absence of any loyalty to nation troubled him greatly. And other aspects of what he called true Americanism required attention—understanding constitutional order here—such as church-state relations and the demand for the English language.

Popular Sovereignty and Globalizing Corporations

Why should we care about the idea of popular sovereignty? Look at Figure 4-1 to see where the people fit into the world when popular sovereignty prevails. The answer is clear—right at the top in the United States. And this is no idle conclusion arrived at by a people who merely discussed the issue. First, the American Revolution did away with foreign intrusion into national sovereignty of all the people here. Second, the American Civil War did away with serious errors and thoughts held in the South about the idea of state sovereignty that Calhoun espoused. As the following will illustrate too vividly, we have to re-learn what history teaches us too well. The other wars reinforced sovereignty of the nation and its popular sovereignty.

The question of sovereignty has been a central concern over the years for one

Figure 4-1
Popular Sovereignty in the United States

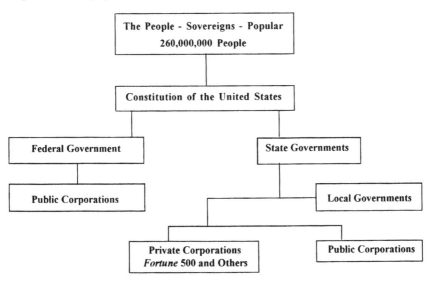

of America's principal scholars of multinational corporations. Raymond Vernon first voiced his concern in *Sovereignty at Bay* (1971), but reflected ten years later on his concern about the relationship of globalizing corporations in various types of nations. Vernon expressed his concern this way in 1985:

Multinational enterprises . . . may well grow in their relative importance in the world economy. Anticipating that development, I am brought back to what I regard as the central question. How do the sovereign states propose to deal with the fact that so many of their enterprises are conduits through which other sovereigns exert their influence? (Vernon, "Sovereignty at Bay: Ten Years After," in Moran, 1985: 258)

Vernon's question may now be answered by examining the question of popular sovereignty implied within it, just as we are doing here. The potential serious clash of nations is really a clash of popular sovereignties—not merely state governments and their leaders who come and go over time. Corporations have power to shift activities from one location to another globally while nation-states, the sovereign people, are fixed to a piece of national turf. Footloose global cosmopolitans in multinational corporations open and close manufacturing plants, shift work hither and yon across nations, and this is a deep source of worry to both home nation and host nation popular sovereignty, to the people and to their leaders. People are rooted to roads, land, churches, mortgaged homes and public debt of their nation. The public infrastructure built and maintained so laboriously and at such great cost—roads, sewers, universities, power lines, water systems, sidewalks, rail lines, public lighting systems and cable services, high schools—are in and on the ground. *Sunk costs* of a dam are truly sunk when a multinational corporation decides to say farewell—that is, close a plant and leave the community with fixed costs of civilization.

Labor's immobility clashes with capital's mobility. The symbiotic relationship of a society, a people and the business actors within it is vividly and clearly an intractable problem of deep seriousness to harmony in a world society—a genuine threat to trust and peace and goodwill. But what is popular sovereignty to a transnational corporation, other than just another risk of doing business. It is mobile. Its capital is mobile.

One could speculate that the central tenet of capitalism—freedom to invest how and where you want with your money without restriction—is resisted deeply by the people in democratic nations where popular sovereignty reigns and public tax cash is joined often with private cash in many large factory investments. Investment control laws from home nations, host nations and others have grown over time (Folsom and Gordon, 1995: 569).

Why dwell on the sovereignty of the people in a book devoted to globalizing corporations in democratic nations? The answer is one of the most fundamental points in the book, and it is responsive to Raymond Vernon's question stated previously. When a people come together in unity in a nation for their mutual benefit and keep doing it successfully for more than 200 years, there must be extraordinary value in what they are doing, especially when they come from all over the world and are literally a nation of nations. The United States is more like the United Nations than the United Nations is itself, because the United States is a powerful governing group of extremely diverse and self-directed people with immense organized power. The propelling motivation of 260 million people is found in their current belief that each of them is first a citizen of co-equal standing. Each has a voice in what is to be done, and each can vote in a democracy where the people rule, rather than some other subgroup like aristocrats, business people, rich people, brilliant people, university graduates, professionals or teachers. All of the other roles we play are subordinate to the citizen—the plain citizen who lives, who is wounded by enemies, who sometimes dies and accepts the risk of death to be an autonomous citizen living under laws of his or her own making. This is the essence of being American, living the American dream—it is no higher or lofty than simply being a citizen.

One could argue that citizenship is elevated too much, but that could never be so. Without your citizenship and allegiance responsibilities you remain a human being, but you are not a citizen of the United States. You are a mere employee of Nestlé or Exxon, not a citizen. Once outside the borders of the United States, it is too clear just how important being a citizen is to every human being. No one asks for your passport from General Motors. Consider the waves of immigrants over two centuries whose dream it was to be a citizen of the United States. Is citizenship taken for granted by many of the 260 million people in America? The one million people in prisons know just how much citizenship rights may be reduced by due process and justice to create death rows, prison cells that take every minute of one's liberty and fines or restitution that impoverish bad citizens who approach that limbo world of "less than full citizenship." The Thirteenth Amendment recognizes this status of involuntary servitude for crime. After all, the last half century of law and order politics in America is a voice within all of us to live peaceably with one another. No one guarantees that every other citizen will live within the law and order of the nation. When citizens falter, there are consequences, but no denationalization except for death sentences. We cannot strip citizenship, as we saw in the case of denationalization attempted but failed in *Trop v. Dulles*.

The rule is too plain. In democratic nations with constitutional order and laws of the majority the citizens, the "demos" of democracy, remain the ultimate authority over all of community life as we know it. They may decide both what is public and what is private—no immutable scientific law decides that for them. They may select any economic or social order or legal order they choose, so long as the selection is done by constitutionally acceptable means, especially in fundamental matters by amending the Constitution. This is what it means to be an American. This is the core of the American dream—the liberty desired to make laws, to vote and to decide whether or not to remain pregnant in the early months. Sovereignty is a broad and populist-based idea, especially the idea of popular sovereignty. Revolutions themselves are based on the idea of a sovereign people.

Sigmund Timberg, in 1945, explained an enlightened view of sovereignty. "There is no single jurist who has contributed as much to the establishment of both the practical and theoretical sovereignty of the United States as Chief Justice Marshall. Yet, his notion of sovereignty is in no way inconsistent with what has just been said [quoting Justice Marshall]:

Government is a mere agency established by the people for the exercise of those powers which reside in them. The powers of the government are not, in strictness, granted, but delegated powers, and may be revoked. It results that no portion of sovereignty resides in government. A man makes no grant of his estate when he constitutes an attorney to manage it. (Timberg, 1945: 397)

During the debate at the Virginia Constitutional Convention, Chief Justice Marshall said:

Is not liberty secure with us, where the people hold all powers in their own hands, and delegate them cautiously, for short periods, to their servants, who are accountable for the smallest mal-administration? . . . We are threatened with the loss of our liberties by the possible abuse of power, notwithstanding the maxim that those who give may take away. It is the people that give power and can take it back. What shall restrain them? They are the masters who give it, and of whom their servants hold it. (Timberg, 1945: 397–398)

Popular sovereignty is rooted in the basic law of America. To threaten popular sovereignty is to threaten the people of the nation. That should concern, as it has, Raymond Vernon and other thoughtful people. Both domestic and foreign corporations could threaten the sovereignty of the people and do so, in fact.

CORPORATE ATTEMPTS TO TAKE OVER POPULAR SOVEREIGNTY

The recurrent theme at the end of the twentieth century and the *storminess* of American political life could now be titled *When Corporations Rule the World*. This was the 1995 title for David Korten's book (Korten, 1995). It was a subtheme of my 1995 book, *Too Much Liberty?* (Saari, 1995). There I reflected on the oligarchies of plutocrats trying to buy public office and control public policy by bribery through campaign gifts to politicians (see also Bowman, 1996).

The central fear of American political life is power that has become un-checked, unregulated, unseparated in form and too influential—all drowning out the voice of the people (Greider, 1992). In America, it is sovereignty of the people, national popular sovereignty of 260 million people, that is being threat-ened once again. President Theodore Roosevelt recognized the threat and fought it by use of the Sherman Antitrust Act of 1890. Too much corporate power was rightly understood then as a threat to the American society. It is no different in 1899 or 1999, and it will be no different in 2005 or 2015 unless political action is taken by the American people to correct the obvious imbalance of power. Vox populi—the voice of the people—is what American democracy is all about, not the "Vox corporatis" or the "Voice of the Master," to use the old RCA little white dog advertising theme. The voice of the master is either the voice of the majority of the people in a democracy or it is some lesser voice, an economic voice represented by giant corporations like Coca-Cola, Budweiser, Ford, DuPont; you name it. They are household words—Kmart, Wal-Mart, Ci-ticorp, American Express. These lesser financially well-heeled voices dominate our television, radio and other media, but they do not and cannot claim to represent the American people who speak *not* through corporations but who speak directly to one another as people without the editorial filtration of big business television and publishers or editors or others. It is the constant attempt by giant corporations to usurp the people's voice and call it their own (through, for example, fictive public interest groups) that so deeply angers the American public; the authentic voices of Ralph Nader and David Korten in the United States, and Vandana Shiva of India and many others across the globe are ig-nored.

There are two basic political lessons to learn about American political per-spectives:

1. Unchecked power does not long go unchecked in America.
2. No one can claim to speak for Americans. Their political sovereignty cannot be bought or sold; it is an inalienable right that cannot be bought or sold in any market. An

inalienable right—what is it? It means in the older language of the Declaration of Independence that you can never be without a birthright. It was *not* sold to you; it is yours by birth alone or by naturalization. You cannot sell it. By swearing allegiance to your new country, you become a new citizen by a constitutionally recognized process before a Judge of the United States District Court. What has commerce got to do with it? Nothing.

It is the corporate threat to monetize, marketize and sell the sovereignty of the American people that is so very treacherous a threat, a political act by the major corporations in America. It has been tried before, many times, and it will be tried into the future. It will never succeed.

Takeover of America's popular sovereignty by giant corporations is the perpetual threat by the *Fortune* 500, now the Global 500, the Forbes 200, the *Business Week* 1000 or the major corporations on the Wall Street stock market. These are the threat to democracy—not some foreign source of trouble, and certainly not the poor, old, disabled, women, students or those on welfare.

The Emeritus Harvard University scholar Samuel Beer, in his 1993 book *To Make a Nation*, is a place to regain a 750-year historical appreciation of the roots of the idea of popular sovereignty. I will explain more of his view in this chapter. The idea is both simple and complex, especially in a federal order such as the United States. "We, the people" in the first line of the U.S. Constitution is the sovereign power of human beings—150 million Americans entitled to vote, flesh and blood. It is not General Motors Corporation, Boeing, Ford Motor Company, DuPont, or CNN, or any of the economic vehicles to support our economy. And our Bill of Rights supports our speaking out. Speaking for Americans is a task each of us is quite capable of doing on our own. We do not need corporations to tell us what to think about the world. Arrogance—political arrogance—is at the heart of the effort to market and take over the sovereignty of the American people. Power is at the heart of it all—the power to control the wealth of the nation. The wealth of nations is directed by the sovereign power of all the people—not by some little economic unit called Caterpillar Corporation. Through the power to regulate and tax, the sovereign voice of the people is heard in every corporate board room, especially when expressed by Congress and the president on our behalf and especially when 50 state capitals voice the same opinion. Smoking lawsuits reflect this voice of rage at this time. Sovereignty cannot be bought or sold on any market—no one can give it to another. It is the inalienable, unsellable, unmarketable possession of every human being from birth to death. Popular sovereignty is the ancient Greek "automonia" that exists in each person's individual breast to strive for national liberty.

Concern over the World Trade Organization as a decisional body to replace popular sovereignty is a most serious concern. Nor is it answered yet today without canceling the GATT and NAFTA "agreements." This may well be the next step in global trade if popular sovereignty means anything.

SOVEREIGNTY PARADOX—"PRIVATE BUSINESS" CORPORATIONS ACTING AS POLITICAL ORGANS

The paradox of this chapter is that I am forced to use political concepts like sovereignty to explain behavior of economic institutions like globalizing corporations. How does one explain the yearning for sovereignty (both national and international autonomy) by economic units (globalizing corporations) that cannot be explored solely with economic concepts such as free markets, comparative advantage, demand and supply or anything derived from Adam Smith's thinking? Sovereignty is primarily a political idea with non-economic roots of its own in Western civilization. Sovereignty does mean the power to put citizens (people and corporations) to death or punish them for crimes, to take their liberty and put them into prison for life and to take their property, seizing it without compensation. All of these are some of the contemporary hallmarks of sovereignty. That is power. Without your life, liberty or property, what are you? You are either dead, a slave or left destitute by order of a state. Modern non-democratic corporations, under incorporation laws, are never authorized or legitimated to issue death sentences to people, to enslave them or to take their property without fair exchange by seizing it. Why, then, the urge among globalizing corporations for sovereignty? Do they want such power?

It was indeed startling to read David Korten's *When Corporations Rule the World*, which blasted an unjust economic global order spawned by globalizing corporations. What, I wondered, has gotten into corporate leaders' minds to get them and others thinking about the politics of ruling the world? Klaus Schwab and Claude Smajda of the Davos World Economic Forum stated:

Economic globalization has entered a critical phase. A mounting backlash against its effects, especially in industrial democracies, is threatening a very disruptive impact on economic activity and social stability in many countries. The mood in these democracies is one of helplessness and anxiety, which helps explain the rise of a new brand of populist politicians. This can easily turn into revolt. (Friedman, 1996: A19)

To put it in other terms, "Are not the important actors in world affairs nowadays the global corporations?" (Kennedy, 1993: 122–123). Are the "old political boundaries of nation-states . . . being made obsolete by an alliance of commerce and technology?" (Wriston, 1992:11). Is there a future for the nation-state? This question, raised before, is on the minds of many. This even seems to be a semi-serious question across the globe, as we previously noted. Let's explore this globalizing mind-set a bit further.

NO FUTURE FOR THE NATION-STATE: A MIND-SET

Some would agree that there is no future for nations. In 1972, Carl A. Gerstacker, chairman of Dow Chemical Company, openly dreamed of owning for his headquarters an island owned by no nation—a place to escape the laws of any nation that restricts free movement of goods, information and profits. He even got offers of islands. The theory seemed to be, if you cannot beat nation-states, join them, become one of them. This dream is possibly all wet, or just a wet dream, or maybe an illusion of a secretive Robinson Crusoe (Barnet and Cavanagh, 1994: 251). Even before the famous Gerstacker outburst, a number of prominent people argued for a ''cosmocorp'' type of globalized corporation— loyal to the cosmos but not beholden to anything as puny as a nation on Earth in the solar system (Ball, 1967). The Honorable George W. Ball, an outstanding American political figure, spoke of the cosmocorp at the annual dinner of the British National Committee of the International Chamber of Commerce in London, England, on October 18, 1967. Ball was a realist, saying his idea was tentative and would surely meet complicated political reactions. It did—it died like any suggestion that vaunts as valuable a peculiar status in its title—''Cosmocorp: The Importance of Being Stateless.'' But it did not die without a host of big names promoting the idea in one way or another—Neil Jacoby, A. W. Clausen, Peter Drucker, Courtney C. Brown and David Rockefeller (Bowman, 1996: 293–296). These people were characterized as corporate cobdenites by Scott Bowman, who named them after the free trader Richard Cobden. Cobden wrote in 1844 that trade was a sure way to stop governments from warring.

The free trade ideology had run rampant in the 1960s through business schools, law schools and businesses feeding off those economists who supported such a free trade ideology. In other words, politics, law, economics and business merged to become a legal business political economy where business dreams of its own domination to rule the world its way and, incidentally, of being a state, a monopoly, a government, a citizen, lawmaker, regulator, judge and jury. What Gerstacker or Ball dreamed of is clearly separated by many constitutions today into separate powers—legislative, executive and judicial. These powers are to be put together once again in a new, business-dominated tyranny—a corporate non-democratic oligarchy that is answerable to no one, not to nation-states, not governments and, most certainly, not to the people as citizens or customers. The CEOs of the great managerial revolution in American business, so well described historically by Chandler, may well be on their final approach to rule the world. Vernon's title, *Sovereignty at Bay*, reflected in 1971 the pushing aside of nation-states by aggressive globalizing corporations, some of whom may be other nations in corporate disguise. In this sense, maybe David Korten is right about the inner-directing motivation of those who rule globalizing corporations—they want popular sovereignty to be replaced by their brand of oligarchy, unelected tyranny.

If a new aristocratic business reality is being joined in law, politics and economy, then the bottom line is not merely profit, but power. And as a consequence, perhaps the standards to judge corporate rule must be expanded by law; new corporate statutes drafted to reflect a new political legitimacy. Some have suggested popular election of CEOs by the people, public representatives elected to the Boards of Directors of the *Fortune* 500, federal chartering and impeachment of disloyal CEOs and imprisonment or death for those caught cheating on the people. After all, business may be asking for other non-profit standards by its political gifts or bribes to Republican and Democratic candidates. There may be a need to publicly elect people as representatives to the Business Roundtable just as people are elected to the legislature, since the Business Roundtable (CEOs of 200 of the largest U.S. corporations) wants it all—both business and politics. Condit of Boeing spoke the truth of business being politics and politics being business. This very mixture challenges separation of powers, federal order, checks and balances among other constitutional norms approved by the people of the entire United States.

WITHERING OF THE NATION-STATE

Let us look at some views of the waning of the nation-state in more depth. Japan's self-styled management guru is Kenichi Ohmae, who holds a Ph.D. in nuclear engineering, and was a managing director of an international business consulting firm. He is the author of several books, including his two latest, which he claims are widely read in the United States and Japan. *The Borderless World* (1991) and *The End of the Nation State* (1995) are two interesting contributions. He argued that developments and forces in business will topple governments that opposed them. He prescribed a role for governments in a borderless world as mere handmaidens to business and nothing more; business politics was paramount to achieve economic dominance. He offered no vision of government or popular sovereignty; he railed against bureaucrats and he offered a simplistic view of human liberty. The closest he comes to truth is decrying the tyranny of modern democracy that tends to give equal weight to votes before contributions to maintaining the society. Ohmae would give the rich more votes. The global economy of value to him is 750 million people earning $10,000 or more a year (*Wall Street Journal*, January 27, 1993: A-6). The other 5 billion people are perhaps irrelevant; it is difficult to say, but it seems likely.

So much for Kenichi Ohmae's view of who counts in the world and who does not count. So much for an Asian nuclear engineer–business consultant understanding of Western civilization and the idea of political sovereignty—popular sovereignty. It was quite limited or non-existent—his literature was mostly citations to himself in 1995. There is virtually nothing of merit in Ohmae's ideas of a borderless world, to state it charitably. Misleading people badly is a more accurate impression, and for this there is no forgiveness, just sadness.

America's well-known professor of business administration at Harvard School of Business is Rosabeth Moss Kanter who, in her twelfth book *World Class: Thriving Locally in the Global Economy* (1995), urged American communities to actively develop amenities and resources to encourage visiting global businesses to feel at home and stay put. That advice is pretty good as a cheerleader for global business, but the feeling contradicts the basically footloose, globe-straddling nature of modern globalizing corporations. Kanter must believe that it is possible to calm the jet setter, cosmopolitan American or non-American business man or woman and keep them down long enough to interest them in investing in America at all. She argued that communities must open themselves to globalizing corporations. It sounds to many like an internal imperative of the commerce power of the federal government of the United States now applied globally or externally. Kanter's extolling of cosmopolitans and her trashing of nativists is clear, but there is no doubt that world class people, the non-democratic oligarchs, are rising, probably in some sort of global oligarchy to take over the world, and she cheers them on. And she says local governments should open their treasuries to such global trotters. After all, *Forbes* magazine tells us there are more billionaires and mutlimillionaires than ever who need such cheerleaders in local communities. No different from Ohmae in attitude but clearly different in empirical study, Kanter views governments as nothing more than doormats for businesspeople. Not even a glimmering of popular sovereignty comes through. So much for Kanter's understanding of sovereignty, though the focus of *World Class* is clearly about the politics of business.

Reminding us of the early work of George Ball's 1967 dream of a stateless corporation, Walter B. Wriston, former chairman of Citicorp, a globalizing bank in the United States, offered his views of nation-states in *The Twilight of Sovereignty* (1992). According to Wriston, the nation-state is headed for twilight—especially in banking with high technology spanning the globe. Wriston seriously wrote that sovereignty is a modern institution, just a few hundred years old, but he did mention medieval roots. Modern sovereigns, he argued, permitted other institutions to exist—like churches, universities, corporations, and voluntary associations. But this "sufferance" will change, he thinks, as information reverses the drift toward the centralizing of power of states. Wriston wrote: "But the power of the state will diminish, particularly its sovereign power: the power to judge without being judged, to delimit the powers and privileges of the other institutions within society" (1992: 34–35).

Does this mean the popular sovereignty must wane before technology? Obviously, Wriston was resentful of government taxes and regulation, expressed by saying that in an "information economy" business may decide to leave a town or nation if unhappy. He failed to note that corporations already do that without warning in our information economy. Plant closing notice laws have had to be passed to temper this action. With Nixon, Shultz and Kissinger extolling the Wriston book, one would think in some way it was a valuable work. Shallow is the only way to moderately describe Wriston's understanding of sovereignty, much less popular sovereignty.

Later, when I will compare Samuel Beer's visions and analysis of sovereignty, we will readily see how flatly mistaken, simplistic and self-serving are the views expressed by Wriston. Ethan B. Kapstein believes that neither technology nor banking have changed the singular ability of nations to tax and make laws and treaties. He believes that in finance, ''no actor is more important than the state'' (Kapstein, 1991/1992: 55–62, 60). That is a contradictory view without equivocation from an expert on the subject of global finance. Especially in Chapter 9 below, it is clear that when looking at banking practices, Kapstein is more wise, honest and understanding than Wriston. A new voice agrees that states are paramount institutions (Pauly, 1997).

HAIL TO THE NATION-STATE

Thomas Jefferson believed that merchants have no country allegiance except to those places where they make profits; Karl Marx thought working men had no country, therefore, workers of the world should unite. Maybe now it should be ''stateless business people of the world unite.'' This means a lot of stateless people will result under modern global capitalism, if true. A sociologist writer from, of all remote places, the University of Tasmania, Australia, Malcolm Waters, brilliantly analyzed world trends in *Globalization* (1995). This succinctly written analytical tool refers to the trends toward multinational enterprises (MNE) or transnational corporations (TNC). Waters reviewed globalizing economic, political and social trends, asking about the existence of a globalized economy, a new world cultural chaos and even post-globalization conditions (when it will be finished) and when the world as a whole could be possibly dissolved into one gigantic cosmocorp organization. Waters observed, however, a disturbing trend in that a global polity is possible, but ''the state remains highly resistant, largely sovereign and a critical arena for problem solving'' (Waters, 1995: 122). In several ways, nation-states are strong, territorial and flexible. Waters thought nation-states may be a final bastion resisting these globalizing trends. The solvent of globalizing can not dissolve something as permanent as nation-states. This does contrast strikingly with views of previous writers.

In a 1995 speech in Tokyo, Professor Brigitte Stern of the University of Paris closed her remarks on the changing role of states by arguing provocatively: ''The nation-state is dead. Long live the nation-state.'' Stern recognized the attack on nations from above by transfers of sovereign powers or duties to multilateral agencies, the globalization of the economy, the development of technology, and the diversified actors of international affairs. And both regionalism and religions provide an attack on the nation-state, but in assessing the strong future of the nation-state, she emphasized the following unique role of the state:

1. As an arbitrator between market and society.
2. As an economic operator of activities (space activities).
3. As a guardian of human values: cultural values of democracy and human rights.
4. As a guardian of human welfare to ensure sharing of wealth and solidarity in times of need (natural disaster, etc.).

This view is solid support for the position that nation-states will not be dissolved by globalizing forces; and it is not merely a peculiar French statist proclivity being expressed by Professor Stern.

The title of Professor Yao-Su Hu's 1994 article, "Global or Stateless Corporations Are National Firms with International Operations," stops you and rivets the mind with its blunt assertion that piling on 30 years of adjectives to describe a corporation in international business is possibly misleading—descriptors such as transnational, multinational, interterritorial, global, worldwide, and cosmocorp (Hu, 1994). The idea of nationality, home state regulation and taxing, the advent of bankruptcy and ownership and control of voting stock suggest the serious significance to *Stateness*, not statelessness. Furthermore, Hu states: "In legal terminology, there is no such thing as a multinational or global company. At present, there is no international law under which a transnational or supranational company can be formed and have legal existence in several nation-states" (Hu, 1992: 115). This surprising and little understood fact of life of a legal entity is supported by Phillip I. Blumberg, who stated, "The contemplation of such a development on the international scale is still visionary" (Blumberg, 1993: 172). With nations controlling the creation of corporations and their death, and those with world business included, the very concern expressed by Raymond Vernon, quoted earlier in this chapter, returns to haunt the idea of a multinational corporation. Nations protective of corporations, calling them "home" companies will resent interference by corporations of other nations not from the home. Canadian companies trading in Cuba are affected by foreign policy of the United States, a perfect illustration of interference—the Helms-Burton Act.

Protecting jobs, human rights and the environment requires that global economic institutions be brought under the authority of political institutions to enhance their legitimacy and the stability of political life (Barnet and Cavanagh, 1994: 421–422). This is a vote for stronger sovereign powers in nation-states. And, those authors argue that to allow business executives the right to exercise political power is an act of affrontery to public accountability for elected public officials. Multinationals thus become everyone's favorite monster, because it is believed their power is not checked, structured and confined. There is a loose worrisome power, especially if governments are weak.

Another clear vote in favor of nation-states and their future is offered by Paul Kennedy, in *Preparing for the Twenty-First Century* (1993). While examining general global trends, such as population explosion, world agriculture, robotics and environmental dangers, Kennedy examined the multinational corporation in manufacturing and finance. While he acknowledged globalization forces, his concern was that one-fifth of the world population, the "haves," may make things worse for the other four-fifths, the "have-nots," in pursuit of a free trade ideology without limits. Can a market for any goods or services concern itself with social justice and fairness? (Kennedy, 1993: 56). This was an excellent question of economic political law. How, he asked, could the footloose multinational corporation, loyal to no nation or employee, to no government, and making alliances, joint ventures and contracts that keep it beyond the reach of local taxes and regulations, be able to look at the faces of hungry and dissatisfied masses in fourth-fifths of the world? (Kennedy, 1993: 58 and 64). Do CEOs of globalized corporations give up the home country so that Ford, Coca-Cola, Colgate Palmolive and IBM become stateless and then put American interests on a plane with 50 or 150 nations? This seems to be the trend—America is no better as a nation than any place on earth in the eyes of the all-knowing, unelected business oligarchies running the global cosmocorp.

Paul Kennedy offered a splendid analysis of what he called borderless world theories by fans of the globalization trends. His answer ultimately was a vote in favor of nation-states: ''It seems, even if the autonomy and functions of the state have been eroded by transnational trends, no adequate substitute has emerged to replace it (the state) as the key unit responding to global change'' (Kennedy, 1993: 134). This was another major reasoned analysis of the future of the nation-state, and it saw none of the future offered by Ohmae, Kanter or Wriston. The opposite votes by reasoned accounts are almost equal in number, but qualitatively the views of Barnet, Cavanagh, Hu, Stern and Kennedy seem certainly more well reasoned—globally powerful and convincing. Most of us would not be entirely sure of what direction to take public policy based on these accounts mentioned so far, and the diversity of viewpoints. This puzzle I understand, and it is perplexing. Trying to find a way out of this conflict is not easy or simple, but let us try to pursue the thinking along two lines. Is there an argument made by reasonable voices in business that urges a stronger future for nation-states? And, are there arguments that can be made about sovereignty and the modern globalizing corporation that make sense based upon history? And finally, must we worry about attacks on the nation-state's authority by terrorists, rebels, freedom-fighters and firebrands of all types—including serious apologists for globalizing corporations that dilute, denigrate and defame the legitimacy of the state in a thoughtless way? Who contributes to the crisis of legitimacy when they find no future for a nation-state? This is the dilemma that faces us today and the questions beg for reasonable answers. This is the question posed by Nicholas Kittrie in his recent book, *The War against Authority* (1995).

One consistent voice of reason over decades is Raymond Vernon of Harvard University. His valuable work on international trade and related issues of globalizing corporations is both illuminating and farsighted. Vernon wrote *Sovereignty at Bay* in 1971, and he said: ''The basic asymmetry between multinational enterprises and national governments may be tolerable up to a point, but beyond that point there is a need to reestablish balance'' (Vernon, 1971: 284). A colleague of Vernon, Ethan B. Kapstein, a former international banker, also of Harvard and Brandeis Universities, captured the quotation above from Vernon to crystallize his own dominant view of international finance and the nation-state in 1994: ''My objective in this book is to provide a contrasting view of globalization. I argue that nation states have created a regulatory structure for international economic activity, and that they remain the single most important players'' (Kapstein, 1994: v).

In his *Governing the Global Economy*, (1994), Kapstein saw international finance developing in the early 1970s with major forces of globalization, innovation, speculation and deregulation coupled with modern technology. The result was ''a vast casino''—a tribute to Susan Strange's description ''casino capitalism'' (Strange, 1986). Luck, not skill, dominated the market and the collapse of the Bretton Woods monetary system, oil price shocks and debt crises raised a specter of a global crash (Kapstein, 1994: 177). And more trauma was in the future. From the June 18, 1982 scandalous death of Roberto Calvi, found hanging by his neck from Black Friars Bridge in London (the then chairman of Italy's Banco Ambrosiano), to the decade-later July 5, 1991 closure of the Bank of Credit and Commerce International (BCCI)—nation-states have wondered justifiably about banking stability. The Daiwa Bank of Japan exclusion from the United States in 1996 and M. Leeson's 1995 trading scandal for London's Barings Bank in the Far East leading to its collapse have shaken regulators of banks. In Chapter 9, this is explained in more detail. Kapstein argued for strong home state bank control and for regulation of multinationals by market-based enforcement, such as the Basle Accord (Kapstein, 1994: 48,184).

In a most volatile international arena—international finance—a voice of reason (Kapstein) votes for nation-states to solve the worst problems—the business crimes of banking multinationals. And, he sees a future for industry-based standards for enforcement. This is striking support for the nation-state, and it is a rejection of the borderless world logic and a further rejection of a purported loss of national identity for multinational corporations by asserting ''international cooperation based upon home country control'' (Kapstein, 1994: 8,184). No corporation loses its home country ever. Daiwa Bank is a good example of a host nation rejection (United States) and home country control (Japan). This pattern of control did actually work in the real world of international finance and crime in 1996. International finance may be losing some of its casino quality in the more sober second thoughts of bank regulators of nation-states and of sound business leadership in industry controls and enforcement. Sovereignty seems alive and somewhat healthy in the perspective of Kapstein due to more recent banking regulatory actions (see also Kapstein, 1991–1992 and Chapter 9 below).

As an eloquent critic of corporate globalization who observed the loss of sovereignty, self and community across the globe and who saw, also, corporate rule undermining democracy, David Korten, in *When Corporations Rule the World* (1995), exposed the illusions of those who lead multinational corporations—the CEOs. The illusions of unlimited growth and domination by corporations were unspoken assumptions by which daily management of giant companies was conducted. The central point of Korten was to see clearly that sovereignty of the citizen, the human being, is challenged by assertion of corporate domination of both the economics and politics of many democratic nations. This argument goes to the heart of the issue that is central to the true meaning of sovereignty in the United States and many other democratic nations where rule is by the many and not the few. The few is represented by the multinational corporation—the many are the people in nation-states.

In a disclosure statement, Korten asserted that an efficient industry and commerce are essential to human well-being, but not with the current dominant global corporations. Korten argued for power restored to the small and local. This came from a person who was a Stanford University Graduate School of Business doctorate and a 30-year global expert on development. It was quite a shocking revelation for many, but completely understandable to others.

Most striking for purposes of this chapter, examining the links between ideas of globalization and the ideas of sovereignty of nation states, is Korten's citizens' agenda: "*When Corporations Rule the World* outlines a citizens' agenda to enhance these efforts by getting corporations out of politics and creating localized economies that empower communities within a system of global cooperation" (Korten, 1995: 13). Korten wanted each person to reclaim his or her political power and spiritual nature. To do this, Korten argued that many CEOs and others of globalizing corporations who acted like cowboys in a spaceship must now be tamed. Transition to a "full" world no longer could tolerate cowboys in business. Growth was at global limits—and we were all sensing this. But corporate power in America still did not get the global picture since it was wedded to sanctification of growth and greed. One could call it cowboy capitalism. One could call the illusions of corporate CEOs cloud-minding: Korten's vigorous argumentation was devastating toward those who mindlessly mind the multinational corporations.

It is too easy to become sidetracked in view of the power and creativity in Korten's work, but it is necessary here to focus on just a small part of his much larger argument, evidence and agenda. Korten develops a set of principles, one of which is the principle of people's sovereignty. He wrote:

Sovereignty resides only with people—all people, real people who need fresh air to breathe, clean water to drink, uncontaminated food to eat, and livelihoods that allow them to earn their keep. Neither governments nor corporations can usurp that sovereignty unless we choose to yield it. (Korten, 1995: 276)

Furthermore, he argued that corporations have no natural or inalienable rights: "We, the sovereign people have an inalienable right to determine whether the intended public purpose is being served and to establish legal processes to amend or withdraw a corporate charter at any time we so choose" (Korten, 1995: 296).

Staying with Korten's thought about the sovereignty of the people and the people's sovereign right to change terms of corporate charters, both ideas may seem a far-fetched view of a global economist businessman who does not grasp what he is saying legally even though he sees the business, economic and global implications. Politically, Korten could be accused of being somewhat naive. Is this true? Is Korten correct in terms of American political history that sovereignty lies with real people, not corporations? For those who may become anxious that Korten is right, I am sorry to confirm that he is right on target with this conception of who is in charge in a democracy. It is the people, not a legal fiction called a corporation. How far have we come since Thomas Jefferson and Thomas Paine and Chief Justice John Marshall to confuse real people with fictive corporations?

AUTHENTIC SOVEREIGNTY IN AMERICA

It now appears that Brigitte Stern, Yao-Su Hu, David Korten, Paul Kennedy, Richard Barnet, John Cavanagh, Ethan Kapstein and Raymond Vernon foresee some important balancing role for nation-states in the future of globalizing corporations. And the idea of sovereignty underlies some of their thinking. Popular national sovereignty was and is now embodied in the first words of the Constitution of the United States adopted in 1787:

We, the people of the United States, in order to form a more perfect union, establish justice, insure domestic tranquility, provide for the common defense, promote the general welfare, and secure the blessings of liberty to ourselves and our posterity, do ordain and establish this Constitution for the United States of America.

This social contract applies to all people born and living here and to people naturalized in the United States. It supports the idea of sovereignty of the people of the entire United States in the most authentic manner one could hope to read.

However, the idea of sovereignty in the Constitution of the United States has been grossly misunderstood in the last 200 years. Winning the Civil War protected the Union of the American people from an erroneous and secessionist view, developed by John C. Calhoun of South Carolina and others, that sovereignty rested in the states and in state governments in particular. Calhoun called the idea of an American people ''mere chimera'' (Beer, 1993: 317). National popular sovereignty did not rest, as Calhoun thought, in part of the people, but instead in *all* of the people of the United States. Article V of the Constitution offered to the people four ways to amend the Constitution and amending is done by voice of all of the people across the nation, not those in one region or one state or one city or county. One type of popular sovereignty is the legitimate power to overthrow and to reconstitute the government—here the people as sovereigns are not bound by government or law. This sovereignty is inherent in the Declaration of Independence. The other sovereignty is found in the laws (constitutions and statutes) established by the people (federal, state and local) in which limits are placed on citizens and governments. As Beer noted:

These two sorts of sovereignty were exercised by the same human agency, the people of the United States, who, exercising their constituent sovereignty, declared their independence and in due course ratified the Constitution, and, thereafter, exercising their governmental sovereignty, governed themselves under its law. (Beer, 1993: 336)

America is still haunted by Calhoun's rejected compact theory of American federalism which posits many "peoples" in the United States and state sovereignty as a consequence. President Ronald Reagan, in his first Inaugural address on January 20, 1981, asserted a new federalism, and he stated: "The federal government did not create the states, the states created the federal government" (Beer, 1993: 2).

This statement is historically false and the Civil War disproved it politically by a resounding conclusion in defeat of some of the states. The Reagan reliance on Calhoun's rejected compact theory of federalism is coupled with his memorable phrase, "Government is not the solution to our problem; government is the problem." He could have said the people are the problem because they are the rulers of the government. The error of Reagan revealed the president's fallibility in basic understanding of the Constitution of the Union and of national history which, according to Samuel H. Beer, Eaton Professor of the Science of Government, Emeritus of Harvard University, required us to review the very different national theory of federalism that Reagan apparently missed in his education. The national theory posits one sovereign power "final say" to be in the hands of the people of the United States, now expressed in the U.S. Constitution and various amendments the people have added.

The people of the United States have dual federal and state citizenship and both governments can tax them, put them to death for serious crimes and control their liberty and property. Sovereignty of the people is exercised through law to which they assent. Consent of the governed is critical, but even more critical is the lack of any view that corporations can vote like human beings. Corporations are not nations in any sense of the word nation. Corporations do not vote in elections as people do—they are not people. No one asks how General Motors voted for U.S. presidents. We will see the dollars corporations use to influence and displace the people's elections. So sovereignty of the people of the United States legally and politically excluded all corporations, from the giant ones to closely held corporations. Sovereignty—as David Korten and now Professor Beer remind us—is a human attribute of real people who think and vote.

The idea of sovereignty is embedded by Samuel H. Beer in his longer analysis of a national theory of federalism—how the American nation was made and why federalism was a central feature worked out by America. The Beer book, *To Make a Nation* (1993) is an extraordinary work of piety for an enthusiastic emeritus scholar who said his grandfathers from Ohio fought in the Civil War for the Union, and this did deeply impress him. Beer stated "I want to state as honestly, clearly and amply as I can the case for what my grandfathers did in the war. And by so stating, it honors them" (Beer, 1993: ix). Beer in his early career was not enthralled by federalism as an idea, but one student from Yugoslavia in his classes in the early 1960s said: "In federal America, you try to make everyone alike. By contrast in Yugoslavia our federal scheme heightens the diversity of its separate peoples, encouraging the cultivation of their different languages, religions, and cultures" (Beer, 1993: ix-x).

In retrospect, the disintegration of Yugoslavia in the late 1980s and 1990s and the ensuing genocide obviously may have had its seeds in the lack of an adequate vision of federalism of the American variety spoken by this student in the late 1960s. The forces spinning a nation apart were much stronger in Yugoslavia than forces of cohesion pulling it together. The Yugoslavia example is one of the most timely offered by Beer to show how foreign students cannot grasp American federalism easily—as he pointed out. Nor can a president of the United States grasp its history, as President Reagan revealed in his inaugural address in 1981. I would argue that the same may be true of the idea of sovereignty becoming confused as well, along with an inadequate grasp of the politics and economics of globalizing corporations and their global dreams.

Sovereignty is not just a few hundred years old as an idea, as Wriston asserted, and it certainly has roots in European medieval life and earlier. Beer starts with the principles of the hierarchic tradition as they were formulated by Thomas Aquinas (1225–1274) and related to their early roots going back to Plato. The principles of hierarchy are both authoritarian and deferential. The opposing view is republican tradition found in John Milton's (1608–1674) *Areopagatica*, which scorns the rule of the wise and holy and offers instead religious individual liberty of conscience as a guide for everyone—the individual citizen is his or her own master of deciding what is truth in religion. If each person is such a sovereign power, how then do these independent sovereign people govern themselves in a joint way with others in a democracy?

PEOPLE OF THE UNITED STATES AS SOVEREIGNS

Here Professor Beer offered the creative view of James Harrington's *Oceana*, written in 1656. Beer found federalism based upon a certain kind of constitutionalism. Sovereignty rested with Parliament in England. By contrast, in the United States both states and federal government (51 major governments) derive delegated power from the federal Constitution which is the prime expression or sovereign voice of the people of the United States. All governments are legally coordinated by the U.S. Constitution and neither is subordinate unless the Supremacy Clause of the Constitution says so explicitly or Congress or the Supreme Court interprets the Constitution to require a form of preemption by national government. Beer stated: "National federalism is possible because of these two key features: the people are the supreme law making power, and the law they make is superior to the law of both federal and state governments" (Beer, 1993: 92). Here the Constitution and Amendments are the superior law.

To allow these individual sovereigns to speak in a government by discussion in an extended republic of continental size, there was a need to listen to the ordinary person say something about the common good which the elite did not know and could only learn from her or him (Beer, 1993: 99). Beer's analysis of Harrington showed how it was possible to have a modern republic with the people in charge and exercising sovereignty through voting and through discussion as one people. Modern communication helps the discussion somewhat as well as it distracts. A nation-state is an evolved modern marvel discovered through trial and error. It is based upon political truths joined in thoughtful ways—federal orders, written constitutions, separation of powers, bills of rights, term limits, voting by people and all the other ideas it takes to make a nation work democratically to hear and to obey the voice of the many while protecting the voice of the individual. Sovereignty emerges as one of the key ideas in centuries of discussions of self-government. People feel powerful in such an order. Autonomia is at work.

By contrast, feelings of powerlessness in state legislatures toward the earlier corporate giants of railroads in the United States parallel the feelings in national governments today in the United States, Europe, Asia and Latin America when they deal with IBM, Ford or Unilever (Bowman, 1996: 301). Bowman stated:

The current trend in the merger movement suggests the emergence of an industrial-financial oligarchy controlling the entrenched oligarchies—that is, an *Oligarchy of Oligopolists*, a structure consistent with a transnational reorganization of markets as the model of corporate capitalism. (Bowman, 1996: 30) (emphasis added)

This creative and independent conclusion of Bowman paralleled but did not draw from David Korten's almost independent, simultaneous observations of a similar character. Bowman cited a "one-stop" merger control regulation for the European community and a European company statute, NAFTA and tariffs phasing out as further evidence of the need to consider where the oligarchy is taking the world.

Bowman stated: "If the corporate internationalists succeed in their mission and economic and political integration of the capitalist world proceeds as planned, corporate power indeed will have achieved its apogee" (Bowman, 1996: 302).

While there may be nothing illogical as Bowman mentioned about a federation of nations linked by common economic interests and bound by international laws and subject to the power of a transnational bourgeoisie (an international oligarchy that commands the wealth of major industrial and financial global corporations), there is something blatantly illegitimate about this state of affairs for rule by the people in the United States where sovereignty must first be given up by the people to achieve such an apogee of corporate power. Would a thousand years of civilization surrounding self-government by the people be so easily and voluntarily *given up* or *thrown away* by the people of the United States, by the English, French, Germans, Spanish, Italian and many others? Here is where, to use an American expression, the rubber hits the road in the life of politics. The probability of such an event is nearly zero without much blood being shed and convulsions of civil war. Nation-states may disintegrate, but not the democratic societies of the world that have been nurtured so carefully for hundreds of years. Certainly, not in the United States will we see popular national sovereignty so lightly cast to one side, even with the votes on GATT and NAFTA already done that suggest the sovereignty be given up lightly. Those were just agreements. The people have not yet fully grasped what is at stake in a global economy. But in 1999 many are finally beginning to see the light.

One could leave the sovereignty paradox where private business corporations yearn to be nation-states at this level of understanding, but it would not serve to enlarge our understanding of sovereignty further. For this reason, we must ask, Will nation-states wane and die? And the answer most assuredly is, *not* without a horrendous fight that is already beginning across the globe. The first International Conference on Globalization in November 1995 at Riverside Church in New York City offered powerful evidence of the beginning of a major global struggle heating up. The reviving of American unions in 1995 and 1996 is further evidence of more warfare in the commercial world against global dreams of corporate oligarchies inside transnational companies. Chambers of Commerce are worried, and they should be. The constant attack on corporate political action committees and the desire to rid American politics of corporate influences are further evidence of the launching of a new public order by the people. The seriously split votes on NAFTA and GATT were not reassuring victories for those who won, because they gave many concessions to get the economic integration agreements passed. A powerful residue of lurking resentment remains in the middle class across the nation toward the victors in these two crucial votes. In 1996, presidential candidates were exploiting the divisions, Patrick Buchanan, in particular. To say the fight has barely begun is perhaps a correct assessment of the lay of the political land at the end of this century (Buchanan, 1998). There are more questions about the future elaboration of sovereignty of the people inside a world order—in a world society that is growing in density and complexity and interaction. A broader international society is emerging, but sovereignty remains strong, as it should. The late 1997 negative politics defeating President Clinton's "fast track" proposal by some 80% of his party members was more concrete evidence of deep political change toward free trade ideology and its corporate sponsors.

INTERNATIONAL LAW PERSPECTIVES ON SOVEREIGNTY

A final vote in favor of the future of the nation-state was one made by Hedley Bull in 1977 in his classic *The Anarchical Society*. Bull, who died in 1985, believed that international relations is the politics of autonomous states without a common superior (Bull, 1995: iii). According to Stanley Hoffman, the editor of the second edition:

Bull's work, for all of its emphasis on common rules, is too firmly anti-utopian, too closely tied to the system of sovereign states—to what it is now a cliché to call the Westphalian system—to please those for whom states are the problem, not the solution, in so far as order is concerned. Bull's work was too "Grotian" for the Machiavellians and the Hobbesians, too statist for the Kantians and the cosmopolitans. (Bull, 1995: viii)

Bull's clear-minded writing addressed three questions in 1977:

1. What is order in world politics?
2. How is order maintained within the present system of sovereign states?
3. Does the system of sovereign states still provide a viable path to world order?

The alternatives to nation-states are several—a new medievalism centered on cities; a world government without nation-states, just provinces, a set of states but not a system; and a system of nation-states but no international society (Bull, 1995: 240–247). Bull examined all three questions and four alternatives and concluded that: "There was no clear evidence that the states system was in decline, or that it was dysfunctional in relation to basic human purposes, provided that the element of international society in it could be preserved and strengthened in the ways that were indicated" (Bull, 1995: 307).

It would be an extreme disservice to think that Hedley Bull could be mentioned without exploring his ideas further, and the temptation is great. But in the interest of parsimony, it is important at least to note that *The Anarchical Society* grows in relevance to us rather than wanes over time. I share the enthusiasm of those who find Bull's work stimulating in general and I find it all the more stimulating because he found little evidence to justify a withering away of the state or nation-state in 1977. Two decades later, this observation can be reaffirmed—there are now more nations than ever recognized by the United Nations and by other nations. International observers and scholars in the post-cold war era remain puzzled about the three questions posed by Bull in 1977. We know, however, that sovereignty still resides on the globe in the system of nation-states.

Before he died in 1985, Hedley Bull began work on a scholarly book that he did not finish, but which was finished by colleagues and others in 1990, *Hugo Grotius and International Relations* (Bull, Kingsberry and Roberts, 1992). In this work, Bull, who was Montague Burton Professor of International Relations at Oxford University and a Fellow of Balliol College, wrote an assessment of Hugo Grotius (1583–1645) in the study of international relations. Grotius wrote *De Jure Belli Ac Pacis* (1625; On the Law of War and Peace), considered to be one of the first great contributions to modern international law, and he wrote many other works on a wide range of subjects. His genius was recognized early, by age 18, at Leiden University. As a Dutch jurist and scholar, Hugo Grotius captured Bull's attention more than 400 years later. The reason Bull was so attracted to Hugo Grotius is not because of Grotius' view of sovereignty—which

Grotius believed was lodged in the sovereign state and did not reside in the people (Bull, 1990: 85). A more anti-democratic view could not be imagined from Grotius. And the sovereign state of Grotius excluded pirates, brigands and entities run by tyrants without a legal system (Bull, Kingsbury and Roberts, 1992: 235). Sovereignty for Hugo Grotius was: "That power is called sovereign whose actions are not subject to the legal control of another, so that they cannot be rendered void by the operation of another human will" (Bull, 1992: 230). Grotius said public war can be waged only by those who have support of the sovereign power. Sovereigns send ambassadors or enjoy the right of legation. No other groups do this. Bull said he had heard that if Grotius were alive today, he would have been in favor of the 1982 Law of the Sea Convention. Bull thought this a rather shallow or superficial historical view of Grotius. For Bull, it was much clearer: "The importance of Grotius lies in the part he played in establishing the idea of international society" (Bull, 1992: 93). States, regional organizations, non-governmental organizations and individual people have a place in the world society—the international society. Even globalizing corporations have a place in the international society conceived by Bull, who said:

Third, multinational corporations are able to operate only in conditions in which a modicum of peace and security has been provided by action of states. It is sovereign states which command most of the armed force in the world, which are the objects of the most powerful human loyalties, and whose conflict and cooperation determine the political structure of the world. *The multinational corporation does not even remotely provide a challenge to the state in the exercise of these functions.* Its scope of operations and even its survival is in this sense conditional upon decisions taken by states. (Bull, 1995: 263) (emphasis added)

The global sovereignty dreams of multinational corporations may include a subliminal desire to act like a nation-state but without conducting war, raising armies, taxing people, issuing passports, settling armed conflict in the former Yugoslavia or conducting International War Crimes Tribunals. As Bull so wisely concluded in 1977, there is no justification to think multinational corporations, "even remotely provide a challenge to the state." Transferring sovereignty from the people of the United States to 1,000 CEOs in the largest multinational corporations would be a transfer of the right of self-governance by more than 250 million human beings to 1,000 people. Conceived in this way, it is hard to think about multinational corporations of America being even slightly guilty of the somewhat treasonous belief that they would like to rule the world in such an oligarchy. But, can David Korten be so wrong? I think not, given the weight of his evidence, the cogency of his arguments and the clear plan of action he laid out to stop globalizing corporations as they currently proceed. Korten's agenda (in summary) for change is broad and precise:

1. Remove corporations from the political sphere.
2. Stop not-for-profit organizations that are corporate fronts.

3. Stop corporate charity organizations.

4. Stop political advertising on television.

5. Limit campaign expenditures.

6. Require public expenditures for elections.

7. Control media ownership stringently.

8. End advertising tax deductions.

9. Stop any commerce at the schools, make them drug-free and commerce-free zones.

10. Start a .5 percent financial transaction tax.

11. Graduate tax upward on short-term capital gains.

12. Require 100 percent reserve requirements for demand deposits.

13. Tighten regulation of financial derivatives.

14. Give preferred treatment to community banks.

15. Enforce antitrust laws harder.

16. Encourage worker and community buyouts of businesses.

17. Tax more heavily resource extraction, packaging, pollution, imports, corporate lobbying and advertising.

18. Require payout of profit to shareholders each year.

19. End all corporate subsidies.

20. Stop corporate monopolization of intellectual property.

21. Reduce debt to low-income nations.

22. Create an international financial transaction tax.

23. Regulate transnational trade and investment very closely.

24. Monitor environmental resources globally.

25. Close the World Bank.

26. Replace the International Monetary Fund.

27. Close the World Trade Organization and replace it.

Korten said corporate libertarians would think all of the above would interfere with operations of transnational corporations and financial markets. "That, of course, is precisely the intent" (Korten, 1995: 326).

CONCLUSIONS FOR THE SOVEREIGNTY PARADOX

To conclude, think of the basic question—are nation-states headed for twilight zones? Some business people, academicians, consultants and economists are sold on the eventual disappearance of nation-states. From 1967 on they have pleaded their case for free trade ideology which made some sense during a cold war and a rebuilding of Europe and Asia. Now that the cold war is over and rebuilding well finished for decades, why pick away further at nation-states, especially the citizens of the one nation-state—the United States—that has generously helped to bring it all about? If Bowman is correct, class warfare by the wealthy underlies the globalization and denigration of egalitarian ethos of government of, by and for the people, a peculiar American popular political perspective.

Perhaps a better answer lies in the exercise of sovereignty and its loss. The implications for a democratic nation like the United States are devastating economically and politically if citizens lose their power to control their destiny—their autonomia. Cosmocorps are designed to do just that—evade the controls of nation-states through deception, confusion and regionalization like the European Union.

The prescriptions of David Korten join the political battle where it should be joined, on the policy level—and the political battles will be fought because giant corporations are political agents by their own admission and design today—not just makers of airplanes and cars, sellers of gas, and software merchants. The fights should be fascinating, and the basic question haunts the policy debates: How much or how little do people want to govern themselves? If millions desire to be ruled by corporate CEOs like those who run Disney World, there will be an easy out from the fight. If millions do want to run their own lives, the CEOs will be downed by a ruinous public agenda that may drive them from all nations. They may become involuntarily stateless. The recent, intense negative political reaction toward rich Americans sheltering their wealth from American taxation by going offshore is but a tiny hint of the political bombshell that will forever shatter American corporate life if sovereignty is taken openly or quietly from American citizens. I fear the outrage that would ensue in both economic and political outcomes. As I suggested, political standards for CEOs, term limits, selection to office by the people of the nation, impeachment for wrongdoing—all of these and more would become highly attractive options. Thus, it is not silly to think that CEOs have gone too far and may one day bring ruin on themselves and shareholders and employees and directors and the public. We shall see.

REHABILITATING SOVEREIGNTY OF THE PEOPLE

Nicholas Kittrie searched, in *The War against Authority* (1995) for a new and exciting grounding for legitimacy of the state in a pluralistic world. According to Kittrie, dated and tired are the political formulas and legitimation doctrines such as "nation-state," "national sovereignty," "social compact" and "majority rule." The inherent inconsistencies in "sovereignty" and other old formulas face new challenges within and without (Kittrie, 1995: 246–247). Political authority requires rehabilitated foundations of legitimacy for institutions that were very long accepted on faith according to Kittrie.

First, Kittrie argued that pluralism is a dominant fact of political life. Second, he argued that vagueness pervades the idea of "peoples," "nationhood," "minorities," "autonomy" and "self-determination." Grotius wrestled with this same problem and pirates 400 years ago. The vagueness needs to be clarified and rethought. Kittrie is correct in saying that standards of nationhood must exist. Third, sound-minded people with a moral horizon of World Wars I and II in their minds may prefer traditional, legal and charismatic leaders with legitimacy grounded in more humane forms of legitimacy and governance (Kittrie, 1995: 251). No one wants Hitler or Stalin again.

The principle of subsidiarity is better known as small is beautiful (a la Schumacher)—that decentralized life is valuable; small units, local control, even home rule is important. About 100 years ago Oregon enshrined home rule in its constitution so cities could thrive. There is nothing new here, just forgotten or ignored for too long. The 50 states represent subsidiarity in reality for 350 years on the North American Continent.

David Korten's political agenda for change in relationships of globalizing corporations to the U.S. government and the 50 state governments is based upon two cogent and relevant beliefs that would satisfy Kittrie. First, Korten correctly assumes that popular national sovereignty of all the people of the United States must be brought to bear on giant corporations—that it is the people's sovereign power that must be exercised in the United States and across the globe to take corporations out of politics and to *confine* them to trade and commerce clearly and unequivocally. Samuel Beer offered extensive rehabilitation of the idea of how the national theory of federalism has evolved in the last 750 years, and how popular national sovereignty of the people of the United States joins with a view of constitutionalism suited to their unique view of American sovereignty in its constitutional framework today. Major rehabilitation is well underway. Kittrie seemed to call for this.

What Kittrie fails to stress in his brilliant book is *the war against authority of the sovereignty of the American people and democratic peoples elsewhere conducted daily by giant American and foreign corporations.* If one adds David Korten's perspective and prescriptions and sees them as new, pluralistic solutions clearly based upon the principle of subsidiarity, there is little doubt that the crisis of legitimacy of the American people to control corporations will force them to examine new solutions for their self-governance. William Greider's *One World, Ready or Not* (1997) lends further support to the need for nation-states to wake up to new realities in governing globalizing corporations.

Furthermore, my earlier suggestions of popular election of CEOs of giant corporations, term limits established for CEOs of giant corporations in public law and publicly set starting salaries for CEOs would begin the creativity called for by Kittrie in searching for new and better ways to develop the legitimacy of governments and their ability to control highly politicized giant corporations that are evolving into organs of governance and government—political institutions. Such policies would begin to rehabilitate the tired, old, but highly popular idea that sovereignty exists in the entire people of the United States. Grotius rejected popular sovereignty and did not then see the European public the way the public is seen today in America and Europe—with millions of college and high school graduates, quite competent to govern, well-informed, with a high degree of literacy, and well organized. The spark of self-governance needs a little recognition and encouragement in this field. Just imagine a public monitoring group that would observe and report systematically to the global public by Internet exactly what General Electric Corporation or Glaxo did last month with its resources. Multiply this group by 1,000 more giant corporations and a more exuberant form of self-analysis and oversight could not be imagined. Public oversight of globalizing corporations is sorely lacking. Here is a way for direct democracy to immediately watch and report just the way pension fund managers do today for Calpers and TIAA-CREF owners. Those in corporations to be observed may think this would be sovereignty gone wild and intrusive. The argument should begin.

No doubt enough valid questions have been raised in this part to start you thinking about the basic inquiry between globalizing corporations and democratic nations.

WESTERN NATION-STATE VISION: A REBALANCED VIEW

Jerry Mander examined the dark side of globalization recently and expressed an idea very clearly, which he called the Western Corporate Vision. Mander wrote in 1996:

But the deeper ideological principles of the global economy are not so new; they are only now being applied globally. These rules include:

• The absolute primacy of exponential income growth;

• The need for free trade to stimulate the growth;

• The destruction of "import substitution" economic models (which promote economic self-sufficiency) in favor of export-oriented economies;

• Accelerated privatization of public enterprises;

• And the aggressive promotion of consumerism, which when combined with global development, faithfully reflects the Western Corporate Vision. (Mander, 1996: 10).

This vision produces global monoculture—a homogenized, golden arches, franchised, standardized existence; and as Mander noted, there will be little reason to leave home—the world will be the same everywhere (Mander and Goldsmith, 1996).

But just as powerful as the Western Corporate Vision and its advocates arguing for its inevitability have become, so there is a view expressed here of the inevitability of a Western nation-state vision. This vision is now emerging and the two competing visions have clashed, are clashing, will clash. There is a slow but inexorable coming together of the nations of the world in reaction to the Western Corporate Vision to oppose it in bilateral treaties and multilateral treaties.

These treaties are the global corpus of law and order (Chayes and Chayes, 1995). The globe will be covered with this vision:

- Many global orders, not just one commercial order.
- A complete rejection of corporate structures and powers in designing a nation-state national operation to control MNCs, TNCs, or any other type (e.g., conglomerates).
- A rejection of the world federalist model or a UN-dominated model.
- A rejection of wild capitalism, free trade and excessive economic integration in the form of GATT and NAFTA and WTO.
- A careful and thoughtful elevation of cooperative, global, popular sovereignty—people-to-people, city-to-city.

The vision of the Western nation-state is beginning to look something like this:

1. National law and national legal structures will predominate and control most of international commercial law except where treaties or customary law are relevant. International law will be enforced in national courts with increasing frequency—not in international tribunals.

2. Where nations want harmony in commercial regulation, they will achieve it by treaty. Where nations do not care, the corporate interest will have to run international business risks knowledgeably.

3. Cross-border cooperative actions (e.g., FBI and Scotland Yard) will grow via treaties and agreements with the UN as observer and commentator, not necessarily enforcer. The enforcer role will continue to be the states.

4. The touchstone of legitimacy in all international affairs is the people of the nation expressed as popular sovereignty. All international systems will be designed to honor this first—as, for example, in the United Nations as a global institution required to recognize this legitimacy of sovereignty in nation-states.

5. The people of the world will be motivated primarily by sustainable development in future conditions of global society. They will produce massive change.

6. The people of the world recognize finally, especially the people of the U.S. that the United States' policy has allowed and encouraged its home corporations to run freely across the globe with very little regulations outside the nation, in contrast to much greater regulations inside the nation. This has led to the growth of anti-social multinationals with very bad ideas and habits. Their bad habits need home-country and host-country mutually respectful taming.

As Louis Turner perceptively noted in 1970: ''What well may become more worrying is the growth of a number of companies which are actively dishonest, and who have gone multinational in order to escape supervision in closely-policed countries'' (Turner, 1970: 212). Turner predicted the invisible Caribbean money laundering, anonymous corporations and tax havens long before they emerged strongly in the 1980s and 1990s where ''shrewd operators'' will operate ''where a number of small 'micro-states' can be played off against each other'' (Turner, 1970: 212). Tax evasion and other criminality now thrives there, but Turner could see it coming over three decades ago. We should be so perceptive and wise.

Chapter 5

Capitalisms, Politics, Taxes and Government Regulation of Major Corporations

Chapter 5 examines the meaning of capitalism as it has evolved for centuries. The 750 giant corporations exist within a capitalist order in the United States and in most developed nations. The United States developed regulated capitalism in the last 100 years, which differs from other types and the difference is quite striking. There are many types of capitalism. Michel Albert and others are right in pointing out the important varieties—the multiple models of capitalism (Albert, 1993; Silk and Silk, 1996). The United States is a regulated capitalism internally; a minimally regulated capitalism externally. Business enjoys an enormous freedom to do as it pleases (Johnson, Holmes and Kirkpatrick, 1998). Labor and management fight globally these days (*Multinational Monitor*, March 1997).

Regulated capitalism naturally draws the regulated capitalists to its center point of global power—the federal government in Washington, D.C. The interchange between the *Fortune* 500 and others and the federal government is obvious, well-publicized and is clearly evolving into a very close financial regulatory relationship—symbiotic in nature (Parry, 1996).

A study of the power, politics and the globalizing implications will allow us to better understand political action committees, and the issue of soft money given by giant globalizing corporations to politicians and political parties. The capitalist order evolved in the United States involves influencing and winning most political conflicts. This order spread to Canada and to Europe and Japan without the same regulatory or legal framework. As we will see, nations do not play by the same rules nor do their businesses or corporations. Deep pockets of millionaires, multimillionaires, billionaires and multibillionaires set the domestic and global agenda for rich nations (*Mother Jones*, March/April 1996).

When it comes to the globalization of giant corporations, none of the 50 states in the United States is powerful enough to handle the regulatory, tax, environmental or labor implications. The relationship requires very large, professional and well-staffed national regulators with a long-term (as opposed to revolving door) central focus upon the public interest every day. The struggle to influence these regulators and legislators is now seen as a major task of both domestic and foreign globalizing corporations. The attention is on internal national control, but the lack of external control of giant corporations is a major problem with global consequences. The international lack of regulation is awesome. An investment broker, Roger C. Altman, who served in the Carter and Clinton administrations in the U.S. Treasury Department, superhyped the point this way: "Markets will be the dominant worldwide force of the early twenty-first century, dwarfing that of the United States or any consortium of nations (Altman, 1998).

CAPITALISMS OF THE GLOBE VERSUS ONE TRUE CAPITALISM

Perhaps it is a naive assumption to think that those who speak of capitalism are of one mind or even that they know what they are speaking or writing about when it comes to the economy. The research for this book long ago put to rest those assumptions. During research on this book I discovered accumulating evidence that "capitalism" is a label applied to whatever economic system you prefer or hate—it has no universal definition, although as I wanted it to have one, and many others assume it has. This lack of universality may be why there is reluctance to use the word capitalism. One true capitalism does not exist except in the minds of a few people. Many capitalisms exist in the minds of many people (Silk and Silk, 1996). Let's explore some of the ideas of capitalism and their implications in this inquiry, keeping in mind the relevance to globalizing corporations.

Capitalism is supposed to express something of the nature of the economy of a nation; it may even express something about the political and social systems of a nation, but the term does not remain fixed as an economic, social, political and legal term. Capitalism is not a constitutional legal word of art in the U.S. Constitution. It does not appear in that text and the closest referent is the ownership of private property protected by the Fifth Amendment public taking clause. The idea of capitalism does have roots, but what "triumphed" over communism in the last few years is not a single thing called capitalism, nor did economic systems alone have much to do with the spiritual battles waged in the last 50 years by the Catholic Church, the Jewish community and others that achieved significant results of their own for the human mind.

Some of the capitalisms to which I refer have been already suggested.

Corporate Capitalism—Irving Kristol

Casino Capitalism—Susan Strange

Cowboy Capitalism—David Korten

These examples are just the beginning of a longer list of adjectives to characterize different capitalisms:

Investor Capitalism—Useem

People's Capitalism—Melloan

Global Capitalism—Ross, Trachte and Greider

Twenty-first-century Capitalism—Heilbroner

Rhine Model of Capitalism—Thurow

Survival-of-the-Fittest Capitalism—Thurow

Jungle Capitalism

Japanese Model of Capitalism

Gentlemanly Capitalism—Greider

Kremlin Capitalism—Blasi et al.

French Model of Capitalism

Ownerless Capitalism—Albert

Bank Capitalism—Albert

Arrogant Capital—Phillips

Speculative Capitalism

Free Market Capitalism

Pentagon Capitalism

Free Enterprise Capitalism

Desert Capitalism—Kopinak

Industrial Capitalism

Mercantile Capitalism

Crony Capitalism—Safire

''The twenty-first century capitalism will be dominated by a spectrum of capitalisms, some successful, some not. The crucial question for Americans, and perhaps for the world as a whole, is where our own nation will be located along that spectrum'' (Heilbroner, 1993: 162–163). Heilbroner adds that the problem of dynamics of competition in markets leads to live and let live, or cartels and state regulation, but as important, the 350 corporations globalizing are what he called the giant beams in the structure of ''world capitalism'' (Heilbroner, 1993: 105). There is obviously a relationship between giant globalizing corporations and the economies of the nations. This inquiry highlights that complexity and interdependence now and in the future. Thus, I conclude the term ''capitalism,'' regardless of the adjective specifically used to modify its meaning, is no fixed north star to guide anyone. But is that multiple nature of capitalism a clue to something more significant? The answer is found in the work of Fernand Braudel.

Fernand Braudel

Fernand Braudel (1902–1985) was a French historian whose initial fame began with his book *The Mediterranean and the Mediterranean World in the Age of Philip II* (1949). Perhaps his lasting fame relates, also, to the prodigious work—three volumes on civilization and capitalism in the fifteenth to eighteenth centuries. Within this work lies an understanding of capitalism's origins that could be described as profound and superbly grounded in history. In the first volume of Braudel's *The Structures of Everyday Life* (1979), he devoted attention to the human population of the world in that period and the forces working to reduce or strengthen it. Daily bread, food and drink, houses, clothes and fashion were coupled with sources of energy, metallurgy and transportation. The last two topics in this first volume were money, and towns and cities that developed in the fifteenth to eighteenth centuries.

Braudel, in *The Wheels of Commerce* (1979), his second volume, wrote at length about the origins of CAPITALE. The word "capitale" (a late Latin word based on *caput* or head) emerged in the twelfth to thirteenth centuries in the sense of funds, stock of merchandise, a sum of money or money carrying interest (Braudel, 1992, Vol. II: 232). Italy was the center of discussions and it was there the word "capital" was first coined in about 1211 and is found, according to Braudel, from 1283 onward in the sense of capital assets of a trading firm (Braudel, 1992 Vol. II: 232). The sermons of St. Bernardino of Siena (1380–1444) mentioned the prolific causes of wealth called capital. Siena was then the center of European banking before 1348. So these historical origins seem truthful to me.

After spreading about Europe, Quesnay said all capital was an instrument of production until Marx referred to capital as the means of production. The word "capitalist" began in 1753, but was referred to in this way—land is the fortress of capitalism, or an economic and social regime in which capital, the source of income, is used by those who work with it through their labor. In 1902 the political side of capitalism emerged to contrast with socialism and with communism, more so after the 1917 Revolution in the Soviet Union.

Braudel noted that in 1926 the *Encyclopedia Britannica* first included the word "capitalism," but its meaning politically grew to mean modern industrial systems. This history is striking evidence of the malleable nature of the meaning of capitalism. Other refinements in definition early on were in distinguishing fixed from circulating capital. Long distance trade, monopolies and mobility of merchants were more definitional refinements. Profits of capitalism from long distance trade were substantial from the beginning (Braudel, 1992, Vol. II: 601). The early character of capitalism relates to international trade, a very significant tack for analysis of this book. This, however, is all by way of background to Braudel's *The Perspective of the World* (1979). In this third volume Braudel examined divisions of time and space in Europe, the city-centered economies of Europe, the national markets emerging in Europe and elsewhere, and it concludes with a study of the industrial revolution.

Braudel sums up his long, searching historical inquiry into capitalism and civilization with conclusions that merit very careful attention because these conclusions easily could guide our thinking about globalizing corporations and their relationship to nations and capitalism. These are some of the significant points of Braudel:

1. Visible since the dawn of history, capitalism emerged and developed through the rise of towns and trade, the creation of a labor market, the increased population density, the growing use of money, the increase in production of material goods, and the development of long distance trade across the globe. Capitalism expanded and contracted to fit pragmatic circumstances. Capitalism began long before the industrial revolution.

2. Forget periods like mercantile or industrial or finance capitalism. Braudel argued that in the long run, "The whole panoply of forms of capitalism—commercial, industrial and banking—was already deployed in thirteenth-century Florence, seventeenth-century Amsterdam, in London before the eighteenth century" (Braudel, 1992, Vol. III: 621). There was little specialization—people in business did it all.

3. Monopoly of earlier capitalism merely took new forms in the nineteenth and twentieth centuries. Braudel stated a most telling and profound view of globalizing corporations from American capitalism: "from trusts and holding companies to the famous multinational firms which in the 1960s tripled their subsidiaries abroad. In 1973, 187 of them, with subsidiary companies in at least five foreign countries, accounted for 'not only three-quarters of United States investment abroad, but also for half the total United States exports and one third the total sales of manufactured goods on the United States market" (Braudel, 1992, Vol. III: 622).

4. A finger in every pie was the way to think of multinationals, especially conglomerates, since they invested in low-wage countries for industrial production and had enormous financial reserves and traded commercially at high levels.

5. In what I consider to be the *most* perceptive of his observations, Braudel stated:

In short, the chief privilege of capitalism today as in the past, remains the ability to *choose*—a privilege resulting at once from its dominant social position, from the weight of its capital resources, its borrowing capacity, its communication network, and no less, from the links which create between members of a powerful minority—however divided it may be by competition—a series of unwritten rules and personal contacts. (Braudel, 1992, Vol. III: 622)

6. Furthermore, a market economy is seen by Braudel to be only partly controlled by capitalism. So, what is the other part of the market economy outside of capitalism and what is inside capitalism? Braudel argued that capitalism can and does change constantly so it focuses upon what it wants—top-level real estate, stock exchange speculation, banking and large-scale industrial production. Agricultural production and transportation vary in interest to capitalists, depending upon, for example, whether flags of convenience exist for ships to escape taxes and are available. Coming and

going of firms is a natural process, but the succession is inherited wealth needing further investment in an endless process of reinvestment.

7. Braudel thinks that capitalism is much more than an economic system—it "lives off the social order, standing almost on a footing with the state, whether as an adversary or accomplice."

8. Capitalism coexists comfortably with the state today—monopolies and big corporations—and doing what comes naturally—leaving the least remunerative and most expensive tasks to the state: roads, communications, army, navy, air force, coast guard, education and research. Plus—capitalism lets the state bear costs of public health and social security. (See Greider, 1997: 322–330, for a vivid contemporary example.) And Braudel said—capitalism shamelessly takes what is called corporate welfare from the state: grants, contracts and large parcels of land, for example, to build the first railroads in America.

9. Capitalism is not premised on equality of social condition for people in a society. Capitalism has no assured future, but it is very adaptable and tough. Capitalism stays out of the basement of the economy where barter, housework, moonlighting, criminal and other factors are working their magic. Capitalism does not organize an entire economy of a nation where cooperatives exist.

Braudel accurately describes the comings and goings of big companies in the U.S. market, the need to place large sums of capital so that it can earn its keep and the persistence of giant corporations like DuPont from the early 1800s to date. Reflecting Braudel's profound insights on capitalism, Charles Hampden-Turner and Alfons Trompenaars, in *The Seven Cultures of Capitalism* (1993) suggest that cross-cultural management is being pressed into service by joint ventures, foreign subsidiaries and alliances among corporations. Globalization shows many ways to accomplish the same goal. This reveals not only the pragmatic, but the ever-changing nature of capitalism. This swirling dervish of a world is not easy for nations to comprehend and get hold of corporations to control, but it may just be the challenge of the twenty-first century for nations. This may be why President Clinton asked for more rapid response from nations—not a decade-long GATT development and discussion. Should nations act so quickly in such basic matters of society? Clinton merely assumes this is "good" for the world.

REGULATORY CAPITALISM IN INTERSTATE COMMERCE AND NOT IN INTERNATIONAL COMMERCE

The United States has spent over 200 years building a regulated capitalism—the evidence is in Table 5-1, titled "Regulated Capitalism—U.S. Style." Step outside the United States and none of it or very little applies to any globalizing corporation with a home base in the United States. Evidence of this is the Mexican maquiladora industrial zone along the southern U.S. border and along the north is the Windsor, Ontario zone of manufacturing. But these inter-

Table 5-1
Regulated Capitalism—U.S. Style

1800	U.S. Customs Service - 1789	**1970**	OSHA - 1970
	U.S. Coast Guard - 1790		Consumer Products Safety Commission - 1972
	Internal Revenue Service - 1862		Clean Water Act - 1972
	False Claims Act - 1863		Equal Employment Opportunity Act - 1972
	Interstate Commerce Com. - 1887		ERISA - 1974
	Sherman Anti-Trust Act - 1890		Magnusson-Moss Warranty Act - 1975
1900	Pure Food & Drug Act - 1906		Commodity Futures Trading Comm. - 1975
	Meat Inspection Act - 1906		Foreign Corrupt Practices Act - 1977
	Federal Employer's Liability - 1908		Equal Credit Opportunity Act - 1977
1910	Federal Reserve Act - 1913		Humphrey-Hawkins Full Employ. Act - 1978
	Clayton Act - 1914		Bankruptcy Reform Act - 1978
	Federal Trade Commission - 1914		Airline Deregulation Act - 1978
	Federal Employee Comp. Act - 1916		Export Administration Act - 1979
1920	Dept. of Agriculture Market Act - 1921	**1980**	Deposit Institutions Deregulation & Monetary Control Act - 1980
	Longshoremens & Harbor Workers Act - 1927		Garn-St. Germain Depository Inst. Act - 1982
1930	Norris-LaGuardia Act - 1932		Federal Computer Crime Act - 1984
	Glass-Steagall Act - 1933		Insider Trading Sanctions Act - 1984
	Securities Act - 1933		Immigration Reform & Control Act - 1986
	Securities Exchange Act - 1934		Insider Trading & Sec. Enforcement Act - 1988
	National Labor Relations Act - 1935		Financial Inst. Reform Recovery & Enforcement Act - 1989
	Social Security Act - 1935	**1990**	Americans with Disabilities Act - 1990
	Robinson-Patman Act - 1936		
	Fair Labor Standards Act - 1938		
1940	Investment Co. Act - 1940		
	Investment Advisors Act - 1940		
	Taft-Hartley Amendments - 1947		
1950	Landrum Griffin Act - 1959		
1960	Clean Air Act - 1963		
	Equal Pay Act - 1963		
	Civil Rights Act - 1964		
	National Highway Traffic Safety Adm. - 1966		
	Age Discrimination Employment Act - 1967		
	Consumer Protection Act - 1968		
	National Environmental Policy Act - 1969		

national zones are all over the globe now, confining the U.S. style of regulated capitalism. This clever state of affairs has some faces smiling, others are glum. It is obvious who is doing what. Managers smile, but labor cannot stand this state evasion by big business. It showed up most clearly in the late 1997 debates over presidential "fast-track" authority to sign trade agreements that then are bulldozed through Congress without amending power. Foreign nations love it as well. Many have no interest in building a regulatory capitalism like the U.S. and they realize how attractive they must be to U.S. globalizing firms. This is where we are today. A yearning to invest outside of the United States grows daily in giant corporations. Witness the global merger efforts being launched in 1995–1999.

Casino Capitalism

In 1986, Susan Strange offered the book *Casino Capitalism* to the world. The financial systems of the world required both skill and luck just as they would in Las Vegas or Monte Carlo. Ethan Kapstein referred to this gambling image as having caught the imagination of the world (Kapstein, 1994: 177). So much speculation, so little regulation, so much deregulation, so much globalization, and so much innovation made the global economy terribly uncertain as a place to do business. Meltdown in the financial sense was a deep-seated worry of calmer heads in financial fields. By late 1998, meltdown of the U.S. stock market approached $2 trillion. Risks had shifted from expropriation by nations or currency devaluations to outright theft or gross incompetence causing enormous financial losses. Since 1986 the birds have come home to roost—the birds are the vultures looking over the dead remains of banks and other financial institutions. In Chapter 8 there is a detailed look at this crime wave, the bones of BCCI are still being picked over in many nations almost a decade later. The Barings Bank, the Daiwa Bank, Sumitomo traders, Archer Daniels Midland, General Electric and General Dotan of Israel—the tip of the iceberg shows too well what deregulation can bring to the world, what globalization of the gambling style means in corporate and human wreckage. Foreign corrupt practices are more than just fancy ways of doing slick business in bribery. The conditions of "casino-ness" exist today.

Regulatory Capitalism and Flea Markets

At least seven markets are not based on trust: the flea markets, the underground untaxed market, the barter market, the black market, the drug market, the patent medicine snake oil market, and the wild west markets dominated by cowboys as capitalists. These are bizarre bazaars. Regulatory capitalism spends its time taming the excesses of the licit markets, the criminal justice systems go after the illicit markets. White collar crime focuses mostly on regulatory capitalism but it rubs shoulders now with transnational crime-control specialists who are looking at the global end of people and drug smuggling, terrorism, nuclear theft and money-laundering to make dirty money clean. As international expert of organized crime Louise Shelley wrote: ''International organized crime groups are the opposite of legitimate multinational corporations. Corporations are based in the industrialized world and market to the developing world, whereas transnational organized crime are largely based in developing countries and market to the developed world'' (Shelley, 1997: 19).

This paradoxical condition is part of globalization that counts transnational organized crime as the most negative consequence of the globalization phenomenon, according to Shelley. Also, the regular business actions that are cloaked in legitimacy but easily transcend it when conditions allow a killing to be made financially have proved to be just as negative. The financial and other corporate debris found in Chapter 9 is too much to be accidental judgment instead of deliberate harm.

A Well-Regulated Society

Owner capitalism of major industries died a long time ago and managerial capitalism has replaced it (Chandler, 1990). Both have lived under regulatory capitalism as defined above. With five major waves of regulation in 200 years and one recent wave of deregulation, the globalizing corporations have organized themselves into 50 supernovas with 450 of the *Fortune* 500 tagging along in a spirited manner, leaving several thousand large companies struggling to survive and a U.S. work force of 100 million not earning daily bread from the giants of industry and service. The political economy of the United States is simply the death of owner capitalism and rise of managerial capitalism and the constant rise of regulatory capitalism (McCraw, 1984). This is the world we live in today from the perspective of political economy. The many references in the bibliography and Appendix B document this, if you care to peruse them. The well-regulated society is just this simple an idea. Business excesses created every wave of regulation, just as they are doing in 1997–1999 in the tobacco regulation furor in the United States. This is the unvarnished truth about both managerial capitalism and regulatory capitalism. It is an excellent example of symbiosis.

VISIBLE HANDS AND VISIBLE POWER: MANAGERIAL CAPITALISM AS A KEY VARIABLE IN A SERVICE ECONOMY

Manufacturing to Service

Whose view of the economy is trustworthy? Who knows reality most accurately? Just as a search was needed to make some sense of the meanings of capitalism, so also is a search needed of the true nature of the economy. Service is what people do when they go to work in the United States. In a work force of 130 million, a handful grow things, another handful make things, about 100 million serve one another. Two hundred years ago, most people grew things, a handful made things and another handful served people. The world has been stood on its head in two centuries and totally reversed itself. The big picture is going from agriculture and manufacturing to service. When you add up the service people they are a mighty public force and private force. The military service, the Federal Bureau of Investigation, the Postal Service, and the rest of government serve the people. Insurance service, stock brokerage service, lawn service, health care service and educational service are massive sectors of the economy. This is the truth; and trouble in unemployment is most likely to be in service areas. Add the imports of things made elsewhere like cars, clothes, and toys and electronic gadgets; the service sector could care less until service starts being imported as in computer programs shot by satellite from India to the United States.

Service finally forced *Fortune* to fundamentally alter its *Fortune* 500 list to add service to industry companies. It rolled out its new *Fortune* 500 on May 15, 1995 and that single change raised the total from 11.6 million workers to 20.2 million or almost a 100% growth. Service companies employ lots of people. *Fortune* justified this move as follows:

In the last half-decade, the massive rollout of cheap computing power has allowed in-dustries to chop apart traditional value chains—outsourcing work they used to do in-house, moving into territories once owned by other industries, and fuzzing up the line between manufacturing and service activities. At the same time, deregulation of trans-portation, telecommunications, energy, and financial services has changed the economics of those industries—in every case in the direction of making revenues, not assets, the best measure of size. (*Fortune*, ''A New 500 for the New Economy,'' May 15, 1995: 170)

This is a sound assessment as far as it goes, but it is essentially incomplete—it misses globalization: the massive shift of manufacturing jobs out of the United States and the massive capital shift out of the United States at the same time. All of this is part of the same industrial policy designed by managerial capital-ism. CEOs did it all. And they tied a ribbon around it with NAFTA, GATT and WTO. And another ribbon will come in MAI (Mulitlateral Agreement on In-vestments) in the next year or so.

Service is not well understood as part of the economy. James B. Quinn, in his 1992 book *Intelligent Enterprise*, suggests that service is valued less, is less capital-intensive, is smaller in scale and it cannot produce wealth—all of these he seriously questions. Since 77% of all employment is in the service category, and 74% of all value-added in the U.S. economy is service work, service com-panies are large, capital-intensive, technology-driven and strategically powerful—all a good description of much of what General Electric does every day and wants to do more of in the future.

Today, the reality of the economy is that it is a regulated capitalism at least in interstate commerce inside the United States, is managed by visible hands called CEOs, and is in a service-dominated economy. This much seems quite true.

CEO Managerial Capitalism and the New Owners

The modern breed of royalty is the corporate CEO. By social, economic, legal and other standards, the twenty-first century will be filled with multibillionaires, billionaires, multimillionaires and the like. No one will care about the millionaires, there will be so many of them. The CEO emerged in this century with immense power in business and in politics; and the CEO takes a larger, more unwarranted and unjustified share of the corporate profits than ever before. This twentieth-century regality rests in anonymity, secrecy, private security and private jets, and they do not like to be hugged by Michael Moore (Moore, 1996). The most interesting question is whether this trend can continue into the twenty-first century and even accelerate the future wealth-taking by CEOs.

There are stirrings to suggest that the next 100 years will see a waning of managerial capitalism to be replaced by new ownership—stewards of pension funds, ESOPS, institutional investors and takeover artists. There could well be a new answer to the question: Where shall we invest the net profits and retained earnings of the giant corporation? Pension funds will not be outsmarted, or outvoted or outsourced. New owners will look over the CEO's shoulder and will initiate a new board of directors more to the liking of the pension fund. This will be most unsettling to the cozy way giant corporations in too many cases are now run. Institutional investors of giant pension funds are no longer sitting by and conceding decisional authority to CEOs (Useem, 1996).

Some very significant choices were made in the past decades when managerial capitalism was unquestioned in its authority. The choices have to do with globalization because the primary agents of globalization have been the managerial classes, some of whom see themselves as nationless in loyalty. Some of these decisions should be noted here:

1. A global reach after a global war in 1945 was normal decision-making in many large businesses.

2. Creating and sending out foreign subsidiaries was more normal business for the managerial capitalists.

3. Overseas direct investment was just a logical choice given the investment numbers with low wages overseas.

4. Downsizing expensive labor in developed countries was another logical choice given the numbers and profit margins.

5. Plant closings are just a part of the same logic.

6. A grand strategy of industrial policy was good for the company, but painful for the local worker and unions. It made good business sense.

7. Industrial policy is the sole prerogative and exclusive province of the CEO.

But the error-prone CEO missed a number of things: the power of the new shareholder owners, the takeover artists and the corporate crime wave of foreign bribery and negative congressional reaction. Just as earlier owners and managers missed the antitrust political wave, the current CEOs made significant mistakes.

Perhaps the greatest mistake is the desire to become so political in business, ignoring the corrupt practices under attack since the first reaction in the 1906 period and the Tilman Act. By 1999 the agenda is bursting with change. CEOs have caused much of the corruption in politics. For this they may pay an extraordinary price—witness tobacco CEOs in 1998.

The Business Roundtable (BRT), which is to be described and analyzed more fully in the next part of this chapter, is a reaction to perceived political weakness and to fear of a consumer movement and Ralph Nader. It is openly seeking political influence and, according to McQuaid, Vogel and others, very successful in its quest to dominate in politics. A cursory look at the last two decades of BRT's existence since 1972 shows that money given to political action committees (PACs) and soft money given to political parties comes to $500 million, and probably much more if the truth were known. The BRT giving through its members is a substantial part of this bigger picture. From 1985 to 1994, who authorized the spending of a half billion dollars on the national political process? These are CEO decisions, of course. Look at the political influence in these numbers: $56 million by banks and finance companies; $50 million by energy groups; $48 million by agribusiness and food processors; $42 million by insurance companies; $40 million by real estate interests; $38 million by communications and media business; $30 million by transportation companies; and $36 million by medical interests. Who earned this money? They did—lobbyists in Washington and a host of related political operatives, media and others (Birnbaum, 1992). The total is $340 million. For what? Add in $82 million by unions in the same time and you get the bigger, long-term picture of acquisition or attempted acquisition of the federal government. The Mankoff cartoon is right on target.

It is precisely here, in the political ambitions of the CEOs of giant globalizing corporations in the richest nation on earth with their unique managerial capitalism, where they must believe in the rightness of their cause, forget the self-interest. If the federal government is not yet bought, and many of the state houses, it will not be long at this rate—and the focus in BRT is on the president and Congress every hour of every day. This translates into 200 men who think it is their job to run the government to their liking and the economy to boot.

But this unchecked power never lasts long in America and as indicated above, the weaknesses are beginning to show.

Managers versus Owners: A New Era Emerging

In *Managers vs. Owners* (1995), Allen Kaufman, Lawrence Zacharias and Marvin Karson examined what they characterized as a struggle for corporate control in America. These authors paralleled Bowman in his political analysis, but reinforced the constitutional acceptance of the business corporation, noted the impact of progressive reforms and observed the changing nature of regulation. They also reinforced the importance of professionalization of managers.

They stressed managerial CEO solidarity with the Business Roundtable (Kaufman et al., 1995: 133). Where they substantially departed is in assessing investor challenges to management—the takeover artists with inside large firms initiating hostile takeovers using junk bonds. Oddly, they go no further in analysis than that group.

Michael Useem went much further in understanding the struggle beyond hostile takeover artists. In his *Executive Defense* (1993), Useem observed that shareholder power was rising and this was particularly true for institutional shareholder power in large pension funds such as Calpers and TIAA-CREF and in mutual funds. Managerial strategies were called into play to defend managers financially with golden parachutes and other stratagems to reduce personal financial risks to them if takeovers succeeded—especially hostile takeovers. Seeking political protection from state legislatures was another strategy born of fear. Useem stated: "Corporate political agendas shifted from fighting government regulation to resisting shareholder intrusion" (Useem, 1993: 1).

Even more exciting was the exploration by Useem in 1996 in his *Investor Capitalism*, where he described the details of corporate managerial capitalism resisting shareholder insistence on attention—from shareholders who will not sell their shares, who represent millions of people, and who will insist on a shareholder's meeting with proposals to be voted upon that may be strenuously resisted by CEO managers. The facts are getting stark: mutual funds and other institutional investors holding stock rose from about 35% in 1985 to over 55% in 1994 in percent of shares held of 1,000 largest U.S. companies. Major companies are vigorously buying back their own stock to control equity voting power which CEOs then vote. Individual investors dropped by about the same amount from over 55% to around 35%. Shareholder power is getting organized and focused (Useem, 1996: 26). Companies with poison pills and states with anti-takeover laws are growing in both categories. The most telling truth about the new era emerging is found in Useem's observation:

Since top executives are elected agents of the company owners, overt rejection of shareholder advice is awkward if not dangerous. Defiance runs against the cultural grain of

American capitalism, and it invites retaliation. . . . The art of politics is saying no without appearing to do so, and company managers have become adept practitioners. (Useem, 1996: 71)

Who will last longer: shareholders with 20- to 30-year retirement plans or CEOs with an average tenure of 6 years? This does present an interesting clash between monied classes (Roe, 1994). General Electric shareholders, at the annual corporate meeting, pushed a 1998 proposal for some limit to executive salaries, to which CEO John F. Welch replied: "We can't put a limit here on me or anyone else . . . of course my salary is enormous" (Murray, 1998). Welch's 1997 salary and bonus was $8 million for maybe 240 days of labor or $33,333.33 per day of work (Buchanan, 1998).

Managerial capitalism is slowly being transformed into investor capitalism in a regulatory capitalism inside the United States. But under the tutelage of CEOs the globalizing corporations have placed a trillion dollars of investment in foreign direct investment in the last 15 to 20 years, and they did so when managerial capitalism ruled the roost. If Useem's brilliant conclusion is correct, as I believe it is, there is a basic new storm brewing over where corporations will invest the profits and retained earnings—an issue no longer exclusively the province of the CEO managers. Patrick Buchanan raises many questions about globalization (Buchanan, 1998). Shareholders will want to be a part of the decision as well and this inevitably means new risks for those CEOs who may wish to go boldly where no man has gone before with other people's money. Even the failed vote in California on Proposition 211 means that shareholders are very willing to hold managers' feet to fire if their promotional promises go sour in new ventures. The U.S. savings and loan and insider trading scandals drove a large number of capitalists into prison. The difference between puffing hype and lying and criminal fraud is very narrow. What this suggests is a revival of regulatory capitalism which has always, especially since 1934 and the creation of the Securities and Exchange Commission (SEC), been on the side of the investor—the entire rationale for the SEC is built on such trustworthy conditions for investing—needed even more today than ever when millions of dollars are invested every day by institutional agents of shareholder owners. The greater demand for accountability of managers caused by shareholders may begin to rectify nearly a century of imbalance caused by managers taking over almost all of the corporate power in America and doing whatever they pleased. This transformation will affect the globalization of corporations when shareholders have little or no enthusiasm for the many risks of the global economy as it was conceived by the few merely to enrich the managers and directors in their futures. Political risks, currency risks and many other risks are much greater in foreign investment. The trend toward investor capitalism is addressing fundamentally who will decide where in the world $300 billion plus in profits in the United States will be made next year and the year after that—*ad infinitum*. These profits are made by the *Fortune* 500 every year and must be placed somewhere to earn more income—the "capital" that rises in capitalism.

POLITICAL ECONOMY OF REGULATORY CAPITALISM; UNEASINESS IN BUSINESS–GOVERNMENT RELATIONS

Businesses and governments are wedded to one another in America, but the relationship was characterized faithfully most recently as an "uneasy alliance," or the parties as "uneasy partners" (McQuaid, 1994; Vogel, 1996). Let us first look back in time in the relationship and then dig more deeply into the current state of affairs.

Early Times—1797–1887

The business–government relationship goes back in time to the origin of colonial settlement on the North American continent; it predates the creation of the government of the United States in 1787 when cities and colonial governments stimulated businesses for colonizing Great Britain. During the 1800–2000 period, the first 100 years of the United States clearly are identified with a powerful and strong business–government relationship:

1. to promote transportation, roads, canals, ports and shipping,

2. to encourage settlement of the mid-western and western United States,

3. to help create manufacturing industries in the United States and thereby reduce reliance on Europe,

4. to protect the flow of commerce on the high seas from pirates,

5. to provide banks, money and credit, and protect patents,

6. to help groups wanting to form corporate enterprise,

7. to launch educational improvements (agricultural colleges),

8. to involve government deeply in three areas—in race and wage slavery, in free labor for its own protection and organization and in immigration matters (Goodrich, 1967).

The Civil War in 1861–1865 was grounded in issues of slavery, in the agricultural labor of blacks on southern cotton, rice and indigo farms—an economic and social issue for slave owners as well as for everyone else in the nation. The first hundred years of the business–government relationship was turbulent, uneasy, and certainly, racial slavery almost broke the United States into two nations. No one could claim that there was not a high degree of political fire in the political economy of America in that period, and that at the central place of heat was the business–government relationship. The Civil War proved that much.

Industrialization—1887–1987

From 1887 to 1987, industrialization and giant corporations settled into America to stay permanently as a major influence in the business–government relationship. The older craft and small business and farm life of America from 1600 to 1887 was fast receding into the quieter corners of America.

Almost every major influence on the key relationships was a tendency to centralize, standardize and federalize or nationalize. A Uniform Commercial Code finally emerged in law—almost a voluntary act by the states and others. Constitutional law was a major determinate in the regulation of interstate commerce and in the creation of a permanent, national, single commercial trading market of the entire United States. The Supreme Court of the United States ruled that corporations were "persons" under the Fourteenth Amendment and their assets and actions were constitutionally cloaked with protection. Transportation by rail, air and land was tied into a series of physical systems, and human communication systems (telegraph and telephone) experienced the same centralization. Wars—World Wars I and II, the cold war, the Korean, Vietnam and other wars—demanded standardized war material so one in ten workers was swept into such systems. President Eisenhower called them military-industrial systems.

Nuclear weapons demanded centralization and they still do today. Energy, communication, computers and satellites all stimulated networks of a national and international nature. Vertical and horizontal integration of businesses was the key to survival. Finally, oligopoly settled into America to stay—with few sellers and many buyers in most product lines. The giant companies bought the smaller ones just as big fish eat little fish. Antitrust has faded into the background in the last 60 years.

By contrast, in the 1887–1987 period there were many businesses marginalized out of mass production, mass distribution and mass commerce. Small businesses, small farming and the like had grave difficulty surviving economically. Small cities died as people left to work in factories in large cities or were swallowed up in the massive suburbanization of 250 large metropolitan areas. The bigger units rose, the smaller units fell in the 1887–1987 era—and many big cities had physically rotten cores, so obvious to everyone today.

The people's constitutional right to free movement inside the nation showed massive migration to the North during the first phase of industrialization and then a western and southern migration in the later years. These are all commonly known facts of life about the American nation.

To sum up, everyone in America knows that by the year 2000, the business–government relationship will be headed in another direction from its first 200 years and the heading seems global in nature. Everyone knows the absolutely gargantuan size of the American economy compared with the rest of the nations. Everyone knows of heavy and increasingly greater American dependence on foreign oil. Everyone knows that without oil the United States is a lesser power.

Everyone knows that governments have grown very large just like all other corporate institutions. And most know of the military-industrial complex that is so slowly unwinding after the cold war ended but seems to want to go on forever as a burden or a precaution, hinting that nations are critical to human beings.

Today—Sizes of Businesses and Governments

After the long period of growth, where do we stand today in the sizes of businesses and governments that relate to one another? There are about 4 million corporate businesses, but the bulk of national and international commerce (about two-thirds by common measures) is found in 500 corporations and their more than 6,000 plus domestic and foreign subsidiary corporations. Their most potent political arm is the Business Roundtable—the 200 CEOs of the largest corporations; and the governments are plentiful—one federal government, 50 state governments, 3,000 plus county governments, over 10,000 city governments plus thousands of special districts, port authorities and similar public corporations. Millions of businesses and 200,000 governments relate to one another. In 1994, the gross domestic product was $1.2 trillion government-related, compared with $5.6 trillion business and private consumption in a 20–80 relationship inside a $7 trillion economy. These numbers alone are a source of uneasiness, but we should look more deeply into other sources of tension that we will turn to next.

Factors in an Uneasy Relationship

In a popular American song there is a reference to a "peaceful easy feeling," something that many people yearn to experience along with excitement from time to time. The theme here of uneasiness in the business–government relationship centers on similar tension of an opposite nature. No one could possibly characterize the business–government relationship as peaceful and easy in tone. It is tension filled all of the time, the supplicants are always pleading for something—there is no rest for the wicked, which some of them must be. Regulatory capitalism means public acts by public actors for non-public interests. The law is automatically part of the tension. Voting is often involved as part of the drama. Some secrecy is part of the climate and money lurks in the wings. All of this spells uneasiness in the relationship. What are some of the factors that underlie the unease?

Uniform Industrial Boredom

The "unease" in the business–government relation rests first upon the long unresolved political tensions caused by industrialization, centralization, standardization, and by the goal of making everything simpler and more uniform. Making the economy uniform, however, makes it easier to control the economy centrally. Irrigation societies find this true—just cut off the water to those who oppose you. The cold war of 75 years was fought to avoid such centrality in a totalitarian mode. Why do we want it so badly here and now? During World War II, wage and price controls were powerful and then were dropped after the war for the most part. We know what central command of the economy is like. But the standardized, franchised, McDonaldized boring sameness is no different from the standard Exxon station or Circuit City store. Boring. No mall differs from any other with Gap clothing assured in every one. Wanting uniformity while hating conformity is not resolved—you cannot have non-boring uniformity. Now it is the world class car or Walkman stereo where uniformity will be pursued on a global scale to reach global boredom. Unresolved uneasiness says we are all going to work hard for something none of us wants. And you will be forced to do it.

Big Business Roundtable versus Nader: 1978

The "unease" in the business–government relationship is related to a second group of major factors. A principal part of the second set of factors is the pressure by Ralph Nader and others in the early 1970s to develop a Consumer Protection Agency, a cabinet-level federal department "to protect nascent panindustrial regulatory programs" (McQuaid, 1994: 154). Corporations then defeated this effort and some associated labor law reform. By 1977, ". . . [those] corporations mobilized against Nader received powerful panindustrial reinforcements. The Business Roundtable was the key new power coalition for elite big business (McQuaid, 1994: 154)." There emerges at least one major conclusion about the 1970s Nader action and corresponding business reaction: "The year 1978 became a watershed year in modern American politics. Corporate politicians, after winning decisive victories, moved on to win offensive ones" (McQuaid, 1994: 155–156).

In this same period, the number of Washington lobbyists rose from 365 in 1961 to 23,000 by the end of the 1980 decade; the legal profession along with others such as public relations firms grew to immense size very rapidly. A new set of tensions for uneasiness came to life.

What the Business Roundtable did was simple. The Business Roundtable developed more complete strategies to buy influence in Washington to more completely control the federal government. This included backing actor Ronald Reagan (who had been a former TV salesperson for General Electric products) for president; increases in paid lobbyists in Washington; and setting major corporate policy priorities in taxes, regulation, monetary policy, federal spending, deficits and economic growth. Political action came in large money flows to promote grassroots networks, lobbyists, lawyers, media acquisitions, controls and influences in the creation of business-sponsored think tanks in Washington as propaganda arms, in the guise of objective research. Since 1975, Washington, as everyone knows by now, has become dominated by big business and not by the public interest groups of Ralph Nader and others (Greider, 1992, Vogel, 1996). And the Business Roundtable has been the submarine force behind it all, lurking in the Potomac River in the nation's capitol.

Looking back, it is clear that the Business Roundtable (BRT) found itself in a crisis in 1975. Then CEOs of major corporations promptly took action (Bowman, 1996). The first four BRT chairmen were CEOs of DuPont, Alcoa, General Electric and General Motors. It is important to note that members of the BRT are limited to the CEOs only and candidates are invited to become members. Its normally secretive operations were and are very effective (McQuaid, 1994: 149–150). The most important political economy point about the BRT is this: "Corporations that lost battles in 1965–75 fought opponents to a standstill in 1975–1978 and then began successful campaigns for reduced taxation, spending, regulation and inflation during the presidencies of Jimmy Carter, Ronald Reagan and George Bush" (McQuaid, 1994: 150).

Irving Shapiro recounts much of the experience he had in establishing the BRT and in serving as the 1976 leader (Shapiro, 1984: 26–46). He said the organization is not secretive and the organization's effectiveness is in great contrast to the 1950s and 1960s in the even more dismal period for business–government relations, from his perspective.

The success of the BRT contributes to the "unease" that others experience in losing to the views of big business. But the failure to stave off the Foreign Corrupt Practices Act of 1977 shows how power is not complete, and fear of the big business agenda still exists (Barnet and Cavanagh, 1994).

Other Factors Leading to Uneasiness

A third factor, in addition to the other two factors of industrial boredom and the Business Roundtable, was the easy escape into international commerce by big business where *very* different rules applied to taxes, regulation, environment, labor, health and safety standards. In the period 1945–1965, the ease of movement overseas with little or no consequences left everyone who was left behind inside the United States suspicious of what was happening offshore. It was thought that none of the governments elsewhere could possibly match the regulatory capitalism of the United States. This has proved largely to be true by 1999.

A fourth factor of unease is the globalization of business that jeopardizes the last 100-year struggle for labor rights found in regulatory capitalism inside the United States. Consider this merely a cursory prelude to Chapter 7 of this book, where much more is to be written about this factor, but think of just one struggle that is put at risk by globalization. Long before the 1938 Fair Labor Standards Act, litigator Louis D. Brandeis (later Justice Brandeis of the United States Supreme Court) won a 1908 decision through hard work represented by his now famous "Brandeis brief" used in cases by him. The Brandeis brief is two pages for standard legal argument, to be followed by fifteen pages for state and foreign laws limiting women's hours at work and that was followed by 95 pages devoted to the social utility of maximum hours at work legislation to protect women (Strum, 1993: 30–34, 59–71).

The extraordinarily important Brandeis case—*Muller v. Oregon* (1908)—proved that wage slavery and working hours needed practical state government regulation in a free enterprise, but predatory, capitalistic economy. Freedom to force a wage slave to work long hours just to keep a job was not considered to be a very American ideal. For over 90 years labor has been considered to be human in the United States and, therefore, entitled to legal protection, but corporations and their CEOs going offshore raises doubts about the entire labor movement in the United States—a grave source of uneasiness, as you could well imagine, in union and non-union circles of workers. In Chapter 7 of this book, we will explore further the implications of globalization for labor.

Part II

Free Trade, Labor and Corporate Investment

Fair Minimal Trade by Globalizing Corporations: Foreign Capital Investment, Services and Goods

Chapter 6 examines the evolving global business regulatory structures, NAFTA, GATT and WTO, as they impact upon business. Both domestic and foreign markets of the *Fortune* 500 are being blended and mixed in new ways. Frequently, market dynamism and allocation of profits are made in ways that are not understood, even seem strange to American citizens who wonder why so many foreign jobs and investments have been and are being made with profits, retained earnings and other assets and debt of American corporations. The loss of millions of manufacturing jobs in America to foreign locations and foreign subsidiaries of American corporations highlights the intracorporate global transfers of wealth. Flat American worker salaries seem to be consequences now widely accepted as a reality. Kodak dumps thousands of U.S. workers while planning to invest $1 billion in China in the 1997–1999 period. This is a perfect example of corporate reality in contemporary life.

Who decides to allocate the annual investment capital (profit) of the *Fortune* 500 ($325 billion in 1997) is of paramount interest. It is the central question of this book. Real trade data show direct investment outside the United States is large and foreign direct investment in the United States is large. Both flows in and out of the United States are significant in the market. The question of who decides on investments—is one result of the international impact on American business and society. Some argue we are headed back to the future—the nineteenth-century future (Schwartz, 1994).

Global capitalism is increasingly more like jungle capitalism than regulatory capitalism. Inside the United States jungle capitalism (each child, woman and man for themselves) is now suppressed by a host of factors: governmental statutes and regulations, consumer and service lawsuits and punitive damages, better corporate strategies and practices and many other factors. But the movement of large amounts of capital around the globe—considered part of the current free trade logic—with virtually no review by nation-states, is a troublesome, risk-enhancing, decision-making process by the visible hands—the CEOs just mentioned in Chapter 5. Let us examine two sets of recent foreign direct investments of large sums of money. These are just two sets of hundreds and perhaps thousands of such major decisional events that are normal for giant globalizing corporations. For a broader review see Alfred Chandler's historical study of the dynamics of industrial capitalism (Chandler, 1990).

TROUBLESOME FOREIGN CAPITAL INVESTMENTS: SOME EXAMPLES

Fortune (Schoenberger, 1996) followed Motorola Company and eleven other of the largest U.S. companies in the investment of corporate capital in China noting that the "players" spent or committed the amounts, as outlined in Table 6-1, by the end of 1996.

Four billion dollars is a significant amount of American capital to move into China, but that is not all. Northern Telecom, Philips, Intel, Boeing, Ericsson (Sweden), Nokia (Finland) and many other globalizing corporations are pouring wealth into China. American imports from China have risen rapidly. It is as if currency risk, political risk, expropriation risk and other risks did not exist in these investments. That would be an absurd assessment, especially in a communist nation.

A second recent example of *Fortune* is the article "If Europe is dead, why is GE investing billions there?" (Koenig, 1996). The story illustrated how a globalizing conglomerate goes about investing capital—a direct foreign investment. Koenig stated that GE began in 1989 to invest in Europe on a large scale. By 1996 more than $10 billion had been invested—about half in new plants and facilities and half in acquiring 50 other existing businesses.

Quoting the then top GE official in Europe, Paolo Fresco, "Since 1987 GE has made about $35 billion in acquisitions and equity investment worldwide, and more than a third of that has been in Europe" (Koenig, 1996: 117). GE Europe includes GE Capital Services Europe, GE Plastics Europe, GE Aircraft Engines Group, GE Medical Systems Europe, GE Power Systems Europe and GE Lighting Europe. Whether one takes the $10 billion more recent European investment or the $35 billion invested by GE across the globe since 1987, the amounts are very large and sustained investments. These are decisions made by the CEO Jack Welch and others in that company. It is called "industrial policy" of a corporate giant.

If one adds China and Europe, the total is at least $35 to $40 billion (plus) in capital recently invested outside of the United States. Even among giant globalizing companies, this is just a very minute part of a larger amount of outward capital flow. This is real money—big money called "foreign direct investment" as opposed to indirect foreign investment in stocks, bonds or other

Table 6-1
U.S. Companies—"China" Investment (1996)

U.S. Company	Capital Investment	Foreign Direct Investment
Motorola	$1,200,000,000	$560 million, semi-conductor plant
Atlantic Richfield	625,000,000	$1.13 billion pipeline
Coca-Cola	500,000,000	23 bottling locations
Amoco	350,000,000	Oil drilling, South China Sea
Ford Motor	250,000,000	5 factories
United Technologies	250,000,000	Elevators, escalators and air conditioning
PepsiCo	200,000,000	12 bottling plants, 87 outlets
Lucent Technologies	150,000,000	7 joint ventures
General Electric	150,000,000	14 joint ventures
General Motors	130,000,000	Auto parts
Hewlett-Packard	100,000,000	12 years of investing
IBM	100,000,000	6 joint ventures
Total	$4,005,000,000 total capital flow outward bound to China	

equity investments of foreign corporations. GE has both types of investments. Later we will examine the foreign direct investment data compiled and analyzed by the U.S. Department of Commerce. For introductory purposes, we should focus on the $35 to $40 billion figure. What does it mean to citizens of the United States?

First, what is going on here? A major globalizing corporation—GE—has such a surplus of funds that it can march across the globe from China to Europe and lay down vast sums of capital all over, even including investments in the United States. If $35 billion had been invested in the United States, such an investment would have meant thousands of new jobs here. That was *not* a choice CEO Jack Welch wanted to make—an investment in the United States is clearly of secondary importance to him and his board of directors.

Second, decisions of investment at the levels noted in China and Europe usually require explicit approval of the CEO and board of directors in most corporations. This may be true of GE, but only an examination of its legal authority could specify authority with certainty. The same would be true of the other corporations. The fact is: CEO decisions of this type typically generate news stories and other publicity because they are so significant. It may or may not be necessary to get shareholder approval, depending upon the legal require-ments of each corporation. Typically, shareholders are not consulted about such major acquisitions or investment decisions. They are usually informed after the fact, if at all. I have never been informed. Thus, the probability that shareholders would be directly involved, apart from the officers and directors who hold shares in the company, is rather unlikely. The full responsibility of such investment choices rests narrowly on the CEO and a few others.

In this context, the reader should remember that the U.S. *Fortune* 500 lost 4,600,000 industrial jobs at a minimum in the last decade and a half while this foreign direct investment has been growing rapidly. At the same time, the *Fortune* 500, including GE, invested American capital directly overseas—it is a part (major) of the trillion dollars invested by American corporations according to data collected by U.S. Department of Commerce. The corporations mentioned above are part of the *Fortune* 500 industrial group. But, we do *not* know pre-cisely from governmental data which company invested how much in what investment—by company. That data is blocked from public view by the government data collection agencies and by statutory proscription by Congress to encourage voluntary corporate reporting to the Bureau of Economic Affairs (Graham and Krugman, 1995).

REGULATED FREE TRADE—FREE-WHEELING FOREIGN INVESTMENT

Globalizing corporations are the principal overseas investors and they prefer free trade logic in the sense of being free to invest beyond borders of the home country and to earn from such investments. The examples are numerous. Foreign direct investment is a large topic with complex data sets. We shall examine this data later. Individual people as investors care less about investing beyond the nation in which they live, but some, like George Soros, an international financier and reputed billionaire, do. The question is for all of us today: What is the relevance of the issues of free trade versus protectionism to our future? The answer for many reasons is simple—the fight over free trade versus having high protective tariffs on imported goods and services is essentially a meaningless conflict. That is because corporate investment is tariffless activity and "intra-corporate." The political facts of life are that to sustain the current American economy we need some types of trade—especially in oil. To save American jobs from being sent overseas, protective tariffs could be used to protect Amer-ican industry and American workers. Such policies could be helpful to the Amer-ican society, as they were in the past. Those policies could be politically desirable, but both are insufficient to guide us into the future, especially after the end of the cold war.

The largest and richest market in the world by many standards is in the United States. Everyone who wants to sell in the U.S. market, or invest in it, across the globe is rather eager to do so. For much of the early history of the United

States, the market was protected by tariffs, starting with President George Washington and the first Congress. This lasted until America's market was opened almost unilaterally in 1960 (Eckes, 1995). Before that, from 1930 to 1960, the United States gradually abandoned the nationalistic tariffs erected after the War of 1812. The need to help Europe, and especially Germany and Japan, to rebuild their economies ravaged by World War II from 1945 onward so that they would not fall into the communist world was the primary motive for the shift toward opening America's markets. From 1960 to 1995, foreign policy concerns continued to be placed ahead of domestic economic interests. Broad national interest was devoted to keeping the international trading system healthy. "Health" meant an open U.S. market regardless of consequence to U.S. workers. At the end of the 1960 to 1995 period, executive discretion was curbed in unfair trade cases by policies of anti-dumping and countervailing duties. There is no grand solution to the trade issues at the end of the twentieth century. However, economic integration is no longer a grand answer today. This truth is extremely difficult to accept in some quarters, especially the White House.

This broad overview is punctuated by two major congressional votes in the early 1990s. The votes were approval of the North American Free Trade Agreement (NAFTA) in 1993 and the vote of approval of the General Agreement on Tariffs and Trade (GATT) and World Trade Organization (WTO) in 1994. These two votes required a supporting lineup of the current and former presidents and secretaries of state and congressional advocates from both Republican and Democratic parties to urge the passage of each trade agreement into law. These famous gatherings were shown on national television with CEOs of major globalizing corporations, and a host of other potential beneficiaries who would profit from global trade, including officials of the World Bank and International Monetary Fund groups. These televised proceedings to urge passage of trade legislation were evidence of *who* benefits personally from free trade. The non-beneficiaries were off television and not present—a much weaker public voice, but a much larger number of downsized industrial employees (4.6 million) were trying to be heard along with their allies, but all of them were essentially drowned out in the hallelujah televised chorus in favor of passage of each act (Nader et al., 1993). American trade politics kept on track favoring the health of international economic trading over domestic economic concerns that were growing in America. The drop of 4.6 million jobs in the *Fortune* 500 from 1979 to 1995—sixteen years—showed how free international trade negatively impacted America at its very most powerful core of industry. The steel industry lost half its production jobs (1,055,500 workers in 1966 to 531,400 in 1992). In the same period, textiles and apparels lost jobs (textiles 886,000 to 580,800; apparel 1,249,000 to 852,000) (Eckes, 1995). According to Alfred E. Eckes, Jr., historian and former chairman and commissioner of the U.S. International Trade Commission: "Contractions in these three industries cost 1,227,000 jobs" (Eckes, 1995: 218). As an American policy the favoring of other nations in trade had a significant domestic hurting quality, contrary to the hoped-for reciprocity in foreign trade without injury addressed by U.S. President William McKinley in 1901: "We should take from our customers such of their products as we can use *without harm to our industries and labor*" (Eckes 1995: 78). The harms visited on American workers and their families from 1966 to 1992 and up to today are the responsibility of both the political parties that allowed this to happen and the *Fortune* 500 corporations. Senator Russell Long in 1976 said that citizens may eventually ignore the "new international trading order" and put in place a new order of their own that places American jobs, security and incomes above those who dealt them a very bad deal (Eckes, 1995: 278). Some have known for more than two decades the fruitless harvest now being reaped in 1999 by the workers of America—lost jobs and stagnant or lowering wages. Deindustrialization and downsizing are now key words (*New York Times*, 1996). Failing to enforce our trade laws at home and failing to demand open markets abroad are major failings to produce such a result. But they are not the full story. President Clinton's export promotion program offset some of the harm, but very little, and too late (Garten, 1997). Deficits in trade are at extreme highs and the Asian downturn obviously makes these trade deficits grow even more extreme.

What is the fuller picture of globalizing corporations that desire free trade? First, let us pay attention to who invests overseas. The profits made in America and across the globe by giant corporations are invested partly in business in other nations. This type of investing is called "foreign direct investment" by the U.S. Department of Commerce, which keeps track of it. The investment of American dollars abroad largely completes the picture of free trade as it is seen by globalizing corporations. First, however, keep in mind that foreign holdings of assets in the United States now far exceed U.S. holdings abroad (Batra, 1993: 172–173). American investment is large in Germany, Canada, the United Kingdom and Australia. However, among many foreign globalizing corporations, those from Britain, Japan and the Netherlands have large investments in the United States (Batra, 1993: 172–173). The presence of Japan's auto assembly plants as direct foreign investments in the United States is a reality that everyone knows. Other examples are the acquisitions made by the Japanese globalizing corporations of significant American businesses and buildings, although some sales of assets have risen due to economic downturn in Japan.

The outflow dollar data available shows a continuously higher amount was set in 1996 in foreign direct investments elsewhere by American globalizing corporations. And, the amount was $85 billion in 1996. Keep in mind who makes the decisions to invest abroad by giant American globalizing corporations. We should ask then—What is the picture like over a long period of time? And, what are the implications of this type of investment for American workers and American society or any industrial nation?

The long-term picture looks like this in table format, as seen in Table 6-2.

You will notice the constant dollar flow year after year to other nations; and, you will recall during the same period the concomitant loss of American jobs

Table 6-2
Foreign Direct Investment Outflows (Millions of Dollars) for the United States
(1985–1990, Annual Average $21,596)

Year	Outflows (in $millions)
1991	33,456
1992	38,978
1993	74,837
1994	51,007
1995	92,929
1996	84,902

in basic industry. This is no random correlation of events. Not investing in America has had consequences. The hemorrhaging of the American industrial economy by foreign direct investment is significant. The lower investment in America by American businesses is evident. Each dollar invested abroad is a dollar not invested inside the United States in the period. The jobs lost in America are a consequence of such investments; and foreign direct investments into the United States add to trouble for Americans by increasing competition.

The desire by American corporations to invest abroad is certainly not new. John D. Rockefeller's oil empire extended itself overseas at the turn of the century, around 1900 (Wilkins, 1974). Rockefeller's was then the second giant globalizing multinational corporation—Standard Oil. Singer Sewing Machine was first. One hundred years later the oil discoveries in other nations show active successors—Exxon, Mobil and others pursuing foreign oil. The practice in the oil industry has not changed for such a precious commodity as oil. Oil and globalization have gone hand in hand for a century. The oil industry is among the most globalized of all industries in America (Yergin, 1991).

What is new is the opening of American markets without automatic full reciprocity in free trade by other trading nations (Batra, 1993; Reich, 1991; Destler, 1992; Prestowitz, 1988; Dryden, 1995: Eckes, 1995). Opening the American market to Mexico in 1994 was the first time in NAFTA history that such a mismatch of economies was made in a common market. Predictably, the results were a disaster. Both of these practices are anomalies that need correction and significant political discourse was not made in the 1996 presidential election campaign to achieve any concrete results of change. So far 1998 and 1999 are much the same.

Another aspect to free trade after the end of the cold war was export controls on arms, atomic weapons and sophisticated military and other technology. In 1991, a panel of experts examined the future design and implementation of U.S. national security export controls. One conclusion was : "Export controls should neither be discarded in the glow of the moment nor retain the rigidity of the past'' (National Academy of Sciences, 1991). Nuclear proliferation, chemical weapons and missiles were a significant concern of the group in the new world structure. Quite often free trade discussions and globalizing corporations ignore this aspect of world peace under conditions of potential atomic and chemical warfare. But free trade is subject to constant overview of nations—especially the United States for export control security purposes. Iraq is a good example of the need for caution in foreign trade. Here is clear evidence that in discussions of free trade, sovereignty of nations remains an absolutely vital topic when exports of high technology to rogue nations like Iraq are considered.

Three policies seem to fit together. First, trade policy favoring free trade exclusively, and ignoring the need for protection from international trade to stop the hurting of domestic industry is obviously unwise in peacetime. Globalizing corporations in the United States will eventually die from international competition defined in this way. The workers' jobs are already rapidly dying. This policy is global competition that drags down pay for lower-skilled workers in all of the higher-pay nations. Impoverishing and destablizing the industrialized world this way through such a policy does not make much sense (Eckes, 1995: 285; Goldsmith, 1993). Employment policy for the twenty-first century is the second most significant policy area (Potter and Youngman, 1995). If trade is restricted through new tariffs, are workers being employed in the most humane and effective manner and is their productivity globally comparable to others? Employment policies will need to be examined again. See Chapter 7 below, where this examination is done.

The third policy that deserves examination, and is central to this work, is how much freedom to invest in the United States should globalizing foreign private corporations have? Should foreign government-owned multinationals be able to invest in America? And, finally, should CEOs and boards of directors of American globalizing corporations have unreviewable and unlimited discretion to invest overseas—in foreign direct investment in their wholly or partly owned subsidiary corporations, foreign joint ventures or in foreign alliances? So far, except for export controls mentioned above, there is a freewheeling policy in the United States, and it is supported by dominant political power. The freewheeling nature of global investment is a policy widely accepted as valid. ''Business knows best about its business''—is probably today a major justification for such a policy. But is the policy of allowing almost unreviewable or unlimited investment decisions into the United States and unreviewable and unlimited investments by American corporations in businesses outside the United States necessarily a good or wise policy to follow into the long-term future? Virtually no discussion is heard today on this set of questions because of the dominant free trade policy and inertia and the complexity of the issues. I would argue that the twenty-first century will see a rebirth of national sovereignty that will expand to include these questions on the top political agendas of both political parties and in terms of national politics elsewhere. And these questions are not the old, erroneous Smoot-Hawley debate to be mistakenly rehashed (Eckes, 1995). Furthermore, these questions are not just the simple-minded issue of free trade versus protectionism. These questions probe the nature of the giant corporation in American society and in societies of other nations; and foreign global giant corporations are under scrutiny in investment decisions. The questions expose the extreme laissez-faire attitude dominating much thinking toward such questions. This attitude of not thinking must stop eventually.

SERVICES

It is obvious that money—capital—is all that has been mentioned in trading lingo so far in this chapter. The word ''service'' is most significant, as was already noted. America is mostly a service-employed economy. Large units of service are offered by globalizing giant corporations. In fact, the aim of GE is to offer services of both a financial and maintenance nature to high-tech products it sells. So service is a subject of international trade—equipment maintenance, legal, accounting, management consulting, computer servicing—you get the picture. Since ''service'' is 75% of the American employment, it is inevitably caught up in the foreign trade policy issues. We will get into questions of service later in this chapter.

GOODS

Apart from money and service, to round out the picture of international trade—goods, products, tangible things, which if dropped may hurt your toes, are the historically significant objects of trade. Spices from the Far East—silk from China, clothing from everywhere, oil from around the globe, automobiles from a dozen nations and thousands of other products from Swiss pocket knives to French eyeglass frames and Canadian pulp in newsprint that rests in millions of Americans hands every day. It is with goods floating across high seas in ships or in the cargo holds of jumbo jets that we most vividly grasp international trade—the trading of wheat and timber and oranges is the most concrete illustration. What about cookies in international trade?

Cookies Are Us: Ship of Fools

The image of cookies passing by one another in the middle of the Atlantic Ocean on ships headed from Europe to America and from America to Europe is a strange idea. It struggles for a permanent place in your memory—and Herman Daly, the well-known ecologist and economist, in his typically humorous way, asked: ''Why not just exchange recipes?'' (Daly, 1996) Why not? This would be just to give up some fictional comparative advantage each cookie maker sees in the greatness of his or her cookie. Maybe this is too hard on

Table 6-3
United States–Japan Automobile Trade

	1994 Value (in dollars)	Assume $15,000/car (# cars rounded)
Japanese new cars to United States	24,020,000,000	1,600,000
U.S. cars to Japan	1,787,000,000	110,000
Difference (ship to United States)	22,247,000,000	1,490,000

cookie makers, and a rush to defend cookie makers' unwillingness to exchange recipes by all of the Famous Amos cookie makers of the world would set the record straight. But, I doubt it.

Most people can readily see the enormous costs of shipping cookies thousands of miles, under expensive security from all types of risks caused by bugs, rainstorms, cookie thieves, and the dehydrating sun. And the expensive packaging and shelf life problems—how great they must be. What, we must ask, will the world be coming to when nobody eats the cookies they make, and everyone of the 5.5 billion people on earth today eat cookies made in some other continent by some other nation? This image of foreign cookie markets is what must dazzle every cookie maker. "Build a better mousetrap" and the world will beat a path to your door. Maybe so, but I think many better mousetrap inventors have been ignored completely. What happened to the QWERTY typewriters, for example?

Cookies are not so heavy. How about moving automobiles? This is the next image to focus on: automobiles at sea passing one another in the night—one ship from Japan headed for Baltimore up the Chesapeake Bay; the other ship headed down the Bay for foreign ports, including Japan, to deliver its Fords, Chevrolets and Chryslers. At least more cookies can fit on a ship than cars. You may think this is absurd. Well, think again. The United States–Japan automobile trade is a simple-minded, perverse trading scheme if there ever was one (see Table 6-3).

A first-grader could get this picture of imbalance or injustice in scales of fairness; and there are other categories of trade with such crazy imbalances.

The greatest imbalance was the 1994 overall negative trade imbalance with Japan. U.S. exports to Japan were $53.4 billion versus $119.1 billion imports from Japan. China is right in the same zone in 1996. And the United States has negative trade imbalances (in the billions) of over $2 billion a year with Singapore ($2.3), Sweden ($2.5), India ($3.0), France ($3.0), Indonesia ($3.7), Nigeria ($3.9), Venezuela ($4.3), Thailand ($5.4), Malaysia ($7.0), Italy ($7.6), Taiwan ($9.5), Germany ($12.5), Canada ($13.9), China ($29.5) and Japan ($65.8), the last being the greatest imbalance. The overall picture of trade is factually very negative for the United States—$150.6 billion in 1994 in just a single year—in just 12 months we imported $663.2 billion and exported much

Table 6-4
Job Exporting by Big Corporations, 1980–1994

Year	Exports ($ billions)	Imports ($ billions)	Negative Imbalance	% Difference Imbalance
1980	229	244	24	10.9
1985	213	345	132	61.9
1990	394	495	101	25.6
1991	421	485	64	15.2
1992	448	532	84	18.7
1993	465	580	115	24.7
1994	512	663	151	29.4

less at $512.6 billion. This is plainly ridiculous and no economist could reasonably justify this strange state of affairs—it is impossible to continue this type of trade into the future. This is a picture of madness.

From 1950 through 1975, everyone knows the United States exported more than it imported from abroad. In 1980 at the beginning of job exporting by big corporations, a negative trade imbalance began to reveal itself clearly, as seen in Table 6-4.

This looks like the race dogs: greyhounds chasing a rabbit—never quite catching it and losing ground in the race over time, but nothing so bad as 1985—the Reagan era. Maybe the United States is a foxhound and the foxes are the foreign merchants.

By principal commodity groupings nothing—*nothing* for the United States is so extreme as crude oil imports and exports. Not coffee, cocoa, sugar, footwear, gem diamonds, iron and steel mill products, pottery, toys and sporting goods, travel goods or zinc. In each of these and many more categories, there are significant trade balance negative to the United States. But there are noticeably large differences in the ten categories just mentioned. However, nothing prepares you for the category of *crude oil* in 1994, as noted in Table 6-5.

Cross out the six zeroes and it's 49: 38,479 or $1 to $785 ratio. Burn those numbers into your consciousness—into your mind. Here are all the massive trucks, sports utility vehicles on America's roads, the big Buicks, large Lincoln Continentals; the Chevy Suburban can carry everything and the kitchen sink with one small woman at the wheel towering over the traffic like some space-world Martian surveying the next four miles of cars parked on a freeway. Is this bordering on insanity or not?

The U.S. driver burns the world's crude oil at such a huge rate it is not easy to comprehend. Take some time to dwell on it. What is $38.4 billion of imports of crude oil? In one year of 365 days it is the burning in every day of 24 hours: $105 million day. This is the bleeding at the gas pumps of America in the

Table 6-5
Trade Balance of Crude Oil, 1994

Crude Oil--1994	
$49,999,000	Export from United States
$38,479,000,000	Import to United States

American economy—the burning bleeding. Oh, we can afford this, you say! I would concede this imbalance is tolerable for a year or two but not for long. This is a tragic and maddening drain of the life blood of the nation for *too costly* transportation. There are cheaper ways to move us—rail, for example, ships and buses. There are few Americans who would not gladly switch to electric cars to get away from some of the huge globalizing oil corporations: Exxon, Shell, Mobil and others. The gas pumps are too costly now for Americans—most Americans. Imagine paying $5 a gallon for gas and "fill'er up" equals $50 to $75. This is what I experienced in Europe in 1996. The wave of the future reflected in Europe's gas prices today is that only the rich can drive a car. It is back to 1900.

In summary, what you already know is rather glaring from a U.S. perspective in world trade and nothing can cover up the dreadful imbalance the United States now suffers. It should be obvious that trade creates wealth for some small groups—and eventual poverty for the masses. This is particularly true of the Middle East oil sheiks compared with American factory workers downsized and looking for work. These are the genuine contrasts across the globe and inside the United States when the billionaires are compared with the poor in any nation.

But, there is a vision that is more than the inequities of who was born over what oil field or no oil field. The rich–poor extremes are in every direction one could imagine. The realities of oil use deserve greater exposition. The vision of China and India on a maximum U.S.-style auto use should be imagined. These are the most arresting ideas of future oil consumption (Karp, 1997).

One final fact should be noted. From 1968 thorough 1994 (26 years) the Japanese sold new passenger cars to U.S. buyers in total: 39,443,000 or almost 40,000,000 new automobiles. And this excludes passenger cars assembled in U.S. foreign trade zones. The *Wall Street Journal* reporter Eduardo Lachica emphasized that the Japanese presence in the United States that grew from direct investment (about $10.2 billion a year) between 1983 and 1992 and Japanese owners of U.S. affiliates in 1993 employed approximately 720,000 persons and paid about $31 billion in wages. Lest we get too excited about the market for new Japanese cars in the United States, think of Germany, Italy, the United Kingdom, Sweden, France, South Korea, Mexico and Canada, who also export to the United States. The total from 1968 through 1994 (26 years) was 85,264,000 autos from all nations importing passenger cars to the United States—the world as a whole outside of Japan imported 45,821,000 or 53.7%

Table 6-6
Passenger Car Production, U.S. Plants, 1993 and 1994

	Passenger Car Production, U.S. Plants	
	1993	**1994**
Diamond Star	136,035	169,829
Honda	403,775	498,710
Auto Alliance	219,096	246,710
Nissan	792,182	312,675
Subaru Legacy	47,117	54,002
Toyota	356,114	399,341
Total	1,454,319	1,681,548
	24.6%	**25.4%**

of the 85 million. This means the 40 million Japanese cars exported to the United States is 46.3% of the total U.S. imports for the 26-year period from 1968 to 1994. Who has dominated the imported auto scene for 26 years in the "richest nation" in the world? Why has the "richest nation," the United States, become a debtor nation? Why is the trade imbalance with Japan so great today? It is obvious: our public policies lack any reciprocity, any sensibility and good for America compared with Japan and the rest of the nations.

By now this analysis may read as if it is "Japanese bashing," but it is intended by an American author to be self-bashing or "U.S. bashing." How dumb can we be as a nation? How very dumb are we in world trade? Very stupid would be my most charitable, calm, rational and probing comment. This is unwelcome honesty in some trading circles. In Chapter 8, I will explore some of the implications of such continued stupidity. But for now, let's look finally at oil consumption—crude oil consumption—very crudely. After all, we needed the imported crude oil to run 85 million foreign-made vehicles. Foreign crude and foreign vehicles do form a transportation system. How far we have come from the Amish horse and buggy days; and how *dependent* we have become on what? Crude oil is an irreplaceable, non-renewable national and international resource that may have, at "current" consumption levels only, 40 years left by current estimates. No cars will run on empty (Hartmann, 1998: 1–18; Campbell, 1991 and 1988); and, global warming is obvious to everyone (Gelbspan, 1997). A transition plan to the twenty-first century is an obviously fundamental need for nations (Boyer, 1984).

One final, final fact before looking at the issues. The United States had total passenger car production: 5.9 million in 1993 and 6.6 million in 1994. Of this total, the groups specified in Table 6-6 are producers of cars.

One-fourth of U.S. total passenger car production inside the United States is

Table 6-7
U.S. 1994 International Investment Position

	Current Cost	Market Value
OUT--United States Direct Investment Abroad	$761 billion	$1,048.4 billion
IN--Foreign Direct Investment in the United States	$580.5 billion	$771.1 billion

foreign subsidiaries of foreign corporations and their branches and joint ventures. Add this to imports made from foreign plants—40 million cars shipped in during the last 26 years and it all spells out one thing: We have been shooting ourselves in both feet every year and never learning. It's a wonder Uncle Sam is still standing.

Even *Fortune* (August 5, 1996: 108) noted that Toyota Motors and Sony Corporation of America did not disclose revenues of their U.S. subsidiaries. One could ask—why not? Does the U.S. government, especially the IRS, want to know? These are interesting questions of public affairs. They involve taxation, of course. We will get to this later, but recall in Chapter 1 the assertion of a U.S. Senator Byron Dorgan—no taxes paid in 1993 by some companies. I wonder how long this has been going on?

TROUBLESOME CAPITAL FLOWS: FOREIGN DIRECT INVESTMENT

So far in this chapter, an effort is being made to elevate capital investment to the highest point in your attention to foreign trade. For many readers this is a ''go-to-sleep'' signal, a boring repetition of money flows and vague inferences. I hope to avoid this since the central point of this book is the question: What should nations do to regulate and tax the flows of capital that move globally both (1) inside groups of related corporations and (2) outside among nations to other families of corporations? Inside flows of capital are already described previously in this chapter by the GE Europe example—money moves from one part of GE to another part of GE crossing national borders in the movement. The example of (2) is the British Airways attempted investment in USAir in the United States or the British Telecommunication PLC attempted acquisition of a U.S. company, MCI. Two families of corporations are involved in capital transfers.

Table 6-7 shows the 1994 international investment position of the United States using two different valuation methods.

As reported by Russell B. Scholl in the June 1995 *Survey of Current Business*, ''The net international investment position of the United Sates at yearend 1994 was [minus] $680.8 billion when direct investment is valued at current cost . . .

Table 6-8
U.S. Net International Investment Position, 1987–1994

	Negative (in billions of dollars)
1987	11
1988	134
1990	251
1992	355
1993	545
1994	680

Source: Scholl (1995): 60.

and it was [minus] 584 billion when direct investment is valued at current stock market value of owners' equity'' (Scholl, 1995: 32). Large net capital inflows into the United States created more negative values. From 1987, the last year of positive value at $44 billion, the year-by-year negative growth is shown in Table 6-8.

This is an unhealthy trend for the United States.

There is no need to over-rely on a single data series prepared by the Bureau of Economic Analysis of the United States Commerce Department because the data is both voluminous and carefully prepared (Mataloni, March, 1995: 38–55). Mataloni stated that total foreign affiliate assets were $1.7 trillion in 1992 and direct investment funded by U.S. parent corporations was $499 billion (Mataloni, March 1995: 39). This must register as a major indicator of the quiet continual growth of globalization by major corporations. In 1992 the U.S. direct investment was largest in the United Kingdom ($83 Billion), Canada ($69 billion) and Germany ($34 billion). Affiliate employment of U.S. parent companies was in the United Kingdom (917,000), Canada (873,000) and Mexico (661,000) in 1992 (Mataloni, March 1995: 46). In 1992, the U.S. MNC-associated trade (in large globalizing firms) accounted for 58 percent of U.S. merchandise exports and 41 percent of U.S. merchandise imports.

How many affiliates of U.S. parent corporations are there? The total in 1993 was 18,698 affiliates, 14,834 of which were owned wholly by the parent, some 2,214 were minority owned by the parent (Mataloni, June 1995). The locations of these U.S. wholly owned affiliated businesses are listed in Table 6-9.

This total is 54.9% of the total of 18,698 affiliates. The other half is scattered in Europe, Latin America, Africa, the Middle East, Asia and the Pacific, and other international areas. This tells you where American foreign direct and indirect investment has gone from 1960 to 1995.

For each of these affiliates and U.S. parent corporation there are rather elaborate inflows and outflows of equity capital, intercompany debt and reinvested

Table 6-9
Locations of U.S. Wholly Owned Affiliated Businesses

Nation	Total Affiliates
United Kingdom	2,185
Canada	1,941
Germany	1,221
France	1,104
Netherlands	904
Japan	842
Australia	777
Italy	680
Mexico	624
	10,278 concentrated locations

earnings. To grasp the complexities see Figure 6-1 prepared by the Bureau of Economic Analysis (BEA) of the United States Department of Commerce (Mataloni, March 1995: 42). To avoid jumping to erroneous conclusions it is worth contemplating the careful analysis of the BEA to assess size of operations and flows of funds. The fact is that it takes a great effort to assemble the few numbers cited here. Beyond this compilation there is a further wealth of data that economists find grist for their mill. There is no need for us to pursue that data here because the reality is clear enough from the data cited. Globalizing corporations are almost everywhere in very vigorous form in the North. That is the empirical reality for nations.

A GLOBAL ECONOMY: WHAT BELONGS IN IT?

Three types of foreign trade seem to emerge: clear candidates for global trade, not-so-clear candidates, and clear candidates *not* for foreign trade. Illustrative lists are as follows:

1. Clear Candidates for Global Trade

Wheat	Investment money	Books
Apples	Coal	Films
Jet aircraft	Oil	Tapes
Oranges	Bananas	

2. Not-so-Clear Candidates for Global Trade

Cookies	Clothing	Semiconductor chips
Cheese	Shoes	Electronic products
Wine	Toys	Steel and ships
Accounting	Legal services	Technical service

Figure 6-1
Components of Capital Inflows and Outflows on United States Direct Investment Abroad

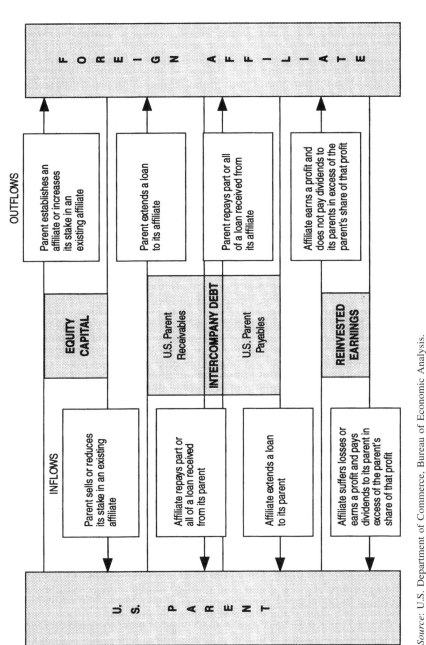

Source: U.S. Department of Commerce, Bureau of Economic Analysis.

3. Clear Candidates *Not* for Global Trade
   Goods made by slave labor, prison labor, child labor
   Goods made by apartheid nations—South Africa in the past
   Nuclear weapons and lethal gases and toxins
   Feathers and hides from endangered species
   Tuna from fleets needlessly killing dolphins and sea turtles

Why is it necessary to be clear about what belongs in a global market and what does not? It may seem to be the height of arrogance for this author to state what is best for the global market and what is not—but a justification is very clear and practical. Some things are completely unacceptable based upon security and human rights concerns—those would be goods that are clear candidates *not* for global trade. Who could assign sensibility for a marketplace that would have a commercial free-for-all in nuclear weapons? That would be arrogantly ignorant to argue for such a proposal and not in the best long-run interest of humanity. The same with human rights. Economics and business take a back seat to politics.

The second category—not-so-clear candidates for global trade—may be a place for reasoned argument. The underlying principle must be self-sufficiency versus dependency of a nation. We raise children and teach them to take care of themselves. We could do no less in nations relating to one another. Teach a man how to fish and he will take care of himself for life. Give a man a fish and forever he will depend on you. This ancient Greek idea is meritorious. In the food, shelter and clothing categories I would presume everyone from Eskimos to Chinese to Italians to Balinese would want first and foremost to be self-sufficient. The paramount need is to take care of one's self in each nation—to be self-contained in a communal sense. With this policy there is great common sense. Global trade of any item that you should produce yourself should be halted or reduced or taxed to discourage it. This is especially true of professional services.

The third category—clear candidates for global trade—is where there are acknowledged surpluses of money, goods of all kinds and scarce non-renewable resources in nation after nation and services critically needed, such as medical services. Transporting people to receive critical medical care is humane global "trade," although we know only a very small fraction of people ever receive it. This part of global trade suffers from too much trade, however. Professional services are an example—the massive and intrusive consulting, legal, accounting and computer services. The one item—oil—is in need of global regulation to preserve it for future generations and to curb appetites of current generations for more and more oil and gas energy.

Thus, it would be helpful to see more self-sufficiency in the United States; for example, only burning every day that oil which it needs most critically and dropping demand substantially from private auto transport systems over the next 20 years. This means substantial growth of public transport systems as an alternative—not just electric cars or more of the same wasteful behavior.

These three categories represent nothing more than an effort to distinguish what nations ought to do on their own and where they ought to consciously create a self-sufficient life and reduce dependency on other people as much as possible. This is a noble goal of self-interest and autonomy—national freedom. We must ask what belongs in global trade and what does not, and what is highly questionable from the standpoint of self-sufficient nationhood. A long, 100-year time horizon is appropriate.

TWO DIFFERENT VIEWS OF A GLOBAL ECONOMY

As this is written, everyone is well aware of the golden word "sustainable," as associated with "development." Everyone is clamoring to claim their ideas and actions are great contributors to "sustainable development." Sustainable development is a good thing—everyone wants to encourage it. A global economy based on sustainable development is the key desire, we are told.

Beyond Growth Global Trade

To his great credit, Herman Daly illuminated one of the two very different views of the global economy. I would describe Herman Daly's steady state ecological economics as the "Beyond Growth" perspective of a global economy. Daly stated: "Once you draw the boundary of the environment around the economy, you have said that the economy cannot expand forever" (Daly, 1996: 7). The global economy is not a free-standing thing without limits of its own—human limits that read: "Thou shalt not trade in products of child labor or nuclear weapons," and environmental limits—"How much poison can you put into a finite body of water before the water will not be fit to drink?" or "How many fish can you take from the ocean before it ceases to be bountiful?" Quantitative growth must slow and cease and give way to qualitative growth. Empty-world economics must give way to full-world economics. Fish at sea face a full world of fishermen depleting fishing stocks on a global scale. Fifty years of global population growth from 2 to 6 billion people has changed everything since 1945.

Daly made a profound point when he stated: "One way to render any concept innocuous is to expand its meaning to include everything" (Daly, 1996: 9). He argued that "sustainable sustainability" is where a worthless definition is headed. Daly reasoned that economic imperialism includes everything in the world inside the economy—the commodification of everything as seen in the writings of Richard Posner or Immanuel Wallerstein (Wallerstein, 1983: 11) or "world peace through world trade" (Polanyi, 1944: xi). There are no alternatives in an imperialistic view of economics (Heilbroner and Milberg, 1995). But they do exist (Duchrow, 1995; Berger, 1990), as will be explained shortly. By contrast, ecological reductionism shrinks the economy to nothing and human choice is reduced to zero so that "natural world laws" can work their mighty way and, as Daly stated: "human extinction [is] no more significant than the extinction of any other species" (Daly, 1996: 11). That position of ecological reductionism is not favored by Daly nor is the economic imperialism viewpoint. I would agree—but where does that lead? Here Daly offers guidance:

The third strategy is the one adopted here—to view the economy as a subsystem of the ecosystem and to recognize that while it is not exempt from natural laws, neither is it fully reducible to explanation by them. The human economy cannot be reduced to a natural system. (Daly, 1996: 11)

As Daly guides thinking about the global economy he stated: "For now, however, the most pressing need is to stop the exponential expansion of this subsystem boundary under the current regime of economic imperialism—but without falling prey to the seductions of ecological reductionism" (Daly, 1996: 12).

These brilliant ideas of Daly guide the definition of a global economy set forth here. There must be limits to global trade—human, moral, legal and environmental limits that are to be discovered, if not obvious now like the three types of appropriate goods, services and capital in global trade mentioned just above in this chapter.

Daly offers a criticism of free trade among the nations that do *not* count social and environment costs and those that do. Free trade, free capital mobility and free migration of people will put into effect an erasure of national boundaries that will creat a power vacuum into which transnational corporations will and have moved—"without any interest in nationhood or community long-term survival" (Daly, 1996: 18). By contrast, in short-term perspective, giant corporations do yearn for sovereignty, but plan for the next five years at the most. Daly's analysis is too involved to pursue it further here, but it is well worth examination (Daly, 1996: Chapters 5, 10 and 11).

What we see are jungle capitalism and neocolonialism rearing their ugly heads in foreign trade and this we know from 100 years of regulatory capitalism in the United States is obviously the wrong direction in which to take global trade. So what direction makes more sense? Daly is not alone in spelling out that "Beyond Growth" perspective. Another set of policy-concerned world citizens, which includes Daly, is found in the International Forum on Globalization. Their recent work, *The Case against the Global Economy and for a Turn toward the Local* (Mander and Goldsmith, 1996) reveals a profound and global concern that current global trade is hurting more than helping mankind. This global group, spurred on by the passage in 1993–1994 of NAFTA, GATT and WTO, joined in forums to examine and address the issues of a global economy. Corporations—especially global corporations—want bigger free trade blocs, more free trade areas—"economic integration" as they call it, to become even more footloose and less answerable to nation-states. Separating production costs from areas of sales of products shifts harm of pollution to low-wage assembly platforms in Mexico and elsewhere. "That is why transnational corporations like free trade and why workers and environmentalists do not" (Mander and Goldsmith, 1996: 235). A system of absentee owners of the earth is being set up by globalizing corporations to deprive communities of the exclusive control of their wealth (Mander and Goldsmith, 1996: 510).

Let me be candid. The view of a world that is beyond growth, where a global trading economy must be severely tamed and regulated and where development is getting a very bad name—"neocolonialism"—is the less well-known perspective on the globe. However, for this book, it is the main point of view on the global economy. For the world as a whole, we are still caught up in a decaying paradigm that urges a perspective that global trade be maximized; then, it is believed, the world will be better off. Nothing could be worse for 5.5 billion people in the world community than the current course of exploding world trade. As Wolfgang Sachs observed: "we now can consume in one year what it took the earth a million years to store up. . . . If all countries 'successfully' followed the industrial example, five or six planets would be needed to serve as mines and waste dumps" (Sachs, 1992: 2). As Thom Hartmann explained, oil is ancient sunlight and when it is gone, 6 billion people or more by the year 2040 will move back to just last year's sunlight for food (Hartmann, 1998).

One must recall the 1945 world population rising—tripling—to nearly 6 billion in just 50 years. A population increase from two billion to six billion people in the world created exceptional resource pressures on Mother Earth—the one planet we have to live upon.

Economic Integrationist of Global Trade

The second major perspective of a global economy is the most well-known. This viewpoint is described by David Korten in *When Corporations Rule the World*. Supporters of economic integration into larger trading blocks want to integrate the non-integratable—as in NAFTA, the North American Free Trade Agreement between the United States and Canada, already highly integrated (too much so for some Canadians; see Clarke, 1997), and the difficult case of Mexico, with its totally incomparable wages and working standards, lack of governmental democracy and corruption. Mexico's scant experience with democracy is a few years in the last 600 years (Krauze, 1997). There is little doubt that economic integrationists have had their day—from 1945 to 1995, but the criticism already noted is rising.

Compared with self-sufficiency (a paramount national goal of self-sufficient independence—a goal of those who wish to turn to local and regional economy rather that the global economy, a goal of those who argue that a sustainable steady state economy is beyond growth), by great contrast the supporters of economic integration are into a policy of new colonialism—a new disabling, dependent, neurotic, manic, frenetic and costly weakening of nations. This type of economic integration benefits only the few, the most wealthy capitalists who are already rich beyond description. NAFTA, GATT and the WTO became the passwords of the economic imperialists. NAFTA has not worked—it has costs and damages far beyond any expectations—it is hated by many in Mexico and Canada and by many in the United States.

Apologists for jungle capitalism include Albert J. Dunlap in his *Mean Business* (1996), and Rosabeth Kanter in her *World Class* diatribe against local economy and *"natives"* (Kanter, 1995). They are a sad commentary on the significant lack of objectivity; but no less so are the last five federal administrations of Clinton, Bush, Reagan, Ford and Nixon. These administrations have shaped the 1970s, 1980s and now 1990s. And, from the perspective of those who see the case against the global economy, these five administrations have marched like lemmings to the sea, causing death for the American economy. Such massive trade deficits, such gross export-import trouble, such a negative position of investment, such gross oil waste, and such horrible downsizing in manufacturing—all of the factors previously explained with empirical detail—all of these troubles can be laid at the doorstep of previous federal administrations and the current one—truly a non-partisan destruction of the American economy and American workers' standard of living. Half of the clothing in America is now foreign made. China makes toys for us. Vast imports of autos clutter our streets and highways. Wal-Mart and Kmart are stuffed with foreign-made merchandise, driving local competitive businesses into the ground and bankruptcy. Steel, semiconductors and many other products are in difficult shape. Raw logs were cut and shipped overseas to Japan. Foreign oil keeps us going. The plunder of the American economy is not merely some worry of Ross Perot and Pat Choate. The economic integrationists are the problem and not the solution.

The wake-up call to America is a vast literature stretching back to the late 1970s when deindustrialization was first detected as a corporate industrial policy. Some 4.6 million jobs lost and a trillion dollars in foreign investment are the minimum sum total of destruction wrought *not* by invisible market hands, but instead by visible hands of CEOs of major corporations downsizing American workers in the industrial core of *Fortune* 500 corporations and hiring millions in other nations. This is the dangerous legacy of the economic integrationists who manage our largest corporations. It is as if they are hell bent on U.S. self-destruction—not self-sufficiency in a global economy.

Furthermore, the overstimulated and overadvertised American markets—surfeit with goods, services and too much of the wrong things—are barraged by a mass media controlled by the wasteful, publicly paid advertising money of giant corporations. The figure is $186 billion for advertising in 1996. This has become a deepening social crisis in America and it is helping to create an ungovernable world (Schiller, 1996). A joyless economy results in people stumbling through the malls of America in endless pursuit of material goods (Scitovsky, 1992; and see Chapter 10 for further analysis). Hyperactive children and hyperactive adults are the product of a mindless, hyperactive culture. How could intelligent CEOs want to create such a social and economic mess? There must be more sane voices to guide the nations if both business and government so totally fail the people. ''Affluenza,'' a 1997 PBS video review of the sick American economy, shows both comical and tragic aspects of consumerism gone wild.

A RATIONALE TO SUPPORT A MINIMAL GLOBAL ECONOMY: WELL-REGULATED

Because the propaganda in favor of economic integration is so well-financed by globalizing corporations who also own major media (GE, for example owns NBC and Westinghouse owns CBS), the rationale to support a minimal global economy that is well-regulated by the nations acting in consort and by treaty must be globally persuasive. The first crack in the propaganda is the lack of vision in modern economic thought, so well described and analyzed by Robert Heilbroner and William Milberg (Heilbroner and Milberg, 1995). The second crack in the massive barrage of propaganda for economic integration is the first major critical work in 1996, titled *The Case against the Global Economy* (Mander and Goldsmith, 1996). The same is true of David Korten's work mentioned before, and of Greider's *One World, Ready or Not* (1997); and for Canada, Tony Clarke's *Silent Coup* (1997). Like the canary in the mine that detects toxic gas, these authors alert the world to the toxic, lethal and horribly destructive side of jungle capitalism practiced by globalizing corporations across the globe. These corporations and their CEOs are in it for themselves, and not for the good of the world as a whole. Globalizing corporations place enormous pressures on people everywhere and all of the pressure is completely unnecessary in a localized economy. In other words, the case against the global economy is forced into existence by the intensive global propaganda machines of the major globalizing corporations. One could easily surmise that this is the work of the Business Roundtable in the United States and its counterpart groups in Canada, Europe, Australia and the Far East. They stand to benefit personally and financially from economic integration schemes. They must believe more billionaires are needed. A rationale must have a form and a substance that is a beginning.

Wolfgang Sachs called the last 40 years the age of development and he believes it is coming to an end. Beginning as an American policy to rebuild a world torn apart by World War II, development is an odd mixture of generosity, bribery and oppression toward the Southern Hemisphere of the globe and its population. The North is developed, the South needs to develop and the obvious model is the Northern Hemisphere nations. The International Monetary Fund and the World Bank believe this to be true in their heart of hearts. So do many in the North in globalizing corporations. However, the ecological misery of Russian nuclear waste, decaying forests blighted by acid rain in the eastern United States and water pollution everywhere are not attractive parts of industrialization anymore than devastated Brazilian forests or fisheries depleted by the United States, Russia and Japan. Modern industrialism kills and it is dying itself in "service" economies like the United States.

Without some guidelines or a vision, the idea of development—"to what?"— is lost. The North is not a goal, argued Sachs, and all we have in his eyes are a flood of immigrants, regional wars, illicit trade and environmental disasters. Who would want this as a goal of development? Sachs stated: "In 1960, the northern countries were 20 times richer than the southern, in 1980—46 times" (Sachs, 1992: 3). World champions in competitive obsolescence, the North always wins and the North and West get richer. And Sachs argued that the westernization of the world is the developmental goal, hardly a compliment to other cultures of the world. These industrial scars are marks against development and the current paradigm must fail, in his eyes, if it has not already collapsed. A better life in some ways has its downsides in other ways. This is a realistic viewpoint.

In *Beyond Free Trade* (1993) the editor, David Yoffie, pulled together a variety of experts to examine many puzzles of global trade—in the context of changing trade patterns, changing capital flows and roles of corporations and changing government intervention. Some of these changes are already noted in previous chapters of this book, but it is helpful to focus on those Yoffie found significant. First was the surge of American imports and explosion of Japanese and German exports. Then 75% of all exports from the industrial world went to the other developed countries—not the South. Manufactured goods were traded with no "comparative advantage." The United States, Japan and Europe ship the same products to each other—why? What is the "comparative advantage?" A third of all U.S. trade with the rest of the world was internal to globalizing corporations, called "intrafirm" trade—not arm's length dealing outside of a corporate parent and subsidiary with others.

Foreign direct investment has risen rapidly in recent years and all that such a practice suggests has been noted previously. Finally, while tariffs dropped from 1950 (10%) to 1990 (5%), tariffs are more complex now, coupled with non-tariff actions of governments:

• Voluntary export restraints
• Licensing procedures
• Countertrade requirements
• Restrictive government procurement
• Technical standards
• Certification requirements.

From the research and writing by many co-authors, Yoffie drew a basic conclusion that to grasp fully what global trade is, "one must also explore the structure of global industry, the level and style of government intervention, the characteristics of leading firms, and the inertia of history'' (Yoffie, 1993: 44). The nature of the trade advantages, the political competition, the business competition type (oligopoly or regulation) and other factors may be significant. There is little doubt that a new eye is being cast upon more realistic factors of global trade in a rather precise and illuminating manner. Yoffie found that lessons of government intervention included:

1. Fostering unilateral deregulation can be destructive of strategic firms.

2. Infant industries can be protected and it works.

3. Managed trade can reverse irreversible trends.

4. Governments can make trade more advantageous (Yoffie, 1993: 443–446).

This work is some of the new and more realistic thinking about trade not necessarily wedded to ideological temperament about free trade shibboleths and mantras. Its objectivity seems clear to me.

This new wave of thinking is found in the work of many others: Tim Lang and Colin Hines, *The New Protectionism, Protecting the Future against Free Trade* (1993), and Chakravarthi Raghavan, *Recolonization, GATT, the Uruguay Round and the Third World* (1990), Ravi Batra, *The Myth of Free Trade* (1993), Ralph Nader and others, *The Case against Free Trade, GATT, NAFTA and the Globalization of Corporate Power* (1993), Alfred E. Eckes, Jr., *Opening America's Market—U.S. Foreign Trade Policy Since 1776* (1995), Charles P. Kindleberger, *Multinational Excursions* (1984), Yuan-Li Wu, *Economic Warfare* (1952), John H. Dunning, *Multinational Enterprises and the Global Economy* (1993) and Laura D'Andrea Tyson, *Who's Bashing Whom? Trade Conflict in High-Technology Industries* (1992). This list is not exhaustive.

Furthermore, there is realism in Stephen D. Cohen, Joel R. Paul and Robert A. Blecker's, *Fundamentals of U.S. Foreign Trade Policy* (1996), where the emerging issues are trade-environment ''green'' issues, ''blue'' issues of labor standards and competition policy—all of 100 years of regulated U.S. capitalism that must be acknowledged in global trade—antitrust, price fixing, market allocation schemes, import discrimination, rigged bidding practices, restricted access to distribution channels and private monopolies' procurement practices and much more. How will American regulated capitalism fit into a world scenario?

More realism is found by John Stopford and Susan Strange with John S. Henley, in their *Rival States, Rival Firms, Competition for World Market Shares* (1991). After examination of the growing reach of multinational corporations in a changing global competition, the authors examined dilemmas for governments and firms. Henley stated: ''Multinationals, perhaps predictably, prefer to employ young, usually unmarried women—on average more than 70 percent below the age of 25 . . . the youthful age structure of developing countries and the prospect of abundant supplies of this type of labour has been a powerful incentive for relocating labour intensive manufacturing industry from developed countries with their rapidly aging population'' (Stopford, Strange and Henley, 1991: 194) (see also Greider, 1997). In their advice to governments and multinationals the authors are very straightforward, asking both to consider ''sustainable'' approaches to governing and business plus other practical considerations. Two shadowed areas needed much more study: foreign involvement in national economies and the idea of a nationality of a firm (Stopford, Strange and Henley, 1991: 232–236). Now we have such a study of the importance of nations in world order compared with corporations (Doremus, Keller, Pauly and Reich, 1998).

DOMESTICATING THE GLOBALIZING CORPORATION: EVOLVING A TWENTY-FIRST-CENTURY POLICY

''Domesticating'' is a wonderful way to describe exactly what must be done to the multinational corporations of all nations including the United States. The U.S. Foreign Corrupt Practice Act of 1977 was the first clear example—you do not allow criminal commercial bribery in the United States, you do not allow it anywhere on earth. You cannot exploit American workers—you cannot exploit foreign workers in any manner. You cannot sell rotten food and harmful drugs in the United States, you cannot do it overseas. Do unto others as you would have them do unto you. Is this so hard to grasp? Is this form of domestication so bad ethically or morally? Is this ''westernization'' of the world? Is this not clear morality not to defraud your fellow man anywhere on earth?

There should not be any action by multinational parent corporations in the United States that is not the identical action of all of its foreign subsidiary corporations that are majority-owned—that is, 51% owned by a U.S. parent. Is this so hard to understand as a form of domesticated globalization of business?

How can human rights be dealt with in a universal manner if globalizing corporations go about the world with multiple public personalities, multiple legal personalities, and different legal, moral and ethical standards in every place they do business? How can they lie, cheat and steal in one place and in another place respect other people's private property, be honest, trustworthy and decent—all at the same time? Is there no such thing as universal integrity, consistent honesty and truth to support honest and truthful behavior everywhere? Do people everywhere want respect, truth and honesty in business dealings so they can proceed with the business deal? Do you buy from the most untrustworthy seller?

Cutting across all of the complaints of multinational corporate behavior is a fault line—an earthquake of a defect that allows parent standards to be rejected by foreign subsidiaries merely because they are foreign, that foreign standards, if lower, must inevitably be the standards. This ''when in Rome attitude'' truly defeats the domesticating of American global business to higher standards, because all global business is local with specific people. There should not be legal, locally relevant factors, or ethical or moral differences. A quality product is safe, trustworthy, fairly priced and good to own everywhere on earth. No one deserves a rotten product or an unsafe one. No one deserves injury at work, no one in any nation.

Much of the resistance to globalizing corporations centers upon this detested, business-behavior status that is lower if it is done outside of the home nation. Anonymous corporations, corporate secrecy and lack of transparent openness in doing business are exceptionally harmful to everyone's trust in business. Scientific truths are universal, and sound, moral and ethical business actions are a universal that should conform to the Universal Declaration of Human Rights—social, political and economic rights and the U.S. Constitution.

Is this one-world federalism? Not by a long stretch of imagination is this to be so labeled in error. Is this American hegemony of business standards? It may be, but with good effect and good reason, especially when American standards are higher. If they are not, then they must grow and change to conform. But there is no reason not to call for high standards of worker safety—a universal standard as well. Who wants electrical energy shocking and killing workers on the job? We know how to do things in a safe manner, why not protect workers everywhere? If others have higher standards, they should prevail in the United States. This is upward harmonization brought on by reason.

So let us be very wary of the lower standards of care everywhere on earth. These must not be allowed to prevail. This is one essential message of this chapter. We see just the opposite in the airline and aircraft industry with global alerts to prevent harm if defects are noted or dangers observed in aircraft operations. We all help one another to achieve high airline safety standards everywhere on earth. This practice of trading up and harmonization makes sense in many fields of commerce. We just have not thought through where such harmonization of national standards fits well and where it would get in the way of unique national policies or local policies. This is not a WTO task—it is a task for people of each nation to exercise their own sovereignty over commerce.

Let us turn next to Chapter 7 to observe the labor norms that impact on global trade and globalizing corporations in democratic nations.

Chapter 7

Labor and Major Globalizing Corporations: Downsizing and Rightsizing as if People Mattered Not at All

Chapter 7 focuses upon the labor equation of globalizing corporations. Labor forces in well-developed nations are finding job shifts to cheaper labor sites in the transitional and developing nations. Democratic nations watch with dismay as the best jobs in salary and benefits disappear through globalizing corporations' decisions to shift manufacturing production from one place to another. Labor negotiations increasingly are threatened by management's open longing to close U.S. plants and to go overseas (Cohn, 1997). Some observers still cannot see the obvious labor harms of corporate globalization (Blustein, 1997). If labor has an obligation to work and to avoid welfare, what then is the corresponding moral obligation of the *Fortune* 500 and others to sustain and to create new good jobs and investment in developed nations as a priority, and within the home country of the globalized corporation as a top priority? Who will set this priority for giant corporations in democratic nations? And what policies make sense for such global investment? Finally, international labor standards are examined in this chapter as they affect children and women. Do we want to go back to child labor and working women as slaves?

This chapter explores the relationship between organized, unionized labor and the *Fortune* 500 corporations. With some 20 million jobs (*Fortune* 500) of the total American labor force of 130 million there is little doubt that labor and the *Fortune* 500 corporations are central to the concern of every worker in America. The best jobs, best benefits and best salaries typically are found in the *Fortune* 500 corporations. This means that less than one in ten jobs (20 million over 130 million) are closely related to the actions of the *Fortune* 500 corporations in the United States and across the globe. The UN reported in 1997 that the top 100 TNCs globally employed 5.8 million (UN, 1997: 28).

What is the responsibility of *Fortune* 500 companies and others to create jobs in the United States first, then jobs in other nations? Who is to tell them to set this priority of business? This chapter examines some of the issues (Lohr, 1997; Uchitelle, 1996; Pasztor and Kravetz, 1996; Buchanan, 1998).

CITIZEN LABOR—HOMO SAPIENS: KUDOKA*

Manufacturing man is the forgotten, unknown soldier in the wars of big globalizing corporations competing against one another in their huge world-spanning, non-competitive, intrafirm trade cartels. The job deaths in this war in the United States alone total at least 4.6 million jobs lost from 1980 to 1997 in the industrial manufacturing core of America that was damaged or hollowed out by the *Fortune* 500 corporations. And that figure of 4.6 million is understated for years 1995, 1996, 1997 and 1998 where consistent data is not readily available. In Chapter 6 of this book the cumulative foreign direct investment by American corporations was listed at about a trillion dollars.

One figure, 4.6 million jobs, represents labor's immobility, the turmoil over plant closings, the shift to non-union labor in the American and global south; to maquiladora labor on the Mexican–U.S. border and to Canada and other low- and lower-wage assembly platforms all over the world, but especially to the Caribbean area and the Far East. And technology is both a positive and negative American job builder and wrecker. As it appears, so far Japan and Asia win in this field. The other figure—a trillion dollars in foreign direct investment—is the highly mobile capital of giant American corporations "going global," taking their U.S. earnings and plunking them down wherever it suits management, not labor. The immobility of labor and the mobility of capital is the supposed "genius" of the capitalist (global capitalism) production system—buy labor cheaply, sell goods dearly in the most wealthy markets with *no* tariff barriers. It sounds like GATT, NAFTA and WTO and free trade ideology. If any theory in terms of public policy sounds one-sided and is fishy-smelling, it is a deal like that for American and other industrial workers; it especially seems that way to labor and unions. Labor cannot do anything but lose, if that is the deal they must take or leave from management. From all indications of this study it is a monstrous bargain, a grotesque deal designed to create a few millionaires, a few multi-millionaires and a group of billionaires and multibillionaires. It is class warfare if I ever have seen class warfare of the rich against the poor; the union-buster against the union creator, the big guy against the little guy. It is wrong and should be stopped. What is a "temporary" worker in this world? The paradigm reeks of unfairness—let us be honest, it is so unequal a bargain that it smacks of injustice and rankles the soul of the worker. Is it any wonder that strong European unions are not taking well to the creeping destruction of their living standards and the debasing of the governments at the destructive levels of the European Union (EU) anti-labor forces they are confronting? And Japanese unions have a large strike fund to stop more kudoka. South Korean workers at

*Downsized or hollowed-out in Japanese.

times are in open revolt. Mexican workers are striking. American unions are finally waking up under AFL-CIO President John Sweeney after a two-decade slumber and a two-decade slide downward in economic status, growing poorer by the day. Unions lost membership—millions of members in the period. The first wake-up call under President Sweeney was clear in 1996.

Chapter 7, of all the chapters, rectifies on my part the typical absence of interest of many in academia in the problems of labor with large member unions. One could not ignore labor's own inattention and some corruption in various forms. But that is no excuse for the fundamental defensive position of labor and organized labor across the world and in particular in American society. American history politically elevated labor to the bargaining table. That is done forever. Capital is important, but as President Lincoln said, labor is more important to society particularly in a democratic nation. And I believe that the last few decades—1960 into this decade of the 1990s—there has been an unwarranted and unjustified attack on all of American labor (union and non-union). The attack is totally unjustified in any respect in view of American public policy and American history reinforcing labor's importance in the United States.

The perspective and understanding of this author must be stated at the beginning of the chapter. Full employment at 3% is a national goal now in quiet slumber even with unemployment at 4.3% in 1998 in the United States. Many are sympathetic toward labor and toward the needs of the working man and woman who are part of the 130 million-person American work force. Many are unsympathetic toward union-busters, downsizing, outsourcing and toward those who want a disorganized, cheaper labor pool and those who think labor standards (especially temps) can be anything wished by management or owners of business. The surest prescription for social warfare is a dictatorial business attitude that is anti-labor and anti-union. In those circumstances, often socialist and fascist solutions gain credibility. This may be where some people and their advisors are today—dreaming the dream of disorganized, cheap and foreign and ignorant labor. Read William Greider's *One World, Ready or Not* (1997) and contemplate fascism's ugly rise described by Karl Polyani in *The Great Transformation* (1944). The dreams are like the dreams of dinosaurs; hopefully they will disappear and become extinct in view of modern public policy toward labor. Meanwhile, the rest of the public and labor must grasp the central questions of this book on investment dreams:

How can mobile capital run away to any part of the globe toward cheaper workers and leave the home worker flat broke and with nothing to pay his or her taxes and his or her mortgage on a home and car? How does a worker feed his or her children? How does a worker educate his or her children or have law and order in the community? How does the worker have time to get more educated? Does it make sense to put so much job stress on labor?

Let me add one precautionary note as this chapter opens. Some doctrinaire political ideologues see free trade as a technique to "screw" the little laborer guy, in an American society whose labor is so vital to the creation of wealth in the society, and when there is such a vast division of labor. This chapter could hardly attempt to win over such strident anti-union and anti-labor "experts" who haunt the halls of Congress and of think tanks, and the business lobby groups in Washington, D.C. This chapter has nothing to do with their perspectives on labor. Being sympathetic toward labor is not a blank-check approval of anything that labor does or proposes, nor does it reflect a belief that labor's voice is the only valuable political voice. Certainly, there are other voices to be heard. This chapter should appear as a balanced perspective—respectful and sympathetic toward equal and just treatment of labor and yet critical at the same time of the need for equal reforms in labor and business. Capital without an intelligent, well-educated work force is meaningless, self-indulgent wealth that could as well lie idle in piles of gold. A democratic society presumes productive use of capital and labor to enhance the welfare of all. This is the anti–class warfare policy that energizes people in a free society. It is one policy that makes sense.

NO MORE JOBS: LEANER IS MEANER WITH 4.6 MILLION U.S. JOBS LOST

What is the global job prospect for 1999–2000? Germany, France and other European nations are at high levels of unemployment—10–12%, some in Europe are much higher.

"The world employment situation remains grim. Unemployment remains stubbornly high in many industrialized countries. . . . Outside Europe unemployment rose . . . among Latin American countries the unemployment rate rose . . . proxy indicators . . . point to a continuing problem of under employment and poverty in many low-income countries in sub-Saharan Africa and parts of Asia" (ILO, 1996: xiii).

The International Labour Organization (ILO) in Geneva, Switzerland analyzed labor issues globally but even this study purposely omitted China and Vietnam and other Asian transition economies (ILO, 1996: 136 n.1). ILO was gloomy about jobs across the globe, although the United States and a few other places are less gloomy. It was Europe and Japan that caused concern as well. The cloud of global unemployment is overhead now and it must be coupled with more insight on China, on downsizing in the U.S., German and Japanese economies, and on an oversupply of goods and services.

First, on China, consider William Greider's report of Chinese authorities that by 2007, China will have 268 million unemployed (5%) in a population of 1.2 billion people (Greider, 1997: 70). The unemployed group projected for China is equal to the size of the total estimated U.S. population in 1997. By contrast, the U.S. work force is now only 130 million people with 4.3% unemployed. Greider had justifiable reason to call this a staggering Chinese estimate. What of India, Indonesia and other nations? Together with China, no industrialized boom involving all of these nations could possibly relieve the global situation very much. Their unemployment problems alone could overwhelm the rest of the world. For General Motors to be investing in China's auto production is like spitting into the wind. What possible good could come of it? Why not help to fix the Chinese railroads, as Greider suggested? And to think of China's current trade surplus with the United States at $34 billion and rising—what if that were deemed excessive and should be halted? As William Greider so brilliantly observed what if the buyer of last resort, the United States, stopped being this cash cushion for the world's oversupply of goods? And he asked: Who would buy the goods on Earth? From China? From Japan? This "foreign aid" form may come to a screeching halt for a variety of reasons, principally due to exceptional trade deficits from Asia. Greider's view is rather penetrating: "The great multinationals are unwilling to face the moral and economic contradictions of their own behavior—producing in low-wage dictatorships and selling to high-wage democracies" (Greider, 1997: 170). PepsiCo is closing its Burma plant in recognition of this (WSJ, 1/28/97).

The central inquiry of this book into the relationship of globalizing corporations to democratic nations must confront the global reality of growing unemployment, global surplus of both goods and services and labor (at prices affordable and wages reasonable), and finally, the use of slave-like labor and wages (to many): perhaps $10 or $15 a month in Asia or $60–$80 a month in Albania. So far the U.S. government has put aside human rights and falsely separated them from trade issues. The way it is said is: relations with China will not be held a hostage to one issue called human rights. How far down this road can the United States go before its sovereign citizens (130 million of whom are labor) catch on to the blatant hypocrisy and it causes deep remorse. Neither Wei Jingsheng from China, who is now in the United States, or Ms. Kyi from Burma think this way (Jingsheng, 1997; Kyi, 1995). Will the $25-*an-hour* European and U.S. industrial wage plus benefits die and find its global level at $10 to $15 *a month* with no benefits if a worker is lucky enough to find a job? That is a most gruesome political question to ask in a democracy. The citizen voters in a democracy simply are not that crazy about unemployment or such ridiculous wages. Why should they be?

But unemployment has a fascinating quality of being able to be seen through several perspectives. The perspective of "downsizing," as it has been called in the United States for some years, is now coupled in most recent years, since 1980, with "kudoka" in Japan and other terms in Germany and other nations experiencing hollowing-out of manufacturing. What has been the total number of jobs *lost* and jobs *gained* in manufacturing across the globe? No one knows. In other words—if you cut manufacturing jobs in the United States, Germany, Great Britain, France and Japan and a few other places and then if you add new manufacturing jobs in Latin America and Asia, what is the net result globally? One study by Adrian Wood concluded that 6 to 12 million jobs were lost and 20 million jobs were gained (Greider, 1997: 72 and 477 n.9; Wood, 1994).

Figure 7-1
Ying and Yang of Global Labor Pools (Sphere: Workers of the World—World Labor Pool)

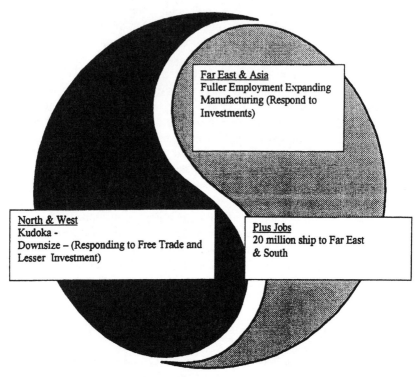

Far East & Asia
Fuller Employment Expanding
Manufacturing (Respond to
Investments)

North & West
Kudoka -
Downsize – (Responding to Free Trade and
Lesser Investment)

Plus Jobs
20 million ship to Far East
& South

This study caused controversy among economists (Laurence, 1996), but it gets at the truth from labor's perspective.

As Figure 7-1 suggests, global labor is related to itself—not necessarily in the concept of a "market," but in the concept of a labor pool as viewed by the International Labour Organization. Ripples in the pool affect everyone—it is like a lava lamp in its movements. Yes, there are local effects, but global effects are the concern here.

But, one may argue, all of the concern over downsizing of American manufacturing jobs is merely so much "anecdotal evidence" (ILO, 1996). The concerned belief is itself sound if non-anecdotal evidence were available, but it is not on a global basis. No one keeps this information—not even the International Labour Organization in Geneva, Switzerland, created early in this century, long before there was a United Nations. So the reality is that unemployment data has enormous global gaps and data is, *by design*, not kept because it is too controversial—it would both embarrass and contradict the free trade ideology and neoclassical economics groups, not to mention the governments and businesses that are responsible for lessening employment in one part of the world. No government is currently designing a new Egyptian pyramid construction program, although maybe China's river projects could qualify. Unemployment in China may just need such projects.

If globalizing corporations merely give out press releases of job losses, what is so wrong with merely totaling up the losses. It is really all the world has, in fact. It is too little data. Some would argue that we forget all the nice 800,000 "temporary" new jobs that Manpower, Inc. has now found for U.S. workers. It is true, but my guess is, few of these jobs are in manufacturing. Few jobs have benefits. The fear of anecdotal evidence not being true is strong among some social scientists, but other social scientists (ethnologists) thrive on stories that people tell of their experiences. What journalist lives on anything but anecdotes (verified if possible) for the most part of reporting, and that is accepted for what it is, a close approximation to truth. Therefore, I relish the truth of anecdotes of massive downsizing reported publicly by major corporations that usually fuzz up the public story by failing to make clear where the people work, how many are citizens of what country in the corporation's labor force and other non-trivial facts of employment. The "submarining effect" I call evasion by corporations is one to live with because everyone wants to put on a happy face even in the worst downsizing circumstances. But who is making these decisions? It should be the CEO. Invest here, disinvest there. Fire here, hire there.

The result of these observations led me to the 40-year data set in Table 2-1 of *Fortune* 500 employment in Chapter 2 of this book. Happily, these numbers do show the rise from 1954 of 7,857,483 jobs in 500 of America's largest industrial corporations to 1979—16,193,344, the peak year. This very respectable 100% plus rise was followed by a respectable decline, hollowing-out, "kudoka" or "deindustrialization," whatever term you prefer, for the plunge from 1979 of 16,193,344 top *Fortune* 500 industrial jobs to the low in 1993 with 11,546,647 jobs—the 11 million lean and mean corporate workers left in American global manufacturing in the highest-paid jobs in the largest corporations at the central core of American industrialization. Some of these jobs are in foreign nations, not the United States. Now, in 1999, we are again in the dark, because *Fortune* decided to change this remarkable figure to include a large number of other corporations in retail and wholesale service, banking and insurance that are large corporations with large staffs. The change in counting added 9.5 million more jobs to the *Fortune* list, but the data is an inconsistent number now.

In Chapter 2, I mentioned that I would explore the meaning of Table 2-1 because the inferences from the data require an explanation. First, the rise and drop of the actual employment count in the *Fortune* 500 annual reports offers merely one consistent single, non-anecdotal data set that spans a 40-year period from 1954 to 1993. Everyone is aware of other data sets from a wide variety of sources. This set is a reliable set of numbers and a good set of numbers insofar as the truth is concerned. But, the data has limits in at least two directions. First, it does not distinguish, inside the *Fortune* 500 corporations, the U.S.

jobs from the foreign jobs. Based on 1993 United Nations data, generally, I estimated a 60% U.S. and 40% foreign job allocation—going back in time, who knows how long?—maybe right to the 1954 start. However, I doubt that, because globalization is not a major business effort across many of the *Fortune* 500 until later in the 40-year period. Again, I do not know—but if Raymond Vernon at Harvard University decided on a project in 1965 to investigate corporate globalization, the phenomenon had to be easily detectable even then, in 1965. For at least 20 to 30 years there has been a growing part of the *Fortune* 500 total employment figure that is associated with workers of these American companies working outside of the United States. That is the general truth. Think of oil companies and IBM. Employees were located outside the United States in the early globalizing groups of those companies.

So, what are the implications of this estimated 60–40% local-foreign split in jobs? The most significant fact is that downsizing is much more severe than it appears from total manufacturing employment dropping by 4.6 million from 1979 to 1993. In fact, if you look at Table 2-1 you can readily see how all the assumptions are that U.S. jobs are lower in manufacturing in 1993 than they were in 1954. That, to put it bluntly, is some hollowing-out job! Some would call it "damn fine" industrial planning and industrial policy and action. Screams from the Rust Belt for the last 20 years of plant closings attest to the pain of closing plants. First, it was New England job loss to the non-union U.S. South, then it was job loss overseas and across Mexican and Canadian borders. So the truth is not established fully with anecdotes, but with hard empirical data volunteered by the companies themselves, year after year to *Fortune*. The meaning of the data is a little fuzzy, but that is by design and by practical limits as well. No one wants to reveal precisely the big picture.

What is almost never explored is the simple, straight-line upward projection of estimated growth in U.S. manufacturing jobs to an estimated 21 million by 1993 if the earlier period from 1954 to 1979 merely were repeated into the 1980–1993 period. Maybe this is wishful thinking, but it makes sense. That figure, some could well argue, is exactly where U.S. manufacturing jobs *should be* in 1993 and by 1999 it should be even higher. But for downsizing—it would be a boon to the nation. Among the most advanced work forces in the world, the U.S. work force was clearly capable of growing somewhat without foreign trade, just based on population rise from 1980 to 1999. But, in fact, the manufacturing work force has declined rapidly at its core from 1980 onward. Who, I wonder, has the capacity to turn the American industrial machine down and around on a dime? Could it be the chief executive officers and boards of directors of the *Fortune* 500 from 1980 to 1997? This is, indeed, a prime suspect group. Across most industrial lines of manufacturing work, the CEO and corporate board control the plant and equipment so labor cannot be responsible, currently, for such an outcome of downsizing. Furthermore, downsizing is not in their interest so much as it is the interest of managers and others.

What is the truth about "lean and mean" or job loss in the United States? If

Ralph Nader and associates could in 1976 quote union leaders who saw runaway factories and 900,000 jobs lost that long ago in the 1960s and 1970s—how could Table 2-1 not reveal that same persistent truth? In my musings on the question, I asked about job creation in manufacturing in Asia and Latin America: do we have another number like this that includes another 150 heavily globalizing corporations of giant size elsewhere in the world? I have not found such a long-range historical set of data, but it does not mean that such a set of data does not exist. It would be interesting to put the 20 million estimated job growth in several Asian countries in Table 2-1 to show how one or more countries lose badly—the United States and others, while many other nations win big in terms of employment gains in manufacturing. What do American workers think of this globalization data? Does it make them glad to be an American or would they rather be a Malaysian? And how many downsized American workers will be leaving for Mexico or Canada—or Malaysia or Thailand or Singapore looking for jobs at $3,000 a year? Yes, what about labor's global mobility? The implications both economic and social of these questions truly are depressing. Just as depressing is China's 268 million estimated unemployed in 2007 with 100 million Chinese people looking for work in 1997—roaming the countryside. If U.S. national unemployment is almost full at 2–3% and it was looking better than previous years in 1998 below 5%—what does it all mean on a global scale with globalizing capital deliberately moving production to the cheapest labor on earth in Asia? But this is just the beginning—think of children's and women's labor in Asia and elsewhere. These are the most competitive workers in the global labor pool.

Jobs shifted to Mexico, Asia and Latin America in manufacturing we could assume went to male adults needing work. The advertisements in Thailand and Malaysia in recruitment banners looked for women—16–17 to 27–30 and unmarried (Greider,1997: 98). The semiconductor world of manufacturing depends on such women. Minolta, Intel and Motorola know this reality and create it, even in the United States (Southwest Organizing Project, 1995). But another result of downsizing in the manufacturing centers of the world must be the stimulation it gives to creation of child labor pools across the globe. Low or no tariffs would do the same. The ILO report in 1996, *Child Labour: Targeting the Intolerable*, stated: ''The Bureau now estimates that, in the developing countries alone, there are at least 120 million children between the ages of 5 and 14 who are fully at work, and more than twice as many (or about 250 million) if those for [whom] work is a secondary activity are included'' (ILO, 1996a: 7).

The 120-million figure of children in 1996 exceeded the 1995 figure of 73 million by such a large margin because ILO was trying some different survey techniques. Most telling was this statement: ''Of those, (120 million) 61% are found in Asia, 32 percent in Africa, and 7 percent in Latin America'' (ILO, 1996b: 7). The location of concern for child labor squares with the shift in jobs out of Europe, the United States and Japan by kudoka or downsizing or hollowing-out. The concern for stopping child labor is old, from the very first

ILO convention on child labor in 1919—the year ILO was founded. Most notable to me was another ILO finding. The ILO report stated: "One of the most striking developments in the last decade and a half is the emergence of a worldwide movement against child labour" (ILO,1996b: 4).

The last decade and a half is from 1980 to 1995—the U.S. kudoka period. This concern squared in time with the 1980 beginning of more noticeable hollowing-out of the U.S. manufacturing work force inside the *Fortune* 500. Later in this chapter we will examine child labor in more depth, but nothing is so moving as the Bangkok, Thailand, May 10, 1993 fire in a toy factory where 188 died and 469 were injured. The dead were all women except for 14 men and the women were as young as 13 years old. Locked doors, lethal leaps from multistoried factories led to a horrific carnage (Greider, 1997: 337–343). Greider called this the worst industrial fire in the history of capitalism (Greider, 1997: 337).

The factory ownership was traced to an Asian businessman ($2.6 billionaire) who owned a number of firms in different nations. Appalling was the management and terribly unfair was the final settlement ($12,000 per person) with the relatives. Amorality of the marketplace like this makes one wonder why Americans and others buy any toys made in such places in Asia. You would think owners and managers of Toys "R" Us, Kmart and Wal-Mart should have their ethical positions examined. Why would anyone stimulate child labor consciously? Does capitalism have no conscience when it is in its most predatory mode (Weissman, 1997)?

MANUFACTURING DOWNSIZING: LABOR IMMOBILITY MEETS CAPITAL MOBILITY

What will happen if you allow capitalists to put capital wherever they wish on earth? This is the central investment question of this book. They will rush to cheap labor—to China and India and their vast labor pools. They will rush to young women and children in Asia. This is the sad truth about where investment capital flows freely without structure, confinement and checking in the name of full employment at 2% unemployment in the home nations of the corporations. Lack of currency controls and capital controls produces what? Downsizing happens in expensive labor markets. An expensive labor pool costs $25.00 an hour. A cheap labor pool costs $1.00 a day or less. Mother Earth has its human variations—this is surely one of them that should be faced directly and thought about to achieve harmony among nation-states. This is a "world order" of a natural variety and how is it remade? We must know more first. Can there be a *global* minimum wage?

There are two books which, if you put them together or close to one another, will make sparks fly. One book is *Mean Business: How I Save Bad Companies and Make Good Companies Great* (1996) by Albert J. Dunlap, CEO of Sunbeam in 1998 and before that Scott Paper. The second book is *Downsize This! Random*

Threats from an Unarmed American (1996) by Michael Moore. Moore and Dunlap are outstanding representatives of labor and management in contemporary America—both are convinced they are right, both are outspoken advocates for their viewpoint. Satirist and straight-guy would be another way to see these two. Moore tried to hug in a friendly way some important politicians and businessmen. They would have nothing to do with him. Moore is creator and host of "TV Nation"—some of which is censored in the United States and shown only overseas. Americans are apparently not mature enough to view it. Moore directed "Roger and Me," the largest grossing documentary film of all time. Moore has other significant credits as a modern social critic with a terrific sense of humor—satire.

Moore's *Downsize This!* is 35 irreverent sketches titled variously as "Corporate Crooks Trading Cards" to "NAFTA's Great! Let's Move Washington to Tijuana!" His thirty-sixth sketch is titled: "Everyone Fired . . . Wall Street Reacts Favorably." The sketch is this: to produce profits for shareholders, mass U.S. firings began at a company and its corporate defenders said no one should turn this issue into class warfare because that could be devisive. A brilliant idea for that company was to get rid of everybody in the company—sheer genius. One company said it had 40 openings in Tijuana, Mexico if anyone spoke Spanish. All of this Moore satire pushes downsizing to a new political level of awareness that most of the public in the working middle class understands easily. There are millions of downsized Americans who get the picture at a glance. The *New York Times* interviewed many in 1995 and 1996 (*New York Times*, 1996) to produce its report.

Albert J. Dunlap is the ultimate example of the CEO-downsizer in America today. Dunlap is a graduate of West Point and then spent a 35-year career in business in seventeen states, Europe and Australia. He worked in many corporations—his most prominently mentioned work was with Scott Paper. In *Mean Business* (1996) he explained how he made a company called Scott Paper into a world class competitor and brought immense value to the corporate shareholders. Dunlap eliminated permanently some 7,000 union jobs (people)—one in every five at Scott Paper ($60,000 buyout per person cost $450 million—a one-time hit on corporate assets (Dunlap, 1996: 172–175). The late Sir James Goldsmith, a friend of Dunlap, called him "Rambo in Pinstripes" or aka "Chainsaw Al" (Dunlap, 1996: 125). This good work is from the son of a shipyard worker from Hoboken, New Jersey. He cares about the 35% let go, but keeps thinking about the 65% who were "saved" in the company. "The harshest critics call me a bastard and say I have no heart" (Dunlap 1996: 23).

For all of the sweat, strain, tension and hard work at Scott Paper, after 20 months, "Chainsaw Al" with his purchases, options and other incentives in Scott Paper "took leave" of Scott and was $100 million richer than when he arrived; no $60,000 check for him. Organizational theorists who clinically examine behavior in organizations call this egocentric economizing. "People love comparing my $100 million against the 11,200 Scott Paper workers who were laid off on my watch'' (Dunlap, 1996: 21). Dunlap argued strenuously against this unfair comparison by pointing out that the few dollars of wealth he earned ($100 million) was a fraction of the corporate value of $6.5 billion created while he was CEO and Chairman. He considers himself modestly to be a superstar in his field of work like Michael Jordan in his line. Then in late 1996 and early 1997 Dunlap began working his special magic again at Sunbeam Corporation. At Sunbeam there is more of the same logic and action (5,100 jobs targeted for cessation). The inner logic of managerial capitalism and Alfred Chandler's ''visible hand'' is clearly seen in this example. This is world class management for the Harvard University Business School and others to study, especially after the Sunbeam board fired Dunlap in June 1998.

The underlying logic is that bloated companies will die if not ''Dunlaped.'' Then, if not Dunlaped, all workers will be downsized in a bankruptcy proceeding—maybe. What is never explained is the added fact that, if possible, downsizing is coupled with ''outsourcing''—getting production from low-wage nations for goods to be sold in high-wage nations. Dunlap confined his book to a description of outsourcing of administration and technical work done inside Scott Paper. The interests of the shareholders are most important and it is the driving force of the logic, on its surface, when downsizing and outsourcing are the strategies.

So here are the antagonists—Moore and Dunlap—in vivid disagreement on the surface. Perhaps a more refined examination would find areas of agreement, and narrower areas of disagreement. Labor's immobile reality of Moore is confronted with ''Dunlaped'' corporate capitalism for shareholders' benefit only. The managerial capitalists come away very happy ($100 million) with their part of the bargain. The worker gets a goodbye kiss and possibly $60,000—a brief economic respite. Such is the glory, forever and ever, of regulated capitalism in the United States, from labor's perspective.

SPECIAL HISTORY OF LABOR: ORGANIZED AND DISORGANIZED

From serf or peasant or slave, the history of labor's growth in power is a long, jagged one. Right now, at the end of the twentieth century, the course is jagged. Before industrialization the conditions of labor were primitive—as they remain in some nations even today. During industrialization modern nations developed public policies toward all employers and employees and particularly toward those employees who unionized or organized themselves to bargain as a group (Selznick, 1969). Unions and corporations go hand-in-hand in this history. Labor's wars against managers and corporations became notorious as in the 1892 Homestead Steel plant strike against Carnegie Steel, near Pittsburgh, Pennsylvania over 100 years ago. Managers' wars against labor are the other side of the coin of permanent mutual antagonism and mistrust. Labor mistrust and unrest and management mistrust and antagonism are two sides of the same coin.

Looking back 100 years, what is a long-term perspective that emerges? From labor's perspective management has won the battle in the last two decades, for sure. Downsizing and outsourcing are two techniques to eliminate union jobs or stop new union jobs. These policies have been vigorously pursued by the CEOs of giant companies seeking global, integrated production with the cheapest possible labor. If one adds technology to eliminate jobs to both the downsizing and outsourcing, then the witches' brew is lethal to a future for manufacturing labor growth in any country except those with incomes under $10,000 a year. The prospect for manufacturing labor in the Northern Hemisphere of the planet Earth is gloomy, cheaper and uncertain as a bargain. This is the economic, social, political and legal future foisted on labor that I see from labor's perspective. It is triumphant, predatory capitalism once again loose in the world of work. It is sad (Kuttner, 1997).

What happened in the United States in the 1975–1980 period that may have triggered or contributed to the triggering of change toward labor and society at a basic level or sea-change level? The change was like the movement of a tide in the sea, slow but inexorable rising or dropping but clearly noticeable after a period of time. There is a special history that is worth noting because the change represents a convergence of events, like rivers running into one another.

As already noted in Chapter 5, McQuaid thought 1978 was a crucial watershed date. Slowly, over years of considering his ideas and reasoning, I have come to the same recognition. What is there about 1978 that is so intriguing and relevant to labor's worries and management's unease?

The Full Employment and Balanced Growth Act of 1978 was finally passed on October 27, 1978. The legislative history of this Act (which is also called the Humphrey-Hawkins Act after then Senator and former Vice President Hubert H. Humphrey and Representative Augustus F. Hawkins) is illuminating. From 1974 through 1978 the bill grew in support and joined other legislative efforts. Support was largely labor and small business and religious and secular social justice interests. Big business, many economists and financial interests opposed it. The conflict was fundamental—to what extent should the federal government in peacetime appear to control production, set targets for employment and unemployment, allocate resources or prices on wages in the private sector? Inflation and unemployment were both simultaneous targets for control. A legislative process involving the president, Congress and the Federal Reserve Board was defined in the Act to accomplish control or to attempt to do so. The 1978 Full Employment and Balanced Growth Act seemed to be a major policy change and on the surface it gave all appearances of combatting 25 previous years of recessionary or lower economic periods of activity. The opponents of the 1978 Act must have been worried—or so it would seem. Something this fundamental in governing the nation and its economy must automatically worry big businesses. The government was trying to control the economy; how terrible a thing to some!

The year 1978 was even more remarkable because big business finally learned how to win in Washington, and this is explained in *Fortune* (March 27, 1978) by Walter Guzzardi, Jr. Top corporate leaders from big business were out in front, among them Irving Shapiro, who was CEO of DuPont and the chairman of the Business Roundtable: "We'll talk to anybody who will listen," Shapiro said.

The legislative successes included defeat of a consumer-protection agency bill and a common situs picketing bill. Most significant was the Humphrey-Hawkins bill winding its way through Congress. By March 27, 1978 it was clear to big business, according to Guzzardi's article, that it had already won its legislative battles in this Act during its development stages as a bill in Congress. The bill was characterized by big business as a bill intended to reduce unemployment but it also gave the government "extensive planning over the economy and virtually ignored inflation" (Guzzardi, 1978). And, inflation was at very high levels then. From March to October 1978 the proposers of the bill met these objections and added training programs for urban youth and blacks. Most curiously this statement appears in Guzzardi's article:

So the Humphrey-Hawkins bill is now reduced to what Richard Lesker, president of the chamber calls "a toothless alligator." But since, according to Lesker, Congress sometimes passes alligators like that and then puts the teeth back in the next year; the chamber and others still oppose the legislation (Guzzardi, 1978: 57).

In 1978, then, long before passage of the Full Employment and Balanced Growth Act in October, it was clear to big business that they had defanged the alligator law.

How do you do this defanging? Look at the strange language of conciliation to big business in the final act on unemployment, inflation and monetary controls:

The Congress hereby declares . . . to foster and promote free competitive enterprise . . . achievement of an improved trade balance through increased exports and improvement in international competitiveness . . .

. . . no provision of such Act or this Act shall be used, with respect to any portion of the private sector of the economy, to provide for Federal Government control of production, employment, allocation of resources, or wages or prices, except to the extent authorized under other Federal laws . . .

. . . to maximize and place primary emphasis upon the expansion of private employment . . .

. . . trade deficits are a major national problem requiring a strong national export policy including improved government policies relating to the promotion, facilitation, and financing of commercial and agricultural exports, government policies designed to reduce foreign barriers to exports through international negotiation and agreement . . . elimina-

tion or modification of government rules or regulation that burden or disadvantage exports . . .
. . . re-examination of anti-trust laws and policies . . . to meet foreign competition . . . and the achievement of a free and fair international trading system. (various Sections of the 1978 Act)

Walter Guzzardi closed his March 1978 review of the great growth in big business political power this way:

Pains in politics are always hard to net out. But in part because of the fresh commitment of talent and money, business certainly has made great advances from the low political estate into which it had fallen a decade ago. It is now outperforming the enemies of those years, gaining on organized labor, environmentalists, and consumerists, whose leader, Ralph Nader, has entered a declining and possibly terminal political phase. (Guzzardi, 1978: 58)

It does seem strange to read the *Fortune* 1978 article and realize that while Nader and labor, consumer and environmental groups are still around today, the actual position of all three and Nader in 1999, about 20 years later, is more marginalized than ever in a political sense. The power of political big business exerted by the CEOs in the Business Roundtable provided a key mechanism to achieve political power beyond their fondest dreams. The political outcome began to be clear in 1978 and nothing has changed much since then. We are just beyond the twenty-fifth anniversary of the creation of the Business Roundtable—a cause for their celebration, but *not* for labor's, however; and not for others, either, who are ''enemies.''

Patricia Cayo Sexton, in *The War on Labor and the Left* (1991) stated: ''During the Carter years, the Humphrey-Hawkins Full Employment Act of 1978 did pass, but it was only a hollow endorsement of the *idea* of full employment'' (Sexton, 1991: 198).

This law came from a Democratic president and a Democratic majority in both houses. An interesting policy, it is, to say the least, ''hollow.'' As downsizing began in 1979; political mobilization of business electing probusiness congressmen; electing Ronald Reagan in 1981; funding and feeding think tanks ($40 million and more); financing political campaigns; organizing workers, managers and stockholders; creating conservative coalitions; increasing the number of corporate lobbyists from 175 to 650 from 1971 to 1979; creating the Business Roundtable in 1972; endowing 40 ''free enterprise'' college chairs; increasing grants to the Public Broadcasting System from $3.3 to $22.6 million from 1973 to 1979; and financing books by conservatives—all of this breathless pace of conservative activism leads in my thinking to one conclusion (Sexton, 1991: 198–199). Big money and giant corporate CEOs were now indirectly in charge of the federal government. The federal government is the grand regulator of American business and it had been captured completely by the regulated. President Reagan fired the air traffic controllers as if to emphasize the political shift in attitude toward labor.

In the context of this special labor history is it any wonder that vigorous outsourcing and downsizing of the manufacturing American work force would become for the next 15 to 20 years *The Industrial Policy for America*, to be set not through the federal government and the Full Employment Balanced Growth Act of 1978, but instead through the business community and its wishes. Those considered as "enemies"—labor in general and organized labor in particular, and consumers and environmentalists were identified and vilified. This is not considered class warfare by big business, but how could the targets or enemies not view it as such? As Chapter 2 indicated, the loss of 4.6 million manufacturing jobs gutted and shuttered many American factories and many American unions. And the industrial policy has continued to 1999—even with new, Democratic President William Clinton elected in 1992 and 1996. The power of big business to obtain what it wants, especially against labor, is so clear—regardless of which political party is in power from Reagan to Clinton—that no one should even begin to question such awesome political power flanked with think tanks, lawyer-lobbyists, trade associations, PACs, soft money, and especially those "objective" academics bought and paid for by business. Charles Lindblom's *Politics and Markets* (1977) put business's political dominance on center stage (Vogel, 1996: 4–5; Lindblom, 1977); and David Vogel's own work reinforces the critical nature of politics in business and where it is headed.

In 1983, Vogel reviewed the power of business in America, noting that the Business Roundtable is the clearest symbol of the heightening of class consciousness among businesses focused on broad policy issues (Vogel, 1996: 281–282). Vogel offered his own analysis and special history of the period before 1983 that is not anything but vivid about the sea change in business politics in the period. The beginning of deindustrialization was so obvious that other academics wrote about it. Their works were just as straightforward—especially Bennett Harrison and the Bluestones (see Bibliography).

The dream of the Humphrey-Hawkins Full Employment law was unemployment at 3 to 4%. Section 104 of the 1978 Act refers to these goals as does the legislative history. Many economists argued against numerical goals for unemployment. For inflation at 12% in 1974 there has been significant progress to a 1998 low U.S. inflation rate of 2–4%. But for unemployment—*not* one year since 1980 has unemployment reached 3 to 4% except for 1997 and 1998. A low of 4.8 in 1997 to a high of 9.7 in 1982 is the best since Senator Hubert Humphrey left the world in 1977. Currently, Canadian unemployment is persistent at 9.5%, Australia at 8.6%, Japan at 3.5%, France at 11–12%, Germany at 6–7% and rising, Italy at 12.5%, Sweden at 9.4% and the U.K. at 8.5%. The reality of unemployment is people and numbers. Let me explain this.

Assume a person works 2,000 hours a year (8 hours a day, 5 days a week or 40 hours for 50 weeks a year of 2,000 hours). Assume various sizes of labor forces as shown in Table 7-1.

Table 7-1
Unemployment Annual Hours Lost

Size of Labor Force	Unemployment Rate	Unemployment Annual Hours Lost
100	4%	8,000 (4 x 2,000)
1,000	4%	80,000 (40 x 2,000)
10,000	4%	800,000 (400 x 2,000)
100,000	4%	8,000,000 (4,000 x 2,000)
1,000,000	4%	80,000,000 (40,000 x 2,000)

In labor forces up to 1 million, the annual loss grows rapidly in hours of work lost—you move unemployed from 4 workers to 40,000. But many labor forces are in the tens and hundreds of millions of people. In the United States the labor force is 130 million—so it would be a staggering loss of 80 million person-hours of labor for each unit of the 1 million unemployed workers times 130 units, for a million people (130 times 80 million) or 10.4 billion hours of potential productivity lost a year. No one could claim a good public policy if fellow citizens just lost *not* 4%, but 4.8 or 5.4% in unemployment rate. And unemployment at this level is staggering for millions of people—devastating to lives of families. The policy is anti-family. The reason for pursuing this point is simple—some people now argue about a "natural" rate of unemployment, perhaps at 6%—an attitude of aversion to full employment (Kuttner, 1996: 95). This is nothing less than astounding that a Federal Reserve system is so averse to full employment by fearing inflation so excessively. But it follows that a lot of people seeking work will keep wages and salaries down to some extent and enhance the hiring capitalists' hand in the employment bargain. Full employment at 3 to 4% is now abandoned in the United States and perhaps globally. Hollowing-out takes many courses. Full employment should be the goal, according to Ray Marshall, a former U.S. Secretary of Labor (Marshall, 1987). Targeted full employment at 4% made sense in 1961 and still does to James Tobin, a leading economist (Tobin, 1996: 48). Some argue that 2% is a desirable goal of unemployment.

LABOR UNDER DEINDUSTRIALIZED AND GLOBALIZED CONDITIONS

Where labor is not well organized—as it is comparatively well-organized in Europe—there will be unilateral unchallenged action by managers to deindustrialize high-wage nations and industrialize low-wage nations. That is global capitalism's industrial policy for the world. This is the essence of kudoka or hollowing-out. Comparing Europe and Japan with the United States, it appears to be infinitely easier to hollow-out the United States—a nation with pitifully little in the way of tough unions or sensible export or import policies, little in the way of tariffs to protect home-based industries and almost no concern except in the last few years over downsizing and elimination of the American manufacturing industry. American businesses fling capital around the globe with little restraint. Presidents and Congresses are almost irrelevant. In clothing, American stores are filled with clothing made in Macao, Saipan, Taiwan, Korea, Bangladesh, Guatemala and many other nations. Jets crash leaving Miami Airport loaded with blue jean fabric for workers in the Dominican Republic. I found, in a recent sampling survey I conducted, that perhaps one in ten women's garments are made in the United States. The reality is that the United States cannot even clothe itself any longer. It no longer makes large numbers of merchant ships, or manufactures steel as it used to, or—the list of products no longer made in the United States, like VCRs, is long. Labor in the United States and increasingly in Europe and Japan is working under advanced conditions of deindustrialization and the condition is global in nature. What are the essential ingredients of this industrial policy of downsizing?

Richard C. Leone, the president of the Twentieth Century Fund, called American capitalism mixed capitalism in the foreword to Robert Kuttner's *Everything for Sale* (1997). The standard policy goals to help mixed capitalism are privatization of government, deregulation of business, downsizing of the labor pool, shrinking government entitlement programs like welfare, health and social security, and lowering taxes for the rich and business in particular. In Chapter 3 of this book, Fernand Braudel said this is just capitalism doing what comes naturally. Robert Kuttner expands this list to include a policy of high unemployment, assaults on unions by business, hostile takeovers of one business by another, junk bond leveraged buyouts of businesses to get their assets, contingent employment contracts, mergers that allow new managers and owners to close down all or parts of businesses and throw people out of work and unilaterally abrogate employment contracts by going out of business or disappearing, like another form of submarining seen earlier in this book. This is called "shedding labor," getting rid of long-term contracts, outsourcing of corporate jobs to avoid employment contracts, becoming a "virtual" corporation—the equivalent of a shell with few employees. The policy is called commodification of labor—people working in factories are not citizens—they are cogs in a big business machine. Add to this set of policy prescriptions those of globalization, a "natural" higher rate of unemployment and an aversion to full employment and the picture is fairly well on the way to being rounded out. Bash the worker in every way possible without saying so. What a pitiful public policy to pursue in business—it is immorality as a foundation for managerial capitalism. The Barsotti cartoon (see Figure 7-2) captures the point exactly.

Figure 7-2
Barsotti Cartoon (*New Yorker*, April 27 and May 4, 1998)

*"There, there it is again—the invisible hand of
the marketplace giving us the finger."*

Source: Charles Barsotti © 1998 from The New Yorker Collection. All Rights Reserved.

The crusade of mixed capitalism includes allowing the stagnation of wages of labor, the creation of growing classes of billionaires and multibillionaires in the world, borderless nations, weakened nation-states and all power not to the people, but to the CEOs and the most wealthy. These conditions of mixed capitalism are supposed to bring peace to the world and global prosperity. It is an oligarchy of plutocrats running oligopolies—nothing more fancy than that.

The fly in the ointment is nation-states and popular sovereignty in democracies, as explained in Chapters 3 and 4. But another fly in the ointment is the labor unions with a different set of policy prescriptions and, finally, the truth in economics about the virtues and limits of markets lends itself to an elaborate argument based upon the economics of the limits of markets. In Chapter 3, these limits were explored except for labor markets. Now we have the good fortune to consider Robert Kuttner's latest thinking about markets. The old argument is that markets are the best way to handle any economic scheme. The new argument, historically speaking, is that governments must tame some markets, eliminate some others that are socially harmful and encourage those that the people want and ignore other markets. The old argument was explored by Robert Kuttner in 1991 in his *The End of Laissez-Faire: National Purpose and the Global Economy After the Cold War*. The new argument is explored by him in 1997—*Everything for Sale*. He explored how market logic underlies much of American business. Kuttner argues that markets are irrelevant to concerns of labor and many others such as medicine and higher education.

Kuttner distinguishes markets where there is no such logic—it just does not apply in labor, in medicine and, I would add, in education or art or music or religion or civic tradition of service to government. Obviously, it is impossible to go into Kuttner's full analysis and argument except in a narrow way where labor is relevant to this Chapter 7. The key was his statement: "A globalized economy, with a weakened state and more flexible and decentralized notion of production, is certainly more vulnerable to the commodification of labor" (Kuttner, 1997: 85).

He correctly focused not entirely on issues of economics, but on political power reflected in inequality in the distribution of the fair share of productivity gains to labor—wage flatness in the last 20 years and extreme salary growth of CEOs at the same time.

In a brilliantly reasoned chapter on the market for labor, Kuttner offered a thorough explanation of how labor has lost its status and significance in the old arguments about the importance of capital, capital owners and business (both domestic and global). The factors he takes into account are globalization of business, high unemployment, the shift from manufacturing to services, the weakening of wage regulation and norms, deregulation in various industries from airlines to hospitals, the assault on unions and the skills debate (Kuttner, 1997: 90–105). A "social" labor market could have policy prescriptions of full employment, stronger unions, wage subsidy and social income, education and training at much more massive levels. Kuttner adds that "gain-sharing" of productivity by equity distribution and responsible corporations would be essential policies. Kuttner was attracted to recent policy proposals by Senator Jeff Bingaman of New Mexico to develop legislation to achieve such policy goals. There are key articles of faith that Kuttner noted would be attacked by such proposals:

that government should deregulate and let market forces take over; that "free trade" is the highest form of free market and an unambiguous good; that federal spending should be cut; and that full employment would be inflationary and bad for financial markets. The free-market ideology has not only needlessly widened society's inequalities, but also entrenched a dominant way of thinking that precludes remedies. (Kuttner, 1997: 109)

What is a dominant way of thinking that precludes remedies? Kuttner offered numerous examples of constraints and blinders in thinking too narrowly that affect economists, labor unions, lawyers, academics and business people. Thinking too narrowly with blinders keeps a horse from being distracted in pulling a wagon. Tunnel vision does block out the "big picture." Specialization prevents people from asking questions about other specialized knowledge because they do not know how to ask questions. How can a citizen prescribe remedies to downsizing of his or her job, if a dominant way of thinking says his or her job loss is "inevitable" or "natural" and "good" for 5.5 billion people on Earth? That is a rather formidable reasoning; William Greider called it the manic logic of global capitalism (Greider, 1997).

The Iron Law of Wages sounds like the Law of Gravity or the Law of Murder but it is not. People cannot change nature very much—Mother Nature makes people change their behavior every day. If it snows or rains you wear different clothes. If it is hot, you dress down and lightly. If it is windy you lean into the breeze. The free trade ideology and the inevitable logic of corporate global capitalism are both defective, non-scientific reasonings from faulty premises. They are cloaked with a veneer of objectivity that is false. They are related to ancient authority in fictional ways; and worse yet, both pretend to be the highest state of human development in a Social Darwinist manner which is done to add a semiscientific patina of truth to the supposedly inescapable and inevitable logic. The reality is the public, labor and unions are sold a bill of goods that is false in order to serve the interests of CEO managers and enhance both their political and business power. Skip the patina, the glossy annual reports and slick TV advertisements if truth is of interest.

Let us recapitulate to this point. This chapter opened on mankind in manufacturing and downsizing—and asked, what is a worker to do? Then we focused on global unemployment growing, persistently staying high. The question of downsizing in one part of the world while upsizing in another is a serious policy question. This happens inside large nations all the time. The meaning of hollowing-out is explored in terms of growth of women's and child labor. The conflict of labor and management today is typical in the Moore–Dunlap interchange. Labor's special history in the United States revolves around 1978 and the Full Employment Act and the creation of the Business Roundtable. Changing political power has been obvious and continuous in the last 25 years. Deindustrialization in its current phase is seen through Kuttner's analyses of markets and the limits of labor markets from an economic and political perspective.

Next let us examine some of the issues of plant closings as a part of the downsizing mentality and industrial policy in the United States Then let us sort out Japanese auto transplants in the United States and Britain to see how they fit. Finally, what all this means requires us to face labor history and labor future.

Plant Closing and Mass Layoffs

Eight years after the hollowing-out of the manufacturing labor force started to show vividly in the 1980s in the *Fortune* 500, the U.S. Congress passed, on August 4, 1988, the Plant Closing Notice Law. The law said: "An employer shall not order a plant closing or mass layoff until the end of a 60-day period after the employer serves notice in writing to affected employees and to local government officials where layoffs or a closing occurs" (29 U.S.C.A., Section 2102). The reality is that industrial planners—the CEOs and staffs of corporate planners simply did not consult enough or discuss plant closing—an extremely unpleasant subject with chaotic overtones for many people. That is the fundamental reason for such a law.

One way to look at the Plant Closing Law is this: as a businessman or woman

I may take three years to plan a plant closing, but need give only two months of public notice to those who work in the plant to be closed. Two months of notice is 60 days and that is all that is needed for workers who may have just signed a 30-year home mortgage on a house for his or her family. This is evidence, once again, of the grotesque "bargain" forced on labor by corporations in the name of mobility of capital, to do what pleases them. This does not sound fair at all from a workers' perspective. It is exceedingly fair to business planners and mobile capital.

Consider the following facts about plant closings:

One study of plant closings notes that from the mid-1970s to 1984, plant closing in large manufacturing firms eliminated over 900,000 jobs each year; in the recession years of 1980–82 this rate of job losses doubled. Using a different data base, another study identifies the closing between 1977 and 1982 of over 650 manufacturing establishments that once employed 500 or more workers. A federal government study concludes that nearly 10 million workers lost their jobs between 1983 and 1988 owing to plant closings and layoffs. (Portz, 1990: vii–viii)

John Portz illustrated the politics of plant closings in the dumping of the social and human problems on local governments where closed plants exist in Louisville, Waterloo, the Mon Valley and elsewhere. A significant literature is now developed over this aspect of investment choices by CEOs, but only in terms of what to do when CEOs decide to close a plant and only in a reactive pattern. Nothing gives rise to the basic question: Who controls investment decisions of CEOs—the public or business?

In a polite and diplomatic way Dale A. Hathaway asked a key question in his book title: *Can Workers Have A Voice? The Politics of Deindustrialization in Pittsburgh* (1993). In the destruction of the Pittsburgh steel-making community in the 1980s, Hathaway examined how the politics were handled. Some surprising things were noted:

1. There was a general rule of dejected acceptance to a decline in the fortunes of the industrial middle class—nearly 30,000 jobs were lost at US Steel in Pittsburgh.

2. A small class of wealthier corporate executives was being allowed to make the plant closing or mass layoff decisions that were unchallenged even by workers.

3. In Eastern Europe Lech Walesa and Vaclav Havel were voices for the worker, yet nothing similar had arisen here in the United States.

Here, too, there is a growing literature focusing upon the lack of "voice" of labor and the need for it.

The belief is that we live in the United States in a privately planned economy—not a free-market economy. Key decisions to close plants are made within huge corporations, not in markets. On July 6, 1892, the Homestead Steel mill labor strike left sixteen dead and scores injured in the Pittsburgh area. Andrew

Carnegie's assistant, Henry Clay Frick, was shot by a labor-sympathetic anarchist on July 23, 1892. The union was busted, however, and not until decades later did a union reappear. As in the past, plant closing politics in the 1980s wanted little of the voice of workers (Hathaway, 1993: 201). The author concluded that labor will have to fight for a voice in plant closings and other matters.

There is a civil jurisprudence being created by legal scholars that may use the concept of trust to be joined with contract law to provide more responsible community controls over plant closings. A leading scholar is Marlene A. O'Connor, whose view is that fiduciary law could promote economic justice in plant closings (see O'Connor, 1995: Ch. 8 in Mitchell, 1995, especially footnote 1). A different and sympathetic legal ear to labor's plight may now be emerging. But, we are a long way from changing the dominance of CEOs making business decisions with absence of any serious governmental review or labor review. There is no German co-determination in labor policy in the United States. There could be if labor fought for it.

Auto Transplants

Robert Perrucci examined the location of Japanese auto assembly plants in six states in the midwest of the United States in the 1980s. Called ''auto transplants,'' Perrucci studied the phenomenon from a social perspective—how the foreign subsidiary corporation worked to find a place for itself in the heartland of industrial (downsizing) America. The social dynamics are a critical part of a successful transplant factory. The six plant locations involved corporate and local and state investment in the millions of dollars to attract about 50,000 jobs paying about $13–$15/hour (Perrucci, 1994: 6–7). This growth occurred while downsizing went on unabated in other American businesses. This example illustrates how peculiar foreign trade with auto transplants has become. But the United States is not the only place experiencing the auto transplant phenomenon.

Brian and Kevin McCormick, in *Japanese Companies—British Factories* (1996), show how Japanese direct investments (about 200 manufacturing plants) in the United Kingdom produced a significantly noticeable U.K. impact in television sets, microwave ovens and car assembly. A broad range of concerns, from labor relations to research and development in business, were studied. The presence of the Japanese investment is opening parallel questions of development in the United Kingdom and United States. Of the 728 Japanese transplant manufacturing plants in Europe in 1994 about a third were in the United Kingdom; France had 121, Germany 106 and fewer plants in 14 other nations. A remarkable Japanese direct investment in plants rests in this data. A global strategy is so clear, and ownership by Japanese firms matters in England (Mason and Encarnation, 1994; Tyson, 1992).

For our purposes, it is important to realize that Japanese transplants are as much a policy decision by Japanese business in the United Kingdom as they are in the United States. What better time to integrate into other economies than when they are downsizing themselves or having significant unemployment. This is a strategy of global dimension that is well thought out and executed with an eye to fitting into local and national interest in jobs. With low unemployment in Japan, both the United States and European transplants made sense as a productive use of capital by Japanese interests. However, another way to view transplant factories is that they help to create a trading presence inside a nation before tariff barriers may rise to affect imported finished products. Get into the house before the doors are closed. The Japaneses are wise with their capital.

LABOR UNDER DESERVICED (OUTSOURCED) AND GLOBALIZED CONDITIONS

The basic problem of service in all of its various forms is that it is easily shifted about the world among nations in many cases. Examples would be Irish or Jamaican data processing groups at much lower wages entering data and transmitting work via satellite to and from the United States on a minute-by-minute basis or programmers in India working on computer tasks at much lower wages than European or American counterparts and linked by satellite to other California service centers. My guess is that the shrewdest capitalists will push this wage difference in services the very hardest in years ahead. What better way to make immense profits?

In the licensed professions, there is enough professional and country control of entry to prevent legal, medical, accounting, architectural and dental services from spanning the globe without significant implications for the control of the professional. The less regulated the group, like computer programmers, the more potential for global approaches to fields such as religion, art, music, consulting, teaching, engineering and other fields. Since being a businessperson is almost totally unregulated in entry, this offers the potential for anyone to offer business services anywhere. And unskilled labor—industry services from non-literate people in the south of the globe—is the most universal in the labor market and least regulated by nations.

Service is the very largest broad category of employment in the United States—it has grown while manufacturing and agriculture and related fields have been a declining part of the labor pool. This fact alone makes service a significant activity—especially the globalizing part. And the government services are linked to regulated public utility services and other non-business groups such as non-profit charitable groups. Unionization of service workers in the United States in both public and private sectors (teachers and janitors) is among the most vigorously growing areas today (Sweeney, 1996: 24). Such unions are typically attacked by business through privatization of government workers.

Focusing upon services—what do we know in general about international trade in services in globalizing corporations? What we know suggests first, that services are a much smaller part of international trade compared with goods.

Total sales by U.S. parents (2,658 non-bank parents and 21,300 non-bank foreign affiliates) were $3.96 trillion in 1994. Of that total, the sales of goods were 69 percent and sales of services were 27 percent (*Survey of Current Business*, December 1996: 21). Of the roughly one trillion dollars in sales of services, there was, in 1994, a figure of $182.7 billion in United States cross-border export sales identified by United States Department of Commerce, Bureau of Economic Analyses (*Survey of Current Business*, November 1996: 70). What is in this services category? Travel expenses, lodging, food, recreation and entertainment, local transportation and gifts; passenger fares on vessels or airlines; freight and port services; royalties and license fees; and "other" private services—education, financial, insurance, telecommunications, business, professional, technical and other affiliated and unaffiliated services (*Survey of Current Business*, November 1996: 73–77). The relationship is $182 billion of sales of services—quite small when compared with goods in international trade, but the total is of some significance. The reason for stressing the minor nature of service sales is that it is impossible to see the growth of service sales affecting employment in the world in a significant way except as noted.

By contrast, the manufactured exports of the South to the North in billions of constant 1980 dollars is striking. From a base in 1960 of a few billion dollars to over $200 billion in 1990 is explosive growth and increasing size of activity (Wood, 1994: 12). The growth from 1990 to 1998, if roughly projected upward, could exceed $300 billion easily. This would be noticeable, and if one added growing manufacturing strength and modernization in developing nations, the question of manufacturing exports to the North is not irrelevant to the question of growing northern unemployment and lack of employment in manufacturing (a decline in proportion) for the last fifteen years. The coin has two sides to its reality.

The real question is captured by Adrian Wood: Are human capital and physical capital to be treated in the same way? Recall that above, Robert Kuttner did not think this was appropriate (Kuttner, 1996). Others have drawn similar conclusions (Mander and Goldsmith, 1996; Sweeney, 1996; Greider, 1997; Tobin, 1996; Eichengreen, 1996; Wood, 1994). Wood's stated hypothesis is:

Unemployment rates in the north rose between the 1960s and the late 1980s. The hypothesis of this book is that the rise in unemployment was caused by expansion of trade with the south (which reduced the relative demand for unskilled labour), in conjunction with the rigidity of relative wages (which meant that the shift in demand emerged partly in the form of shortages of skilled workers and surpluses of unskilled workers, rather than simply as wider skill differentials in wages). The underlying reason for relative wage rigidity is the widespread view that people's incomes should not be too unequal, which is translated into practice, especially in Europe, by unions, minimum wage laws, and social security income floors. (Wood, 1994: 321–32)

Wood characterized optimism and pessimism in the understanding of the impact of "free trade" on rising and constant high unemployment in the North. Do manufactured goods from China, Japan, Korea and Taiwan, for example, impact negatively on British or German or U.S. unemployment figures, that is, keep them high? (Wood, 1994: 3–4). The argument through much of this book is pessimistic—there is a relationship in goods, services and capital flows out of the North and flows into the North of manufactured goods from the South. But protectionist trade barriers may make sense only if both North and South could redirect their energies harmoniously, and especially if capital investment by the North was structured, confined and checked by the nations more carefully than it is now. There is virtually no concern for outward capital flow by public authority in the world, with few exceptions. Only a few lines in the 1998 Business News of The *Washington Post* mentioned General Electric's plan for $40 billion more in Asian investments.

There were 7 million workers in 1994 in the 20,000 plus non-bank foreign affiliates of U.S. parents—to use the category of the U.S. Bureau of Economic Analysis. Of these 7 million workers, there were the following: in Europe, 2.8 million; in Asia, 1.5 million; in Latin America and others in the Western Hemisphere, 1.5 million; in Canada, 886,000 (*Survey of Current Business*, December 1996: 15–16). Of these 7 million workers, 4.1 million were in manufacturing, that is, foods, chemicals, electrical equipment, industrial machinery and transport equipment. There is no question that these jobs are the ones at the center of the job-shifting conflict. Without foreign investment by globalizing U.S. corporations and others in Europe, would the jobs exist in the United States or Europe or elsewhere at all? The demand may have been met by firms in those nations and very likely will be met in the future as they grow and U.S. and northern influences wane.

There appear to be two schools of thought about the great issues opened in this section. One set of scholars is raising a serious question about unemployment and international trade—especially unregulated trade and free global capital investment. Is it true that "Universal male suffrage and the rise of trade unionism and parliamentary labor parties politicized monetary and fiscal policymaking?" (Eichengreen, 1996: 4). If so, the political issues cannot be made neutral by business judgments pretending to be private in a world of unlimited capital mobility. The global study of these issues is unresolved but new questions are being asked. David Bailey, George Harte and Roger Sugden, in *Making Transnationals Accountable* (1994), exposed lax British policies of control toward multinationals and how they should be strengthened, including labor issues and investment issues. A comparable examination of French- and German-owned multinational enterprises found more need than ever to grasp the corporate political, economic and other powers (see Sally, *States and Firms*, 1995). In Bernard M. Hoekman and Michel M. Kostecki's *The Political Economy of the World Trading System* (1995), it is clear that a WTO member is free to pursue any investment policies that are not discriminatory (Hoekman and Kostecki, 1995: 251).

Finally, in Jonathan Michie and John Grieve Smith, *Managing the Global*

Economy (1995), the editors focus on how in 1944 the mass unemployment in the world and the need for currency stability gave rise to systems of control that are now abandoned by 1999. The contributors examined this history in detail, the role of labor and capital and corporations and the nation-state from a new perspective—suggesting a reimposition of international controls (though some contributors disagreed). In *States against Markets* (1996), editors Robert Boyer and Daniel Drache and contributors examined the limits of globalization, expanding the horizon to the issues of national sovereignty but including labor policy and new politics. Adrian Wood (1994) is opening new avenues of exploration in world trade in a most creative manner—centrally concerned about labor. Those are mostly authors from the United Kingdom. In the United States, Jeremy Rifkin, in *The End of Work* (1995), asked about jobs in the information age and sharing of productivity gains. The rebirth of the American union movement may now depend upon women—the suffrage movement of 1910–1920 period may give way to a new labor movement in 1990–2010. Rifkin is critical of the politics today that ignores these issues.

Of course, William Greider focused upon labor heavily in his *One World, Ready or Not* (1997). The questions are not merely the economics of worldwide economic integration, but the political implications. He supported James Tobin's view of vigorous governmental action on many fronts to regulate capital and labor. Editors Mander and Goldsmith, in *The Case against the Global Economy and For a turn toward the Local* (1996) opened a broad critique with many contributors on the impact of globalization, the supposed panaceas of free trade, why globalization is so harmful and what can be done to relocalize production, manufacturing, trade, business and employment.

The next is a set of voices in the second school of thought or second set of scholars who want free trade, WTO and GATT, want neutrality toward corporate investors by nations, by states in the United States and cities and who see free trade as the exclusive route to Nirvana—with all of the negative implications for labor and investment—and who want a wide open world for the most part. These scholars are mostly American economists. They include Ronald G. Ehrenberg (*Labor Markets and Integrating National Economies*, 1994), who saw a need for labor to change to achieve integration. In Robert Z. Lawrence (*Single World, Divided Nations?*, 1996), the answer for labor is more integration, even though he grasps hollowing-out arguments explicitly.

Graham and Krugman, in *Foreign Direct Investment in the United States* (1995), explained foreign direct investment into the United States by firms across the globe. Why firms invest directly, the economic impact, the political affects, national security concerns and current federal policies and alternatives are set forth. Their view is essentially an open world logic and free trade as a good national policy to follow. It is a standard view. Financially, Edward M. Graham examined, and argued for, in *The Global Corporation and National Governments* (1996), an investment accord being proposed (MAI) which may be a central goal for nations since there are no global rules to govern foreign direct investment, a significant point already made in Chapter 2 of this book. This study by Graham is focused on money—not people, or labor and unemployment.

The differences in the two sets of scholars is quite interesting to an outside observer. The truth must be somewhere and it is now not entirely clear where it lies. The choice will be achieved by political concerns—not exclusively business or economic concerns, but driven with a wholesale review of the 50-year free trade policy effort of industrial firms in the North—principally in the United States, Europe and Japan. As suggested, the fly in the ointment is labor and unemployment, and the public policy question is not a "natural" 5 or 6% in unemployment, but full employment with as little as 2 or 3% or less in unemployment. Public policy debate is needed on lost hours of work by workers and how to minimize drastically any such hours lost.

THE INTERNATIONAL LABOUR ORGANIZATION (ILO): GLOBAL WORKPLACES FOR CHILDREN AND WOMEN— FAIR LABOR STANDARDS

From the perspective of some in the United States, the International Labour Organization (ILO) is moribund in a slumbering condition. Its relevance to the real concerns of labor across the globe has become marginal since 1919 when it was created. If the ILO is to promote social justice and contribute to universal and lasting peace, many ask: Where are the results? The global unemployment picture is dismal. Some argue that globalizing corporations have been successful in marginalizing the ILO. These views are real among some experts.

However, there appears to have been a reawakening of the social justice implications of child labor and women's labor in the last few years; and the ILO is a part of this reawakening movement. It is this aspect that is most hopeful because the code of international labor conventions and recommendations on freedom of association, conditions of work, social policy and security and industrial relations administration are not outdated, even though globalizing corporations have been successful in reducing worker protections that are based upon social justice. The ILO keeps social justice in the forefront in the labor field involving children and women, and this emphasis is to its credit.

The United Nations Convention on the Rights of the Child in Article 32 explicitly recognized the right of the child to be protected from economic exploitation. Exploitation included hazardous work (say with chemicals or electricity) or work that interferes with a child's education. Exploitation included work that is harmful to a child's health or physical, mental, spiritual, moral or social development. This international norm is very broad. Article 32 urged nations to take legislative, administrative, social and educational measures to achieve the goal of protecting children and especially suggested that nation-states do three things:

1. Provide a minimum age or ages to be admitted to work; and
2. Provide regulation of hours and conditions of work for children; and

3. Provide sanctions—including penalties to enforce employment ages and working conditions.

This treaty was ratified by 107 nations and signed by 35 additional nations in the two years prior to January 1992. "No other treaty, particularly in the human rights field, has been ratified by so many states in such an extraordinarily short period of time" (Alston, Parker and Seymour; 1992: viii). Even the idea of rights for children is gaining broad acceptance across the world. No doubt this accounts for vigorous new attention to children at work.

The ILO in 1996 stated that child labor is a serious problem—120 million children ages 5 to 14 are working instead of learning, playing and going to school (ILO, 1996b: 3). The details are gruesome: deformed growth, deficient growth, exposure to chemicals and biologicals, diseases like lung cancer (Asbestiosis) or endemic epilepsy (chronic exposure to pesticides), early death and abuse—sexual, verbal and physical. The emergence of concern against child labor exploitation is new in the last fifteen years. Consumers are reacting by boycotts of child-made products and are demanding corporate responsibility to international norms. "World-renowned manufacturers such as Levi Strauss, Reebok, Sears and others in the sporting goods industry are now looking into the conditions under which their products are being produced" (ILO, 1996b: 5). Action by consumer and trade groups, unions and businesses and governments is starkly different from just a few years ago. A ban on goods produced by prison and slave labor, a respect for trade union rights and a prohibition of child labor are central focal points for the European Union. The United States has pending legislative proposals to prevent importation of products made by children. While linking trade and labor standards is a subject of widely differing views, there is agreement on action to stop child labor. The ILO has a program to eliminate child labor.

The background is striking. The population of working children under age 14 in industrial establishments was the subject of the Minimum Age (Industry) Convention in 1919. Law in minimum ages and a broad legal framework exists today in conventions and treaties. Gabriele Stokov, the ILO expert in child labor, observed that for the last two decades child labor has grown. "Employers are willing to hire children not only because they are cheaper but because they are more docile" (Zachary, 1996: A-2). In *Child Labour: Targeting the Intolerable* (ILO,1996a) there is such a detailed review of the "intolerable"—those children in hazardous work sites on the seas and in the mines and factories, in forced or bonded work and in child prostitution, sex tourism and the sale and trafficking of children and child pornography—that one is left to wonder what happened to religion, morality and ethics inside the human species? The current tragedy may stir the nations and peoples to take more extreme steps, but for globalizing corporations it will take both host and home nation coordinated work. More resources for governmental regulation will be needed to achieve social protection of children.

Particularly noteworthy is the ILO child labor collection with films and pamphlets to stimulate public awareness. The same intensity appears to be emerging in women in the ranks of the working poor across the globe. The global facts and figures on women working appear in compact form in Figure 7-3 relating to 1996 from the International Labour Organization.

Women entering the labor force in greater numbers and being paid less than men are two outstanding characteristics on a global level (ILO, 1996b: 4–7). There is little question that women and children are a central concern in social justice issues as they impact on globalizing corporations and international trade. The story of the delays and obstacles in the Bangladesh garment industry's efforts to become "child-labor-free" is an illustration of the need for executive and legislative governmental leadership in importing nations to regulate the trade in the "best interests of the child." There is no doubt that without government intervention, little would be done by business in home or host nations (ILO,1996b: 1, 8–9).

SUMMARY: AS A POLITICAL SOVEREIGN, WHAT IS A WORKER TO DO?

Popular political sovereignty of citizens in democratic nations who are in the labor force is the grounding for their independent political judgment about full employment, fair wages and salaries, decent hours and conditions of work, secure medical care, pension benefits for old age and security for injury at work. These concerns and many more must be judged by workers to be fair, to offer social justice and to be in the best interests of the worker. Ultimately, on issues like plant closings, auto transplants and capital investment choices—the worker will have to express his or her desires for the world in which he or she wishes to live. Managers of capital will make their choices and so will labor and other citizens.

The World Bank, in 1995, explored the world of work in "Workers in an Integrating World": "But one fact is indisputable: capital crosses borders more easily than labor and despite the best effort of national governments to control it" (World Bank, 1995: 61). Is capital mobility a blessing or a curse? This simple question is perhaps attractive, but misleading. In this book I ask: What can be done to structure, check and confine capital mobility, because I am not willing to concede that unlimited freedom in capital mobility is an unmitigated good for global society or for workers in nations. The World Bank takes into account that industrialized countries have used the lion's share of global savings to the 1980s. But private capital has been moving in recent years in record levels to low- and middle-income nations. The figure was $175 billion in 1994 which is four times the 1989 figure of $42 billion, all on a net basis. Foreign direct investment at $67 billion, higher portfolio investment at $47 billion and bonds at $42 billion in 1993 exposed a dramatic shift. In 1996, the same rapid growth in foreign direct investment occurred (UN, 1997).

Figure 7-3
Facts and Figures on Women in the Economy

● In 1994, approximately 45% of the world's women between the ages of 15 and 64 were economically active.

● In the OECD countries, the number of women in the labour force grew by more than twice the rate for men between 1980 and 1990. Within the European Union, women accounted for 7 million out of the 8 million newly employed.

● In Central and Eastern Europe, both male and female activity rates fell in comparison to their pre-reform levels. However, only in the Czech Republic and Bulgaria did female participation rates decline more than those of men.

● In east and south-east Asia, women provide up to 80% of the workforce in export processing zones.

● In international labour migration, the ratio of females to males is 12:1 among Filipinos migrating to Asian destinations, 3:1 among Indonesians and 3:2 among Sri Lankans.

● In developed countries, women work at least two hours per week more than men and often five- 10 hours per week more. In developing countries, women spend 31-42 hours in unpaid work, while men spend between five and 15 hours in such work.

● In Latin America and the Caribbean, 71% of economically active women are concentrated in the service sector. In developed countries, the figure is about 60%. The concentration of the female labour force in the agricultural sector is

more than 80% in sub-Saharan Africa and at least 50% in Asia.

● Everywhere, women are paid less than men, and there is no indication that this will change soon. The majority of women continue to earn on average about three-fourths of the male wage outside of the agricultural sector.

● Women hold 14% of administrative and management jobs and less than 6% of senior management jobs in the world.

● In industrialized countries, much of the growth in women's labour force participation has been in part-time jobs. Women make up between 65% and 90% of all part-timers in OECD countries.

● In Africa, more than a third of women outside of the agricultural sector work in the informal sector. The figure is 72% in Zambia and 62% in the Gambia. It is 41% in the Republic of Korea, 65 % in Indonesia and over 80% in Lima, Peru.

● In about two-thirds of the countries in developed regions, unemployment rates among women are higher than among men; about 50-100% greater, in general. In Eastern and Central Europe, unemployment rates are higher for women except in Hungary, Lithuania and Slovenia.

● Women make up nearly 70% of the world's poor and more than 65% of the illiterate.

● Only 5% of multilateral banks' rural credit reaches women.

Source: The World of Work, International Labour Organization, Geneva, No. 17 (September/ October 1996).

At the heart of these investment shifts are multinational corporations. As the World Bank expressed it:

Multinational corporations have been a major vehicle for globalizing of manufacturing, in which relatively cheap labor in developing countries has been equipped with capital and modern techniques—of storage, management and telecommunications, as well as of production. Recently most of the expansion of multinational corporations has occurred in developing countries: 5 million of the 8 million jobs created by multinationals between 1985 and 1992 were in the developing world. The number of workers employed by multinationals in developing countries now stands at 12 million, but the *TRUE NUMBER who owe their livelihoods to multinationals may be twice that, given the prevalence of subcontracting.* (World Bank, 1995: 62) (emphasis added)

The World Bank is rather honest about the enhancement of mobility of capital—export processing zones make it even easier to be mobile with capital, since ties and taxes to the host country are so slight. Capital has, also, moved on to a new generation of export processing zones in newer countries with even cheaper labor such as China, Sri Lanka and Morocco. William Greider noted the same flight of mobile capital (Greider, 1997). One must ask: When does capital become dangerously mobile for other human beings? The World Bank uses terms like "hot money," "financial blowouts," "crisis" and others to describe mobile capital. The interest in labor standards is minimal, but is called "structural adjustment" with implications that labor adjusts—business does whatever it wants with capital—labor adjusts to mobile capital, not the reverse, that mobile capital would adjust to labor. In this sense, the World Bank has reversed the social justice issue and turned it on its head. This is why many call for an end to the World Bank—labor is not much on its agenda except to react to whatever the World Bank and business wants. Others reveal this same World Bank bias (Lawrence, Bressand and Ito, 1996: 82–84).

What is needed is a new way of looking at mobile capital to ask what limits must be imposed on it by nation-states. There are numerous examples of how social justice concerns of labor could easily slow down mobile capital. Getting rid of export processing zones would be a good start. Develop an international regulatory strategy for global capital flows to control the flows in ways that nation-states and labor find mutually acceptable. Such a strategy was conceived by Allyn Taylor for global tobacco control (Taylor, 1996). The same change in public policy may be needed to overcome corporations that argue "when in Rome, we must do as the Romans do." Thus, if antitrust statutes, securities regulations, civil rights acts and age discrimination or sexual harassment laws and environmental protection are not done in Rome, the American corporation located in Rome can just do as they do in Rome. Laws of the United States do not apply beyond its borders. But some argue—the laws of the home company parent should apply beyond U.S. borders, should have what is called an "extraterritorial effect" in the host nation over the subsidiary companies of the U.S.

parent (Turley, 1990). *The Global Factory* (1990) by Rachael Kamel puts an action plan together with a clear understanding of labor rights, and social justice for workers in host and home nations of corporations trying to globalize in maquiladoras.

Other strategies include the ESOP (Employee Stock Ownership Plans) where employees own the company stock and employees are owners—as in United Airlines and other large, modern multinational corporations. A balanced analysis of the pros and cons of ESOPs is offered by Joseph Blasi (Blasi, 1988). Another strategy is to come to terms with one of the biggest social upheavals of the twentieth century—the decline of the traditional company man (Sampson, 1995). Ex-company men faced what Karl Marx saw in 1848: "It (capitalism) has pitilessly torn asunder the motley feudal ties that bound man to his 'natural superiors' and has left remaining no other nexus between man and man than naked self-interest and callous cash payment" (Sampson, 1995: 308–309). Coming to terms with a nearly total lack of genuine corporate concern for labor's welfare is pure honesty and realism. A new political reality emerges in which popular sovereignty is trump for the worker joined in powerful unions and communities of workers.

Because labor rights are issues that do not go away in international trade, they must be confronted directly and dealt with openly. This is the advice from an expert like Virginia A. Leary (see Leary, 1996: 177–230 in Bhagwati and Hudec, 1996). A "social clause" in all trade agreements is just as "natural" as the "natural" rate of unemployment. Leary cites historical evidence from 1833 where a member of the British Parliament, Charles F. Hindley, proposed an international treaty on hours of work. In 1838–1839, a French economist wrote of the need to harmonize labor legislation. Both proposers saw this as a way to promote international trade where trade is wanted. Is the twentieth century, and will the twenty-first century be, so different?

Pension funding protection is critical as an aspect of labor rights (Ferguson and Blackwell, 1995). Recognition of the impact of free trade on jobs is vital (Cavanagh, Gershman, Baker and Helmke, 1992). The labor movement must rebuild itself (Tasini, 1995). Even the idea of *The Maximum Wage: A Common Sense Prescription for Revitalizing America—by Taxing the Very Rich* (1992) by Sam Pizzigati does challenge our assumptions about egalitarian ideas—a minimum wage needs a maximum wage—part of the same global logic of no more billionaires—no more people like Bill Gates or Sam Walton or George Soros, or plundering political leaders who make themselves corruptly wealthy.

Finally, the very successful experience of South Africa and the global disinvestment policies pursued to end racial apartheid as a social policy offers a permanent window of insight into the question of taming mobile capital for social justice reasons. There is a body of literature that deserves mention here because it does add deeper insight into South Africa: Ann and Eva Seidman, *South Africa and U.S. Multinational Corporations* (1977); Jonathan Leape, Bo Baskin and Stefan Underhill, *Business in the Shadow of Apartheid. U.S. Firms in South Africa* (1985); Desaix B. Myers, *U.S. Business in South Africa. The Economic, Political and Moral Issues* (1980); and Richard W. Hull, *American Enterprise in South Africa. Historical Dimensions of Engagement and Disengagement* (1990).

To close Chapter 7 on a recommendation to study the issues further, as if the chapter has taken you very little forward to advance your understanding, is what is intended. As a professor, one constantly reminds students that subjects are understood by opening windows of inquiry. That is the entire purpose of this book and Chapter 7 has opened another window to let in some light just as a genuine inquiry should do for the reader. Because it is so global in nature and so firsthand in its accounts of international corporations, trade, manufacturing and with its deliberate focus on people, William Greider's *One World, Ready or Not* (1997) offers a good way to open even more windows.

Greider is a realistic observer of humanity in an objective sense. He does not bring the narrow biases of some economists to the table. He writes for the general public from firsthand observation and discussion, which lends authenticity to his account. And, fortunately, he adds real flesh-and-blood people to the story which is also one of human motivation in all of its own complexity. Finally, he explicitly lets you know his political biases and long-term beliefs. This means his work is offered with grains of salt.

When Greider wrote that law is degraded by global capitalism I thought of Chapters 8 and 9 of this book. When he argued for re-regulating financial capitalism as a first priority I thought of the central question of this inquiry— controls needed over capital flows. In contrast to Greider, this book does focus on governments and the usual and unusual policy debates (Greider, 1997: 17). The Dark Satanic mills mentioned by Greider evoked an image of the mills where I lived and worked some years ago. One of Greider's sources, Albert Wojnilomer, a retired economist, said: ''I don't think the good Lord could stop this trend, short of nuking Southeast Asia'' (Greider, 1997: 42). The trend Wojnilomer refers to is the rush of northern manufacturing to cheaper southern labor from North to South. One would hope mankind could do better than war, especially the insanity of nuclear war, to slow or stop such a trend. The Asian slowdown in 1997–1999 is evidence that seeds of internal self-destruction may lie in the global rush to cheap labor in Asia. These developments bear careful monitoring by citizens everywhere on earth who have democratic power. Indian and Pakistanian nuclear explosions in 1998 make Wojnilomer's comment eerily haunting.

Part III

Law, Order and Globalizing Corporations: Risks of Foreign Investment

Law, Order and Globalizing Corporations: The Civil Side of Global-Local Jurisprudence— Regulation of Civil Harms and Legal Responsibility

Chapter 8 examines the stark global complexity of the legal web of relationships created by globalizing corporations. Changes underway in understanding the liability of globalizing corporations as a single enterprise spread across numerous democratic nations are examined. The largest globalizing giant corporations have an astounding web of thousands of subsidiary corporations across the globe where they own 51% or more of the subsidiary. Chartering of globalizing corporations is now receiving a new wave of attention from many sources. History of chartering and its current development are explored in light of local interest. Finally, liability for harm is one issue, but issues of regulation, employment, taxation and related financial issues lend themselves to study here. The world class tragedy of the Bhopal, India poisoning by Union Carbide and hot laundered money are examples explored, along with transfer pricing practices of global corporations.

Most peculiar, *even weird*, is the posture of law toward the globalizing corporation. Many scholars and practitioners miss this point completely. Most law is territorial-based and this is natural enough since nation-states creating the law are turf-bound inside a part of the globe. In contrast, international law is so "consent-dominated," that is, nations must agree to it to be bound by law, and even then enforcement institutions are usually very weak. The resulting situation is that there is very little powerful law and order created in international law to govern multinational corporations outside their home countries, compared with domestic national law inside a nation. Furthermore, as we will see, the corporation, in the field of international law, is merely an NGO—a non-governmental entity. As tax havens protect some interests internationally, so do "law havens" protect others who seek international legal anonymity, asset protection, secrecy and an "alegal" environment with nearly zero demands of accountability. I think the Cayman Islands may qualify as such a tax and legal haven.

To illustrate: it took over 25 nations acting in concert to shut down BCCI— the corrupt money-laundering Pakastani bank—on July 5, 1991 (Bhala, 1994: 9). By July 29, 1991 offices of the bank were closed in 44 nations. No single international authority could do that. Concerted joint national action is paramount in controlling corporations, especially the corrupt ones.

The peculiarity or weirdness of corporations in international law is expressed in a number of ways and has been noted for decades—it is nothing new. What is most significant at the end of the twentieth century is the *persistent* nature of the peculiarity. In 1993, one way to express the peculiarity was this:

The growing power of the TNCs (transnational corporations) also poses a challenge to the notion that the primary focus of international law should be relations between states. Such a narrow view of international law allows TNCs to evade accountability for their actions at the domestic level by shifting production between different sites. *The absence of clear international standards means that they can also avoid regulation at the international level.* (emphasis added) (Grossman and Bradlow, 1993: 9)

Both Grossman and Bradlow are legal scholars with international expertise. Another way to understand peculiarity is to see it through the experience of Seymour J. Rubin, the U.S. delegate to the U.N. Commission on Transnational Corporations for the period 1975–1986. In 1995, Rubin expressed it this way: "Transnational corporations and the issues surrounding their treatment and conduct continue as a worthy theme of serious international discussion" (Rubin, 1995: 1276).

Rubin believed that privatization of governmental activities does not create better business and higher ethical standards, that more regional economic integration (such as the European Union) may result in less government control and that honesty in transborder securities markets, and honesty in transnational insolvency or bankruptcy must be found in national policies that are harmonized, or if not harmonized, subject to international agreements. Issues of sovereignty, nationalization, standards of compensation, regulation of business conduct, environmental concerns and investment regulations remain on the agendas of international organs for consultation and norm formulation (Rubin, 1995: 1277– 78). But as Rubin noted: "The relationship between corporations and governments has often been uneasy" (Rubin, 1995: 1278). We have already noted "uneasiness" in Chapter 4 and in other contexts. There is no resolution of 20 years of uneasiness even if, "Almost all nations agree on the desirability, if not the necessity, of some form of international regulation of TNCs" (Rubin, 1995: 1282). As a result, a business law UN code for TNCs was proposed in 1984 after nine years of major study and deliberation and shouting matches, according to Rubin. By 1993, the UN Center on Transnational Corporations (UNCTC) was absorbed into a larger UN body. The draft code remains still a proposed code. One wonders who won what? This is indeed peculiar—the intentional inability to give a common voice to the international voice of nations. Someone must be saying no. Who could this be?

Another expression of peculiarity was found in 1970 by Louis Turner who titled his book: *Invisible Empires: Multinational Companies and the Modern World*. Turner believed that one should know more about invisible power in multinational corporations, whom he said were in a poker game with governments (Turner, 1970: 135–157). As late as 1994, the invisibility of the transnational corporation (TNC) was stressed again by Fleur Johns: "The transnational corporation (TNC) does not have a concrete presence in international law" (Johns, 1994: 893). Johns referred to the multinational corporations as an apparition sifted through the grid of state sovereignty into a variety of secondary rights and contingent liabilities. This corporate status is exceptionally anomalous for the TNC—reputed to be the most powerful agent of internationalization of human societies that the world has ever known. How come? Is this TNC invisibility not peculiar? Or, is it designed obscurity? Perhaps it is like a submarine or stealth fighter in its design? We should know more about this strategy.

In 1970, Detlev F. Vagts confronted the peculiarity being addressed here by stating: "As the literature about the MNE (multinational enterprise) grows exponentially, the question arises whether the legal profession should not be developing responses to it. As yet it has not; statutory or case law reaction is virtually non-existent and the secondary coverage is thin" (Vagts, 1970: 739).

Fortunately, the constitutional statutory and case law corpus is somewhat less thin in 1999—some two and a half decades later—but the peculiar nature of the TNC has not disappeared in the slightest (Steiner, Vagts and Koh, 1994). Later we shall get into the growth of this law. Vagts believed the MNE, as he called the TNCs, was a largely post-1955 creation. Except for United Fruit Company, MNE operations were characteristically large-scale overseas investments under an integrated management organization. Charles Kindelberger offered a simple but clear classification of such firms: (1) national firms with foreign operations, (2) multinational firms that take the local color wherever they go, and (3) international corporations that are aloof from identification with any nation or nations. Some call these third-category TNCs "anational" (Munkirs, 1985: 188–216). National firms tend to use their own nationals in foreign operations, while multinational firms use local citizens in foreign operations and international firms look anywhere for competence (Kindelberger, 1984: 234). These different corporate creatures respond to law in different ways. "Home country" has a different connotation for each, although the legal norm remains the same—the parent corporation nation is usually home. Across half a century of thought and action the peculiarity just outlined remains in law and especially in international law toward the TNC.

Looking back over the previous chapters in this book, there is virtually nothing to warn us about the peculiar nature of law and multinational corporations.

There were hints in the economic work of Korten in Chapter 4, but no real advance warning. Business analysts did not prepare us for anything like the very different way law operates or does not operate upon the international corporations; and no one spoke of the grave shortcomings of international law. For these reasons it is necessary to examine the multiple perspectives of law and multinational corporations in much more depth.

It is increasingly clear to me that many economists and business people, some of whom were mentioned previously, may never have examined the peculiar way the multinational corporation is treated by the law. This is not true of some international law experts who have developed a rather clear and traditional view of the multinational corporations. Nor is it true of some business school scholars, legal scholars and others, as we will see. There is a global jurisprudence evolving slowly into which globalizing corporations may fit most appropriately. The next task is to explain these multiple perspectives.

MULTIPLE LEGAL VIEWS OF THE GLOBALIZING CORPORATIONS

Let us begin by looking at the traditional subjects analyzed by lawyers and law and other teachers in business schools. These would include perspectives of Spiro, Folsom, Weidenbaum and others. In contrast, we will next compare the views of international relations and international law experts—Bull, Johns, Chayes, Falk and Cleveland. Then we will examine the historical legal literature and contemporary legal literature for another set of perspectives on the law and multinational corporations. Finally, we will finish with the views of Phillip Blumberg, whose ideas of the multinational corporation parallel European perspectives to some extent. Finally, a summary of these perspectives will be in order.

Traditional Views

The Legal Environment of Business (1993) by George W. Spiro broadly surveyed the nature of law and the legal system, organizing business, regulating it, business crimes, employment law and legal environment of the marketplace in antitrust and other areas of law. The topics for international business of trading relationships (import-export, licensing and dumping), corporations, host country regulations, foreign corrupt practices, international contract agreements and forums and trade restrictions (import and export controls) were analyzed as a part of 850 pages of text for undergraduate business school students (Spiro, 1993). By contrast, in just two pages, *The Essence of International Business* (1993) by James Taggart and Michael McDermott covered the legal environment for five bulleted topics: industrial intellectual property rights, trade obstacles, product liability, monopoly and restrictive trade practices and home country legislation (Taggart and McDermott, 1993). That is quite a contrast in brevity.

Murray L. Weidenbaum, a professor of business and former U.S. presidential economic advisor, in the fifth edition of *Business and Government in the Global Marketplace* (1995), offered a broad examination of government regulation of business, the global marketplace, government promotion of business, the business response and the future of the corporations. Few other basic texts are so realistic in assessing the relationship of government and business showing the complete interweaving of business and government in every aspect of each other's operations. Symbiosis is the way Weidenbaum sees the reality—thus a law proposal is designed, drafted and promoted into a public statute in concert by both sides. The business–government relationship is almost a complete marriage of interests, supposedly in the public interest. In Washington, D.C., the marriage is complete today. "Government still has a vital part to play, but it is as a supporting player and facilitator" (Weidenbaum, 1995: 249). This political viewpoint is from one of the creators of government deregulation.

Finally, Ralph Folsom and Michael Gordon, in *International Business Transactions* (1995), offer the legal profession a "hornbook" approach, supposedly to summarize the law in 967 pages. This non-brief summary has 31 major topics, one of which focuses upon the question of branches and wholly owned subsidiary corporations. The work is generally silent on the corporation in international business in the same way economists and business people analyze it. There is little guidance beyond selling goods or services or capital investment—the core of international business transactions. The omission is most telling—it is a gaping void in coverage.

The traditional view hardly or barely examined the multinational corporation. However, exceptionally probing is an article by Yao-Su Hu, a professor of international business who stated: "there is no international law under which a transnational or supranational company can be formed and have legal existence in several nation-states" (Hu, 1992: 115).

More vividly than anyone I have read, Professor Hu stated: "In legal terminology, there is no such thing as a multinational or global company" (Hu, 1992: 115). Why no one had stated this quite so clearly before is surprising. That may be why for 30 years so much confusion has developed about borderless worlds, and stateless cosmocorp corporations. Professor Hu would agree only to this— there are national firms with international operations—that is it! Everything would flow from this premise of home country control. In the Chrysler–Daimler-Benz merger the most difficult issue, according to Robert Eaton, CEO of Chrysler, was where to incorporate the new corporation—Germany was chosen over the United States or other nations. Why? (See interview: *Fortune*, June 8, 1998: 146).

The traditional views just examined are not fully conversant or consistent with other perspectives on corporations, which will be examined next. The disciplines do not communicate with one another sufficiently.

International Law Perspectives

One of the more brilliant books on international relations by Hedley Bull, *The Anarchical Society*, written in 1977, was a study of the idea of order in world politics. He asked such basic questions as: Does order exist in world politics? Is there a world society developing? What alternative paths are there to world order? While we cannot hope here to summarize his main points, we should note his basic belief that nation-states are not in decline and are not obsolete. Bull characterized several developments as a ''new mediaevalism,'' namely—regional integration of states on various topics (NAFTA), disintegration of some nation-states (Yugoslavia), restoring private international violence (airline terrorists), development of transnational organizations called corporations (Shell Oil), and finally technological unification of the world (global satellites). The insights of Bull into the transnational organization in world society are very significant because they may help to explain why the TNC is so peculiar in the law, especially in international law. Operating across international borders, sometimes global in nature, these organizations try to disregard the national borders. Who are these organizations? Bull included General Motors, Unilever, the Communist Party, Tricontinental Solidarity Organisation, NGOs of all types—Greenpeace, scientific and professional bodies, religious bodies like the Catholic Church and intergovernmental agencies—the UN, World Bank, the IMF, or the U.S. Air Force or NATO (Bull, 1995: 260). Thus, among the groups of organizations that he mentioned, Bull focused mostly upon the multinational corporation because of the widespread promotion then of the idea that the TNC was clearly overtaking the nation-state—ignoring its boundaries.

What did Bull take into account in concluding that transnational corporations could not possibly displace nation-states in the world society? First, he readily acknowledged the power and size of the multinational corporation to 1977, but he argued that none of them came close to the English East India Company with its own armed forces and the territory it controlled. While some like George Ball argued for the constructive force of the TNC, J. J. Servan-Schrieber from France argued that it was merely American imperialism or imperialism of advanced nations. To the date of Bull's book in 1977, many nations had constrained corporations somewhat, particularly Australia, Canada and Western Europe; Japan notoriously prevented foreign corporate market penetration into Japan. Politics of nations did not give way to technology or ethnicity in all cases.

Next, Bull stressed that the agreements that nations press upon multinational corporations to condition entry into the nation are viable expressions of sovereignty, not an impairment of sovereignty. Nations do not allow corporate entry due to weakness in the face of technology. Finally, Bull argued that the command of the armed force in the world, that being objects of intense human loyalty and that being the centers of conflict or cooperation in the political structure of the world, meant that nation-states remained very powerful in the face of corporate wishes for power. Bull stated: "The multinational corporation does not even remotely provide a challenge to the state in the exercise of these functions. Its scope of operations and even its (TNC) survival is in this sense conditional upon the decisions taken by states" (Bull, 1995: 263).

Bull's work is a major downgrading for the borderless-world advocates whose work has already been mentioned—Ohmae, Kanter and others. The legal control over entry into territory is a key feature as well as all of the rest of the significant factors mentioned by Bull that put TNC operations into a proper perspective, subservient to control by nation-states. It is Bull's perspective as an international relations expert that gives exactly the right type of insight into the actual international law framework already mentioned—the peculiar invisible and subordinate nature of the TNC in international law. Let us next explore this more carefully.

Under existing international law, a transnational corporation is a "juristic personality" as a "national" of a nation-state (Johns, 1994: 894). This is the same legal status as a human being. Diplomatic protection for "nationals" may be exercised by a nation-state for its "nationals." The nation-state and territory (e.g., Delaware) under traditional rules attribute and recognize both corporate rights and liabilities if they are the place of incorporation and have a registered corporate office. Furthermore, TNCs are objects of international law with a derivative legal personality—they do not create international law or possess international legal rights and duties as nations do. A code for TNCs would be enforced by nation-states. The UN addresses itself to nations whenever a TNC's troublesome actions disturb it. Nations ganged up to kill the corporation BCCI. Johns stated: "Thus, the effect of these international regulatory efforts is to affirm rather than challenge the assumption that it is a state's prerogative to deal with TNCs through its national legal systems" (Johns, 1994: 899).

Financial experts agree on strong home country control (Kapstein, 1994). Customary law may recognize a transnational corporation, but states are unwilling, also, to elevate corporations to the status of a nation. TNCs may be a party to a contract recognized by international law and possibly become a subject. Finally, TNCs may consult with other nations in the making of international law or with the ILO where they have membership, but this does not invoke legal capacity to act like a nation.

Thus, TNCs are legally not more significant than a single human being or a non-governmental organization like Greenpeace. TNCs are just nationals like other nationals in international law.

Johns made clear that TNCs can break norms of international law—have the legal capacity to do it—without becoming legally liable. Actions catalogued include intervening in political affairs of nations, making political contributions to public officials, bribing and other monetary benefits, dominating media with advertising and interfering in many other ways (Johns, 1994: 906). Also, TNCs interfering with the people's right of self-determination, especially by mining and oil companies, was common practice. Finally, violations of international human rights law by TNCs arises frequently: "a political power without responsibility, a state within and above the state" (Johns, 1994: 910).

The TNCs are anomalous because if they were equal to nation-states, this status would move international law from the category of law to politics and economics. This recognition of TNCs as nations would recreate the plague of the pre-Renaissance Europe period, with too many non-state participants in the international legal system. Thus, the most exclusive club on earth remains the nation-state, but consistently knocking on the door for more and greater recognition is the TNC. So far the door is closed under international law, thus the peculiarity continues today.

We are left with the UN charter, which in Article 2(7) provides: "Nothing in the present charter shall authorize the United Nations to intervene in matters essentially within the domestic jurisdiction of any state." The TNC is inside the nation-state acting as a national by conducting private affairs where international law does not interfere or intrude. The way Johns saw this is as follows: "The effect of this is to grant those men performing ostensibly "public" roles of great influence worldwide, an *international anonymity* that allows for their continued exercise of power without international accountability (Johns, 1994: 918) (emphasis added).

Later in this chapter we will see how the CEO of Union Carbide fits the "international anonymity" status in the Bhopal case. This is another way to understand the truly peculiar nature of multinational corporations under international law, which has been examined from an international perspective and also, may be a non-perspective. One could call it the *laissez-faire* view or the "leave-TNCs-alone" point of view into which TNCs have artfully crafted their existence in the "ether" between nation-states. They are "offshore"—somewhere out there, wherever that is. Peculiar indeed!

Harlan Cleveland, a very well-known international relations expert, expressed some of the "leave-TNCs-alone" attitude. This is worth examining for its merits because of his stature in the international arena. Cleveland devotes an entire chapter to explaining the world economy he foresees—"managing with nobody in charge." First, he observed that transnational companies have adapted to the evolving world economy quite well (Cleveland, 1993: 34). In contrast, nations have not adapted well because power leaks from them in three ways:

1. From the bottom to the people and NGOs;
2. From the sides to TNCs and a third of their trade is "intrafirm";
3. From the top—to international treaties, agreements, agencies.

But, Cleveland identifies a dozen areas where the birth of a new world order for nations is very successful, even with such leakages of power.

A list of the success stories by cooperating nations seen by Cleveland includes: weather forecasting, eradication of infectious diseases, international civil
aviation, allocation of the frequency spectrum, globalization of information
flows, agricultural research for development, UN peacekeeping and peacemak-
ing, cooperation in outer space, the law of the sea, the High Commissioner for
Refugees, the Ozone Treaty and the Antarctic Treaty. Here the people of the
world work together well in a world society and this list is not exhaustive. Ten
common threads, according to Cleveland, produce better cooperation and each
of them has some bearing on the TNCs in a variety of ways. "Pooling of
sovereignty" is found in the closure of the BCCI bank; this is one example.
"Flexible, uncentralized systems work best" is another idea that Cleveland believes works in the marketplace—with complicated tasks and diverse players—
in commodities, financial instruments and money. This could lead to casino
capitalism as well as joint national action to close a corrupt bank. Cleveland
stressed the need for a loose world economy with nobody in charge coupled
with a "global public sector"—collective standard-setting by international public authorities to produce globally acceptable norms alongside of market norms
and standards. The place of the TNC in all of this is not clear, but Cleveland
does recognize the law and order aspects required to conduct trade in goods,
services and investments. If TNCs were demanding a UN code of behavior they
could get one almost overnight. It has been drafted and awaits adoption. The
reality is different: no one wants a code—no one wants standards and norms,
otherwise we would have them—is perhaps closer to the truth. For the present,
no one in charge is good public policy, according to Cleveland.

Something like the regime offered by Harlan Cleveland appeared in Ethan B.
Kapstein's *Governing the Global Economy*, which in 1994 provided exceptionally clear advice on a contrasting conception of financial globalization. "I argue
that nations-states have created a regulatory structure for international economic
activity and that they remain the single most important players" (Kapstein,
1994: v.). The political structures of nations give underpinning, a safety net to
the economic activity, and without them who knows what would result in a
casino called a bank. International banking is based not on laissez-faire capitalism but managed liberalism (Kapstein, 1994: 182). This shows up in national
regulation of pollution from oil tankers to nation-state control and international
communications. The result in banking is as well a policy of home country
control responsive to international norms and interdependence and national responsibility to assure trustworthy banking. Kapstein wisely stated: "The evidence provided in this book suggests that our way of conceptualizing economic
globalization is in need of fundamental reexamination. The world economy does
not operate somewhere offshore, but instead functions within the political framework provided by nation-states" (Kapstein, 1994: 184). The very solid foundation for law and order across the globe emanating from strong, networked and
informed nations means a set of economic norms or standards that all understand. The TNC loses its mysterious globalizing "offshore" glamour of being

a cowboy capitalist out on some global frontier where there is neither law nor order in business, just pure greed as a norm and deception and fraud as a standard (Korten, 1995). It may well be that Kapstein offers further reason to think of globalizing in a sounder manner, fitting the reality of nations interacting with each other to monitor and control TNCs across the globe. We may actually be getting somewhere more solid at the end of the twentieth century by carefully crafting a better legal conception of globalization and its relationship to corporations and nations.

Richard Falk, a prominent international law scholar, in *On Humane Governance* (1995), observed: "The breadth and depth of the banking scandal [BCCI] disclosed the extent to which transnational banking operations take place in a regulatory vacuum" (Falk, 1995: 180).

So far the evocative words are "global," "offshore," "ether" and "vacuum" to describe doing business internationally. Falk believes that the BCCI case shows just how lax national and world finance regulation was—companies escaped state control, eluded democratic responsibility to depositors and governments and produced great human costs and turmoil in many nations. Environmental and human rights concerns were center stage while finance was backstage causing trouble. This state of affairs will not produce humane governance in the long run. Falk did not focus on the peculiar nature of the corporation, but instead asked how one can get economic and social rights taken seriously (Falk, 1995: 181–189). This may be a good direction but it is not so clear as Kapstein's direction. It does offer a broader framework of human rights, although somewhat divorced from the mundane concerns of this book inquiring into the relations of globalizing corporations in democratic nations. It may be that Falk's international law perspective keeps the corporation at the NGO periphery of consciousness, the corporation is a mere "national."

There are other relevant international perspectives found in the book *The New Sovereignty* (1995) by Chayes and Chayes, and two books by Bailey, Harte and Sugden: *Making Transnationals Accountable* (1994) and *Transnationals and Governments* (1994). These works finally get to the point that Cleveland, Kapstein and Falk all seem to suggest—toward a more consciously, carefully crafted set of standards and norms in a regulated worldwide capitalism that is emerging as a vision of a world law and order—all of which structures, checks and confines the business discretion of the transnational corporations all over the globe. Let us next examine these two approaches.

In *The New Sovereignty* Abraham Chayes and Antonia Handler Chayes focused on ensuring reasonably reliable performance of treaty obligations—sanctions for failure to comply with state treaty obligations. Treaties with "teeth" is another way to view the focus, but they believed that is not appropriate. Instead, they offered a model of treaty compliance that injects constant dialogue into treaties and creates pressure to resolve non-compliance. By contrast, coercive sanctions—trade embargoes—are less than effective sanctions. Beneath the motivation for nations to comply is a clear recognition of sovereignty—a participation in regulating the international system—of being without isolation (in a North Korean or Albanian sense) and of being connected to a world society. Being in good international standing through justification, discourse and persuasion is the goal of Chayes and Chayes. They stated: "An essential component will be robust, active well-endowed institutions to manage the intricate network of political and social interactions required for implementing complex regulatory treaties" (Chayes and Chayes, 1995: 284). In many fields—the chemical weapons convention in particular—the staff of several hundred and an annual budget of $100 million would evidence the serious nature of the undertaking (Chayes and Chayes, 1995: 285). GATT and WTO follow this same logic of continual dialogue (Chayes and Chayes, 1995: 214, 218–221). Active management with transparency, norms, reporting, data collection, verification and monitoring and reporting all would contribute to a more robust legal norm enforcement regime that would certainly be a promising new world order without teeth but with constant dialogue and pressure. This makes sense for the TNCs of the world in their actions—a more vigorous international regime of oversight in many regulatory fields. We have yet to achieve this state.

In 1994, David Bailey, George Harte and Roger Sugden, from Britain, examined very carefully the recent policies toward transnational corporations over the last 30 years in Japan, France, Germany, the United States and Britain. As part of a larger project to study how to monitor transnational corporations in Britain, the authors tried to classify the national approaches in *Transnationals and Governments*.

This work is germane to the present book on globalizing corporations in democratic nations, but of a much more refined and manageable scope. What did they learn?

At one end of the spectrum, Japan and France have been relatively more worried about transnational alleged disadvantages and hence relatively more willing to attempt to influence their activities. At the other extreme, Britain has been very relaxed. In between have come Germany and the US, the latter being very similar to Britain in its actual policies. (Bailey et al., 1994: 2)

The authors found: Japanese policy is to pursue its own interests and not give transnational corporations a free rein in investment, although some barriers have been reduced in the last 30 years, but concern in Japan remains high. France has kept national interest in the forefront of variable regulation and investment by TNCs. Germany is also keenly aware of investment and protects key sectors by a series of techniques—supervisory boards, workers councils, limited voting rights, banking sector involvement, governmental ownership, a cartel office— all designed to watch over German interests. The United States operates an open-door policy toward incoming capital investment flows, except in national security areas. U.S. structures are the Committee on Foreign Investment in the United States and legislation called Exxon-Florio. The U.S. concerns are not consistent but instead cyclical. Finally, Britain has an open door to investment, but is both incoherent and fragmented in approach to TNCs over the period studied.

In Chapter 5 of *Transnationals and Governments*, the authors examined U.S. policy from 1960 to 1993 with a clarity only foreigners could achieve, to expose the relations over incoming capital investment to the U.S. through transnational corporations (see also Graham and Krugman, 1995). A waxing and waning of United States public concern while foreign capital investment into the United States rose to very high levels over the period 1973–1993 is most obvious— but there was very little real regulation, and very little legislation and very little national control. Over the period 1960–1993, the labor unions, the Senate, the State Department, the International Chamber of Commerce, the U.S. Department of Commerce, the Treasury, the president and many others weighed into the issues—balance of payments, acquisitions, technology transfer, real estate and national resources being purchased by foreign interests.

In Chapter 6 of this book an analysis of the incoming foreign direct capital investment was made and in this chapter it is so clear—there is virtually no control, and compared with other nations—*no* control of any significance (except security) over foreign investment into the United States. The policy is one of mostly private capital interests determining for themselves who owns what worldwide among the large and small companies. Germany, France and Japan (much smaller) are not so foolhardy as the United States, according to Bailey et al. Their analysis is carried over into a second volume: *Making Transnationals Accountable* (1994). This volume provides an overview of British efforts, such as they are, a most fascinating examination of Glaxo, the second largest pharmaceutical company in the world, located in Britain as a home country although a third of its sales are in the United States. The authors' solution for all transnationals is to promote supranational cooperation in monitoring—for Britain in itself and in the European Community, action is appropriate on a regional level in addition to national monitoring. Perhaps the reality these authors found deserves repetition:

As regards Britain's policy toward British transnationals, there has been relatively little discussion in the literature. Our assessment is that these corporations have essentially been given free rein to do as they wish (although their activities have been influenced in the ways applicable to firms in general). Governments have seen this as beneficial for Britain, a view which is not undisputed. For example, the activities of British transnationals are arguably associated with deindustrialization, and with divide and rule tactics against employees. Moreover, the free rein has not been based on good information; governments have been ignorant about transnationals' effects. (Bailey et al., 1994: 217)

What a tribute to the governments of Britain—operating in ignorance. Is it any wonder that both the United States and British assets are swiftly becoming owned by corporations of other nations. Recall how greatly the U.S. TNCs invested in Britain. It ought to be called mutually assured self-destruction; that sounds vaguely familiar. Recall how impossible it is to invest in Japan. There is nothing about visible or invisible hands in all of this and it turns out that economics is but a small a part of the politics of it all. Let us next move to another perspective on corporations.

The legal perspective of international law toward the transnational corporation is expanding across a wide front of legal topics. A sampling of law review articles from the earlier era of 1945 to 1970 reveals a fascinating and profound examination of TNCs. The period of 1970 to 1995 illustrates the expansion of topics and the persistent nature of legal issues about TNCs. There has been no resolution of the invisible nature of TNCs to date (Johns, 1994). Their absence from legal discourse is less than in the past, but there is no resolution in that discourse. Even Johns' solution of recognizing TNCs in international law more fully is no real answer in the long run. Maybe Rubin's efforts to develop a UN legal code will come to fruition (Rubin, 1995). There are plenty of misgivings about being propelled backwards toward a more cluttered and medieval people-centered and religious-centered transnational legal order (Grossman and Bradlow, 1993; Bull, 1995).

From the 1945–1970 period of articles, let us reflect first on the work of Sigmund Timberg, Wolfgang Friedman, Arthur S. Miller and Detlev Vagts. In May 1945, Sigmund Timberg analyzed a proposal for an international trade tribunal—perhaps a precursor idea to the World Trade Organization today (Timberg, 1945). In 1946, Timberg deeply probed the idea of corporate fictions and their broad implications (Timberg, 1946). Legal fictions both true and false were examined in great depth. In 1947, Timberg wrote about international combines and national sovereigns (Timberg, 1947). The combine defined by Timberg was a business with operation in two or more countries, unified top direction, legally distant units (subsidiaries), but economically tied together. Holding companies, parent-subsidiary operations or personal identity like Armand Hammer's business: each qualified as a combine or multinational corporation (Timberg, 1947: 578).

Timberg raised questions then in the mid-1940s that are still asked today, some 50 years later, about combines or TNCs.

1. Why has the combine wrested the substance of sovereignty from the nation?

2. Why no combine political loyalty to the nation?

3. Why so much trouble with combines?

4. Why is national action alone insufficient?

The level of sophisticated grasp of the international corporation was very significant. Timberg stated that TNCs were international economic states but that national law could not bind them. What he meant was "it merely means that the parties to international commercial transactions by and large apply a private and reliable law of their own, which assumes the varying contours of codified business usage arbitration, standard form contracts, selection of 'appropriate' legal rules, manipulation of conflict of laws criteria and internally binding law of the corporation'' (Timberg, 1947: 588).

Timberg stated four propositions to explain why TNCs are not loyal to nations and why they cannot be controlled by nations:

1. TNCs make a deliberate choice of forums and legal devices in the geographic places suited to them. Nations do not have this choice of forum.

2. TNCs are not mercantile expressions of the state called "home" country or "host" country—they reflect primarily economic vertical and horizontal integration without concern for home or host country or people.

3. TNCs are simpler than nations and more easily managed without political considerations.

4. A corporate personality is a bundle of legal fictions—that only a technical expert could sort out fact from fiction.

Timberg's analysis of the TNC and nation-state in 1947 is so good and so thoughtful, it could only be described as way ahead of its time. No attempt will be made here to explain Timberg fully, except to quote how he would solve the TNC regulation problem: "the territorial scope of the regulatory and enforcement power should in the main be co-extensive with the territorial impact of the activities regulated and interest to be protected" (Timberg, 1947: 620). You will see later how elegantly this fits into enterprise law developed by Blumberg. James Madison, president of the United States, said regulation of commerce was indivisible; Timberg added that there can be no unregulated gaps in any national-international division of power to regulate TNCs. Finally, in 1952, Timberg wrote about the use of a "Govcorp" institution to improve international administration (Timberg, 1952).

Timberg was a part of the post–World War II exceptionally mature reflection on corporate action before, during and after the war. Some of his examples are worth reciting here to remind us of times in corporate behavior when capitalists acted like genuine capitalists in exactly the manner described by Braudel in Chapter 5 of this book. The globalizing corporations are in no way naturally responsive to the political needs of states or nations—their principal concern in war is survival and protection of their assets with any conceivable strategy. Here are some of Timberg's examples of "deft" nationality of TNCs:

1. The Suez Canal, owned by an Egyptian company, majority control by the French, yet, the British considered it their instrument, but the British could not waive fees for U.S. ships to pay back lend-lease accounts in Britain.

2. Unilever (600 companies) was controlled by twin holding companies in England and Holland—dual national control reminiscent of the English East India Company.

3. The suicide of a Swedish industrial magnate precipitated insolvency of Swedish company A/B Kreuger and Toll (150 companies in 28 countries) which took 13.5 years to unravel in a global puzzle of assets and liabilities hidden by business secrecy.

4. Non-existent values and inflated profits in fictitious accounting entries in non-existent Canadian warehouses audited by a responsible firm, all of this was in a U.S. company—McKesson and Robbins, and it led to an SEC report in 1940.

5. NV Phillips of Gloeilampenfabrieke was an 80-subsidiary corporate holding firm in the Netherlands with operations in Europe and South America. Headquarters were moved to Curaçao in the Dutch West Indies before World War II. "When war came, therefore, the leading executives of the organization were able to leave Holland and assume active management of the British and American trusts and of the Curaçao companies" (Timberg, 1947: 588). Swiss companies and Argentine companies appear in various forms. "Well may such corporations be envied their amoebae-like fecundity and the psychological and political ease with which they are able to change and neutralize their nationality" (Timberg, 1946: 583).

These examples are perfect illustrations of the chameleon (changing skin color) national character of TNCs *before* the modern era from 1955 onward in time. Corporate purpose and national policy simply did not square. Favoritism to major industrial powers, using TNCs for fraudulent purposes, becoming an enemy in another nation with a corporate disguise were not likely to engender faith in TNC behavior. Timberg stated:

Corporations with global connections, singly or in concert, have been able successfully to ignore or to circumvent numerous other economic and social policies of similar broad import, including taxation, price control, the stockpiling of essential materials, antitrust policy, prohibitions against trading with a resistant enemy; and disarmament activities sought to be imposed on defeated enemies. (Timberg, 1947: 584)

When national systems of law try to control the TNC, the obvious lack of an integrated international economic system and the incomplete national systems are no answer, because private law systems take over and the real loser becomes the national state. The TNCs became economic nation-states without territorial boundaries. The official law, however, remained national law—very ineffective beyond the nation (Timberg, 1947: 587).

Timberg's analysis of TNC actions to evade national control used a submarine to represent the TNC and by analogy compared them with the fixed locations of shore batteries (nations). When national regulation is dormant, when books need to be cooked, when incorporation in nation A is better than nation B, when shifting offices across borders helps the TNC, when legal abstractions help the TNC raise questions with many possible answers, when ownership of assets needs to be papered over with contracts and leases and corporations, and when a nation is peculiar in favoring some business—all are circumstances favoring TNC maneuvering, cover, deception, and obfuscation with deliberate plans and actions viewed as rational solutions to protect capital from nations (Timberg, 1947: 589–598). Modern organizational theory would call this rational maximizing of strategy within a rapidly changing environment. It reminds one of the Daimler-Benz-Chrysler merger.

The seeds of Timberg's ideas are found in Phillip Blumberg's work, to be examined later in this chapter, but first we must pay attention to Friedman, Miller and Vagts.

The early period includes a challenging examination of excess corporate power, an assertion that corporations are private governments in the world community and that TNCs challenge national policy so that new regulations are needed (Wolfgang E. Friedman, 1957; Arthur S. Miller, 1960; and Vagts, 1970). Miller concluded that neither legal theory nor constitutional theory had caught up with the corporation in America (Miller, 1960: 1571). Vagts explored the legal framework for TNCs and flows of goods, management data and reported earnings as points of potential conflict.

In 1970, Vagts articulated a global strategy for nations if TNCs would flourish. Obviously, if TNCs had failed, this book would become just a history. But from 1970 to 1999 TNCs have flourished; thus, Vagts thought: "If it does proceed, nations will have to order their priorities more stringently, pool their information more liberally and iron out their substantive differences so as to present the MNE (multinational enterprises) with a common front" (Vagts, 1970: 792). This has not happened in fact, so 29 years is just more of the same—no coherent international approach to TNCs, no organized common front to date; no agreement on anything, or almost anything to do with TNCs. Some could argue that is the way it should be (Kindleberger, 1995). It is not for a lack of brilliant analysis of law that there is no common front among nations toward TNCs today. Vagts offered a balanced view of home and host country policies on the most critical phases of international operations of a TNC and even suggested various models of the future TNC (Vagts, 1970: 756–787). These may offer a foundation for thinking through the peculiar nature of TNCs in the law (see Johns, 1994). And more recently, a greater breadth of jurisprudence is being created.

The greater breadth of global-oriented jurisprudence is found in the traditional legal issues that are involved in corporate globalization. "Forum shopping" is needed to locate the best nation for labor and human relations, for product liability, for financial and contractual issues, and for communication issues (Pincus et al., 1991). Nike Company is founded on this strategy. The work of Seymour Rubin has already been examined briefly and others argue for global legal codes (Rubin; 1995; and Charney, 1983). Extraterritorial reach of national law is explored in some depth (Turley, 1990). A World Health Organization code of breast milk substitutes is a specific example of a set of global norms emerging (Del Ponte, 1982).

Significant changes internationalizing law and law practice and the resulting impacts on law firms in various nations was documented carefully in Europe and United States (Trubek et al., 1994). Constitutional Fourth Amendment issues in searches and seizures affecting non-citizens abroad remains a point of legal debate (Bentley, 1994).

Torts (civil harms like *Exxon Valdez* oil negligent spills) committed by TNCs are a broad area of concern to be mentioned here in passing, but to be developed more fully in a later part of this chapter addressed to the Bhopal poisoning. Labor in the North American Free Trade Agreement (NAFTA) was examined in Chapter 7 of this book, but it too has generated concern (Perez-Lopez, 1993). The rotation of Japanese managers in and out of U.S. subsidiaries of Japanese firms has raised a challenge under American employment discrimination law for non-Japanese employees (Mullen, 1993).

Real estate purchased by foreign interests is alien land ownership—a subject of complex federal and state laws in the United States (Mason, 1994). Health and environmental protections were expressed by CERES—a group responding to the *Exxon Valdez* March 24, 1989 oil spill by an Exxon company tanker in Alaska's Prince William Sound. The Valdez Principles arose out of this event and were subject to analysis (Carpency, 1991). Patrimonicide, stripping wealth from a nation by taking its resources through acts of national leaders is a multibillion-dollar issue that is inadequately handled by domestic law, but international law may provide a solution (Kofele-Kale, 1995). International bribery will be examined in Chapter 9. Scholarly analysis of the Foreign Corrupt Practices Act of 1977 has begun. Transfer pricing is the topic of a growing literature in the law (Elliott, 1995; Davlin, 1994). Taxation of TNCs in the United States is a vigorously debated topic after a decision by the U.S. Supreme Court in the *Barclays Bank* case (Husain, 1995).

Economic integration agreements are a major topic of legal analysis (Whalley and Hamilton, 1995). The topic of foreign direct investment is broadly generating legal interest in a general agreement, dispute settlement procedures, regulation in central and eastern Europe and reduction in Japanese investment barriers (Geist, 1995; Brewer, 1995; Gray and Jarosz, 1995; Roehrdanz, 1995). An international organization for multinational enterprises was examined (Scaperlanda, 1994). Issues of sovereignty on the conclusion of the Uruguay Round Agreements and their implementation were studied (Aceves, 1995). The impact of NAFTA, GATT and WTO are unknown (Hansen, 1996).

New and old issues are found in this overview, but most significantly there is a growing body of literature of very high quality emerging with a balanced perspective, both national and international in nature. Global jurisprudence is rising.

To summarize to this point in the chapter, we have noticed the peculiar place of TNCs in the legal world—especially the last five decades of dealing with them since World War II ended. Scholars along the way repeatedly raised the same questions, starting forcefully with Sigmund Timberg. Many have tried to provide a seamless domestic-international web of control only to be thwarted by TNCs too clever to be controlled by nations so far. The evidence mounts in global jurisprudential thinking that the idea of globalization is neither intelligently conceptualized nor is the law intelligently adapted to TNCs conceived of as economic states beyond domestic law. But, the reality is, man has constructed all of this—there are no immutable natural laws like the law of gravity at work. There is one scholar in the United States, Phillip Blumberg, whose work could become the foundation for a major transformation of the legal personality of corporations, especially those that are a parent of many subsidiary corporations (51% owned by the parent). Globalizing corporations are rarely just one corporation with many branches (parts of one corporation) scattered across earth. Instead, as is pointed out in Appendix B, the top 50 U.S. corporations are 50 families of 6,000 other corporations. These are the schools of submarines that Timberg mentioned, who go above and below the consciousness of nations, their governments and the people of a nation. Because the law operates so slowly and because there is much covert resistance among TNCs who believe they are private institutions, there is every reason to believe that American regulatory capitalism (described in Chapter 5) and the model of TNC governance represented by it, will be slowly unfolding from the national arena inside the United States into the international arena in the next 50 years in a clear, unmistakable and thoroughly profound expansion. Every thoughtful critic from Raymond Vernon to Fleur Johns clearly casts such light on the relationship of globalizing corporations in democratic nations so that we must question the laissez-faire approach and start to grasp the need for regulation in many forms, regulation found in treaties of all kinds, and in UN-articulated norms covering all aspects of international trade in goods, services and investment. Investment controls today are unsuitable for TNCs from a national perspective of all nations toward the 750 largest TNCs. The Multilateral Agreement on Investment, to be proposed formally by the OECD in 1998 or at a later date, offers a peculiar and undesirable approach that we will examine in Chapter 10.

Phillip I. Blumberg's Search for a New Corporate Personality

In 1975, the then Dean of the University of Connecticut School of Law, Phillip I. Blumberg, wrote *The Megacorporation in American Society*. This is rare from two viewpoints—first a law-educated scholar probed financial and economic data thoroughly just as A. A. Berle, Jr., a lawyer, had done previously in the early 1930s or as Justice Brandeis had done before Berle earlier in the century. Books like *Global Reach* (1974) by Barnet and Mueller, and Ralph Nader and others in *Taming the Giant Corporation* (1976) were noticed more in that period, perhaps, but no other legal scholar demonstrated so clearly as Blumberg the factual grasp of economic power in large corporations—megacorporations.

Second, Blumberg was a dean of a law school within a state where many giant corporations have home bases. He lived amidst or close to the corporate power, but maintained an independent intellectual stance of his own. Of course, his 1975 findings were clear and did not appear to be earthshaking. The role of major corporations changed in American society. By 1975, the very size in sales, assets, net profits and market value revealed the central role of industrial corporations—significantly larger than all other businesses and highly concentrated in market controls in basic markets. Blumberg noted growing concentration of shareholders in institutional investment groups like pension funds and noted their potential for becoming future centers of control (Blumberg, 1975: 84–144). This was far in advance of others (Useem, 1996). Finally, Blumberg observed growing managerial power in a self-perpetuating style coupled with interlocking directorates—an old problem in giant companies. The book concluded on a wish to tame corporate power in America:

In summary, I have endeavored to set forth the dimensions of corporate power in the United States, the concentration of economic power in the hands of the megacorporations, and the emergence of potential corporate control in the financial institutions. *The concerns that these developments present for a free society are fundamental.* The extent of corporate power is plain. The basic issue is how to limit it in a way that will be compatible with the preservation of free institutions. (Blumberg, 1975: 178) (emphasis added)

If Blumberg had never done anything further, his contribution at least demonstrated a deep understanding of the nature of power and of the U.S. society so that the political economy of large American corporations was clearly and unequivocally evident in his work. But that was just the beginning of his search.

From 1975 to 1993, Blumberg entered into another major phase of intellectual development. *The Law of Corporate Groups* began emerging in 1983 in five volumes appearing in 1983, 1985, 1987, 1989 and 1992. Articles of Blumberg appeared in 1986 and 1991. Finally, in 1993, Blumberg authored *The Multinational Challenge to Corporation Law*. This single volume more than any other work offers a brilliant and easily understood analysis of the jurisprudential view of the legal personality of the corporate group (not just a single corporation). Blumberg's analysis is the missing link in the peculiar nature of TNCs in both corporate law and international law that was explored earlier in this chapter. It is easily demonstrated through Blumberg's work how he has reached a new paradigm of the large corporation group that fits a new economic reality, which he explained nationally in 1975 in his earlier work. If I seem to dwell too long on Blumberg, it is justified by the significance of his thinking about enterprise law. His work is a major transformation in thinking about corporations.

Traditional entity corporate law fit the earlier economic reality—one corporation—one business in one nation. By contrast, most TNCs are one parent and dozens of subsidiary corporations wholly owned all over the world. Blumberg noted:

Thus, with the application of traditional entity law to corporate groups, the older concept of legal entity no longer matches the reality of the economic entity. The traditional law no longer reflects the society that it seeks to order, and implementation of the underlying policies of the law inevitably is gravely impaired. (Blumberg, 1993: ix)

This observation of the weakness of traditional corporate entity law led to the development of what Blumberg described as "enterprise law." The giant corporation and all of the family of corporations that it owns are viewed when necessary as a single enterprise and if the law must view them as a single enterprise it does so; but if the law finds enterprise concepts unhelpful it still has traditional entity law for single corporations. *This is a major, earthshaking change in legal thinking.* The whole idea of firewalls and safe harbors would be in jeopardy. The serious risks of nation-states confronting one another because of in-country activity by families of corporations means that national law with extraterritorial effects could lead to international controversy. Enterprise law may help to reduce this conflict and provide the seamless web of policy control the law must provide to be effective. Timberg called for this policy in 1947.

It is important *not* to see enterprise law in a fight with entity law, they supplement one another, if the historical insight is properly understood. The corporation and the rise of limited liability both developed together in American jurisprudence, along with constitutional formation of the corporation. As corporate groups emerged in fact, both judicial and statutory response were sympathetic toward enterprise ideas, in the "piercing the veil jurisprudence," in unitary tax cases, in bankruptcy law and other fields. All of this is directed internally inside the United States toward families of companies with U.S. home bases.

The world dimensions of enterprise law are clear—more of the nations are adopting it in select areas which places Europe, Australia, Canada, New Zealand and the United States in the same jurisprudential direction. In a series of decisions, enterprise law and extraterritorial extensions of home and host country national laws have arisen (Blumberg, 1993: 168–204). Individuals, physical objects and organizations are involved in enterprise law. Enterprise law matches the law and the economic enterprise as one. Enterprise law is a form of agency law, which partly eliminates limited liability, operates like a privity idea and imposes derivative liability. The courts and legislatures in the United States and elsewhere are formulating a legal system capable of dealing with activities of giant, worldwide corporate groups (Blumberg, 1993: 253). This practical response of enterprise law is an adaptation to change just as antitrust law was a response to illegal business trusts in the United States.

In summary of the multiple legal perspectives on multinational corporations, we are finally beginning to see a major creative idea of jurisprudence arise globally—enterprise law. Still too new to predict where it will end, enterprise law offers a seamless web of domestic and international legal control and fits extraterritoriality into a legal framework. Legal policy can flow across borders just as easily as TNCs flow across national borders. Cross-border joint national action, policy, treaties, coordinated enforcement, exchange of data, high technology monitoring appear in the legal winds of change coupled with enterprise law—indeed, this is an exciting prospect at the start of the twenty-first century. Domestic international issues and international domestic issues will be viewed as global/local in nature. There will be an interweaving of interests of nations because of this change in legal thinking.

Finally, the same TNCs may face chartering norms from local, national and international agencies all registering corporate activities in a coordinated global pattern of enterprise law applied to the important topic of corporate existence.

The next part of this chapter is devoted to regulation of TNCs. This topic is developing very rapidly due to economic integration agreements of NAFTA and GATT in the mid-1990s. The WTO forces considerations of mutual regulations.

GLOBAL CORPORATE ORDER UNDER NATIONAL LAW AND INTERNATIONAL LAW: HARMONY AND DISCORD

Most of the argument so far in this book has been that trade among nations should be reduced because it would be better for everyone on earth to take care of themselves first and foremost. Then, if some small items are desired, like spices or silks or a peculiar fruit, then trade in goods makes some common sense. Trade in services makes no sense at all—each nation should cut its own hair, have its own doctors, lawyers and account for itself. And investment should be made at home first; then a government-business policy set by Congress and the president each year should determine how much total capital should be directed away from the United States to other nations and how much can enter the United States from foreign corporations. Capital export controls make sense in view of the loss of 4.6 million jobs and the large sum of a trillion dollars in outward foreign direct investment, and equally unregulated large amounts entering the nation. This view is not widely accepted at this time, nor are the following ideas.

Our world of foreign travel makes sense if *not* done by plane, but by ship because of the massive number of people now seeking air travel. It is far too expensive and wasteful of jet fuel to boost so many people into the air and fly them globally. Boeing will be building ocean ships, not 777s. Efficiency in use of resources is a central concern. I am certain these observations and ideas are likely to drive rabid casino capitalists mad; the predators would have nothing on which to prey. But it is healthy to state these simple ideas and policies in foreign trade for the United States compared with the anxiously strained arguments of those madly in love with maximum free trade, and the excessive preoccupation with growth and with odd globalization ideas bordering on attacks on nations and responsible business. So let us see how the free traders think about regulation of trade.

First, tariff barriers to trade are not examined here since they are so direct and easy a method to control foreign trade. While out of favor, I favor them. The focus is upon non-tariff barriers to trade—where a few efforts are made to study national regulation in an international context. Trade and national regulation are now linked in the United States because of the GATT tuna-dolphin decision in 1991 and the intense debate over the NAFTA (American University Conference, 1993), and then GATT. There is a question not settled: Do economic integration agreements like NAFTA and GATT weaken and displace national, state and local regulatory standards? Some argue they do, others argue the opposite—the politics is not settled. Let's examine a couple of recent analytical accounts.

Is it harmonization, standardization, homogenization or recolonization? That is the question. The favorite word in 1999 is "harmonization." It is used to say that nations in the world in trade regulation will "harmonize" their regulations to make world trade flow more easily across national borders in a borderless world. Harmony sounds so peaceful, who could be against harmony? The real question is: Is it harmony up to my high standard or harmony down to your low standard? One auto executive said—Should the glass in autos be the kind that breaks into no bigger than ¼" pieces or ⅛" pieces? Harmony here may just split the difference—3/16" is acceptable. However, not all trade disputes are this simple or easy to resolve. For example, the European Union struggled over a standard for electric connections.

Two recent major works explore the idea of harmonization. Jagdish N. Bhagwati and Robert E. Hudec edited a two-volume work appropriately titled *Fair Trade and Harmonization: Prerequisites for Free Trade?* (1996). David Vogel wrote *Trading Up: Consumer and Environmental Regulation in a Global Economy* (1995). What emerged is a thoughtful analysis of many issues within the context that assumes promotion of global trade is a good thing in itself. Assuming that one wants more global trade, the question is, how to do it in case after case of disagreement about all types of issues. Harmonization raises more and more issues. Global trade generates an endless sense of issues that produces conflict among nations, which nations the traders then join into their fights in the commercial arena. One could question initially whether traders ought to stop trading if they are going to generate so much conflict among nations. Should Kodak be allowed to drag the U.S. government into its disagreements with Japan over the sale of film in Japan? Multiply this fight by the hundreds and one can see immediately that foreign trade may not be worthwhile from a national perspective, which leads to the conclusion that each nation ought to make its own film and stop exporting it. This is the easiest way to stop all the turmoil in the marketplace for film. No nation is obliged to buy from or sell anything to any other nation—there is no natural law to this effect.

Vogel questioned whether trade liberalization or, as it is also known, opening national markets to foreign competition, automatically meant a "Delaware effect" downward in both nations trading, or a "rush to the bottom" or the lowest standards would apply in any given market and trade once trade starts. He argued that there may be a "California effect," a raising of trade standards to the highest level. For example, food with the least trace of pesticide, autos with highest gas mileage and cleanest exhaust emissions are examples of a "California effect" as Vogel defined it. Tuna caught without killing porpoises or sea turtles is another issue. Beef without growth hormones introduced by man is another. The list of topics is endless in the environmental and consumer areas of trade.

As I reviewed Vogel, it occurred to me that the entire lingo used in trade talk is conducive to further confusion. "Economic protectionism" was a term he used, Baptists and bootleggers defined a certain common trade event, and trade barriers are becoming works of art that cover the way products are produced reaching back into the manufacturing process. The greening of GATT is a peculiar idea. National health, safety and environmental regulations, statutes and other policy expressions of national law are being undermined—the national sovereignty of the people defined in previous chapters is being set to one side by global traders (Vogel, 1995: 1). Many U.S. public policies that affect trade are old public policies:

- 1897—no importation of wild birds or animals without a permit.
- 1907—no import of pests injurious to crops or forest.
- 1906—no sponges from beds where taking harmed the bed.
- 1913—Underwood tariff—no plumes or feathers from wild birds can be imported.
- 1926—no import of salmon caught in violation of U.S. fishing regulations.
- 1930s—no Argentinean beef in the United States because of diseases in animals there.

Vogel's examples do suggest a law of sorts, as he stated: "The greater the commitment to economic integration, the more trade agreements will intrude upon domestic policies" (Vogel, 1995: 9). This is a very important truth articulated by Vogel. But vast expansion of trade in the last 50 years is pressing everyone in every nation—from protection of tropical rainforests, ozone layer protection and bootlegged CFC containers and disposal of hazardous waste and many other subjects. It has become a legal jungle and this must mean that multinational corporations have found ideal legal conditions to exploit inherently ambiguous regulations that become, unwittingly, "trade havens." There is a virtual forest of exploitable legal opportunities for business. Their lawyers must be cheering.

BIG TOBACCO

Vogel reviewed the several-decades-long trade fight over the export of American cigarettes to Thailand and other Asian nations. Attempts to discourage and stop such exports of American corporations are met with vigorous American tobacco industry efforts to sell cigarettes to Asians—exporting them by the billions. The fight began in the 1960s and by the early 1980s the USTR (Office of the United States Trade Representative), at the request of the United States Cigarette Export Association, began investigating regulations and found quotas, protective tariffs and foreign illegality by owning or selling American cigarettes (Vogel, 1995: 199). Threats to impose "301 sanctions" liberalized some of the trade restrictions in Japan, Taiwan and Korea, but Thailand stuck by its 1966 Tobacco Act—no imports without a license and no licenses were issued for ten years. This caused the United States in 1990 to file a GATT complaint. This GATT action set the stage for further escalation of the tobacco trade war with Thailand—since GATT allowed Thailand's ban on advertisement (Vogel, 1995: 200). Then the Thais went to the American Cancer Society, the former U.S. Surgeon General C. Everett Koop, and the American Heart Association for help, which they got. Congress reacted negatively to USTR, but the U.S. GAO (General Accounting Office) said they were just doing their job. The U.S. Department of Agriculture promoted cigarette exports. The inconsistent federal government international policy is obvious in this trade warfare with Thailand on one side and U.S. tobacco multinational corporations on the other side. It reminds one in retrospect of the 1997–1998 tobacco "settlement" fights in the United States.

Glenn Frankel, in a four-part series in the *Washington Post* titled "Big Tobacco's Global Reach" in November, 1996, focused attention on the American cigarette export promotion to Thailand and its resistance to presence by three American multinational corporations—Philip Morris, R. J. Reynolds and Brown & Williamson (Frankel, 11/18/96). A Thai doctor, Prakit Vateesatokit, noticed as early as 1985 the targeting in advertising of Thai children—tee shirts, kites, baseball caps and school notebooks. Philip Morris denied its involvement in what it claimed were pirated logos stolen from them. By 1989 secret talks produced imports of American cigarettes into Thailand through government negotiations. Prying open a market for exported American cigarettes was accomplished by threatening trade retaliation under Section 301 of the United States Trade Act. The Geneva GATT panel said Thailand violated GATT rules and only then did Bangkok voluntarily lift the ban on foreign cigarette brands in 1990. Frankel noted: "But in practical terms, Thailand won an enormous victory" (Frankel, 11/18/96: A14). Thailand has the strongest anti-smoking laws in the world and only 3% of their cigarettes are imported—not 25% which was anticipated.

People in Asia united over Thailand's resistance to what the Section 301 threat implied. Thailand had a $2 billion annual trade surplus with the United States— it would be threatened. Carla Hills, the USTR head, was a non-smoker as was Clayton Yeutter, the previous head. Yet Hills pushed to open Thailand along with congressional pressure and then referred the conflict to GATT in Geneva. Dr. Prakit Vateesatokit found in GATT some language to protect Thailand's health and welfare and a GATT decision agreed—Thailand could justifiably restrict sales of cigarettes and ban advertising if both domestic and foreign producers were equally affected. "By 1995, 33 of 35 Asian countries had tobacco control laws . . . laws were prompted not just by health concerns but by a sense of righteous Asian nationalism" (Frankel, 11/18/96: A 15). Frankel quoted David Yen, a Taiwanese businessman: "We think it's a pity that with so many wonderful products to sell, you have insisted on pushing disease instead" (Frankel, 11/18/96: A 15).

The tobacco trade warring is not finished because cigarette content rules are now being examined in Asia, enacted in some nations, found in Canadian law, and tobacco trade activities in Eastern Europe, Romania and Poland are showing the frank inconsistency in American foreign trade behavior in the Clinton administration (Frankel, 11/18/96: A 15). The basic question is—do we need smoking in the American society or in any other society on earth? Is trade so important—the export of American cigarettes, for example? This is the real issue and the answer is probably *no* in any practical sense, and everyone realizes this except for tobacco farmers and cigarette manufacturers, especially the more aggressive among them who see no harm in preying in good capitalist fashion on young Asian men and women. Such are foreign trade disputes in vivid reality.

It should be clear that harmonization in the cigarette export business leads to politics of a global nature. Trade is viewed by some as colonization or recolonization. Standardization of the world is demanded—a level playing field to do whatever business deems desirable becomes the norm—not medical or health or environmental standards, or moral standards not to hook children on smoking. The borderless world is not so wonderful a place for young Asian lungs. Yet, this is the purported cultural harmonic homogenization that is supposed to bring good things to life. Cigarette export promotion is but one of many examples of trade regulation harmonization that starts to ring political bells across the globe in the Asian cigarette markets and Asian capitals.

Raymond Vernon, one of the wisest voices in foreign trade suggested that once a foreigner invests his funds in another country, the investment sets in train a stream of events that defies measurement. In other words, the country is never the same again. We ought to think very seriously about the process of change because it has a very dark side of harmful consequences for some of mankind (Rogers, 1995). Cigarette exports are just one of a number of examples of a similar nature and trade wars are filled with other examples. And there are harmless goods—pants, tee-shirts and athletic supporters from Costa Rica that the World Trade Organization said must be admitted into the United States. But some things ought to be barred from international trade, as suggested in Chapter 6.

Fair trade and harmonization—are these prerequisites for free trade? This is the question presented in the two volumes by Bhagwati and Hudec, a lawyer. To quote Bhagwati, an economist: "This is the key question before us today: Is a move toward harmonization, or what is sometimes called 'fair trade,' or 'level playing fields,' a prerequisite for free trade?" (Baghwati and Hudec, 1996: V1–1). Legal and economic analysis by more than 25 authors follows in almost 1,200 pages. Their focus was upon environment, labor and competition in trade—with side excursions into tax policy, aspects of a race to the bottom, Japanese and European experience in trade, the GATT legal framework and fairness concepts. The work is serious, probing and satisfying to economic, legal and political concerns. The overview of these large, interrelated topics does force one to rethink the meaning of harmonization in much greater depth. Unlike Vogel, whose political focus brought to light the Delaware and California effects, the political aspects were not dominant in these two volumes; nor were corporations of much interest; nor were the Thailand–Asian cigarette export disputes discussed. This supports a belief that some economists and lawyers are removed totally from some trade realities of tobacco corporations insisting on cigarette exports in the face of determined national opposition. One would think this or the tuna cases would be more interesting. They may argue that trade must be "de-linked" from everything else in life, but many do not accept the idea of isolated trade norms.

One conclusion is certain—harmonization may well offer that "golden" legal and economic opportunity to argue endlessly and ambiguously about trade regulation without much of a conclusion. This is a sport for the long-winded, or long-writers. It favors those who can hire economists and lawyers to argue the fine points and invent more. Some would argue that corporate colonialism is the real aim with harmonization not being anything more than a disguise to get one's imports into every national tent (Korten, 1995: 121–179). The cigarette dispute in Thailand is a good example just described. Others may genuinely believe in borderlessness:

But I see no virtue in the implicit position of most political scientists that the nation-state as it exists today is sacrosanct and eternal and that other world forces should be bent to its preservation. If the scale of political efficiency changes, why should not the nation-state follow the county not into oblivion but into the museum of antiquarian interest with the city state? (Kindelberger, 1984: 32)

That would be a good question for some interests and not others in trade regulation by nation-states.

Others may believe that global trade regulation in the GATT and NAFTA economic integration models merely reflects how far we have come since 1975 toward the twenty-first-century "benign" mercantilist model—when the nation-states are stirring to action as the gradual demise results in what Robert Gilpin called the "sovereignty at bay model" and the "dependencia models" (Gilpin, 1975: 230–262). As Gilpin noted:

In a world economy composed of several major centers of economic power, economic bargaining and coalitions will predominate. Through the exercise of economic power, each center of the world's economy will seek to increase benefits of interdependence and decrease costs. Trade, monetary and investment relations will be highly politicized and the subject of intense negotiations. . . . It is within this post *Pax Americana* world of intensified economic conflict that the American multinational corporation must seek its new, albeit reduced, role. In such a world, American multinationals will have to be nimble and quick indeed if they are to escape suffering the fate of the British East India Company. (Gilpin, 1975: 261–2)

Gilpin's belief in the reduced role for multinational corporations means that nations will have to supply the political and economic will to reduce stalemates and reduce tensions, strains and conflicts that emerge from economic issues, trade issues and regulatory conflicts. This further suggests that nations will have to provide capital for research and development to improve innovation potentials and to direct the benefits more broadly.

As if in response to Robert Gilpin's sage forecast in 1975, Alex Rubner, in *The Might of the Multinationals* (1990) stated:

Chapter 20 recalls that the protagonists of the TNC have linked the blossoming of multis with the emasculation of the nation-states and the advent of world government. In my prognosis the nation-state will strengthen and tighten its grip on the international corporation. (Rubner, 1990: 227)

Rubner's witty and caustic but always informed view offers some confirmation to the benign mercantilism theory or, as some would prefer to call it, the plain rebirth of healthy, cooperative nationalism and intergovernmental cooperation with disappearing xenophobic fears long gone in a developing world society with strong counties, cities, states, regions and nations and a UN hard at work. This is the harmony that counts most to tighten the grip on multinational corporations.

WORLD CLASS CORPORATE TRAGEDY: CIVIL WRONGS; BHOPAL, 1984–1999

The world's worst industrial accident or disaster waiting to happen, or event or civil wrong or tort or crime, or all of the above, was found in the tragic massive leakage (tons) from Union Carbide Corporation's subsidiary plant in Bhopal, India in the early hours of December 2–3, 1984. What burned so many lungs was an insect poison—a pesticide called methyl isocyanate (MIC). As Anwar Fazal from Malaysia stated: "Like Auschwitz and Hiroshima, the catastrophe at Bhopal is a manifestation of something fundamentally wrong with our stewardship of the earth. Its ghosts will be with us forever" (Weir, 1987: xii).

Death, permanent injury and temporary harm were spread by the toxic MIC gases over the city of 800,000 people in Bhopal. Estimated deaths ranged from 3,150 to 10,000. A 1990 report said continuing deaths resulting from the toxic injury were 50 per month. Over 200,000 people were exposed to toxic gases that left 86,000 more people permanently disabled (Dembo, Morehouse and

Wykle, 1990: 86; Mitroff and Linstone, 1993: 111–113). The Bhopal horror is one result of industrialism and it clearly reflects the globalizing of multinational corporations seeking growth in foreign markets. World class harm was visited on an innocent local people. Because of its global significance the Bhopal disaster deserves very careful attention—just like the *Exxon Valdez* oil spill in Alaska, the *Amoco Cadiz* oil spill near France, the asbestos liability and many other corporate torts, not to mention Three Mile Island and the Chernobyl atomic energy plant disaster of mixed ownership.

To shield a corporate group like Union Carbide Corporation and others in a corporate group from massive potential liability in high-risk activity like that of making insect poison, the dangerous operation is placed in a separate corporation, a subsidiary corporation, to create a "safe harbor" for a family corporate group seeking to externalize the cost of a high-risk subsidiary's negligence in making poison. Limiting tort liability is the goal—limiting liability to the assets of only the single corporate subsidiary in India. But "piercing the veil jurisprudence" in tort cases makes safe harbors of such subsidiaries very unsafe. Ultimately, the shareholders of the corporate group as a whole—worldwide—may lose their assets to judgments obtained by persons injured by the negligence of the high-risk subsidiary in India. In other words, without insurance, there is no way to shift or externalize liability for risks or harms to others—to the government, the consumers, the victims or others. Tort creditors who get judgments to be satisfied take their just due amounts to compensate for harms from all shareholders of all corporations in the corporate group (Chopra, 1994).

The leaking Bhopal plant was 50.9% owned by Union Carbide Corporation of the United States. The corporate subsidiary in India was called Union Carbide (India) Ltd. or UCIL—the rest of UCIL or 49.1% was owned by other shareholders, some Indians. In 1984 the plant in India was large—10,000 employed in the twenty-first largest company in India (Mitroff and Linstone, 1993: 112).

Who was legally responsible for the harm?—the thing speaks for itself—*res ipsa loquitur*. Lawsuits brought by the Indian government and many plaintiffs asserted direct liability of the U.S. parent for its action in owning and controlling UCIL—this was five of the six causes of action in U.S. lawsuits. The sixth cause of action, relying on the enterprise doctrine of liability, sought intragroup liability of the parent for torts of the majority-owned Indian subsidiary. In the United States, a federal court refused jurisdiction on grounds of forum non conveniens and dismissed the case. In India, the Supreme Court of India upheld in 1989 a $470 million settlement judgment against Union Carbide of the United States and the Indian subsidiary corporation, both on direct negligence and an intragroup liability under enterprise law (Blumberg, 1993: 190). Blumberg stated: "Bhopal, shorn of it catastrophic dimensions, was simply a case involving the assertion of enterprise principles to impose parent company liability for a subsidiary's torts, a result frequently reached in the United States through 'piercing the veil jurisprudence' " (Blumberg, 1993: 190). From the legal viewpoint of Blumberg, there was nothing new in the Bhopal case. But others saw some more lessons to be learned—the World Council of Churches saw TNCs creating problems, not solving them (Dunning, 1993: 540). "As in the Bhopal accident, the parent company agreed that because the plant was under the control of local management, they accepted no responsibility" (Dunning, 1993: 540). Dunning was also referring to a 1982 case in Malaysia of a plant partly owned by a Japanese company, Mitsubishi Chemical Company, where radioactive thorium waste was dumped on open ground in plastic bags that were easily broken up. Public reaction was outrage and boycotts followed. The environmental demands on corporate groups will place more stress on management in handling risks of high magnitude, without safe harbors for financial liability risks.

Mitroff and Linstone probed the organizational managerial, chemical and personal factors in the case of Bhopal. Thirty separate factors could be potential causes. But they concluded that extremely complex systems are catastrophe-making enterprises (Mitroff and Linstone, 1993: 111–135). Human error cannot be eliminated and it expands with fatigue, multiple languages, and many other normal factors plus intentional sabotage potential. Many of the ingredients in technical design and supposedly "fail-safe" equipment features in Bhopal never worked. The separate factors joined together in an unmanageable disaster.

A special study of Union Carbide, titled *Abuse of Power* by David Dembo, Ward Morehouse and Lucinda Wykle (1990), offered a historical profile of Union Carbide corporate-group global performance, from the creation (on November 1, 1917) of Union Carbide and Carbon Corporation (four companies and subsidiaries) (Dembo et al., 1990: 12). Activities of the corporation with Hawk's Nest Tunnel, with atomic energy in the Temik poisonings, with West Virginia and with Puerto Rico offered insight into corporate performance. It was a troublesome profile. By 1987, Union Carbide parent was 130 subsidiaries in 36 countries, and 44% of its work force was outside of the United States with a third of total sales and a third of profits non–U.S. in origin. It had become truly a globalized corporate group—ever ready to do its work. India, Canada, France, Belgium, Australia and Indonesia presented significant findings of double safety standards. Even a leak in a West Virginia operation after Bhopal made for general concern in the United States.

Financially, the $470 million settlement in 1989 meant that Union Carbide's liability insurance covered all but $20 million and small amounts set aside each year while litigation arose (Dembo et al., 1990: 98). Profits were made in 1988 of $662 million. The proportion of the settlement to one year of profit by Union Carbide meant another major evasion of corporate social responsibility according to Dembo, Morehouse and Wykle. In 1994, Union Carbide sold the government-seized Indian subsidiary for about $90 million. The literature about the Bhopal disaster continued to mount as more was learned about the views of Carbide workers (Chouhan et al., 1994) and further reports released (Morehouse and Subramanian, 1986).

In April of 1992, *Chemical Week* reported that an extradition warrant was issued by the Indian government for the former Union Carbide chairman, Warren Anderson, to stand trial on criminal charges growing out of the 1984 Bhopal incident (Chouhan et al., 1994: 163–164, 210). One report stated: "Conditions at the plant were so bad that according to Warren Anderson, chairman of the corporation, it 'should not have been operating' " (Shaikh, 1986: 62).

My research revealed no further resolution of this issue into 1998. David Weir, in *The Bhopal Syndrome* (1987), cast the Bhopal tragedy into the context of the global pesticide industry and previous chemical disasters. With 1983 pesticide sales of $13 billion the businesses were rising rapidly. After a thorough review of the tragedy from many perspectives, Chouhan included many horrifying eye witness accounts reported by Claude Alvarez (Weir, 1987: 159–182).

Weir examined the past seven decades in an illuminating examination of the major industrial accidents, as summarized in Table 8-1 (major evacuations are omitted).

The devastation from these events is a partial picture of a much larger reality and the reality in the ten years from 1986 to 1996 is not presented. Bhopal was predictable. Corporations usually operate such facilities. The inference is clear— the impact of high-risk activities is borne by thousands of innocent people every year—externalizing the cost of industrial harms to citizens. The Bhopal financial costs imposed on Indian people are not begun to be paid by a $470 million dollar settlement under standards of tort liability imposed on corporations in the United States with perhaps the highest global standards. Very few TNCs are prepared to pay the full cost of doing business—the tort liability merely highlights the cost-shifting practices. This may, in fact, account for DuPont Corporation's difficulty in August, 1991, when a GOA group in India wanted no part of a nylon factory proposed (Alvares, 1991). The PONDA Declaration provides very significant local opposition to multinational plans of Dupont.

A global civil jurisprudence is beginning to appear in the area of civil wrongs or torts. Editors Campbell McLachlan and Peter Nygh offered *Transnational Tort Litigation* (1996) that explicitly examines the difficult jurisdictional issues in transnational pollution (Chernobyl), the forum issues in the Bhopal disaster litigation, the international fraud cases, product liability, intellectual property protections and transnational personal injury. This development along with Phillip Blumberg's exploration and statement of enterprise law for corporate groups augers well for a new intergovernmental cooperation among lawyers and legal institutions involved in multinational legal responsibilities across the globe. In this critical tort area the nation-state control over corporate actions is getting much stronger, as it should be getting stronger to protect the people more completely.

EVOLVING CIVIL JURISPRUDENCE: WHAT LAW TEACHES OR COULD TEACH

One could argue that law teaches very little about the nature of the globalizing corporation in democratic nations. Law is and was slow to understand TNCs,

Table 8-1
Major Industrial Accidents

No.	Date	Place	Type of Disaster	Dead	Injured
1.	12/6/17	Halifax, NS	Ship explosion	1,654	
2.	9/21/21	Oppau, Germany	Factory explosion	561	1,500
3.	10/20/44	Cleveland, OH	Gas tank explosion	131	
4.	4/16/47	Texas City, TX	Ship explosion	576	2,000
5.	7/28/48	Ludwishafer, Germany	Railcar explosion	207	4,000
6.	8/7/56	Cali, Columbia	Truck explosion	1,100	
7.	6/1/74	Flixborough, UK	Railcar explosion	28	89
8.	7/10/76	Seveso, Italy	Plant reaction	100,000 animals	
9.	7/11/78	San Carlos, Spain	Truck explosion	215	
10.	4/8/79	Crestview, FL	Railcar explosion		1,000
11.	11/10/79	Mississanga, Ontario	Railcar explosion		8
12.	4/3/80	Somerville, MA	Railcar spill		418
13.	6/5/80	Port Kellang, Malaysia	Cylinder explosion	3	200
14.	6/6/80	Garland, TX	Railcar explosion		5
15	7/26/80	Mildraugh, KY	Railcar explosion		4
16.	7/27/80	Newark, NJ	Railcar explosion		
17.	5/19/81	San Juan, PR	Plant toxic release		200
18.	8/1/81	Montana, Mexico	Railcar explosion	29	1,000
19.	4/10/82	Belle, WV	Plant toxic release		13
20.	8/28/82	Livingston, LA	Railcar explosion		
21.	4/3/83	Denver, CO	Railcar leak		43
22.	2/25/84	Cubatao, Brazil	Pipeleak explosion	500	
23.	11/19/84	Mexico City	Gas tank explosion	452	4,248
24.	12/23/84	Bhopal, India	Plant toxic leakage	10,000	86,000*
25.	1/6/85	Koratly Kerly, India	Plant toxic leak		40
26.	1/26/85	Cubatao, Brazil	Plant toxic leak		400
27.	8/12/85	Institute, WV	Plant toxic leak		135
28.	4/5/86	Chernobyl, USSR	Nuclear explosion	unknown	unknown
29.	10/11/86	Basel, Switzerland	Rhine pollution	unknown	unknown

Sources: Mitroff and Linstone (1993); Dembo, Morehouse and Sykle (1990).

and failed as late as 1970 to develop much for them in law, according to international law expert Detlev Vagts. International law had nothing much to offer NGOs—non-governmental organizations like private corporations or families of them called corporate groups. Law never taught economics a thing and it taught business even less. And international law still cannot produce a universal code of rules as late as 1999. So the logical question is: Why bother with law? The answer is simple and yet profound: we, as citizens of many nations, have found no other way to join into common expressions of what we want other than by speaking through law to one another—as imperfect a tool as law is, in fact. A Uniform Commercial Code emerged in the United States from such a desire to speak one coherent business language so that we could understand one another better. International airline pilots use English to communicate globally and most of the time it works, too, as imperfect as language is. In the same sense that airline pilots need conversation, nations need a common language of law to navigate and to avoid national collisions. In the case of nations, law is their joint voice to both agree and disagree with one another. That is why law is so very important to the international discourse about multinational corporations. Furthermore, that is why the law as one expression of the sovereign people in its national constitutional and statutory order is central to an understanding of how globalizing corporations relate to nations. The UN code that has been labored on so long and still is not adopted illustrates how complex and difficult the task of understanding and communicating is in the real world of nations and corporations.

The law is stumbling along, nonetheless, toward a path that I believe will develop much greater clarity in the decades ahead. First, the development from entity law along with enterprise law headed in the pathways Phillip Blumberg suggests will make much clearer the nature of the corporate personality in entity law and enterprise law. After all, we have pretty much lost most of the old corporate law that meant substantial and serious charter limits on a corporation's powers (Nader, 1976). Chartering of corporations is a dormant subject now even though it had surfaced first in 1906, then at other times—1937, 1973 and again in the 1990s (Grossman and Adams, 1995: 374–389 in Mander and Goldsmith, 1996). More conversation is needed here.

The corporate personality of a corporate group was central in the Bhopal case for the Supreme Court of India. The work of entity and enterprise law joined together. Thus, transnational torts may now have a newer legal framework that draws in corporate tort liability in a sensible manner across national borders. Cross-border extraterritorial effects may be on the verge of being handled more intelligently than ever before, recognizing the judicial powers of two independent nations attempting to achieve justice in concert across borders. This certainly is the wave of the future—closer judicial contact and understanding among nations for corporate groups that often are international in nature these days.

The issues of harmonization of law will work their way into the many areas where law must be the common language of treaties, conventions, statements and declarations of a nation or groups of nations. Economic and business concepts will be needed and crucial in the communication growth to enhance common understanding of practices and procedures the law attempts to put into legal form and content. Harlan Cleveland pointed to success in many international efforts—and there would appear to be no reason for not repeating the success in many fields of joint concern—in foreign direct investment, in taxation, in regulation, and in civil law and crime. What I see going on in every field of law is translation in all domestic areas of law of the implications for international law, and vice versa, the translation for international law of all the domestic implications of concern inside a nation. The European Union is experiencing the translation process now that the United States has experienced in a different way for 220 years of federal-state development. The taxation power of states over interstate commerce took a long period to resolve peacefully through legislation and litigation in America. The supremacy clause of the Constitution of the United States helped to define our national domains and preemption areas, while the full faith and credit clause among other provisions supported strong judiciaries and legislatures of each state eventually blended into a more coherent governance scheme. The Constitution of the United States spells out this intergovernmental cooperation and mutual respect. The UN Charter does the same.

Economists like Charles Kindleberger and Stephen Hymer, lawyers like Seymour Rubin and Phillip Blumberg, international finance experts like Susan Strange and Ethan Kapstein and international business experts like Raymond Vernon and others add the deep levels of experience and support that political economy and law together could give to nations and globalizing corporations to support a regulated capitalist order that avoids the extremes David Korten pointed out in *When Corporations Rule the World*, or those mentioned by many authors in *The Case against the Global Economy*. The work of Bull, Chayes and Chayes, and Bailey and others along with newer economic insights by Edward M. Graham in *Global Corporation and National Governments* (1996) should aid in further growth of a global civil jurisprudence based upon realities of law, economics, politics and international relations in conjunction with insights from other fields. Wolfgang Reinicke, in *Global Public Policy* (1998) offered a meaningful discourse on the importance of law in general.

Chapter 9

Eternal Global Corporations: Crimes, Regulatory Harms, Sentencing, Ethics and Morals

Foreign corrupt practices illustrate the way globalizing corporations face and somewhat overcome the criminal regulatory legislation of a democratic nation—the United States. Cases of foreign corrupt practices also illustrate the lack of compatibility of actions by globalizing corporations in some nations and the questionable nature of ''when in Rome, do as the Romans do'' practices. In this chapter, the ultimate sanction of dissolution of corporations of any size is examined, both voluntary and involuntary dissolutions. Furthermore, world class chaos spurred by global banking corruption are classical cases for the growing field of global world class corruption in business. Should giant corporations be dissolved because of repeated felonious acts? Should some of the *Fortune* 500 companies be ended or are they too big to fail, as some argue? What happens on dissolution? Do assets evaporate? Does debt disappear? Do people who have jobs just vanish? What do we mean by ''dissolve'' a corporation? Is dissolution any more scary than merger or acquisition? This is a thriving field for Wall Street lawyers and investment bankers (Wasserstein, 1998). When should people exercise popular sovereignty and say to any giant corporation—enough is enough, you are finished as a corporation?

SEE NO EVIL, HEAR NO EVIL, SPEAK NO EVIL

Legend of the Three Wise Monkeys, Sacred Stable,
Nikko, Japan, seventeenth century

No greater universal reason (stress universal in reason) exists today than to stop cold the white collar crimes of globalizing corporations. Of all topics brewing today, none carries more hope of global governmental cooperation and progress than development of something like a global approach to crimes and civil harms of globalizing corporations. What is needed is a person of the prominence of President Clinton or Vice President Al Gore or Bishop Desmond Tutu of South Africa or some other independent-minded man or woman to care as much about crimes as Clinton cares about world trade or Gore cares about the environment or Tutu cares about ending all vestiges of racial apartheid in South Africa. Just as we, the world society, needed a Law of the Seas or a Biodiversity Treaty, we the people of the world need a *treaty ending corporate crime* to face straightforwardly the eternity presented by eternal global ominpresent corporations.

No one yet seems to have the political courage (except for William Greider or Ralph Nader and a few others) to step up to the plate and slug away at the problem of repeated corporate crime. So far, everyone on earth seems to have struck out when trying to stop repeated criminality of giant globalizing corporate actors; no one seems to be getting solutions right, not even the International Forum on Globalization. Maybe it is just too obvious, like the nose on your face, that this policy area is one of the keys to national control of harmful corporate actions. Excellent examples are the joint national action in 44 nations, as we have already seen, taken in order to close a corrupt bank (BCCI); or in the recent coordinated attack on money laundering in over 25 nations, which we will examine later; or in the nascent transnational organized crime field where some action is now stirring. While we have watched money laundering grow for over 20 years (a precise example of repeated corporate crime), and have removed government controls over currency in general at the same time, in an unwitting manner, a much more stringent control and norm of global intolerance for corporate corruption should be the goal. Bumbling tolerance for corporate crime is gradually losing its hold on nations.

The basic policy issue could not be clearer. Why allow any corporation to directly invest in plants, or factories or facilities, or indirectly invest in securities inside another nation if the corporation has committed *even one* felony or serious civil harm in a home or host nation or a third nation? Why allow the global spread of corporate groups with criminal records? We do try to bar pirates from international commerce—right? (Mueller and Adler, 1985). What about people bent on crime using the corporate shield to harm others in the world for their own selfish gain and greed?

Chapter 9 focuses upon the repeated felonious action committed by agents of *Fortune* 500 types of corporations with stress based upon repeated criminality involving the corporation—parent or subsidiaries. Eternality is questioned. Examples include General Electric and other companies involved in incidents that are indictable criminal actions on a wide front over the last century right up to the present. Comparisons of individual and corporate liability expose significant unjustified differences in habitual crimes. Federal sentencing guidelines for organizations are also studied.

THE POLICY ISSUE: INVESTMENT AND CRIME; KEEPING THE BAD BOYS AT HOME—SEE, HEAR AND SPEAK OF EVIL

Economics, international relations, business literature and globalizing sociology generally do not associate crime with their field's major concerns. Neither do business and international law in the private and corporate sense usually associate with criminal law concerns. Both of these propositions fit together in a conclusion that crime and business are rarely, if ever, thought of together in much of the literature. Crime is a domestic concern, not an international concern. Waters, in his 1995 study of globalization from a sociological perspective, omits a reference to crime (Waters, 1995). Dunning, a major scholar in global business studies, in his significant 1993 work on multinational corporations, pays little or no attention to business crimes (Dunning, 1993). Graham, an economist, in a very recent study of globalizing corporations, omits any meaningful reference to multinational corporate crimes (Graham, 1996). This is normal for these types of analyses, but very limiting. Corporate crime demands an open mind of all fields of study and action.

Folsom and Gordon, in their major legal work on international business transactions, refer to a single, major area of criminal activity—foreign corrupt practices—bribery. But that is about the extent of crime for those legal co-authors. This example should reinforce a basic assumed norm—when writing or talking about economics and business, purposely ignore criminal subjects, by and large. The subject of crime is just too difficult to handle for many people; and there are good reasons for that difficulty, which will be mentioned in this chapter. I characterize much of the ordinary reluctances the three wise monkey syndrome: "hear no evil, see no evil and speak no evil."

Therefore, if the experts have trouble coming to terms with reality, many readers who are not experts will find it diffcult to associate business corporations and crime—an association that has been a normal, daily and academic chore for me over the last three decades. What is second nature to me may not be to your way of thinking, and it is important to recognize this potential gulf in thinking at the beginning of this chapter, which is so heavily loaded with business crimes. It would not be much different if I were a brain surgeon and wished to discuss the details of my work with you. You may cringe at the prospect.

If you have read through the previous chapters of this book, you have seen an occasional reference to the main policy issue, but cast not in terms of crimes. If you glance ahead in this chapter, there is an overwhelming amount of evidence of corporate global crime that far transcends the word "ordinary" crime. Next, it will be pointed out how the investment issue was framed in previous chapters and then how it was related to crime which is the principal focus of this chapter. Let us look back for a quick review of the investment policy issue as it has been framed so far.

It was stressed in Chapter 5 that the central inquiry is: can 185 nations allow

750 giant corporations to invest the profits of the corporations in any way they see fit, or must public authority in every nation check, structure and confine all investment decisions by 750 giant corporations as they move about the globe? There is a lack of cross-border police to examine such decisions on investment, and a lack of regulation or criminal sanctions for most of the corporate transfers of wealth. Should there be the public policy limits over investment decisions and the types of decisions within an industry, especially the auto and jet aircraft building industries? The implications for a sovereign people in a democracy of such unilateral business investment decisions were examined.

In the context of casino capitalism in Chapter 7, the issue of control of corporate foreign direct and indirect investment was examined. The advent of pension fund shareholding of globalized corporations was explored. By what right do corporations invest the profits when owners have one view in one nation and managers in other nations have another view? When owners become large pension funds representing the life savings of millions of people, will managerial capitalism give way to the wishes of these owners, or will managers buy up stock outstanding and vote the shares as a corporate asset? Can equity control of outsider owners (common stock shareholders) be reduced to zero? Or should a company become totally private again (get out of the stock market) to avoid any potential owner interference in managerial capitalism? That is the game being played by CEOs today in many companies.

In Chapter 5 the international investment decisions we saw are free-wheeling, but inside a nation they are much more constrained. Investment into the United States is explored by non–U.S. globalizing corporations. Public policy is almost moribund here. The question is critical in foreign direct investment inside and outside of a nation. Comparative examination of investment policies of Germany, France, Britain, Japan and the United States was reviewed that pinpointed the U.S. and British laxity in regulations over investment compared with other nations—the civil jurisprudence has never developed, even though the United States is internally well prepared with more than 100 years of regulation to accomplish regulation of investment rather easily. An expansion is all that would be called for, but no doubt would be resisted by business. Next let us explore the investment issue in the context of crime.

The policy issue of cross-border investment and crime is complicated by major trends in law. John C. Coffee, Jr., is a well-recognized expert on corporations and crime in the United States. His view is that substantive U.S. federal criminal law over the last few decades has witnessed a much less clear line between civil and criminal law (Coffee, 1992). The construction of this chapter and the previous chapter was very difficult to conceive due to the waning distance between crime, regulatory offenses, civil harms and torts in a traditional sense. The use of the criminal sanction in regulatory capitalism is much greater now than 30 years ago. The implications of this are not clear. But this trend should be recognized as real in the first look at the crime—investment nexus.

Coffee points to three significant trends: (1) white collar crime in federal law is a growing, judge-made law based upon federal statutes that demand interpretation like mail and wire fraud statutes, because of the generality of the criminal proscription; (2) *mens rea*—the intent to commit a crime so critical and central to major street crime felonies like murder and robbery—is less influential in white collar crime in some areas, like those of strict liability that do not probe into actor intentions looking for a guilty mind; and (3) the upgrading of "public welfare offenses" to felony status in statutes thereby expands more strict liability with consequent expansion of criminal liability. Coffee argued against too great an expansion of criminal liability and criminal law and sanctioning since criminal law may lose its inherently blameworthy character if used too widely—people may just begin to ignore it. Vicarious liability for acts of others is growing as well. This may jeopardize individual blameworthy acts and guilt which people would associate less with white collar crime.

Corporations (as legal entities), their officers, their employees and even their subsidiary corporations in corporate groups are all liable for—reponsible for—their own criminal actions. Corporate crime was initially conceived in 1949 as white collar crime, the core root was corporate criminal responsiblity in today's world. The literature has expanded considerably since Edwin Sutherland's *White Collar Crime* book was first published in 1949 (Sutherland, 1983). The corpus of the main literature is now large and it has become recently international in nature. Sutherland's 1949 work was republished by Yale University in 1983 (Sutherland, 1983). Other early authors include: Clinard, 1990; Clinard and Yeager, 1980; Geis, 1967; Mueller, 1957; and Stone, 1975 and 1980. Very prolific is John C. Coffee, Jr. (1977, 1980, 1981, 1983, and 1992). That is a partial list of his work. Other authors and works are of more recent vintage, although some of the authors are long-standing in the field (Blankenship, 1993; Brickey, 1990; Fisse and Braithwaite, 1993; Geis, Meier and Salinger, 1995; Pearce and Snider, 1995; Pearce and Woodiwiss, 1993; Podgor, 1993; Simon and Eitzen, 1992, Spencer and Sims, 1995; Tonry and Reiss, 1993).

To enter into this body of fairly new material would sidetrack us from keeping our eye on the ball of the globalizing 750 plus corporations. Later in this chapter we shall launch our own inquiry in some of the cases. To illustrate the growing global concern over the use of corporations to commit crimes, the literature examines many aspects of crime and how this form of crime may be spreading across the globe. Furthermore, it shows the very complicated job of nations enforcing their criminal laws. Globalizing corporations have a very dark side that sometimes starts domestically and then spreads its shadow across the globe like a lunar eclipse.

LINKING INVESTMENT AND CRIME

Investment and crime are linked to one another inevitably, and eventually that tie should become a major topic of treaty-making and domestic law in nations that care enough to want to stop it. Nations that do not care will soon be marked.

The policy is this: debar any corporation of any nation from making direct or indirect investments inside a host nation if the corporation, either the parent or any of its subsidiaries, has a felony record of one or more crimes. Keep the bad boys of international commerce strictly confined to their home states so that they cannot spread crime among nations with corporate groups. This would make it easier to enforce domestic criminal law. The year 2000 would be a good date to start such a forward-looking global policy because so many globalizing corporations today have some criminal records in their past. With adequate sunshine on past corporate felony behavior, a nation could tap into an international internet corporate crime data bank and decide whether it wishes to allow investment by any corporation or individual on earth. The rule would be no more anonymity in corporate life, and no way to dissolve the records made, by any legal device such as dissolution, reincorporation, merger or acquisition. There would be no way to hide by submarining with a new corporate form.

There would be strict accountability on a global basis that could never be shed or ignored ever again through any ruse of any kind. With civil harm records displayed as well, it would be easy to see how, where and when a corporation skirts the criminal law and regulatory law in any nation where it does business. Civil harms would be clearly noted. This finally will provide everyone on earth, through the Internet, a "blacklist" of corporate criminal groups that would be banned from international investment. Dirty money owners would be marked as such for the world to see. Laundering money would be ended. The last thing the world needs in order to achieve peace is a spread of corporate groups with criminal records of felonious actions. Special attention will be needed for tax haven corporations that ought to be barred automatically from international commerce. This type of coordinated national action could seriously weaken the criminal element in business very significantly and stop its spread across the globe. The guilty would become global business pariahs or outcasts. And two nations (Japan and the United States) should take action immediately with a bilateral treaty to cover the investment practices of 300 of the 750 giant corporations.

Debarring corporations after criminality is a U.S. technique and it was used notably for brief periods of debarment in the defense industry scandals called Operation Ill Wind (Pasztor, 1995). My suggestion in this inquiry is not a brief debarment for short periods of time. The global public policy should be a *permanent* debarment forever from international direct and indirect investment for the life of the corporation and for its high-level remnants including officers and directors that may move or be sold in commerce to others who would themselves be tainted by acquiring dirty assets. Insider trader's money would be unwelcome if tainted. No corporate shuffle to avoid sanctions by dissolution, bankruptcy, merger, acquisition or makeover or takeover or spin-off could clean the funds. The aim of this proposal would be a global, permanent and perpetual attack on criminal elements in business who too often merely put on another face or disguise or who work in a different corporate legal personality. There would be a serious need to heed public labelling and public concern and obey public global policy and public laws of all nations in both domestic and international business. Nations would certainly mean business for corporate criminals with a policy of this gravity.

Let us next examine the principal corporate actors that have thrust themselves upon the world in a most aggressive manner and, by so doing, warrant special attention by everyone in the world—a careful look at the facts is most important.

GENERAL ELECTRIC: WORLD CLASS CORPORATE HABITUAL CRIMINALITY WITHOUT CROSS-BORDER POLICE

General Electric (GE) is a U.S. company at the leading edge—it is number one, two or three in many fields like medical imaging and it is a very large, conglomerate-style, aggressive globalizing corporation. The plaudits for the company are many and these will be mentioned first to give you a balanced perspective. However, the picture would not be complete without mentioning the many harms brought to life by GE—these too, are just as real. As we saw in Chapter 6, GE in Europe and China is a global investor of tens of billions of dollars of its profits. The company is a splendid example of many reasons why one would link investment and crime into an international treaty norm to prevent spreading practices of such a corporate group into new nations from its home base. But first, some good things about GE to illustrate why it exists at all and has continued to exist for a very long time in various forms.

The 1892 origin of General Electric Company gives it 107 years of existence by 1999. At its start Thomas Edison was a director—the great inventor of America. Research and development at the dawn of the age of electricity was GE's strong point because it produced a myriad of products—light bulbs, toasters and elevators, to name a few. Sales of $2.6 billion by 1952 meant GE was always one of the largest U.S. corporations in the industrial sector. As it conglomeratized itself over the years the company has bought and sold many businesses. Its record in this area includes sales of businesses in: air conditioning (1982), housewares (1984), and semiconductors (1988). It bought an investment security firm in 1990 and sold it in 1994. There is an obvious strategy of positioning itself in a dozen or more very lucrative markets in the United States and across the world. The markets are: aircraft engines, appliances, broadcasting, industrial products, materials, power generation, finance, technical products and services. It has over 30 major competitors. Table 9-1 compares GE's financial position in 1985 and 1994.

The GE 1994 sales were $49,920 million in the United States, $13,290 million in other countries or a 79/21 ratio of domestic to foreign sales (Hoover, 1996). Not surprisingly, in April of 1997, *Fortune* reported GE to be seventh largest in the *Fortune* 500 national ranking, with $70,028 million in 1996 revenues, $6,573 million in profits and with assets valued at over $228 billion. GE had 222,000 employees in the same report. By 1998, it registered number five in

Table 9-1
General Electric Financial Performance

	1985	1994
Sales ($mil)	28,285	60,109
Net Income ($mil)	2,336	4,726
Dividends/share	.55	1.49

the *Fortune* 500 by revenues of $90,840 million, profits of $8,203 million, assets of over $304 billion and earnings per share of $2.46 (*Fortune*, April 27, 1998: F-1 and F-2). Surely this is a picture of success in capitalism's terms. GE employees rose to 276,000, a 15% rise from 1996—but where on earth in the GE conglomerate's sphere they were added is hard to tell from *Fortune* data.

On December 11, 1995, *Fortune* gave warm accolades to Jack Welch, the CEO of GE for creating a $52 billion market value added to the company (Morris, 1995). Morris noted: "By 1988, he [Welch] had bought and sold scores of companies and reduced his work force by 100,000" (Morris, 1995: 90). In 1980 when Welch began as CEO there were 402,000 employees (Tichy and Sherman, 1993: 261). Thus, the Welch downsizing record exceeded that reported by Morris by a great margin. In any event, two significant books came out in 1993 praising the efforts of Jack Welch as CEO (Tichy and Sherman, 1993; Slater, 1993). That is the good side, next the bad.

In recent times, one of the studies of GE was by William Greider in his popular book *Who Will Tell the People* (1992). Major activities of GE of a bad nature involved illegal activities, unjustified political influence, and pollution. Chapter 15 of Greider's book is titled "Citizen General Electric," an obvious comparing of GE to a regular flesh and blood citizen sovereign voter of the United States. In the case of GE, Greider thought that the corporation, as with many others, had taken the place of political parties (Greider, 1992: 331), portraying themselves as "good citizens." However, in a stark manner Greider followed: "Like many other major companies, 'Citizen GE' does its every day politics despite its anomalous status as an ex-convict" (Greider, 1992: 332). What is the ex-convict status of GE? Let's look at the record.

As of 1975: "At least 67 suits have been brought against General Electric by the Antitrust Division of the Justice Department since 1911, and 180 antitrust suits were brought against General Electric by private companies in the early 1960s alone" (Woodmansee, 1975: 52; Clinard and Yeager, 1980: 59–60). Clinard reported, "In 1959, the courts convicted the company [GE] and its executives of massive price-fixing in heavy electrical equipment" (Clinard: 1990: 16). Also, Clinard listed illegal contributions in 1972 to the Nixon presidential campaign, bribery of foreign officials, and discrimination against women in violation of civil rights laws. In 1981, there was another criminal conviction for bribery of a Puerto Rican official, and in 1985 a defense contracting conviction. In 1988, other cases of false claims and involvment in toxic waste sites arose (Clinard,1990). Greider cited a 1990 criminal fraud conviction of GE and several other defense contract problems settled. Other actions involved insider trading and discrimination of various kinds. Pasztor explored Pentagon contracting scandals in 1986–1990 called ''Operation Ill Wind''—more than 190 individuals and over a dozen major corporations caught in defense contracting scandals, including GE (Pasztor, 1995). A 1992 diamond scandal arose involving price-fixing accusations and investigations (Slater, 1993: 263– 264). In 1992, the Israel scandal with top GE officials required GE to pay ''$69 million in civil and criminal penalties'' according to CEO Jack Welch (U.S. Hearings in House of Representatives, July 29, 1992).

Greider asked a simple question in 1994: How can a repeat felony offender like GE keep doing business as a citizen, when many other human citizens with a three-strikes (three felony convictions) record are out of society forever and labelled ''habitual criminal''—and then suffer permanent imprisonment for the rest of their natural human life with no probation or parole or rehabilitation? Greider asked this question in an article in *Rolling Stone* titled, ''Why the Mighty General Electric Can't Strike Out'' (April 21, 1994). There is no just answer, but unequal justice is the most obvious consequence. Rank favoritism toward giant corporations is clear from these facts. Many could fear that GE (especially its 270,000 employees) could not suffer a permanent end or disso-lution for repeat criminal acts, but that is a false form of thinking. If AT&T and ITT and others can voluntarily dissolve into new corporate beings—several— there is no reason that dissolution and split-up with new officers could not occur for other corporations involuntarily if only there were the political will and the criminal record to justify the result. We have the record in the case of some corporations.

The most worrisome part of a corporation with a record like GE is its pro-jection into nations beyond the United States with such a long and serious criminal record here repeating itself decade after decade for a century of exis-tence. Capital export controls or an absolute bar over such a corporation would seem to be a wise public policy, especially given the loose regulatory world outside of the United States into which GE is now projecting direct capital investment and indirect capital investment on a global basis. Everyone knows of transfer pricing schemes and lax law enforcement and conditions of no reg-ulation. GE presents a most distressing example of serious and irresponsible corporate actions over too long a period of time that is now being shaken loose from its home nation moorings where regulation is often strong and effective and criminal law is enforced. And this is just a single corporate example among 749 other giant companies.

Greider included these corporations as recidivists—repeaters of crime: Boeing, General Electric, Gruman, Honeywell, Hughes Aircraft, Litton Industries, Magnavox, Martin-Marietta, Mcdonnell Douglas, Northrup Raytheon, Rockwell International, Teledyne, Texas Instruments and United Technologies (Grieder, 1994: 36). There are others. The major corporations listed are *Fortune* 500 types of companies—many are globalizing corporations, and since the United States is home nation to most of them in the sense of origin and some current sales and employees, the task of governmental regulatory control is even more critical for the United States than for any other nation except Japan. Free trade with ex-convicts leading the way is a silly and changing image for the United States to present to the world. The president of the United States, sitting in a golf cart with a CEO, cannot give comfort to America's trading partners that all bodes well for the future of international commerce.

COSMOPOLITAN POLLUTERS: WORLD CLASS TRASHING

Concerns about the environment are not new. Yet only in recent years have ecological crises reached such pervasive, disruptive, and potentially disastrous levels that "suddenly the world itself has become a world issue." Thus, today's environmental problems are closely interlinked, planetary in scale, and, literally deadly serious. (Plowman, 1992 in Weiss, 1992)

Edith Brown Weiss is a former president of the American Society for International Law and a professor of International and Environmental Law—one of the global experts on cosmopolitan polluters. Pollution of major concern that crosses national borders is in air, land and water. Acid rain is an example. To her great credit, Weiss focused upon intergenerational issues in her award-winning book *In Fairness to Future Generations* (1989). This focus is most important to bring order out of self-serving business chaos.

Weiss did target her attention on corporations in their pollution activities (Weiss, 1989: 135). Briefly, the theory is worthy of review. The earth and its resources are both an investment opportunity and a trust—a planetary trust—"passed to us by our ancestors, to be enjoyed and passed on to our descendants for their use" (Weiss, 1992: 395). Both rights and responsibilities emerge from the trust (corpus of the earth) for current generations (trustees) and for future generations (beneficiaries). The idea of a trust brings order to this chaotic field and it is most important for crime, although Weiss did not draw this inference. Trustees who harm beneficiaries can be removed, and, if committing crime, can suffer the criminal sanctions for breach of trust. A trust concept would apply well to corporate officers and directors of polluting corporations. This is one element of control and law that has been particularly active in the last two decades in the environmental fields in treaties.

Aaron Sachs, in *Upholding Human Rights and Environmental Justice* offers evidence of recent physical attacks of environmental activists in Russia, Peru,

Philippines, Kenya and the United States. In Nigeria death sentences were executed for environmental resisters in November 1995. Ken Saro-Wiwa was among the more prominent killed by the Nigerian government over Shell Oil activities harmful to the Ogoni people (Soyinka, 1996). Political action ensued around the world objecting to such an atrocious action. In Siberia, Wales, Taiwan, Ecuador and Malawi, Sachs noted community-level injustices. Finally, he noted transborder pollution troubles in salt-water fisheries, CFC emissions, and thinning of the ozone layer, carbon emissions and global warming impacts. The *Multinational Monitor* in 1996 alone added stories about environmental and other problems associated with multinational corporations operating within the Dominican Republic, El Salvador, India, Kuwait, Russia, Mexico, New Guinea, Brazil, Haiti, Pakistan, Canada, South Africa, Lesotho, Zimbabwe, Burma and Indonesia. Asian timber firms set sights on the Amazon in Brazil (Friedland and Pura, 1996). The field is extremely active with conflict building across the globe in many fields—including environmental problems at the forefront.

In the face of this environmental turmoil on the globe, the laws in environmental treaties were strengthened, according to Hilary French (Brown, Flavin and French, 1996: 126–127). Decarbonization of the global economy is believed to be occuring. The U.S. Business Roundtable flatly objected to restrictions on oil, auto, energy and other businesses and it persuaded Congress to pass a sympathetic resolution in 1997 before the meeting in Kyoto in December 1997. Meanwhile, Principles of Environmental Justice were adopted on October, 27, 1991 in Washington, DC, by the First National People of Color Environmental Leadership Summit (Southwest Organizing Project, 1995: 101–103). Environmental activism is a rapidly growing political discourse in world society (Litfin, 1994; Wapner, 1996; Stone, 1993). Stone offered little hope for legal means to combat transboundary pollution (Stone, 1993: 33–70). His global view does not include criminal law solutions—instead he thinks solutions lie in calamity insurance, global trust funds, and specific healing treaties on various subjects like ozone. The Exxon Valdez oil spill and other spills on the Rhine River and elsewhere merely reinforce the transborder impacts and the need for global national accords (Burger, 1997).

International waste trade in nuclear wastes is a major problem, as are other types of waste. The United Nations, in 1992, at the first conference on the subject of control of transboundary movements of hazardous wastes and their disposal, heard from the head of the India delegation, member A. Bhattacharja. He suggested that industrial countries have been asking developing nations to do many things for the global good—to stop cutting down forests, to stop using CFCs. Now, he proposed, it is time for the developed nations to do something for the global good: keep their own waste. While this position lasted from 1992 to 1995, it was revealed that India's opposition officially to transboundary shipments of hazardous waste collapsed in 1995 from its initial opposition in 1992. Zinc in waste from Germany and the Netherlands is processed in Bhopal, India.

This may have influenced the outcome in policy. There is a certain insanity in ships at sea carrying waste that no one wants, and there have been such nautical vagabond ships with *no* home port.

GLOBAL CORPORATE CORRUPTION—WORLD CLASS FRAUD: BCCI, BARINGS BANK, CREDIT LYONNAIS, DAIWA AND SUMITOMO

As the world speeds to the twenty-first century, there seems to be no cooling of the casino capitalism of the 1980s that Susan Strange identified so well. Quite a lot of criminal corruption came to a head, so to speak, in globalizing corporations and it popped up in the United States, Britain, Singapore, Japan and France in odd ways. Those cases involved BCCI, Barings Bank, Credit Lyonnais, Daiwa and Sumitomo—all banks and one trading firm. First, there is a need to distinguish major U.S. domestic business corruption cases, since there are so many of them, in order to focus more sharply on the cases that are more global in nature. Second, it is necessary to distinguish the cases of global price-fixing, money laundering, tax evasion and transfer pricing and other transnational organized crime, which will be studied later in this chapter.

A word is needed about the sources of the five cases. As a group of cases, the five examined here are well-publicized in general media, and those journalists or reporters did a magnificent job of explaining the five cases to the public. We will draw on their work to understand what no person alone could ever hope to grasp by solitary labor, field visits, interviews and writing up notes of firsthand conversations or looking at original records. That was not done here for this book. The breadth of their research is enormous. That means the following cases are secondary in nature of sources. But, as five cases of great interest to globalizing corporations and their national citizens and leaders, they cannot be surpassed for their human interest. Multiple sources provide some rational cross-checking of publicly reported events in responsible news media and other sources. To ease reading of this chapter, most of the news references are listed in the text with the author (if stated), the news media source, date and page (if available). The sources are abbreviated: NYT (*New York Times*), WSJ (*Wall Street Journal*), WP *(Washington Post)*, and MM *(Multinational Monitor)*.

To begin and by contrast to the five cases developed later in this chapter, the following cases are mostly domestic U.S. cases and they precede the five cases in time and are not connected to them so far as I know (except for one savings and loan scandal):

United States Domestic Major Business Scandal—1980–1990s

• Bank of Boston, 1986—Money Laundering

• E. F. Hutton, 1987—Check-kiting (writing a check with insufficient funds in a round of checks and banks)

- Paul Thayer, late 1980s—Insider trading scandals
- Dennis Levine, late 1980s—Insider trading scandals
- Ivan Boesky, late 1980s—Insider trading scandals
- Michael Milken, late 1980s—Insider trading scandals (Stein, 1992)
- Drexel Burnham, late 1980s—Insider trading scandals

Savings and Loan Scandals, 1980s and Early 1990s—Financial Fraud and Mismanagement

- Charles Keating, Jr.—Criminal violations and prison time, 1980s and 1990s
- Salomon Brothers, 1991—Irregularities and rule violations in auctions of treasury securities

For our purposes these should all be "put behind us," the favorite phrase of those who are finally sentenced: "Well, I'm glad that is behind me so that I can now get on with my life." This classical expression dominates the accounts, although it is doubtful whether anything of this magnitude could be brushed aside in the public memory or in future social and business intercourse.

It is *not* true that the United States is the mother of all business scandals. At the same time, in the 1980s and early 1990s, there were business scandals in many other nations: Britain (Ernest Saunders and Guiness affair, Robert Maxwell), Ireland (Michael Smurfit), France (Triangle Corporation), Germany (Deutsche Bank official), Italy (Carlo DeBeneditti), Japan (Toshiba Corporation, Hisashi Shinto, Nomura Securities, Nikko Securities, Sumitomo Bank, Hiortomo Takai, Sagawa Kyubin) and Australia (Ian Johns, Laurie Connell, George Herscu and Alan Bond) (Vogel, 1996: 91–112). The world was a bubbling place for business people and for prosecutors bringing criminal charges and obtaining convictions and sentences for crimes in business. The United States led the world in crime business.

In reaction to this corruption, lawyers made it their business to study all related topics in business crimes with a renewed seriousness. Since 1983 there have been anti-corruption conferences in seven major cities. Transparency International, a Berlin-based organization with ties to twelve similar groups, aims to focus public attention on business corruption and bribery. Action and reaction are widespread.

But there is endless pressure to downgrade safeguards. A recent example will illustrate this problem well. Louis Lowenstein, a legal expert, cautioned investors, the leaders of American industry and of the New York Stock Exchange, not to lower the strong accounting standards required by the U.S. Securities and Exchange Commission (SEC) that allows public stock to be listed and sold on the major exchanges. Lowenstein referred to James L. Cochrane, Chief Accountant of the Exchange, who suggested that 2,000 foreign companies would be eligible to be listed on the Big Board were it not that the Securities and

Exchange Commission now requires much more financial data for those companies.

An effort is underway now to weaken such accounting standards with potentially disastrous results for simple trust in the stock market. For example, unstated liabilities of $35 billion for one corporation did not show up on the corporate books in globalizing corporations. Pension liabilities were unstated in many corporations until a 1990s funding forced their statement. Allowing loosely crafted account books of foreign corporations into the U.S. stock market could be a potentially crippling act. There are plenty of accounting shenanigans, even with good and tough U.S. accounting standards (Schilit, 1993). Not less, but more transparency and data are needed (Estes, 1996).

Recent Events

The universe of global corporate corruption is immense. Before getting to the five cases there is a need to sample some of the late 1995 and 1996 cases of actual or potential business scandal in about 20 nations. Business corruption is very widespread. China convicted and sentenced James Peng, an Australian businessman, to 18 years in prison for corruption and embezzlement and seized his $230 million business. Three former employees of a U.S. unit of a Dutch Philips Electronics NV were indicted on U.S. federal charges of conspiring to defraud by falsifying testing data for missile parts. A South Korean major industrialist, Chung Tae Soo, was charged with bribery in South Korea (WP, 11/28/95: A3). The South Korean government did convict top industrialists for various crimes in August of 1995: Kim Woo Choong, Lee Kun Hee, Choi Won Suk, Dong Ah Group, Chang Jin Ho and Chung Tae Soo (WP, Sugawara, 8/26/95).

Coopers & Lybrand in London agreed to pay $68 million to settle litigation related to its dealings with companies tied to the late Robert Maxwell—"We are pleased that the matter is behind us," said a spokesperson for the firm (WSJ, Rose, 1996: B5). An Australian mining corporation, BHP, settled in Australian courts a mining pollution case in 1996 involving a Papua New Guinea mine and massive pollution there (MM, September 1996: 5). The U.S. Justice Department is examining how Citibank in New York handled more than $100 million in funds of Raul Salinas de Gortari, the brother of former Mexican President Carlos Salinas de Gortari, who is now living in exile in Ireland (WSJ, Hays, 9/23/96: A4).

McDonnell Douglas Corporation and China were being investigated by a U.S. federal grand jury to determine whether licensed special equipment was sold to China and diverted to military use (WP, 10/31/96: A6). The ex-chief of India's program to privatize phones was arrested for possible bribery (WSJ, Jordan, 9/17/96). Ferruzzi Finanziaria of Italy settled a class action lawsuit in the United States for manipulating soybean futures in Chicago and possibly paid in settlement $21.5 million (WP, 10/14/96). Jersey (45 square miles) is in the Channel

Islands off the coast of France and is part of Britain, but Jersey is a tax haven—
no sales, wealth, gift or inheritance taxes; most investment profits are exempt
from a 20% tax, and Jersey is the best example of bank secrecy with 77 banks
having $140 billion in deposits, and it is also home to $270 billion in mutual
fund and trust assets. The British police arrested a financial trader, Robert Young
of Jersey, to face charges of concealing information and making false statements
to investors. Losses to investors in the United States were large (WSJ, Sesit,
9/17/96: A10).

A U.S. company, Continental Grain Co., and a Swiss-based affliate (63%
owned by Continental) paid $35 million to the U.S. government to settle a fraud
case involving U.S.–backed loans to help Iraq buy animal feed in 1990. The
affiliate, Arab Finagrain Agri-Business Trading Ltd. of Geneva, Switzerland,
pled guilty to conspiring to defraud the U.S. Agriculture Department of export
credit guarantees for which it was not eligible. The Swiss company will pay a
$10 million criminal fine (WP,11/26/96). Italy's Montedison was accused by
the SEC of hiding bribes on its books (WSJ, Robichaux, 11/22/96: A4). There
are too many more to recount here.

These cases just mentioned illustrate the tangled web of international commerce better than anything I know. These cases whiz by everyone, but each is
a little universe of intrigue within a globalizing corporation inside a democratic
nation trying to make an illegal dollar or two. Most obvious examples show
how foreign corporations run into very different standards that may lead to grave
civil and even criminal action against them. This is often deliberate and often
stumbling and halting and error-plagued globalization. One wonders whether the
game is even worth playing with such risks of financial and legal harm to the
players. The next five cases show in great detail how the stakes can be raised
to much higher levels.

Case No. 1—The BCCI Case

Time magazine, on July 29, 1991, called BCCI (Bank of Credit and Commerce International) ''The World's Sleaziest Bank''—just four days after it
began to be involuntarily closed by many governments. On June 22, 1991, an
audit report called ''Report on Sandstorm'' in England reported widespread
fraud and other improprieties and illegalities in BCCI's operations. By July 5,
1991, bank regulators in the United States, Britain, Luxembourg, Cayman Islands, Canada and Spain decided to close BCCI. By July 6, 1991, eighteen other
nations closed BCCI down or restricted the operations. By July 29, 1991, a total
of 44 nations shut down BCCI (Bhala, 1994). This was the equivalent in banking
to the Chernobyl fire and meltdown, or the Exxon Valdez going aground or the
Amoco Cadiz grounding or the terrible Union Carbide insecticide poisoning in
Bhopal, India in 1984. It was a major potential criminal event in world history,
as the facts later revealed.

Closure of the BCCI operations was followed in the United States on December 19, 1991 by BCCI pleading guilty to U.S. and State of New York criminal charges pertaining to secret and illegal acquisition of the First American Bank—the precise crimes were fraud, lying to the government by falsifying bank records and larceny—all rather homely charges. BCCI pled guilty to secretly acquiring National Bank of Georgia and Independence Bank of Encino, California.

What followed was precedent-shattering because the largest criminal forfeiture to 1991 was paid—$550 million by BCCI. This went to creditors and others. Then Congress passed the Foreign Bank Supervision Enhancement Act of 1991 altering drastically the rules for foreign bank entry into the United States. Like clockwork, one thing followed another, but it was a little too late for Congress. The harm had already been visited on the nations.

The newly enacted statutory controls and the Federal Reserve Bank regulatory controls included: a permit or prior approval from the Federal Reserve Bank before establishing an office of a foreign bank in the United States. The International Banking Act of 1978 regulated foreign banks, the 1991 Act enhanced the regulation. The Federal Reserve passed Regulation K to implement the statutory framework. The regulations logically covered entry requirements, deposit insurance, termination and enforcement examination and disclosure. These five areas of control are criticized by Bhala (who worked on the BCCI case) as overcontrol (Bhala, 1994). The argument has begun—do extreme cases make bad law, or do such cases make some law and real regulation where excessive laxity prevailed? Recall (in Chapter 6) that the United States is at the too-loose end of public controls.

BCCI represents, just like the Bhopal poisoning cases, a steady stream of findings. Truell and Gurwin reported that in December of 1991, liquidators from Touche Ross estimated BCCI's total liabilities at $10.64 billion and its assets at $1.6 billion. The difference of $9.48 billion vanished—one of the biggest larcenies ever committed in banking (Truell and Gurwin, 1992: 391–392). They also reported the rippling losses in Britain and other countries. The Truell-Gurwin chronology of BCCI starts in 1922 with the birth of Agha Hasan Abedi in India—the man who started BCCI. It ends on October 22, 1992—70 years later in a Luxembourg court approving claims of BCCI depositors.

An important and bizarre twist of this case included in July of 1992—a grand jury indictment of seven individuals in New York and two in Washington. Clark Clifford and Robert Altman, both very prominent Washington lawyers, were named in each place as indictees of grand juries. By 1995 almost all of these criminal proceedings against the individuals were concluded as some began to plead guilty immediately, some were eventually convicted and some were being acquitted or released. Clifford was not tried, but had major heart surgery. Altman was acquitted in 1993 of criminal charges (Frantz and McKean, 1995). Both were caught in a web of civil lawsuits in 1995 stemming from the BCCI collapse (WP, Walsh, 9/18/95: 7). Work still went on winding down this case in 1996–1997 in London, where a treasurer of BCCI was released. This case of BCCI is banking globally at its very nightmarish worst in casino capitalism. So much for borderless worlds and world class business as a model.

Case No. 2—The Barings Bank Case

From Germany, Nick Leeson, age 28, was turned over to the Singapore police, who took this British Barings Bank financial trader back to his Singapore trading world on Wednesday, November 22, 1995. On Friday, December 1, 1995, Leeson pled guilty and was convicted of fraud and forgery in the $1.4 billion collapse of the Barings Bank of England. Leeson deceived auditors and misreported to the Singapore International Monetary Exchange the trading position of his firm on February 1. On December 2, 1995, Leeson was sentenced to six and a half years to Tanah Merah prison in Changi, Singapore (Leeson, 1996; WP, 12/1/95.). Barings Bank, Leeson's former boss, is now merely a unit in acquiring ING Group NV of the Netherlands. It is no longer a 233-year-old bank of England. How could something so drastic arise from the acts of one person?

Leeson wrote a book published in 1996 that shows a long pattern of fraudulent deception of his bank—a rogue trader in the genuine sense of the word who worked mostly on his own with a little help from a few inside people, coupled with bad supervision and poor auditing. From 1993, when the fraud started, to February of 1995 when he fled Singapore to Brunei and on to Frankfurt, Germany where he finally gave himself up and was caught by authorities, Leeson must have thought the world was his oyster. "Error Account 88888" was used by Leeson in conducting the fraud and, also, used by his publisher to hype the book (WSJ, Reilly, 2/9/96: B13). The 233-year-old bank suffered so greatly it had to be sold to a Dutch bank after bearing $1.28 billion in losses caused directly by Leeson. A critical report showed only too clearly that Leeson's supervision was inadequate and numerous managers were dismissed or forced to resign in May 1995 (WSJ, Bray, 7/22/96:A8). One manager, Ronald Baker, was cleared of most charges (WSJ, Parker-Pope, 11/13/96: A-18).

The subtitle to Leeson's book read: "How I Brought Down Barings Bank and Shook the Financial World." It says something about his cocky hubris in this case, a rather dangerous attitude. In his book he admitted his wrongs and crimes and then wrote: "And then I'd come out on the other side and put it all behind me" (Leeson, 1996: 262). The famous refrain pops up again and suggests an amnesia that most white-collar criminals hope will be their glorious future. They certainly must think the rest of us have little or no memory and would not think of holding a grudge for years. Or, Leeson wrote: "I had to accept and atone for my crimes and then put them behind me" (Leeson, 1996: 262). Either way—there seems to be a belief in automatic forgiveness and redemption in this rogue trader, maybe a faint glimmering of morality.

Casino capitalism is epitomized by this case. Neither co-workers nor family, friends or wife could be proud of him as he sits in the Singapore prison. For many others harmed by the confluence of sloppy banking and rogue traders, there must be even other conclusions one could draw from this case, or other wishes one could dream.

Case No. 3—The Case of Credit Lyonnais Bank of Paris, France

As a private French bank started in 1863, Credit Lyonnais (CL) grew to a first rank size by 1929, but then was nationalized after World War II. It planned privatization in the 1990s, but remained a state-owned bank in 1996—a French government institution. CL employed 70,000 in 1993, but lost money in 1992 and 1993. It operated 4,500 offices in 80 countries. CL owns a part of Areospatiale and other banks, industrial firms, information services, hotels, and software and security firms. It is a diverse conglomerate bank. In 1992, CL took control of the stock of MGM (Metro-Goldwyn-Mayer) in the United States after the film production firm foundered. A Dutch branch of CL lent Giancarlo Parretti a sum of $1 billion to buy MGM in 1990 (*Hoover's Handbook of World Business*, 1995: 184).

David McClintick (*Fortune* 7/8/96) explored the MGM connection of Credit Lyonnais in an article titled ''Predator.'' In an unflattering and brutal exposé of Giancarlo Parretti's corrupt management of MGM, and his eventual ouster by CL, McClintick opened a fascinating inquiry into the world of state-owned globalizing corporations in democratic nations. By January 10, 1991, signals of serious trouble appeared—another $1 billion of CL loans was needed to set MGM afloat. In 1996, McClintick reported: ''Today the Parretti affair occupies a United States grand jury, two federal prosecutors, and a group of FBI and IRS agents in Los Angeles who are weighing evidence of racketeering, criminal securities fraud, tax fraud, and money laundering by Parretti and others. It is also the focus of criminal proceedings in France, Italy, Switzerland and the State of Delaware'' (McClintick, 1996: 130). There is civil litigation underway as well.

The tumultuous circumstances of this case are so convoluted and hidden from view by sealed depositions it would be well to conclude at this time that there will be more heard of this scandal that is truly global in nature. Even with what is known, it shows how vulnerable any business is to corrupt managerial influences, to dummy corporations and bribery. Some of the casts of characters in this case are in prison in Europe writing books about the case. The French government issued a warrant for the arrest of Giancarlo Parretti who was seized in 1995 by U.S. federal agents. Extradition of Parretti was on appeal in mid-1996. MGM was put up for sale and bought by its previous owner. Parretti is thought to have fled to Europe after losing a Delaware civil case.

Case No. 4—Daiwa Bank Ltd. Case

From the fall of 1995 to the fall of 1996, Daiwa Bank Ltd., a Japanese bank firm's U.S. banking operation with about $10.5 billion in U.S. assets, was barred from doing any banking business in the United States and officers of the bank were indicted for crimes. This barring action was by far the most prompt, vigorous and well-known action taken by a nation against a globalizing bank in recent times except for BCCI. Real teeth exist in the banking laws to bite hard those who flaunt the law. This case is unlike the Barings Bank case reviewed above—there was no single rogue, although that at first appeared to be the case. It is similar in some respects to the BCCI case, thus reinforcing the continued casino capitalism already noted in other cases.

On September 26, 1995, Toshihide Iguchi, an executive vice president of Daiwa Bank Ltd. in New York, was indicted for criminal fraud, arraigned and held without bail. Covering trading losses of $200,000 since 1984 appeared to be the initial problem. The total cover-up was $1.1 billion when the full amount was known. It looked like a one-person scandal at first. Daiwa's officials initally expressed "deep embarrassment" that Iguchi had not been caught by internal accounting controls and management supervision. The plot thickened because a July 1995 letter by Iguchi to the president of Daiwa Bank in Japan, Akira Fujita, confessed his errors. But both skepticism and fear of such a practice were voiced in the first public airing of the scandal (WP, Fromson and Sugawara, 9/27/95: F1). Fromson carefully analyzed the pattern of bond-trader fraud—too much freedom at work, fear of antagonizing a good trader, complexity of trades, voluntary compliance schemes, trading and record-keeping combined in a single trader's role and trades for customers and for the firm mixed in one employee's role. This is one prescription for disaster in casino capitalism—world class fraud at work in a democratic nation. But Daiwa did split Iguchi's job of trading and record-keeping, or so they said (WSJ, O'Brien and Shirouzu, 9/29/95: C-1).

By October 9, 1995, Daiwa discovered more bond trading losses of nearly $100 million in New York. Daiwa closed its 20-person downtown Manhattan office on October 9. The $100 million in losses were secretly disposed of through a dissolved "entity" (WP, Sugawara, 10/10/95: D-5). Daiwa Chairman Sumio Abekawa, in late 1995, announced his resignation, to be effective by March 1996 (WP, Sugawara, 10/10/95: D-1).

By October 19, 1995, Iguchi pled guilty in a federal court to falsifying records and selling securities owned by bank customers to hide losses, misapplying bank funds, making false entries, money laundering and conspiracy. A U.S. senator asked the chairman of the Federal Reserve Board, Alan Greenspan, to look into the matter (WP, Berry, 10/20/95:1). Everyone was getting into this growing scandal. A second criminal charge was filed October 20, 1995 (WSJ, O'Brien and Ono, 10/20/95: B-13).

Then the most significant action of all was taken by the Federal Reserve

Bank—it issued an order giving Daiwa Bank Ltd. just 90 days to close the bank and to get out of the United States (WSJ, 11/3/95: A-5). This meant that 15% of the Daiwa Bank Ltd. global operations were stopped by an order of a nation— one of the more important nations—the United States. No smoke and mirrors about borderless nations was heard on this occasion. The financial blow was one thing—the public image of Daiwa Bank was very damaged. It asked Sumitomo Bank to take over some U.S. operations. A New York senator asserted: "They know the law was being violated and they tried to sweep it under the rug" (WSJ, 11/3/95: 1). Both Japanese and U.S. bank regulators did an ineffectual job. And then Daiwa Bank itself and Mashahiro Tsuda, a Daiwa manager, were charged in a criminal indictment on November 2, 1995 (WSJ, 11/3/95: A-5), and on December 27, 1995 (WSJ, 12/28/95: C-15; NYT, 12/28/95). The legal tension was at the breaking point by this time.

U.S. Attorney Mary Jo White announced the criminal indictment making front-page headlines in the *Washington Post* on Friday, November 3, 1995— "DAIWA BANK INDICTED, BARRED FROM U.S" (WP, Blustein, 11/3/95, and 11/4/1995: A-1). The 24-count indictment was made against one of the world's largest banks—alleging a cover-up by top bank officials, secret meetings, phony transfers of money between the New York branch and Japanese headquarters. The familiar legal crimes were: mail and wire fraud, conspiracy, falsifying bank records and failing to report and concealing federal crimes. The "book" was being thrown at the bank in the criminal charges. Prosecutor White was quoted in the article as saying: "Law enforcement will not tolerate financial institutions [that] unlawfully attempt to mislead regulatory authorities and to cover up criminal misconduct by their employees." Daiwa Bank said it would fight such charges.

In Japan the Ministry of Finance took several actions to control Daiwa Bank; the bank chairman resigned and a new one was named. The details of the cover-up were explained in some depth and included an earlier use of the Cayman Islands for a "big accident" in trading—in other words, a "loss." Daiwa Bank was a $300 billion–asset bank, the fifteenth largest in Japan. The *Washington Post* editorialized on November 4, 1995: "The Daiwa case demonstrates that international cooperation in financial regulation still isn't working well enough to be reliable." (WP, 11/4/95: A-6). The Japanese began to question their own trust system in banking (WSJ, Sapsford, 11/6/95: A-21, and Sapsford and Steiner, A-21.).

Finally, Federal Reserve Board Chairman Alan Greenspan, in what was labelled as an unusual statement before a Senate Banking Committee, said: "The bottom line is that we did not succeed in unearthing Daiwa's transgressions where we might have" (WP, Blustein, 11/28/95). Transworld world class transgressions may be thought to be so sophisticated no bank regulator could ever catch on to the financial shenanigans that it is required by law and paid by the taxpayers to stop. But no high-tech mumbo-jumbo here. Something as simple as not taking a vacation to cover up fraud was under consideration as the subject of a new regulation. Iguchi did not vacation for long periods and then took off only brief days at a time. Obviously, this helped to cover up bond trades, but where was the vaunted Japanese management?

By January 21, 1996, Daiwa Bank Ltd. was expected to move for dismissal of the criminal charges against it. Iguchi had not yet been sentenced and Tsuda waited for his trial (NYT, 1/21/96). On January 29, 1996, Daiwa sold its U.S. assets to Sumitomo Bank Ltd. for $3.37 billion—ending its business in the United States—in New York, Atlanta, Baltimore, Boston, Chicago, Dallas, Houston, Los Angeles, Miami, Minneapolis, Philadelphia, Pittsburgh, St. Louis, San Francisco and Tampa. Then Masahiro Tsuda pled guilty, was convicted and sentenced to prison for two months and fined $100,000 and placed on probation for one year (WP, 10/26/96).

As if the case was becoming a complete disaster, Daiwa Bank Ltd. of Japan pled guilty to charges of covering up trading losses of $1.1 billion at its New York branch. The bank agreed to pay a fine of $340 million on February 28,1996, a few weeks before a scheduled April 15 trial date. Daiwa's new president said: "Years of future litigation would benefit no one, we accept responsibility for our actions." U.S. Attorney General Janet Reno said: "Banks doing business in the United States must abide by the rules." The $340 million fine compares favorably to the $650 million for the Drexel, Burnham and Lambert case, the $550 million fine for BCCI and the Prudential Securities $370 million sum for its transgressions. White-collar crime is certainly alive and well and so is the enforcement community, but how much is missed in world class crime is, perhaps, the greatest unknown. The bad boys were sent back home and evil was seen, heard and spoken about in very public ways, as is demonstrated by this case. The missing element is the broad and permanent debarment policy mentioned above. Daiwa could return to the United States.

A dramatic saga was the essence of the Daiwa Bank Ltd. case (WSJ, Shirouzu, 1/1/97). As an inquiry into how globalizing corporations behave in a democratic nation, the case deserves very careful attention by those who claim there is such a thing as a borderless world or that there should be such a world, and that nation-states are on the wane in the face of high technology, especially in the banking and financial area. The sovereignty of the people of the United States or any nation amounts to much more than a hill of beans in this case. Every aspect of the Daiwa Bank case reinforces the sound views of Ethan Kapstein, mentioned previously in this book, that nations are the foundation for global world order, not banks or financial traders. The former president of Citibank, Walter Wriston, should put the Daiwa Bank case in his pipe and smoke it.

The Case of Sumitomo Corporation, Trading Co.

No one knew the size of loss created by a trader in copper, the metal widely used in the world. When the story broke into public view on June 14, 1996, Yasuo Hamanaka was accused of creating $1.8 billion in losses to his employer,

Sumitomo Corporation (WP, 6/14/96; NYT, 6/14/96; WSJ, 6/14/96). But by September 20, 1996, the losses were put at $2.6 billion (WP, Sugawara, 9/20/96). Finally, by late fall of 1996, Japanese authorities indicted Hamanaka for document forgery charges (WSJ, Shirouz, and Steiner, 11/13/96: A-19). At the time of this writing the case is pending. But the parallels drawn among the cases of Barings Bank and Leeson, and Daiwa Bank and Iguchi were in wide public speculation (WSJ, Sapsford, 6/17/96: A-11). Some thought the internal corporate controls were very weak or non-existent. No one mentioned weak or lax public controls. Others saw nations being incapable of controlling the actors inside corporations with enough public regulations. Regulators in the United States, Britain and Japan began to review just what could be done and who was involved. The copper market sank in value as this case unfolded—showing too clearly that one person could influence prices in the metal merchant world. On Tuesday, May 12, 1998, the U.S. Commodities Future Trading Commission fined Japan's Sumitomo Corporation $125 million for 1995 and 1996 for illegal manipulation of copper prices (WP, Fromson, 5/12/98). The commodities world is fraught with great laxity, minimal regulation and great wealth to be earned (Copetas, 1985; WSJ, Copetas, 6/21/96). Marc Rich, a metal man in global commodities trading, made over ten billion dollars, hardly paying any taxes, according to author A. Craig Copetas. Other ventures of Rich, such as fleeing the United States in 1983 to Switzerland while under indictment, reveals a rather strange world of business (WSJ, Ignatius, 3/9/93: A-14). The role of the Swiss extradition policy was odd in this case. Intergovernmental international cooperation was a global joke. Who knows how it will be for the copper trader?

WORLD CLASS FIXED PRICES: ARCHER DANIELS MIDLAND, INC.—SUPERMARKET TO AN ODD WORLD

The case of Archer Daniels Midland, Inc. (ADM) is so tangled a web of human interaction it defies simple description as only a case of price-fixing, and the case remained open in 1999. The corporation ADM pled guilty on October 15, 1996 in a Chicago federal courtroom to illegally fixing prices of two commodities (WP, Walsh, 10/15/96). Judge Ruben Castillo said: ''This is not a good day for corporate America'' (*Business Week*, 10/28/96: 52). ADM agreed to pay $100 million to the U.S. government—a criminal fine of very notable size in itself, but not much compared with ADM profits. The chairman of ADM, Dwayne O. Andreas, had, surprisingly, not to that point been a target of criminal prosecutorial action. The Chairman's son, an executive of ADM, Michael D. Andreas and Terrance Wilson, another top manager of ADM, were notified that the government would seek an indictment against them (WSJ, Burton and Kilman, 7/16/96: A-2). It subsequently did so and they were convicted in a Chicago federal trial court on September 18, 1998.

Companies—globalizing corporations—two Japanese and one South Korean, signed plea agreements on August 27, 1996 in Chicago with the U.S. attorney. The companies admitted to conspiring with ADM to illegally rig worldwide price and sales volumes of a livestock feed additive called lysine, from June 1992 through June 1995. Lysine promotes faster growth in poultry and hogs, where it is used in the feed. Those charged were:

1. Ajinomoto Co. of Tokyo and Kanji Mimoto, then manager of feed additives. Fine: $10 million for company, $75,000 for Mimoto.

2. Kyowa Hakko Kogyo Co. of Tokyo and Masaru Yamamoto, then manager of agricultural products. Fine: $10 million for company, $50,000 for Yamamoto.

3. Sewon America Inc. of Paramus, N.J., a unit of Sewon Co. Seoul, Korea, and Jhom Su Kim, former president of Sewon America. Fine for company not available, $75,000 for Kim.

4. Cheil Jedang Ltd. of South Korea, conspiracy to fix prices, $1.25 million fine in January, 1997 as a separate case.

These officials were a part of the price-fixing conspiracy (WSJ, Burton, 8/28/96: A-3; WSJ, 1/15/97). The sentencing judge expected cooperation by these persons with the U.S. attorney in the prosecution of the ADM officials. The relationship to ADM executives of these persons was associated with meetings in Paris, France, Mexico City, Zurich, Vancouver, B.C., and it revealed a fine global texture to the case. There are unnamed co-conspirators as well. After a June 27, 1995 search of the ADM headquarters in Decatur, Illinois and the finding of much to seize, and after review of hundreds of secretly made video and audio tapes of meetings with ADM executives and others with Mark Whitacre (who made the tapes), the FBI and Justice Department group apparently needed even more evidence to proceed further to convict ADM executives.

The rolling consequences of this turmoil inside ADM resulted in many resignations, and changes in the board of directors, changes in management and leaves of absence and settling of many civil lawsuits triggered by shareholders and citric acid customers for $65 million (WSJ, Kilman, 9/30/96: A-3). One director, Brian Mulroney, former Prime Minister of Canada, had troubles of his own (Cameron, 1995). There were 28 lawsuits filed against ADM at one point in August of 1995. An acrimonious annual meeting was another result in October of 1995. But that is not all that happened.

Mark E. Whitacre is being sued by ADM for $30 million and Whitacre is suing ADM for an amount not reported (WSJ, Kilman, 9/23/96: B-12; WP, Walsh, 11/23/96). The clash of employer and whistleblowing employee is of major proportions with accusations of embezzlement, libel, broken contracts and more flying in all directions. *Fortune* featured Whitacre on its September 5, 1995 cover that headlined: "My Life As A Mole for the FBI." In that major investigative report, Ronald Henkoff of *Fortune* got Whitacre to speak on the record in a most damaging way about ADM and others and about his work with the FBI as an informant—secret, no less. What a bizarre supermarket ADM is to the world. By late 1997, Whitacre pleaded guilty to stealing $9 million from ADM (WP, Walsh, 10/11/97: A-1).

Even more fuel to the conflicts is the extremely high political prominence of Chairman Dwayne Andreas in American politics as a major campaign contributor to the Republican and Democratic Parties (WP, Carlson, 7/14/96). Corporate "pork" or welfare accusations were directed toward Andreas for ethanol by *Mother Jones* magazine and by others (Mother Jones, Carney, 7/8/96: 44–47).

As the case further unfolded, the two ADM top executives—Michael D. Andreas (son of Dwayne) and Terrance S. Wilson—took leaves of absence from the company on October 17, 1996 (WSJ, Kilman and Burton, 10/15/95: A-3; WSJ, Kilman, 10/18/96; WP, Walsh and Mintz, 10/18/96: F-1). Finally, on December 3, 1996, the U.S. government indicted Michael D. Andreas, Terrance S. Wilson and Mark E. Whitacre (the government's mole), and Kazutoski Yamada of Anjimoto Co. of Tokyo. A further plea agreement was made with Cheil Jedang Ltd. of Seoul (WP, Walsh, 12/4/96; WSJ, Kilman and Burton, 12/4/96; NYT, Eichenwold, 12/4/96). As indicated, a two-month trial in the summer of 1998 produced convictions in September of 1998 for price-fixing crimes.

Some argue that antitrust enforcement is dead. Maybe it became dead in the Nixon, Ford, Carter, Reagan and Bush years of the presidency—but not in 1996–1999. The antitrust laws in the ADM case so far reached to South Korean and Japanese companies and officials rather easily by their own plea agreements and admissions of price-fixing of a criminal nature. The laws called antitrust are intended to keep hope alive—hope that giant globalizing corporate cartels will not stamp out competition completely in the name of capitalism, free trade or predatory versions thereof. But it should be abundantly plain by this point in this chapter—global corporate corruption is rampant in some markets and ADM continues to advertise itself on PBS every evening as a supermarket to the world. The world they seem to serve is a self-serving criminal world of greed with cosmopolitan overtones. It is an odd world indeed.

FOREIGN CORRUPT PRACTICES ACT OF 1977: UNITED STATES AND GLOBAL BRIBERY IN WORLD CLASS BUSINESSES

The Foreign Corrupt Practices Act of 1977 (FCPA) aims to stop bribery (illegal payments) by American businesspeople to foreign government officials. While few cases have arisen under the 1977 law and it was amended in 1988, the FCPA remains the law today. The reason for the FCPA rests upon a history of bribery before 1977 that was certainly a dramatic epidemic and damaging to the interests of the people of the United States. We will examine that pre-1977 period. After 1977 there was a gradual small stream of cases coming to light, even in 1996. The Dotan case in 1992 involving Israel and General Electric is a particularly significant case to review. And significant global action by European and Organization of American States nations was taken in 1996 in support of the basic anti-bribery policy of the FCPA. Let's look back first.

Before 1977—Corrupt Practices in Business

A study of corporate political payments abroad revealed widespread bribery and extortion in world business. The payments were pervasive—special terms were reserved for just such payments: in the United States, pay-off; in Japan, wairo; in Germany, trinkgelt; in Italy, bustarella; in Mexico, mordida. The list is longer and goes back some time in history (Jacoby, Nehemkis and Ells, 1977: 3–44). "Grease payments" are supposed to be social lubricants to get business accomplished smoothly and swiftly. "When in Rome do as the Romans do," is the spirit of the payments. Jacoby and co-authors were convinced that American businesses must conform to local business norms to win any business—in other words, bribe to get business if that is required and permitted by local customs and law. Their proposals were elaborate, but directed more to reduction of foreign political payments by reforming governments, not businesses (Jacoby et al., 1977: 250). Jacoby examined the case of ITT in Chile in 1970, the case of United Brands in Honduras in 1974, the case of Gulf Oil in South Korea in 1973, the case of Exxon in Italy in 1975, and the case of Boeing in 1976 and Lockheed Aircraft in 1975 (Jacoby et al., 1977: 103–117). The Lockheed Aircraft case opened to public view in 1975 the payments of $22 million in bribes from 1969 to 1975. Some payments were to Prime Minister Tanaka of Japan and some to Prince Bernhard of the Netherlands. The purpose was to sell aircraft and very elaborate cover-ups were concocted to conceal such payoffs for business contracts. Large companies with 1974 gross revenues of $1 billion or more made a total of $93 million in payments of illegal or questionable nature (Jacoby et al., 1977: 120–121).

Foreign relations of America were seriously impacted by payments to Tanaka and Bernhard. Criminal prosecutions of Tanaka and others in Japan were successful, and destabilization of the Dutch government was the result of bribery there (Clinard and Yeager, 1980: 168–186). Over 450 large U.S. corporations—many in the *Fortune* 500 class, disclosed illegal payments during the late 1970s and 1980s. The total was over $1 billion in payoffs (Clinard, 1990: 121–122). Disclosure of one bribery case in Honduras resulted in the chairman and CEO of United Brands jumping to his death from the forty-fourth floor of his New York city office in 1975 (Clinard, 1990: 123). "The shock waves of these disclosures were felt by foreign government officials, corporate managment and the United States government, and public reaction to these revelations was quite strong" (Spiro, 1993: 776). The Foreign Corrupt Practices Act of 1977 was a practical, logical and politically reasonable outcome—criminalizing the illegal payment practices and requiring corporations that issue stocks and bonds with the SEC to keep accurate records of such illegal transactions. Controversy continues over the act in 1999. In 1988, amendments pushed by business clarified ambiguous provisions, but today the law remains on the books much as it was intended originally, to stop transnational corporate bribery of public officials.

The Post-1977 Era

The current attitude toward the FCPA varies from antagonistic to resigned to realistically cautious. Edward M. Graham, an economist, stated: ''U.S. business executives are particularly galled by the fact that illicit payments to foreign governments and their agents are essentially forbidden under the United States Foreign Corrupt Practices Act, whereas certain other advanced countries not only fail to forbid such payments but in some cases even allow home-country tax benefits to offset or partially offset such payments'' (Graham, 1996: 67). Being galled is being antagonistic.

Resignation to the FCPA is evident in the attitude revealed by international law experts Ralph H. Folsom and Michael W. Gordon, who stated: ''Any full repeal of the FCPA seems as unlikely as replacing the American bald eagle with the rattlesnake as a national symbol. The FCPA breathes morality. Who in Congress wants to attach his or her name to the bill which abolishes prohibiting *corrupt* payments? If it is ever abolished, it is likely to be by burying its demise in an omnibus trade bill with little discussion of its repeal'' (Folsom and Gordon, 1995: 336–337).

The cautious realism of Donald R. Cruver is most notable in his *Complying with the Foreign Corrupt Practices Act* (1994). Cruver saw the Watergate case and the Nixon era political payments linked to the eventual passage in 1977 of the FCPA. He cited bribes involving Textron Inc. in Ghana, General Tire & Rubber in Venezuela, Mexico and Algeria and Exxon Corporation in a number of countries. The criminalization by nearly unanimous vote in Congress was needed, according to Senator William Proxmire, since many thought bribery would continue, rewards were great, penalties minimal, nobody had gone to jail and only three corporations even bothered to fire their CEOs over disclosed bribery. The up-hill battle over congressional control of globalizing corporations outside of the United States through the FCPA is a significant incline that has not been overcome (Cruver, 1994: 4–5). To quote Cruver: ''Despite the obvious importance of the Act, actions under it have been brought relatively infrequently since its enactment'' (Cruver, 1994: 54).

However, even with minimal enforcement energy, Cruver suggested not becoming complacent in the illegal payments area even though things seem quiet now (Cruver, 1994: 57).

General Electric and General Dotan of Israel

The year 1992 gave a wake-up call to everyone when General Electric Company (GE) admitted that it conspired with Israeli General Dotan of their air force to create bogus bills to pay for projects that were questionable in nature. GE pled guilty to federal charges of FCPA violations and federal money laundering charges. GE agreed to pay $69 million in fines and other restitution to the U.S. government (Cruver, 1994: 56). CEO John Welch testified in hearings before the Oversight and Investigations Subcommittee of the House Energy and Commerce Committee about the case of General Dotan in Israel and a key high-level GE employee (U.S. House of Representatives, Hearings, 102nd Congress, 2nd Session, July 29, 1992).

In the Hearings before Chairman John Dingell (D-Michigan), he reviewed the $1.8 billion in foreign military loan assistance by the United States to Israel and the diversion of tens of millions of dollars of U.S. military assistance in a conspiracy with top GE corporate (former and later fired) manager Herbert Steindler. Other companies were involved in similar schemes—Dingell mentioned Pratt & Whitney, Textron and others. The illegal diversion for GE began in 1984 with $40 million. Elaborate money laundering schemes were established in Latin America, Europe and the United States to clean the dirty money. Even the Israeli government was resistant initially to U.S. probing. General Dotan of Israel was convicted and is serving a thirteen-year term as a private in an Israeli military prison. His conviction is clearly established. In July of 1992, GE pled guilty. And a whistleblower, Edward Walsh (a GE employee), informed Congress of these illegalities and received an award called *qui tam* of more than $13 million ordered by U.S. District Court Judge Carl B. Rubin of the Southern District of Ohio on December 4, 1992 (*United States v. GE*, 808 F. Supp. 580, 1992). The existence of this award says little good about GE management at any level.

The Congressional Hearings included the testimony of John F. Welch, Jr., chairman and CEO of GE. Welch was blunt: "Today I am not here to give excuses for an event I regret. There are none" (Hearings, 7/29/92: 5). Welch stated, "GE regrets what happened and accepts that liability" (Hearings, 7/29/92: 6). Since GE's employee, Steindler, injured both taxpayers and the 275,000 GE employees, Welch explained the approach taken by GE when it discovered what one of its own supervised employees was doing: GE laid out its knowledge to the Defense and Justice Departments, GE hired outside counsel to investigate the case, GE cooperated with the government and disciplined the employees (some 20 or more), GE pled the corporation guilty of the felony crimes and agreed to pay $69 million in civil and criminal penalties. Welch asserted that employees who were caught broke company policies, or ignored them or were not alert. Welch gave a strong defense of GE's good side before the committee and it clearly outweighed the bad in his view.

No one was certain how much money had been stolen by Dotan and Steindler—an estimate of $11 to $12 million was made during the hearings, out of $30 million involved that would end up in a Panamanian shell company or in foreign bank accounts in Switzerland. The reasons GE failed to catch the Dotan-Steindler theft sooner than 1990 were attributed to several factors: inadequate executive performance review, leaving a GE executive too long (15 years) in one area of business, and excessive personal friendships developing. But no one was sure of why a trusted, long-term employee failed GE. Welch said the then 275,000 GE employees were equal to a city the size of Tampa, Florida. Size alone made it difficult to ferret out individual evil. GE's size has never been so severely slammed by those who nurtured congomerate global size. Recall GE global investments in China and Eastern Europe detailed in Chapter 6—$40 billion more to watch over very carefully.

Yet in the GE and General Dotan case no one asked who was responsible for making GE ungovernable in this specific case and evil at the same time. No one took real responsibility by resigning. It still looks to me as if it was more of the artful dodging in which top management is so skilled. And everyone probably fell for the gamesmanship, or so it seemed.

Cruver listed "high-risk" countries where bribery may be a problem, although he intended no blanket condemnation. His "be careful" and be prudent because of previous history list included: Australia, Belgium, Canada, Colombia, Egypt, Germany, Greece, India, Iran, Israel, Italy, Jamaica, Japan, Kuwait, Mexico, Nepal, the Netherlands, Nigeria, Oman, Pakistan, Saudi Arabia, Spain, Surinam, Togo, Turkey, United Arab Emirates and Venezuela. One not on the list is Argentina which in 1996 became involved with IBM Argentina in an unfolding scandal of potential bribery in a computer contract including, among others, Banco de la Nacion Argentina (WSJ, Friedland, 12/1/95; WP, Escobar, 2/10/96, and 4/3/96; WSJ, Friedland, 4/3/96). An Argentine journalist was beaten outside of his home and his chest slashed 20 times with the letters I-B-M carved into his skin (WP, Reuter, 8/1/96: A-20). IBM Argentina was accused of scandals in the April 30 indictment of 30 former IBM officials.

Some nations are now giving evidence of coming around to the U.S. viewpoint on bribery after 20 years of waffling around. A welcome first in a multilateral effort (26 nations—major and industrialized) sought to eliminate tax deductibility of bribery payments as a normal business expense. On April 11, 1996, the Organization for Economic Co-operation and Development (OECD) took such a position. The OECD in Paris, France recommended that member countries disallow tax deductibility of bribes to foreign public officials, treating bribes as illegal.

On April 15, 1996, the Organization of American States adopted an Inter-American Convention Against Corruption signed in Caracas, Venezuela on March 29, 1996. The Convention defines transnational bribery and requires OAS members to prohibit and punish it. Other acts of corruption are proscribed as well. Not invoking bank secrecy by member states when investigation is underway was a part of the agreement. This is a second major multilateral effort underway in Europe and North and South America. Furthermore, Robert S. Leiken believed that top U.S. officials want the G-7 nations to criminalize transnational bribery—to make something like the U.S. Foreign Corrupt Practices Act of 1977 a more universal requirement among such nations (WP, Leiken, 4/16/96: A-15). Nations have come a long way since 1977; whether globalizing corporations have moved their morals upward remains the key question.

Vogel wondered why the United States is faced with heavier oversight of business compared with Europe or Japan. Public interest in business misconduct is very intense and lingering in the United States. He claimed that in the last fifteen years more U.S. businesspeople have been jailed or fined "than in all other capitalist nations combined" (Vogel, 1996: 103). Vogel sees Americans wanting home nation control for foreign subsidiaries of U.S. multinationals and the standards to follow abroad are U.S. standards. At least in the Foreign Corrupt Practices Act of 1977, the U.S. standards were the highest globally—criminalizing illegal bribery payments—no more "payoffs" by American business to governments inside the U.S. or in any other nations where United States corporations operate. This bold American action in 1977 and persistent insistence that it is right has had a demonstrably good influence on the OECD and the OAS in their actions.

The FCPA is woven into educational programs for lawyers and new materials are being developed. Jeffrey P. Bialos and Gregory Husisian authored *The Foreign Corrupt Practices Act: Coping with Corruption in Transitional Economies* in 1997. They concluded: "Hence, we believe that now is the time for the United States to enhance, rather than slacken, its efforts to end illicit payments in international business" (Bialos and Husisian, 1997: 170). The argument of this entire chapter and book is in agreement with that point of view.

HEAVENS ON EARTH: TRANSFER PRICING, TAX HAVENS AND MONEY LAUNDERING—CLEANING DIRTY MONEY AND EVADING TAXES

Transfer pricing and tax havens are different sides of the same coin (WP, Farhi, 12/7/97). Transfer pricing is a polite accounting terminology to say we are avoiding and evading taxes—escaping from taxes and reducing tax liability to governments. Globalizing corporations working inside 120 nations find the transfer policy technique alluring. Tax havens are nations that like to hide the ill-gotten gains of criminals from the eyes of other nations—a place to squirrel away the financial nuts acquired, especially those acquisitions of assets that result from tax manipulations and crime. The basic question is: Who needs such business or such nations?

Hot money from illegal drug sales is perhaps the largest flow of dirty money on earth—the cash is not useful until washed or laundered as to its source so that it may once again be used in legitimate commerce. Drug money, insurance scam money and other sources of tax or contractual evading money (people on the verge of divorce hiding assets) is hot money. Estimates of the underground economy to support hot money are in the multibillion-dollar range. Anonymously owned corporations set up in the British Virgin Islands, for example, are one of the many tools used to launder money as we just saw in the Dotan case. There the bribery money needed cleansing. Secret bank accounts and even some credit card systems are designed to support laundering. The tools combine to fit together into a pattern of criminal fraud.

Transfer Pricing

On November 25, 1996, the *Wall Street Journal* reported that "Japan's Tax Man Leans on Foreign Firms—Coke, Goodyear Charged with Moving Profit Abroad." Robert Steiner reported that Japan's National Tax Administration enhanced its search for tax revenues by examining the Japanese subsidiaries of non-Japanese multinational corporations. Specifically, the Japanese tax authorities were looking for "transfer-pricing" which Steiner artfully described as an accounting trick in which a company in Japan will artificially depress its Japanese profits in its subsidiary corporation and then move the profits to the books of some home-country parent corporation or some other entity such as a trust in a tax haven outside of Japan with no taxes or much lower taxes (see also WP, Blustein, 3/26/94).

Some 50 corporations—foreign to Japan as of June 30, 1996—were facing allegations of unfair transfer pricing and Japan wanted $492.4 million in back taxes from the 50 companies. In the previous eight years only 80 cases were filed. The Japanese tax authorities tripled their auditing teams in 1993. In 1994, Coca-Cola of Japan was hit with a $140 million tax claim in Japan. Other companies included Goodyear Tire & Rubber Co., Procter & Gamble Co. and Roche Holding AG. One could speculate that a collapsed real estate market, depressed stock market and banks with losses and in trouble in Japan forced tax authorities to search for other sources of revenue. This could be true anywhere on earth when governments run short of tax resources.

Experts on transfer pricing call it intracorporate transfer pricing between members of a corporate family group—a parent and subsidiary corporations. The transfers are raw materials, finished and semifinished goods, allocations of fixed costs, loans, fees, royalties for use of trademarks, copyrights and patents and other items (Radebaugh and Gray, 1993: 492). Prices are based on production costs in theory, but reality is that transfer pricing systems vary across the world based on cost or market price, inflation and other factors. "To be sure, transfer pricing is a matter of great concern to governments" (Radebaugh and Gray, 1993: 498). The U.S. tax code Section 482 refers to "arm's length" prices as a formula. Blumberg finds this tax provision suitable for corporate groups (Blumberg, 1993: 112).

The global taxation of business is a major subject of concern among nations. Sol Picciotto, an expert on taxes, devoted considerable effort to exploring the "transfer pricing problem" (Picciotto, 1992: 171–229). Problems involving Citibank were analyzed (Picciotto, 1992: 206–207). Vito Tanzi showed that a parent corporation in nation A can set up a subsidiary corporation in nation B with loans either from a low-tax nation C source or another tax haven source (with no taxes) as a source of capital. Tanzi said that the parent corporation in home country A can watch as its subsidiary corporation in nation B will show lower profits as it repays the loan. Loan proceeds would show up in the tax haven nation C where taxes are zero. This is a classical case called "thin capitalization" (Tanzi, 1995: 100–101). "The manipulation of transfer prices has become a major concern of international taxation" (Tanzi, 1995: 100). And developments in transfer pricing are pushing the OECD and the United States toward conflict (Elliott, 1995). Runaway manufacturing plants from the United States are, it is claimed by some, encouraged by U.S. tax policies of deferral and foreign tax credits (Secor, 1992). Further conflicts are emerging with blocked foreign income that reduces a U.S. parent's U.S. corporate taxes (Davlin, 1994).

In 1992, James D. Harmon, Jr., asserted that Japanese cartels, or keiretsus, as they are called, illegally developed transfer pricing policies that cost American taxpayers billions of dollars in lost tax revenue and at the same time placed American domestic business at a significant competitive disadvantage. Labelled "predatory trade practices"—transfer pricing was a possible candidate for the federal act called RICO or Racketeering Influenced and Corrupt Organizations Act to combat the obvious tax evasion that results (Harmon, 1992). Harmon noted the extensive underreporting of income by foreign corporations in the United States by a range of as much as $4.4 billion to $16.5 billion in 1987, almost a decade ago (Harmon, 1992: 10). One foreign-owned company sold more than $3.5 billion in goods in the United States, had gross profits of almost $600 million and paid only *$500.00* in federal income taxes during that ten-year period. The U.S. international trade deficit obviously partly reflects these obscene practices of ''free trade.''

Hearings held on March 23, 1993 before the Committee on Governmental Affairs of the United States Senate, 103rd Congress, 1st Session, showed a breakdown of U.S. Internal Revenue Service tax enforcement toward multinational corporations. The Senate Committee found substantial revenue losses, excessive litigation and unfair burdens placed on individual and smaller domestic businesses in the United States. This involves foreign subsidiaries in the United States of parent corporations of other nations—not paying taxes fairly in the United States. The host nation (in this case the United States) gets taken by its guests who steal a lot more than hotel towels. This unsavory business cuts across every nation that hosts globalizing corporations who design their tax lives to fail to pay their way in the world. The attitude of such companies is predatory and they should be kept at home (see U.S. General Accounting Office, 1995 [April and July]).

Finally, as if this dismal thieving picture is not too sordid to behold, there is a final touch that hurts just as much. If one adds the lower tax bill of American corporations in the United States over the last two decades, there may be great problems of getting any ''voluntary'' tax compliance from the ordinary taxpayer who sees the tax base walking and leaving him holding the bag (Barlett and Steele, 1994: 137–173). Table 9-2 is a listing by Barlett and Steele of the tax bills (1990–1992) where American companies pay more in foreign taxes overseas than in the United States.

Table 9-2
Comparison of Taxes Paid by American Companies

Company	Foreign Taxes (in millions of $)	U.S. Taxes (in millions of $)
American Home Products	675	545
Black & Decker	15	6
Citicorp	1,400	214
Coca-Cola	1,700	784
Exxon	6,900	2,100
Ford	1,300	876
Gillette	456	339
Johnson & Johnson	1,200	483
United Technologies	789	530

Source: Barlett and Steele (1994): 180–182.

Tax Havens and Money Laundering

The other part of the coin of the realm is nations that actively entice criminal actors to place their stolen money, drug money and fraudulently obtained money and tax evading money in the banks of the nations—to clean up the money. As long ago as February 1983 there was an important Staff Study of *Crime and Secrecy: The Use of Offshore Banks and Companies* that was made by the Permanent Subcommittee on Investigations of the Committee on Governmental Affairs of the United States Senate (U.S. Senate Staff Study, 1983). A decade and a half ago this study broadly opened the door to global criminality. By 1983 it was clear to probing congressional staff that crime which exploits offshore tax haven banks, trusts and corporations was extensive and growing. The shield of operations outside the territory of the United States prevented detection of crime, stopped investigation of crime and blocked prosecution of crime. The collection of tax revenues was stifled by the underground untaxed economy which was estimated in 1983 to range from $100 billion to $300 billion. The foreign commerce sector was thought to be $9 billion to $40 billion. Nine major federal agencies were then concerned and the State Department was not even mentioned as an enforcer. The principal tax havens in 1983 were the nations of Antigua, Bahamas, Bermuda, Monserrat, Panama, Switzerland, Cayman Islands, and other nations had bank blocking laws such as Austria, Costa Rica, El Salvador, Dominican Republic, France, Germany, Hong Kong, Lichtenstein, Luxemburg, Netherlands Antilles, South Africa and the United Kingdom.

Within the decade preceding September of 1992, the National Institute of Justice (NIJ), a research arm of the U.S. Justice Department, reported on research and investigation of international money laundering. The BCCI case mentioned earlier in this chapter was just breaking open with some money laundering convictions. If other crimes were added—bribery, fraud, securities manipulation, tax evasion and others, the estimate of such crimes rose to $300 billion a year. In 1991, the FBI joined the NIJ with eighteen nations to study money laundering. The Money Laundering Control Act of 1986 created the crime of money laundering. The Bank Secrecy Act of 1970 was used previously. The Anti-Drug Abuse Act of 1986 and the RICO statute added further strength to the field. The Money Laundering Prosecution Improvement Act of 1988 helped the Treasury Department in its tasks.

Other important steps to expose tax havens have arisen in recent years and these need to be taken into account. Swiss code changes in August of 1990 related to money laundering and reduced secrecy. Mutual legal assistance treaties (MLATs) were developed to foster bilateral and multilateral investigations (Nadelmann, 1993: 313–396). Internationalization of law enforcement was rapidly underway in this decade of the 1990s. The emerging transformation of U.S. foreign policy and U.S. criminal justice agencies was becoming deeply entangled. The UN Convention Against Illicit Traffic in Narcotic Drugs and Psychotropic Substances was ratified by 100 nations by 1995. The convention requires extradition of money launderers. G-7 action, OAS action and other multilateral approaches arose. Extradition treaties were expanded. A review of extensive global developments by Bruce Zagaris is well summarized in an analysis of an international anti–money laundering regime as it is called (Atkins, 1995: 127–218; Shelley, 1998). While somewhat slower than globalizing corporations to adjust to newer conditions, the nations are doing quite well in their new search for improved global law and order under more intergovernmental cooperation than ever, and this bodes well for the future (U.S. General Accounting Office, May 1996).

PURE EVIL: TRANSNATIONAL ORGANIZED CRIME

On October 22, 1995, President Clinton announced a Presidential Decision Directive (Number 42): United States Initiative Against Organized Crime. The pure evil toward which PDD 42 was directed was terrorists, narcotic traffickers and other international criminals. The concern included smuggling of aliens, nuclear materials and weapons of mass destruction such as some biological agents. President Clinton's directive aims to foster a global response, eliminate sanctuaries and creatively and aggressively combat international organized crime. Five initiatives in the directive included: money laundering initiatives, no trade with front companies, increased international assistance, enhanced U.S. legislation and development of international statements and declarations of common purpose for nations. President Clinton expanded the effort further in May

1996 with more initiatives. The purpose for mentioning PDD 42 here is not obvious and should be explained.

The borderline between legitimate and illegitimate is never very clean, neat and orderly. As mentioned previously in this chapter, the middle ground between criminal and civil law is growing blurred (Mann, 1992; Coffee, 1992). Some want to shrink the criminal law, others want to segregate a new civil sanction into a clear category. Still others hope to expand and criminalize more of human activity without much in the way of principled limitation on government power in a democracy with a constitution of limited-delegated powers to people's representatives. The new sweep of asset forfeiture laws in both civil and criminal law is caught in the blurred area. As internationalization of criminal agencies and sanctions grows, there is no corresponding U.S. constitutional limit to hold other governments strictly accountable to the people in various nations. Unprincipled and unlimited crime fighting tears at constitutional order and is more like war than civilization. This condition creates real fears for societal stability at the end of the cold war.

Business corporations conducting international operations that blend more and more into international money laundering zones will run into the growing anti–money laundering regime now being developed by nations to combat criminal money laundering. As successful criminal money launderers use illegal proceeds to buy legitmate businesses, the line gets even fuzzier between legitmate and illegitimate. The potential conflict here is filled with disaster for legitimate businesses that cannot account for assets in their possession or control due to some accounting error, some rogue employee or a failure to keep records. The pure evil of transnational organized crime may mistakenly overwhelm and sweep away some legitimate businesses and even some smaller nations in the future as the worldwide war against business crimes and transnational organized crime brush into one another (Shelley, 1995, 1996, 1997, 1998; Kerry, 1997; Elliott, 1997; Reinicke, 1998: 135–172).

CORPORATE CRIMINAL RESPONSIBILITY: ENTERPRISE CRIMINAL LIABILITY, RICO AND U.S. FEDERAL SENTENCING CORPORATE GUIDELINES AND COMPLIANCE PROGRAMS

A U.S. revolution is now underway in the sanctioning of corporations as organizations. Officers and employees of corporations are subject to traditional criminal and civil sanctioning separate from the corporation as a legal entity with assets and a legal life of its own. Now there are both a people-centered sanction system and a corporation-centered sanctioning system running side by side. Now there is a corporate body to hurt and kick, and a soul to torture in damnation of public hell of the organization itself. This potential national impact on 150 giant globalizing U.S. corporations and foreign visitors is already having a substantial impact in development of what are called compliance programs that may well be globally corporatewide, that is, global in nature to match the corporate spread in the world. And alliances, joint ventures and other organized approaches to doing international business will be affected. Foreign corporations doing business in America are clearly affected. Just as rapid internationalization of law enforcement was spelled out above, the same process is at work here in corporate criminal sentencing.

By way of background, it should be clear that the Corporate Sentencing Guidelines were finally effective on November 1, 1991. The politics of corporate punishment were great, and few outside of big business were effective in voicing concerns (Miller, 1992). The guidelines are new in concept and the emphasis is toward corporations as organizations. The guidelines provide for fines, probation for the organization and restitution. So new are these guidelines the effect is still to be seen, but guidelines apply only to organizations and not the people (officers and employees) in the companies who are governed by other parts of the federal sentencing guidelines. The topics for organizations are: restitution, remedial orders, community service, victim notices, special fining practices for corporations, disgorgement provisions and other topics (Podgor, 1993). The main point to focus upon here is the mitigation of criminal liability and fines by corporate adoption of compliance programs (Spencer and Sims, 1995).

The compliance programs have generated a lot of interest because they indicate how corporate assets may be protected to some extent from the solitary or ''rogue'' employee like Nick Leeson whose work wrecking a 233-year-old bank revealed few accomplices. This case differs from the Daiwa Bank and the Dotan cases reviewed above in this chapter. Corporations argue endlessly that they cannot control all of their employees and should not be held to criminal liability exposure of corporate assets from fines generated by a rule-breaking employee who commits a felony at work while being employed by a corporation. Always the aim is to protect corporate assets from liability exposures (LoPucki, 1996). Differences of opinion among courts as to the use of compliance programs exist, but their value is worth arguing (Huff, 1996; Wray, 1992; Walsh and Pyrich, 1995).

The acronym RICO stands for Racketeering Influenced and Corrupt Organizations Act which was passed as a part of the Omnibus Crime Control Act of 1970. It was directed toward disabling the criminal organization through forfeiture of assets gained by dirty money, allowing civil enforcement and treble damages and allowing the costs of the lawsuit to be awarded. While initially directed toward labor rackets and organized crime, prosecutors found the law to be an effective weapon against white-collar crime (Brickey, 1990: 353). Enterprises with criminal flavoring in their makeup may find themselves under governmental attack because of investments of a dubious nature from criminal elements. The RICO statute enlarged the potential criminal liability of U.S. corporations and all of their subsidiaries around the world. The same is true for U.S. subsidiary corporations of foreign parents—some parents of whom appear in the appendix to this book. The universe is expanding here. The tools exist for prosecutors to ferret out criminals in domestic and international venues. The corporate shield is of little or no protection for the assets of the corporation and personal criminal liability may result as well. The world is changing rapidly toward expansion of criminal liability no matter how hard the various Business Roundtables of the world would like to squelch such legal responsibility. Their success to date in the United States is minimal.

THE CORPORATE SHUFFLE: DANCING INTO DISSOLUTIONS, MERGERS, ACQUISITIONS, BREAK-UPS, TAKEOVERS AND BANKRUPTCIES—GAMES OF ETERNAL PERPETUITY

The game played by corporate executives is to avoid civil and criminal liability to the extent legally possible. It could mean even a disappearing act. Domestic corporations inside a nation are stuck with that legal system. But, domestic corporations with a large number of foreign subsidiaries in corporate form are particularly well-suited to shift liquid assets around the globe. The games played are enormously complex, especially to outsiders to the company. Mergers and acquisitions are billion-dollar activities on paper making no product or service except fees to the transaction insiders. Corporations break up into smaller units. Sick corporations like Pan Am or Eastern Airlines or Mansville or Robins seek the sheltering arms of the federal bankruptcy courts to protect assets. But rarely does a corporation face an attorney general of a state armed with an order to dissolve the corporation for cause—usually because it is a criminal enterprise of some kind. The activities of corporate transformations are in the tens of thousands every year, and year after year. Who keeps up with this corporate shuffle and games? Few people even try, but creditors must. As a consequence, the anonymous corporations become even less understandable and even more remote from the ordinary citizen, regardless of the warm and fuzzy advertising cloak many large corporations use to conceal themselves.

The relevancy of these observations is this. As corporations in large international families haunt the earth—and as they constantly transform themselves as legal entities, as holders of corporate assets or corporate debt, and as their employees and officers change—those persons who are criminally and civilly harmed and affected by corporate actions are placed into a very difficult position of seeking justice inside their own nations and inside other nations. Years may be required to sort out an international bankruptcy or a transnational tort or resolve other matters such as airline crashes or oil spills or other toxic waste. The bewildering legal world for the ordinary citizen and even for the legal expert is a formidable real barrier to justice. It is too bad that was and is the intent behind such designed confusion. Evasion has a very dark side in corporate form. ''Catch me if you can'' is the attitude of the criminal mind in corporate crimes. Floutingly arrogant is one way to describe the corporate shuffle of evasion.

CORPORATE GLOBAL VISION: NO EVIL IS BEHIND US

No memory is the best memory for all customers who may think or recall that your corporation is crooked. Recall how desperately President Nixon painfully insisted that he was not a crook. Corporations insist that they are not crooks in the same sense. Recall, also, in this chapter how it was stressed repeatedly that those in business who are caught and convicted of serious crimes wanted just as desperately to *"to get it behind them."* Fixation on this attitude reveals a universal complusion to "rub out that damn spot," a clear denial of responsibility and a denial of evil attitudes and actions and emotions and intentions. After decades of observing white-collar criminals in action and seeing them led off to prison, or paying a fine or sanctioned in some other way—I see that the denial just never ends. There are significant examples every month. Civil sanctioning now carries with it the journalist's mantra—"And the corporation denies any wrongdoing even though it has just paid horrendous civil fines and jumped through other legal hoops." A corporation may deny being a convicted felon, an ex-con, as Greider put it. Those who work for the corporation cannot easily stand the constant embarassment, humiliation and shame, so denial must be a way out of such tension. But in some cases the shame is so terrible and widespread—the disappearing act of merger, acquisition or even dissolution may exist by necessity. The perfect example was E. F. Hutton, an old Wall Street premier brokerage house that was caught in a massive fraud, criminal in nature. "When E. F. Hutton talks . . . people listen." This ad campaign was driven home to the public on television. Check kiting is a crime (insufficient funds in an account) and everyone listened as E. F. Hutton admitted to doing it (Stevens, 1989: 170). After decades of success, E. F. Hutton & Co. bit the dust in May of 1985. It picked itself up until October 1987 when the market crashed and further weakened the firm. After eight decades E. F. Hutton was sold: "The firm that Edward F. Hutton had founded eighty-three years before would be sold for $960 million" (Stevens, 1989: 291). Shearson bought E. F. Hutton and in a month 4,800 employees were discharged. Presumably for their gifted oversight, directors got a golden parachute (Stevens, 1989: 295). Thousands of dollars were involved in parachutes. The evil was behind the corporation forever—it was gone to the place where dead corporations go. The people scattered to the four winds in the aftermath of evil or were absorbed into another firm.

Ethics and morals are interesting subjects of the business world, although decidedly of an extremely minor nature. Given the record reviewed above in this chapter, no ethics institutes, or preaching, or codes of behavior, or training seminars could do much to overcome an autocratic and downsizing management that insists on strict performance to arbitrary standards or goals at any cost. This was described as being Dunlaped or neutroned. The organization climate could become a breeding hot house of crimes to accomplish corporate goals. Given the new international forums for escape, the globalizing corporation can often escape responsibility. So, too, managers survive.

Edwin Sutherland argued for the ancient idea, "As ye sow, so shall ye reap." The autocratic corporate empires reaped exactly what they sowed in the last 30 years. The problems of ethics and morals in business are studied (Elfstrom, 1991; Haslett, 1994). The basic persistent question is whether anyone in management in any country is at all serious about seeing corporate evil, hearing about corporate evil and speaking about corporate evil (Wells, 1993: 149; Küng, 1998). It is citizens of nations that must care and their governments in the nation-states must care as well, for they represent the people who will not stand for corporate crimes. Commercial corruption is now of threatening size and scope— an epidemic of global proportions (Leiken, 1996–97; WSJ, 1/2/97).

Part IV

Future Corporate Investments: Twenty-First-Century Risks

Future Relations of Globalizing Corporations Inside Democratic Nations

NEW WORLD ORDERS: 2000 TO 2100 OF GLOBAL POPULAR SOVEREIGNTY

Chapter 10 advances the inquiry into globalizing corporations inside democratic nations in several major ways. Are nations ready for one world? Will environmental justice and labor concerns be considered important enough to be put on the agenda? Do free traders have different views from those who question the importance of free trade? Will nations be able to keep up with the changes? What should nations consider to be important to control international commerce? Finally, who should be making investment choices—just business or should nations and their citizens become deeply involved in the many choices affecting the public interest? Consider Cuba where there are limits of commercial engagement—''Cuba's defaulted debt offers a prime example of shortsighted and greedy capitalism at work'' (Werlau, 1997: 66).

The surge of investment on a global basis is remarkable: ''Multinational corporations, led by the United States and Britain, ventured into the developing world last year with a record $129 billion spending stretching from Latin America to China'' (WSJ, Bleakley, 9/22/97: B18B). The United Nations, in its *World Investment Report 1997* released in September of 1997, offered data about 1996 and the data shows more great expansion just as it has for years since the 1995 report. The big investments in Middle Eastern oil fields in the 1980s and the direction of investment toward the developed world later on are different from the 1996 investments. China attracted $42.3 billion, the second most attractive behind the $85 billion into the United States. That truly is news. But just as important are the major U.S. companies acquired by foreign companies—seven of the ten largest were U.S. corporations. In 1997, U.S. acquisitions of foreign companies showed $56 billion invested in 1,067 companies. This level is high compared to $65 billion in 1995 and $53 billion in 1996. Wal-Mart Stores Inc. bought a Canadian chain in prior years and in 1996 bought a $1.2 billion stake in a Mexican retailer, Cifra SA. It is globalizing as it sees fit. Hochst AG, chemical giant of Germany, thinks of itself as a non-national company, according to its chairman, Juergen Dormann, and it creates few German jobs and downsizes there and upsizes elsewhere (WSJ, Steinmetz and Marshall, 2/18/97).

Another way to see what is at stake is to note the 23% rise in profits of the *Fortune* 500 in 1996, from $244 billion to $301 billion in 1995. In 1997, *Fortune* 500 corporations generated profits of over $324 billion. Only 150 of the *Fortune* 500 were big enough in 1996 to be considered global giants, but these firms generated $202 billion or 66% of the $301 billion profit record. That left 450 firms to produce 34%. The profits are after taxes, and after extraordinary credits or charges if they appear on the corporate income statement (*Fortune*, 4/28/97: F-21; Henkoff, 1995: 193). There are another 184 nations and another 600 giant globalizing corporations in them to be added to the U.S. total of profit. Capitalists have much work cut out for themselves to successfully place all of this hard-earned profit so that it multiplies. Some observers, such as Jessica T. Mathews, still write: "Unhindered by ideology, private capital flows to where it is best treated and thus can do the most good" (Mathews, 1997: 63). This fallacy of non-ideological capital ignores the ideology of capitalism itself (WSJ, Lehner, 9/18/97).

Looking Back Briefly

What has been learned from the previous chapters? Looking back briefly, here is what was intended. Chapters 1 to 4 invited one to focus upon giant corporations, not all of them. The very largest economic organizations, it turns out, are genuine political organizations as well. The foreign and domestic corporate invasion of Washington, D.C. threatens the sovereignty of the people of the United States. A very serious imbalance now exists and it must be addressed by the people in a political way. There is a great need to find a Western nation-state perspective in self-governance, not corporate interference.

The empirical reality described in Appendices A and B of giant corporations reveals only part of the truth for many reasons stated there. The intentional disguise or submarining must be addressed while aiming one's attention on the key set of issues—those related to investment and control of its direction of flow.

Chapter 4 shows just how political the economic organizations called globalizing corporations have become in the United States in the last 25 years. The rise of the BRT, the Business Roundtable, is the best example one could hope to know more completely. A new way of managing the business–government relationship creates uneasiness or tension that just cannot be imaged away by public relations firms. The sovereignty of the people will not disappear by calling citizens stakeholders or customers. The big money corruption aimed to capture the federal government is deeply unsettling and international trade fights are symptomatic of grave unease, reflected as well in William Greider's important book: *Who Will Tell The People?*

Chapter 6 challenges traditional thinking about trade, and what should be traded to create self-sufficient independent people who can take care of themselves. A pattern of extremes in trade outlook is explored—all with a view to encouraging citizens of all nations to get more active in thinking through what kind of trade makes sense in the long run.

Chapter 7 is focused upon a single message: labor's problems are global in nature if globalizing corporations feel free to do anything they wish with labor's time and energy and goodwill on a global basis. Labor cannot be suboptimized to a nation's boundaries on any fair and just rationale while management is acting globally and customers are free to buy globally. The lowest global labor standards are likely to result from this type of policy myopia. We are beyond labor exploitation in moral stature in 100 years of labor law development in the United States and Europe, and this must now become a global standard to protect men, women and children from predatory capitalism that was crushed in the twentieth century, but not completely crushed, as we see sweatshops from Asia and Mexico creeping into the workplaces of the United States. Regulatory capitalism is the goal for control of globalizing corporations everywhere on earth. A nation like Russia is seeking its own form of regulatory capitalism, not a kleptocracy (stealing public assets for private gain).

Then in Chapter 8 the theme of law is central—law for the multinational corporations that suits the needs of 185 nations to control actors in corporations. The civil jurisprudence needs revitalization so that cases like the Bhopal poisoning are handled much more intelligently with justice. Transborder torts and corporate identity and taxation need a major overhauling to meet the needs of the sovereign people in all of the nations. And Chapter 9 shows just how bad casino capitalism has been with crime and corruption haunting the globe through money laundering, tax evasion and cheating run rampant, goofy transfer pricing schemes, bribery of governmental officials, price fixing, monopolization, cartelism, fraud and habitual corporate criminality. Stopping this dirty money and dark side of the globalization process is no job for corporations alone; it demands that the people and their governmental representatives step in boldly to bring the snowballing mess to an end (Kerry, 1997). The corporate malefactors must be confined to prisons and to their home nations and not be allowed to export their criminal and civil harms on a global basis. The alternative is deepening corruption and malaise in democracy that could be pushed aside for more tyrannical governments. Nations must work together in every way possible to stop crime.

Those who flack for multinational corporations see a happy picture and good old days and being on top of world. This nonsense is not justified based on the facts outlined in the previous chapters, nor is it justified when the lives of 4.5

240   Future Corporate Investments

billion human beings outside the "happy" world are considered just as important as those lives inside that world (Sakamoto, 1997: 475–502 [Richard Falk]).
Yes, it is true that 1 billion people are much happier than those who lie outside
the blessed part of the globe; the 4.5 billion in the Asian, African and Indian
parts of the globe do not share in the prosperity and health and wealth (Hartmann, 1998). This state of world affairs calls for moral and ethical judgments
that transcend the commercial world. And settling international investment disputes is rarely just a domestic issue (Brewer, 1995; 660; Geist, 1995).

Ready for One World?

Are we ready for one commercial world? To use a version of my favorite
author, William Greider's title of his significant book in 1997 as a launching
pad for focused inquiry, my answer is no. We, as a world society, are not yet
ready for one commercial or business or trade world or finance world or manufacturing world (Greider, 1997). What evidence is there to support this very
negative view? Look at the main evidence and arguments in the previous chapters in this book.

We still have giant corporations pretending to exercise sovereignty of the
people—having "foreign policies" of their own to conduct operations. In a
Harvard Business Review article on Greider's book *One World, Ready or Not*,
by Jeffrey Garten, a former government official and now Dean of Yale University's School of Management, we find a direct assertion by Garten of a need
for foreign policies by globalizing corporations. Foreign policy is believed to
be a function of the nation-state; the Constitution of the United States makes
this very clear. It is not a task for business. So why would Garten think this
way? He lays out a very unpersuasive case in his last book (Garten, 1997). This
is generating confusion at the very highest levels of thinking and it is completely
unnecessary. The idea of popular sovereignty has not even begun to be asserted
by people in democratic nations to control business except inside nations—so
what about powerful national charter controls that keep businesses where they
belong? Such powerful controls are ignored completely.

Now consider the argument in the balance of the chapters. We do not agree
on the nature of the capitalism we supposedly are enacting into life in the
business community. There are many models of capitalism (Silk and Silk, 1996).
We do not agree on the importance or desirability or need for foreign trade for
anything—even for oil. There are a couple of competing models to attract our
attention from the model of minimal international trade to the exuberant maximal models of world trade. The argument for self-sustainability is not interested
in maximum trade, but those who want maximal trade are the cheerleaders for
tight global interdependence, maybe too tight for anyone's sanity, security and
relaxed, enjoyable living in place. Who is to decide how much trade is enough
for a people in their sovereign role of controllers of their own trading destiny?
One would think the people should make these choices and not have self-

appointed experts telling them what to think or business people telling them that trade is an "inevitable" good. And we still suffer from a myth about the corporations from different nations called multination corporations (Doremus, Keller, Pauly and Reich, 1998).

Warren Anderson, who was CEO of Union Carbide during the 1984 Bhopal poisoning disaster, is still wanted in 1999 by Indian authorities to answer to criminal charges from that 1984 incident. Just as in the United States, criminal charges in India do not disappear or vanish just because they are old. These charges are valid in 1999 while certainly not as fresh. Here is a perfect case where the past is not forgotten, business leaders just cannot "get it behind them." On the other hand, no other person on earth could get it behind them either. So equal justice beckons U.S. authorities to listen to India. Harboring fugitives from foreign demands for justice is a U.S. practice that is not very likely to change, and this means the U.S. government leaders are not ready for one world for CEOs. Nor are the CEOs ready for one world of criminal law and institutions. They want to do foreign business, but not run the risks of criminal liability in other nations while the citizens in those nations clearly run such risks. Why ask for such unequal treatment as a business merchant? We must like our little harbors, safe from the petulant storms of public outcry for justice for the harmed and dead in India, and the living with their sad memories of dead friends and families. This attitude does not speak well about the courageous one world we may want to foist on others for our own selfish financial well-being while we ignore oneness in criminal matters.

More pointed is the lack of one commercial legal world. The evidence shows clearly the business community does not want one at all. And it never has, according to the evidence in Chapter 8, and one could say it never will want one world in law. Nations may need to take this bull by its horns.

And the ultimate lack of one world and the world not being ready for one world is the weak position of the United Nations that is purposely kept weakened by the member nations. The blue helmets of the UN may be many more in number, but the number of places needed for civil strife overwhelms those few, much less asking them to become the cross-border commercial cops of the world. That job would require them to add thousands of regulators overnight just to begin to make a dent in oversight of business across the globe. In those few areas like the Law of the Seas or CFC ozone regulation, the international cooperation may be great enough to accomplish goals, but not in broad commercial areas of regulation and corruption and crime in business.

We must be cautious about the twilight of sovereignty for laborers and workers in the Northern Hemisphere who have no idea of what will be the further impact on their jobs of hundreds of millions of Chinese and Indian citizens also needing work. The arbiter in the case of labor at this moment is an exceedingly small number of people, a clique of about 750 CEOs of the corporations who think their rightful job is to shift work globally as they see fit to do it. Cheaper and less protected labor is their aim or has been until public outcry to companies like Nike shakes them enough to wake up their moral conscience and they may even close plants with disturbing practices.

For all of the reasons just mentioned the world has a long way to go to become one world. The world federalists found out long ago how true this is in their failures to persuade the world to adopt one government. The world has never had such illusions and the United Nations safely stays away from such a position. What has been tempered is the military delusions of grandeur—Iraq is the latest to learn a very hard lesson of what the world will not tolerate. Bosnia and the others are hopefully learning as well. What has not been tempered is the open and underground colonial desires springing anew in the hearts of the capitalists who want to conquer the world in a commercial sense. This nonsense still wafts around the globalizing corporations as a smouldering fire not yet put out. There is every reason in the world to be concerned over the exhibition of such a mentality because it is so archaic and out of synchronicity with the times. Dilbert, an American cartoon character, shows us how bad things can be inside a company; we need a Dilbertina to show us how bad things can be outside the company in international trade. We are not ready for one world yet, for all the reasons mentioned. No one knows when we will be ready, if ever.

Environmental Justice and a Simple Love of Nature

Environmental justice and love of nature are two important themes to weave into this final chapter. Pressures on Mother Nature's natural resources—oil, water, air, land and minerals are higher than ever to serve vastly increased total populations that have risen so rapidly in the last 50 years, but a billion of 5.5 billion people place even more extraordinary stress on the finite sources of the Earth's bounty. These richest Northern Hemisphere people have not yet learned to say no to the materialism that is rampant. The sport utility trucks replaced the finned Cadillacs of the 1950s and 1960s (NYT, Wald, 1/26/97). Oil spills despoil the world; Ogoni people of Nigeria lived with Shell and General Abatcha in great oil flares and political assassinations; the Ecuadorian natives live with their government and formerly with Texaco in great oil destruction; and the natives of Indonesia suffer in the same way through natural resource exploitation for a handful of gold nuggets and other minerals out of a vast world of waste rock and chemical burning of rivers. These 24-hour-a-day mining operations are getting worse. These modern attitudes must be contrasted with someone who showed much more gratitude—St. Francis of Assisi.

St. Francis of Assisi, who is the patron saint of Italy, is recognized by the Catholic Church as a saint who could be called the first environmentalist (Gottlieb, 1996: 236–237). Born in 1181 in Assisi before it was known as a part of Italy, he died in 1226—on October 4 of his forty-fifth year. So great was his influence that Pope Gregory IX canonized him in 1228. The great basilica of St. Francis was begun shortly after he died. G. K. Chesterton wrote a tribute to St. Francis in 1924:

For that is the full and final spirit in which we should turn to St. Francis; in the spirit of thanks for what he has done. He was above all things a great giver; he cared chiefly for the best kind of giving which is called thanksgiving. If another great man wrote a grammar of assent, he may well be said to have written a grammar of acceptance; a grammar of gratitude. He understood down to its very depths the theory of thanks; and its depths are a bottomless abyss. (Chesterton, 1990: 156)

Chesterton was very perceptive about the enduring qualities of St. Francis. One the qualities for which we can be most thankful is his creative poetry; *The Canticle of the Creatures* is one of his most important poems. Because it is impossible to grasp the environmental significance of this poem without reading it, it is set forth on the next page in order for the reader to appreciate it explicitly (see Figure 10-1).

The poem of St. Francis (Figure 10-1) has inspired those who love Mother Nature and all of its gifts and those who feel passionately about protecting our commons and common heritage. Friends of the Earth are important friends of all the people. In today's world of harsh global capitalism with "no one in charge," which some suggest is a sane way to live, there are those who want to tear the earth apart and despoil the rest with pollution. The world desperately needs love instead. Civilizations disappear because they cut down too many trees and begin a cycle of massive, destructive erosion that sweeps away the land in the next flood, and the people perish. Whole civilizations have disappeared. No love of nature is a sure death sentence for future generations. Global capitalism simply has no future if future generations do not count and when it is the hateful kind of predatory capitalism.

We are not ready for one world and we must be smart enough to take very precious care of the one we have. We have only one world. Space research confirms that fact of life. No corporation that wants to globalize at your expense, to pull out more billions of dollars of your resources and labor, is worth having in any nation. They ought to be dissolved promptly. The era of neocolonialism should never get started again now that it is so thoroughly discredited as a way of exploitation of fellow man and woman and child. Unfortunately, the world is filled with plenty of misguided souls who want to make a fast and not an honest dollar.

A simple love of nature was expressed by Rachel Carson in *Silent Spring*, published in 1962. She quoted the famous physician, theologian and musician Albert Schweitzer who said: "Man has lost the capacity to foresee and to forestall. He will end by destroying the earth." Solemn words these are, indeed, from such a religious figure cited by a modern scientific woman. Then Carson cited E. B. White whose sentences are prophetic: "Our approach to nature is to beat it into submission. We would stand a better chance of survival if we accommodated ourselves to this planet and viewed it appreciatively instead of skeptically and dictatorially." As we all know Rachel Carson was among those who spoke out against reckless and irresponsible poisoning of the world by a

Figure 10-1
The Canticle of the Creatures

Most high omnipotent good Lord,
   to thee Praise, glory, honour, and every blessing.
To Thee alone Most High do they belong.
   And no man is worthy to pronounce Thy Name.
Praise be to Thee my Lord with all Thy creatures.
   Especially for Master Brother Sun
   Who illuminates the day for us,
   And thee Most High he manifests.
Praise be to Thee my Lord for Sister Moon and for the stars.
   In Heaven Thou hast formed them, shining, precious, fair.
Praise to be thee my Lord for Brother Wind,
   For air and clouds, clear sky and all the weathers
   Through which Thou sustainest all Thy creatures.
Praise be to Thee my Lord for Sister Water.
   She is useful and humble, precious and pure.
Praise be to Thee my Lord for Brother Fire,
   Through him our night Thou dost enlighten,
   And he is fair and merry, boisterous and strong.
Praise be to Thee my Lord for our sister Mother Earth,
   Who nourishes and sustains us all,
   Bringing forth divers fruits,
   And many-coloured flowers and herbs.
Praise be to Thee my Lord for those
   Who pardon grant for love of Thee
   And bear infirmity and tribulation,
   Blessed be those who live in peace,
   For by Thee Most High they shall be crowned.
Praise be to Thee my Lord for our Sister Bodily Death
   From whom no living man can flee;
   Woe to them who die in mortal sin
   But blessed they who shall be found in Thy most holy Will;
   To them the second death can do no harm.
O bless and praise my Lord all creatures,
   And thank and serve Him in deep humility.

St. Francis

chemical for killing mosquitoes called DDT. Permanent contamination of our world by massive outdoor spraying and by the progressive buildup of chemicals in our bodies and the bodies of all other creatures has led to cumulative poisoning of much of life on earth. The ''Silent Spring'' of her book was the deaths of songbirds and fish and fish-eating osprey eagles whose eggs cracked from bird weight alone. Carson quoted Schweitzer and White because they showed that beneath the objective and quiet facade of science and chemistry was a desire to control nature since nature is supposed to serve man. The key attitude identified by Carson is arrogance based upon ignorance—beating Mother Earth into submission is the extreme point of the greatest arrogance.

Arrogance—what do we mean by using such a word to describe those who despoil and wreck Mother Nature? The key characteristics of the arrogant are:

1. Making unwarranted claims or pretensions to superior importance or superior rights,
2. Being an overbearing and blindly assuming human self-centered being, and
3. Being proud and insolent about it as well.

We think of the meek who shall inherit the earth—not the proud—not the people who are brazen, imperious, haughty and presumptuous. These are the attitudes of people who wreck the Earth for themselves and for their own puny individual gain (Tokar, 1997). Avarice was *pleonexia* to ancient Greeks—an old problem of politics described by Aristotle 2,500 years ago.

Looking back since 1962, which is now over thirty-seven years ago, how was the message of *The Silent Spring* received by the chemical industry? With arrogance:

Back then, the chemical industry's efforts consisted chiefly of deploying friendly scientists to attack Carson in the press and distributing a sarcastic rebuttal to the book. Today, manufacturers are infinitely more sophisticated, carefully choreographing legions of lobbyists, lawyers, scientists, public relations experts, and mass-media marketers for maximum effect. (Fagin et al., 1996: xx)

Dan Fagin, Marianne LaVelle, and the Center for Public Integrity recently attacked the chemical industry again for threatening the public with toxic chemicals that are pervasive in everyday lives of people: atrazine, alachlor and perchloroeythlene. The story is one of arrogance, not humility, by globalizing corporations. In other fields male sperm counts are dropping along with other effects on people's hormone systems—Carson's legacy goes on (Colborn, Dumanoski and Myers, 1996).

GLOBALIZATION TRENDS OF MAJOR CORPORATIONS: FREE TRADE IDEOLOGY

Globalization trends of major corporations are now embedded in a century of increasing activity. Commonly held beliefs about globalization—especially in the last fifteen years, are that it is working splendidly for the United States and rather well for Europe and Japan and by 1999 less well for some other Asian nations like South Korea, Thailand, Singapore and Hong Kong and Taiwan. The late 1990s shows Asian strains in globalizing. Export promotion is the main theme of the collection of ideas cobbled together as a free market trading ideology. One hears the president of the United States pleading for export promotion for U.S. workers as if their national market of 260 million comparatively rich people did not them give a lot to do at home. One should begin to wonder. Other ideas thrown into the grab bag of free trade ideology include:

1. Suppression of government ownership and control of productive assets and services with a technique called "privatization." In Russia it's called selling off at bargain prices the wealth owned by all of the people. Some is stolen, thus kleptomaniacal kleptocracy.

2. Export your wealth and import your oil, soft drinks, clothing, food and other necessities and luxuries.

3. Encourage investment in the assets of your nation by outside investors who do not live in your nation—sell off your patrimony.

4. Create non-taxable export processing zones inside your nation so foreign traders pay little or no taxes—like the Mexican maquiladoras, and so that local business and local citizens pay all or most of the taxes.

5. Give up on popular sovereignty and local laws in favor of business-made foreign laws embodied in treaties and agreements that preempt all national and local laws.

6. Buy into the various trade agreements now in place including GATT, NAFTA and WTO so you may be governed by agreements never discussed by and voted upon intelligently by U.S. representatives in a "fast track" mode. And be ruled by others, forget democracy and self-rule and autonomy.

7. Downsize, hollow-out and outsource production and service so that local unions have no jobs to fight over and this will in turn eliminate unions without you having to say a thing about your preferences for or against unions. It is a nice cover.

These modern personnel policies are premised upon laissez-faire brands of economics with Darwinian survival-of-the-fittest morality in a jungle-like marketplace. Everything could possibly be for sale in such a highly commodified place—there are no students just customers, no patients just customers, no clients just customers, no citizens just customers—ad infinitum (Greider, 1997; Kuttner, 1997; Korten, 1995; Mander and Goldsmith, 1996; Clarke, 1997; Daly, 1996). The corporate globalization message is: "Get out of our way!" No one can stop the corporate globalization juggernaut now on its way to worldwide conquest—the forces are as inevitable and unchanging as the laws of nature—the law of gravity. This bombastic chorus of free trade ideology reminds us of the Marxist and Communist utopias that are now dystopias (Berlin, 1997: 37).

Closer to the truth about corporate globalization is William Pfaff, a noted American author and columnist who believed that any questioning of conventional wisdom spelled out just above on free trade usually would rule one out of the debate, such as it is. No one cares to hear the downside of globalization any more than they want to see downsized employees. Pfaff questioned the current condition of utopia—he said people and nature are being destroyed at an unprecedented rate. Pfaff wrote: "I myself believe this is immoral, another manifestation of the characteristic immorality of the 20th century, which has been to cause positive harm to people today out of unproven and unprovable theories about the distant future'' (Pfaff, 1996: 23). We should never actively do harm to people, but what is plant closing and its ruthless mentality? The globalized marketplace, casino capitalism, and CEO political conduct of business corporate affairs do not strike Pfaff as sound—"It Isn't Working" (Pfaff, 1996). Also, the old capitalist paternalism is back once again to tell the world it knows best—"father knows best"—"the colonial master knows best." This old and deep-seated arrogance based on ignorance is stalking the planet—now in the guise of corporate globalization. It is the pre-Teddy Roosevelt plundering of forests, mining with abandoned haste and waste, sweeping the seas clean of life, polluting the air, nuking the Arctic Ocean, and pulping the south (Carrere and Lohmann, 1996). Who needs this free trade ideology but a few billionaires and multibillionaires and multimillionaires? Surely it is nothing but a game to the ordinary person, but a deadly game they should fear.

THE GREAT DIVIDE

Badly split apart over the truth about free trade and corporate globalization are the various strands of business people, journalists, writers and economists. They fall into so many warring camps one wonders how it happened (NYT, Uchitelle, 2/16/97). No side seems to have much of a hold on the truth, so the safest position is to suspend judgment on the entire intellectual mess until more is known and thrashed out. The United States is creating greater risks for everyone by its policies (Mandel, 1996). Skepticism ought to rule the day on free trade. Here is why.

Those Who Favor a Free Trade Ideology

There are many economists and business people who think corporate globalization is just fine—without limits under maximum conditions of free trade. The Institute for International Economics in Washington, D.C., is just such an organization that promotes a free trade ideology. As of the spring of 1997, the Institute fine-tuned its published work to meet what some say will be the next greatest debate on foreign policy—globalization. Dani Rodrick, an economist, wrote one of the more sensitively attuned works on globalization. His *Has Globalization Gone Too Far?* (1997) asked economists to consider the consequences of international free trade for labor, for domestic social arrangements (child labor and blocked exchanges such as prison labor, and social insurance), and for other factors. Rodrick asked whether social disintegration is the price of economic integration when the only market not regulated by an overarching political authority is the international trading and intracorporate market (Rodrick, 1997: 69–71). Note that this point has been examined in Chapter 5 at some length. Rodrick suggested roles for economists, labor advocates, and national governments in resolution of conflicts over globalization. Particularly clear are his prescriptions: strike a balance between openness and domestic needs, do not use "competitiveness" as an excuse for domestic reform and do not abuse "fair-ness" claims in trade (Rodrick, 1997: 77–81). This is a start—a good start. The answer tentatively struck is that maybe globalization has gone too far in some peculiar ways. At least it is an admission, however mild it may have been.

It is much less clear that globalization may be in trouble in another recent Insititute for International Economics offering by Edward M. Graham titled *Global Corporation and National Governments* (1996). This analysis is a mixed grouping of ideas that favors more of the same international investment, but with some new rules and institutional arrangements. However, politics gets in the way of a global investment accord; maybe it is the Multilateral Agreement on Investment sitting in the wings in late 1997, 1998 and 1999. Graham wrote: "At root is the clash between the objectives of sovereign nations and those of global corporations. Such clashes makes the need for an effective enterprise-to-state dispute settlement mechanism paramount: creating such a mechanism (or upgrading existing ones) would be the chief end of an international investment accord" (Graham, 1996: 119). This suggestion makes me very uncomfortable after this lengthy study of the slippery nature of the corporate entity, and after studying the American judiciary for the last 30 years, because it is merely an economist's view of popular sovereignty and justice—ideas quite capable of being sidestepped and subdued by globalizing companies. Just select the proper forum and the whole scheme will come undone. See Chapter 8 for ample his-torical evidence on what could control multinational corporations. It would take a whale of a lot more than a simple international accord that everyone would probably ignore.

From the same Institute and generating even less comfort is Robert Z. Lawrence's *Single World. Divided Nations?* (1996a). And his earlier work en-titled *A Vision for the World Economy* (1996b) is no better at producing un-derstanding for labor except perhaps among some economists who seem satisfied with his views. Labor seems not justified in its concerns over both globalization and stagnant wages—a claim by Lawrence that is unjustified from almost every-thing presented in this book. Finally, again from the same Institute for Inter-national Economics, came the third edition of Edward Graham and Paul Krugman's *Foreign Direct Investment in the United States* (1995). These authors exhibit a "cool" attitude toward foreign inward investment in assets in the United States. Do little or nothing is their basic advice—little should stop for-eign investors from doing as they please. Non-investor others in the United States should avoid hysteria. This is a questionable type of "economic" advice from Graham and Krugman. It sounds more like psychological counselling. Oth-ers add their fuel (Garten, 1997) to the flame of misunderstanding. Finally, some of the more balanced voices for exuberant free trade in the expansive sense say also that there is a genuine role left for government, labor and environmental concerns and other issues (Barshefsky, 1998; Yergin and Stanislaw, 1998).

These works just cited are among many more studies of a similar nature—

all with a bias streak so wide and obvious it bears repeating—be very skeptical of such advice. Your skepticism is justified by merely noting how a few thousand miles of ocean or a national boundary can produce simultaneously a vastly different viewpoint on globalization in Britain, Canada and Europe. There one finds real fears and profound dismay expressed by a series of recent works by other economists and allied professions in the following work. Please take note of the extreme contrast in outlook.

Those Who Question a Free Trade Ideology—Not the United States

A fresher view of globalization is being generated mostly outside of the United States. Robert Boyer and Daniel Drache joined 20 other scholars in economics, business and other fields to challenge the conventional wisdom being fed to the world by the free traders. In their *States against Markets* (1996), the authors centered on four questions to illuminate their inquiry:

1. How can nations manage their economies in the face of globalization?
2. What is the relevance of markets to governing a society?
3. International cooperation and a strong economy—is free trade the best way to get these conditions?
4. Is the nation-state relevant any longer?

Boyer and Drache asked excellent questions and they were very clear:

Hence, the nation-state can not be easily replaced by the market for any significant period since it is the only institution society has to organize itself, protect the social solidarity of its citizens and safeguard its values which cannot be "traded" like commodities. (Boyer and Drache, 1996: 13)

As clearly as possible, these authors and many of their co-authors concluded upon a recognition of the importance of globalization, but rejected its newness and power, rejected casino financial markets, supported labor's need for governmental cooperation, and argued for a renewal of a democratic polity. This work is a remarkably objective and thorough examination of the issues (see also Gray, 1998).

Another European view is that of Razeen Sally in *States and Firms: Multinational Enterprises in Institutional Competition* (1995). Globalizing corporations are tied into the political economy of nations—noting, among other things, that corporations do not lose their national nature in globalizing (Sally, 1995: 211–214). The focus was upon German and French firms. Others assert the belief that governments do not lose their significance and often play a vital role in firm globalization (Stopford and Strange, 1991: 7; Pauly and Reich, 1997).

Firm national identity remains very influential during globalization of giant corporations (Pauly and Reich, 1997; Pauly, 1997; and Doremus, Keller, Pauly and Reich, 1998).

Added to this Canadian-European view are the British researchers David Bailey, George Harte and Roger Sugden who looked at the last 30 years of policies of nations toward transnational corporations—in Japan, France, Germany, Britain and the United States in their *Transnationals and Governments* (1994). Some eighteen criteria were studied—and nations varied—Japan, Germany and France were much more vigorous in their controls than were the United States and Britain. The United States is a sporadic actor and Britain is just plain lax. When the authors produced a sharper look at Britain they urged stronger public policies in many areas (Bailey, Harte and Sugden, 1994).

Within the context of history and international finance, the interplay of labor and capital and the current international finance systems, Jonathan Michie and John Grieve Smith, in *Managing the Global Economy* (1995), provided a cogent analysis of the role of governments along with their co-authors. Chapter 6 on Transnational Corporations and the Nation State is a brilliant historical exposition of the growth of international production and the continued role of nations and governments in allowing such production to thrive. Richard Kozul-Wright did much of this work. Cooperation, not antagonism, marked the relationship of state to corporation.

This European tour continues with the final two scholars. The worry expressed by Titus Alexander in *Unraveling Global Apartheid* (1996) is significant and should be heard. Alexander saw separate development of forced trade in the economics of global apartheid found in labor policies that discriminate unfairly, in tariffs that tyrannize, in world trade rules made by others, in managed financial markets and in many other policies and practices. Alexander believed the world politics of elites keeps these items off the table: the regulation of transnational corporations, the arms trade, disarmament, global inequality and reform of international institutions—all kept in the margins (Alexander, 1996: 210). Does the West know what is best for the world, he asked? To Alexander, it sounds as if the answer may be an ideology of apartheid and colonialism reborn under a new rubric: a corporate command economy (Alexander, 1996: 87). Do you now find this a fresher view of world politics? Does corporate-managed trade begin to be a worry?

From far afield either left or right or a blend of both, comes Ulrich Duchrow, *Alternatives to Global Capitalism* (1995), in which he identified the harms of the plutocratic world economy and searched for alternatives outside of the conventional economics of industrial policy in a return to alternatives in every aspect of labor, land, money and politics to bring life back to human scale. The Bible offered suggestions for new pathways for Duchrow. There are shades of E. F. Schumacher's *Small Is Beautiful* in this work, that are being heard once again.

Oddly enough, Duchrow is not unlike George Soros, the billionaire financial investor who explored a market-dominated society in an article titled: ''The Capitalist Threat'' (Soros, 1997). Unmistakably he was referring to himself, one would think, from a European or Malaysian perspective (Millman, 1995). But he argued that an open society is open to new ideas—it possesses no ultimate truths, just good working ideas, but it needs a renewal from the period when philosopher Karl Popper developed the open society idea. Soros does think laissez-faire capitalism excessively and aggressively promoted is a threat to institutions that provide a foundation for markets to exist—namely, nations. Casino capitalism is now an ideology, not a source of truth—it promotes robber capitalism to sack Russia and it is a temporary phenomenon, according to Soros. Three cheers for this view! But reality is that capitalists prey in a global hunting style on troubled corporations in troubled economies from the Far East Asian countries to Mexico (WP Torres, 9/30/97).

From Canada the author, scholar and activist Tony Clarke confronts transnational corporations in *Silent Coup* (1997). Clarke's analysis traces the takeover of key parts of the Canadian economy by large corporations and how the global managers worked their own special magic. The political abandonment and growth of corporate rule happened with swift action to create a corporate state. Clarke designed a strategy for citizen reinvolvment in the Canadian struggle. This story in Canada reveals how quickly the attack on democracy can be carried out by business interests intent on domination (Clarke and Barlow, 1997).

The rich, varied and fresh set of views of globalization and free trade from such diversity mainly outside of the United States tells us that nations can get worn down talking with one another inside and get duller by the minute. This continental boredom among those who have given the topic some thought is fascinating to behold; it suggests that we may not be at the end of history at all, but just preoccupied turning the page. Some pages are very large and heavy. They take forever to turn, it seems. Let's turn to some U.S. authors who have a lot of steam.

Those Who Oppose a Free Trade Ideology—U.S. Style

Irreverent is Kevin Danaher's book *Corporations Are Gonna Get Your Mama* (1996). This is an edited series of brief articles by well-known writers such as Noam Chomsky, Richard Barnet, Ralph Nader, Jeremy Rifkin and many others who flatly attack globalizing corporations with every argument posed so far in this book and more. The Institute for International Economics will never refer to this work. Free trade ideology takes an enormous pounding from all sides. Most of the authors spent the last two or three decades observing globalizing corporations so the insights are irreverently profound and well grounded in reality often hidden from public view by corporate public imagery. For a brief effort to reach a large audience, one could not do better. In the same fresh style, Mark Zepezauer and Arthur Naiman list about 20 major areas of public policy that ought to be changed to *Take the Rich off Welfare* (1996). The rich they target are giant globalizing corporations or what some call corporate welfare addicts. These two books are evidence of desire to move from ideas to actions in the United States—to bring the debate to a head as quickly as possible. The political aim is crystal clear.

Perhaps the most widely researched criticism of free trade ideology is found in the edited work of Jerry Mander and Edward Goldsmith with the long title *The Case against the Global Economy and for a Turn toward the Local* (Mander and Goldsmith, 1996). This award-winning (American Political Science Association Best Book Award for 1996) 550-page book is an outgrowth of two major global meetings of the International Forum on Globalization in New York in 1995 and in Washington, DC, in 1996. Leaders with a similar view of globalization from across the world—Chile, India, France, Britain, Malaysia, Japan, Canada and many other nations—examined and compared often identical notes on how globalizing corporations behaved in their nations. The ideology confronting each nation was the same old free trade ideology mentioned above in the start of this section. Reports from the planet revealed this much to everyone. The backlash against free trade ideology was not merely trading of one idea for another, but trading away badly misguided policy in the disguise of free trade. The serious negative impacts of globalization are described and defined in the work of Mander and Goldsmith. There is not a hint of ''protectionism'' as some call it. These leaders are in constant contact with one another across the world. With labor and environmental interests joined, this new political force may well become not just a backlash, but a positive force for change in its own right with its own agenda. Thousands of people over the world are connected to this movement and it is an auspicious start.

Free trade ideology was attacked by William Dugger, an economist, in his *Underground Economics* (1992). Dugger found the most pressing problem for Western democracies is to curb corporate power amassed in the last 50 years and then bring corporations back under social control of the society they were designed to serve—not master and control as they have done with political energy and wealth devoted to capturing the federal and state governments.

Prominent economists Robert Heilbroner and William Milberg, in their profound 1995 study titled *The Crisis of Vision in Modern Economic Thought*, offered a most troublesome perspective on the decline of economics caused partly by extreme mathematical modelling in which the vision of society is both an unarticulated premise and obliterated by a forest of numbers. As applied to free trade ideology and globalizing corporations these authors wrote: ''This 'globalization' of production carries unsettling implications for all advanced capitalisms, including the lowering of social, environmental, and labor standards through the forces of market competition, and the rise of newly industrialized countries as major rivals for market shares'' (Heilbroner and Milberg, 1995: 121). With an adequate vision, one could see how nations must react to immigration pressures caused by large population growth in some nations, ecological global problems and the political outfall from all of this as terrorism and national unrest arise. They argue that as economics becomes an instrument for the attainment of politically chosen goals, it then becomes the "indispensable" servant of the socio-political order that it ministers to. Economics in the West is embedded in various types of capitalisms and cannot escape the political order—which they assert is never apolitical (Heilbroner and Milberg, 1995: 127). Economics is just the servant of whatever political order exists—monarchical, communist, capitalist, socialist or Amish. This warning from economists themselves is reason enough for skepticism about who is speaking the truth. All sides want the truth, but when one side starts to assert "inevitability" of their truth, that act by itself raises serious doubts about the truth.

James Tobin, another prominent economist, in *Full Employment and Growth* (1996), renewed in his latest work his views on macroeconomic policy, monetary policy, fiscal policy, international economic relations and social policy. Tobin has fought as a Keynesian, during his entire career, against the extreme revival of classical economics in that profession. He repeated his 1978 suggestion for a 1% transfer tax on financial markets. He wrote that the invisible hand of the market needed help—"a helping hand"—in fields like long-range planning, external costs of pollution, addressing world population growth, exaggerated and glorified free market ideology and finding the right and good place for human social and economic equality in a democracy (Tobin, 1996: 176–179). The voice of Tobin has been missed in the debates over sound policy.

At least three more significant dissenting voices need to be heard against the free trade ideology and its broader agenda. First, there is Robert Kuttner, a well-known economist and journalist whose previous work was mentioned in Chapter 7 of this book. His latest, *Everything for Sale* (1997), summarized the mottos of a free market economy with some of these terms: privatization, deregulation, downsizing, shrinking entitlements and lower taxes. Markets are good and markets are imperfect, inappropriate or unattainable and nations, he argued, must rebalance their public institutions, strategies and political coalitions to adjust to conditions in the real world—to achieve a good society with a mixed economy. Globalization does impact labor in a variety of ways, thus Kuttner questioned free market utopias and suggested strong nations and a vigorous polity are much more important than a hands-off policy toward any market. This is strong support for the thesis of the present book.

Herman Daly, whose work has been used in previous chapters of this book is thinking way beyond everyone in his latest book called *Beyond Growth* (1996) The field of economics is set within planet Earth which is a closed and finite system. That basic premise shapes every thought. Sustaining life has limits, as does every other human activity. And he noted David Ricardo's basic thought that capital was not mobile among nations (Daly, 1996: 152). Nothing is less true today about capital, thus Ricardo's views of comparative advantage are limited by a new reality of vast sums moving about the earth electronically. Japan has no comparative advantage over Korea in manufacturing, nor does the United States. Integrating economies and mutual vying for scarce natural resources puts nations at one anothers' throats as in the Persian Gulf. Daly puts it so well: "National production for the national market should be the dog, and international trade its tail" (Daly, 1996: 157). Given the identical analogy used in Chapter 2, the view of Daly makes great common sense to me.

The third economist is Martin O'Connor, who asked *Is Capitalism Sustainable?* (1994). He thought there was irreconcilable conflict between free trade ideology and sustainable growth within limits. A free fox in a closed chicken coop is not freedom for chickens. A thoughtful business person, Paul Hawken, raised similar concerns in 1993 and in a more recent forthcoming work about the need for reducing waste to zero by reusing everything (Hawken, 1993).

Who Is Playing by Different Rules?

The Office of Technology Assessment (OTA) of the U.S. Congress is no more—Congress abolished it in September of 1995 (Doremus, Keller, Pauly and Reich, 1998: xii). What could possibly have gone wrong with the OTA? Before abolition, OTA researched and published many fine studies including one very important one: *Multinationals and the National Interest: Playing by Different Rules* (September 1993). A distinguished Advisory Panel to the report included historian Lawrence Friedman from Stanford University; Alfred Chandler of Harvard Business School; William Greider, author and journalist; Theodore Lowi, political scientist, Cornell University; Raymond Vernon, Harvard University and many others. This undertaking was no trivial chore since it was commissioned by the U.S. Senate Committee on Commerce, Science and Transportation and the U.S. Senate Committee on Banking, Housing and Urban Affairs. The results are found in a 157-page well-researched and thoughtful study. The question of who was playing by different rules and what were the consequences of this unlevel playing field were well examined.

Multinational enterprises play by rules that are very different in America— whether they are American, Japanese or other companies. The rules are related to growth, profits, proprietary technology, strategic alliances and market power—and not to a deep corporate concern with advancing the goals of the people of a nation. The study observed that trade frictions were on the increase and that nations were sucked into trade conflicts of businesses. MNEs (multinational enterprises) in Japan and Europe follow different trade rules from those of the United States. There is an asymmetry and disharmony among globalizing corporations in democratic nations. Because there are trade barriers to U.S. firms outside of the United States, while at the same time the United States promotes openness toward outsiders in the United States, there results a no-win situation for the United States. This leads to three possible policy choices: (1) continued unilateral national treatment and open markets, (2) enhanced protection of the United States and (3) specific reciprocity (OTA, 1993: 17–19). The United States is doing a little of each with a dominant free trade ideology. The OTA staff report was not impressed.

Some of the findings of the OTA study are valuable and for that reason are worth summarizing here:

1. MNEs are chameleon in nature—fitting wherever and however they may do so in nations. This submarining character was noted in Chapter 8.

2. Government policies may be decisive in determining which MNEs prosper in global competition.

3. With no globally coherent system of government policies, various trading regimes emerge that affect market access, foreign direct investment and other financial and industrial policies.

4. Restricted foreign direct investment in some OECD nations is the rule, especially for Japan, but in other nations in Europe as well.

5. The United States was the most influential global trader 25 years ago—but is no longer since other foreign MNEs and nations have asserted global trading power. Japanese MNEs have arisen to take the place of U.S. globalizers.

6. MNEs are increasingly "multi" and less "national"—a divergence between MNEs and nations is growing.

7. The U.S. government has not specified what interest it has in international trade and U.S. MNEs do whatever they believe is proper—selling off key U.S. assets and placing research and development facilities and advanced manufacturing plants abroad. (It should be noted that this industrial policy is favored by U.S. MNEs and their CEOs.) The proof is in the Mexican maquiladora plants in Tijuana that are ISO 9000—the highest state of the art of electronic plants.

8. Strategic alliances were increasing rapidly, were not well understood and some generated fears of harmful transfers of technology against the public interest.

9. MNEs play the international financial markets as never before with derivatives and other international arbitrage schemes. Casino capitalism lies within the MNEs.

10. If nations decide to regulate international finance more thoroughly the MNEs would be forced to adapt to these policies.

11. Japanese MNEs have used both domestic government support in Japan and the support of the keiretsu corporate ties to move aggressively into U.S. markets such as autos, semiconductors and consumer electronics. This has crushed some American businesses. The reciprocity shown by Japan is minimal and it is an "intellectual closed shop" (Hall, 1998).

The OTA findings confirm those of the independent study by Bailey, Harte and Sugden that on a spectrum of potential policies to control MNEs, the British are least involved, the United States next and the nations of Germany, France and Japan most involved in controls. The implications for trade frictions and labor unemployment are significant (OTA, 1993: 38–41).

The OTA study stated that U.S. national economic sovereignty may become more illusive as dependence on alliances that control strategic assets grows (OTA, 1993: 115). The history of weakening governmental controls over MNEs in the United States does not augur well for the country (OTA, 1993: 135–158).

OTA told the truth as it saw it. OTA died. The UN rules for corporations died about the same time. There may be no conspiracy afoot among MNEs who do not want to be exposed, but it surely looks like one. After further research and reflection, some of the former OTA group have concluded: "The global corporation, adrift from its national political moorings and roaming an increasingly borderless world market, is a myth" (Doremus, Keller, Pauly and Reich, 1998: 3). This adds a hint of confirmation to the views explained in previous chapters of this book.

SOME NATIONAL TRENDS

When the big picture unfolds on globalizing corporations in democratic nations, it is only the nations that are the source of public global law and order for 750 large companies at work 24 hours a day in all of the nations where they have allowed entry to make a profit. The justification for global law and order in international commerce is rather clear—there is very little if any public law and order—there is no "overarching" political authority to force companies to behave on a worldwide basis, as Dani Rodrick mentioned. This is still a field where anything goes, a field where everything is relative, a field where nothing is sacred and everything is commodified and everything has a price. Furthermore, justice is often absent, and one cannot appeal to universal truths. Chapters 8 and 9 are the extension of the views laid out here in summary fashion. Because of this stark and bleak law and order terrain, nations face an unparalleled opportunity to make law and order by treaty and other agreements, by increased global communication among nations through regulators conferring regularly and by vastly increasing the public staffs to achieve the globalization of regulation in taxation, finance, and many other fields. There will be a renaissance of what is called regulatory capitalism that will become global regulatory capitalism.

The question is, out of what could nations construct an improved law and order for international commerce? This section offers nine areas to consider that carry within them the seeds for a new world of law and order for global business. Those nine areas, to be examined next, are: extraterritoriality, democratization, egalitarianism, transparency, sovereignty, regulatory capitalism, taxation and due process. Let us go through each of these factors to see what this law and order would portend compared with what we have already seen that arises with international commerce under free trade ideology.

Extraterritoriality

This mouthful of a word—extraterritoriality—is intended to express how public policies of a nation end at the nation's boundaries to respect another nation's sovereignty of its people. Occasionally, extraboundary or extraterritorial effect is very desirable, especially when interacting nations have the same or similar public policies. A current example to illustrate a wise extraterritorial effect is the case of *United States v. Nippon Paper Industries Co.*, decided March 17, 1997 in the U.S. Court of Appeals, First Circuit in Massachusetts. Let us examine this case briefly.

A novel case, the U.S. Attorney as prosecutor was attempting to convict Nippon Paper Industries Co., a Japanese corporation and a foreign corporation under the U.S. Sherman Antitrust Act, for allegedly committing criminal price-fixing acts in which (although the acts took place in Japan) there were substantial effects that occurred in the United States. The lower U.S. District Court dismissed the indictment because of the wholly extraterritorial conduct in Japan that it thought was not indictable in the United States. The U.S. Court of Appeals reversed the decision of the trial court.

A striking holding is that Section One of the Sherman Act (15 U.S. C. Sec. 1, 1994), applies to wholly foreign conduct which has an intended and substantial effect in the United States. Quoting the U.S. Court of Appeals:

We live in an age of international commerce, where decisions reached in one corner of the world can reverbrate around the globe in less time than it takes to tell the tale. Thus, a ruling in NPI's favor would create perverse incentives for those who would use nefarious means to influence markets in the United States, rewarding them for erecting as many territorial firewalls as possible between cause and effect. (*U.S. v. Nippon Paper Industries Co., Ltd.*, 109 F.3d 1 at 8 [1997])

This is a brilliant conclusion to extend the power of the criminal law to circumstances clearly warranted by a scheme to fix prices of thermal fax paper sold in North America through Japanese trading houses and then sold into their U.S. subsidiaries. The indictment stated that NPI monitored the paper trail to make certain of fixed sales prices to the end user. This would be clear restraint of trade and a criminal violation in the United States. The Nippon case follows the case of *Hartford Fire Ins. Co. v. California*, 509 U.S. 764 (1993) where the U.S. Supreme Court determined that it is "well established by now that the Sherman Act applies to foreign conduct that was meant to produce and did in fact produce some substantial effect in the United States." The conduct in the Hartford Case in London met the test for civil antitrust actions in the United States.

The decision in the Nippon case represents the precise type of difficulty faced by prosecutors attempting to stamp out price-fixing activities in a global economy. And it illustrates how firewalls could protect a foreign corporation from criminal liability. The reality now is that no firewalls can be constructed, and no safe harbor can be reached from the oncoming storms of criminal liability for globalizing corporations in democratic nations with a law like the Sherman Act of 1890: "Every contract, combination in the form of trust or otherwise, or conspiracy, in restraint of trade or commerce among the several states, or with foreign nations is declared to be illegal." This means extraterritorial impact of this criminal law of the United States all over the world, but only when the criminal acts of price-fixing produce effects in the United States. For other nations with antitrust laws—U.S. globalizing companies violating foreign laws will face very probably the same consequences of extraterritorial effect. The global salubrious result would be that price-fixing may not prevail, which would in turn benefit consuming citizens everywhere and it would be a great boost for honest prices and honest business. This would mean national public control, but not international business corporate control and no relevance would exist for the WTO. Some scholars want a role for the WTO, but such a role seems superfluous in the light of the Nippon case (see Fox, 1997: 1).

To strongly reinforce the wise linking of significant competition policies with any trade liberalization, the UN, in its 1997 *World Investment Report*, emphatically stressed this key policy linkage. Kofi A. Annan, the Secretary-General of the United Nations, believed that competition policy has a key role to play when there is liberalization of foreign direct investment in host nations because such host nations are responsible to their citizens for maintaining the proper functioning of the markets to avoid monopolies, cartels, oligopolies and a wide range of anti-competitive strategies that destroy fair markets. The UN Conference on Trade and Development (UNCTAD) stated that foreign direct investment liberalization creates "more space for firms to pursue their interests in markets—as it invariably does—it becomes necessary, as a rule, to put in place competition laws to ensure that the former statutory obstacles to contestability are not replaced by anticompetitive practices of firms" (UN, 1997: 210). The broader policy implications center on the global importance of competition policies among nations and the many ways that international cooperation may be achieved among nations. The 1997 report must be praised for its forthright examination and analysis of the complex issues and its relevancy to the Multilateral Agreement on Investment posed by the OECD. It is now abundantly clear that there cannot be national unilateral disarmament by trade liberalization without simultaneous strenuous exertions of competitive law and policy demands on all market actors to behave properly. Trade liberalization is not surrender to markets in any intelligently conceived public policy. Mergers and acquisitions need intense scrutiny everywhere on earth. Public interests far exceed those of markets. The rule of law must be imposed vigorously on the markets and their actors (Fox, 1997).

Democratization

In the 1997 International Forum on Globalization, John Cavanagh summarized the motto of the third way of globalization: *dismantle corporate rule and democratize our economies.* This means that public policies must reflect the soul of the democratic nation and that trade policies must follow that soul looking for the best interests of the people, looking for trade policies that are in the best interests, the public interest of the people of a nation. Just nation-states must be benevolent to the people in them and trade policies must be just and benevolent, first and foremost, to those people who live on the land inside the nation. Most nations do not exist for international trade or commerce, particularly the geographically larger nations that are more self-sufficient like Brazil, Russia and the United States. It is clear that island nations like Britain and Japan or very small nations place trade much higher on their agendas of public policies, because they are driven by the circumstances of a lack of resources. They roam the globe for trade out of basic necessity, not out of a sophisticated love of the peoples of the earth. These behaviors are not much different from colonial actions of an earlier era with Hudson Bay and East Indian trading corporations haunting the globe during the colonizing centuries.

Trade policies do reflect national peculiarities, but they should reflect foremost the self-determination of the peoples of the nation to be *autonomos* in the world to the extent possible. It is better public policy to have trade policies reflect human nature which grows from complete dependence at birth to much greater independence as years pass by. Maximizing human desires to be *autonomos* is one way that trade policies would fit better into democratic nations that remain independent for good reasons. The laws of each nation are a touchstone of national sovereignty and of human autonomy to make laws of one's own choosing. This is what is meant by liberty (Saari, 1995).

Egalitarianism

A fundamental guideline for trade policies is to promote egalitarianism to the extent feasible in trading relationships. A democracy thrives with greater equality among citizens. Justice Thurgood Marshall's operating premise was based on equal justice under law. Justice is part of trading; fairness is a reason to trade with another, even to trust another person. Fairness promotes cooperation among people who wish to trade and competition is placed in a secondary role because of enhanced cooperation. From egalitarianism we derive reciprocity and comity—two ideas that appeal to our sense of fairness or justice. And reciprocity in trading is a vital factor to continued relations among people who trade with one another. Trading internationally is a repeat business when done successfully. Traders have to learn to give and take within limits of reciprocal giving and taking by others. The OTA study of MNEs showed how the world has not yet learned reciprocity because nations take from each other, but find it hard to give in return. Their globalizing corporations reflect the attitude of the nations. There is much value in designing trading rules that respect the mutual need of all peoples for reciprocity. Life is a lot better with it; trust becomes justified.

Depoliticization

The word is hard to pronounce, but depoliticization means reducing partisan politics to the extent feasible in trading rules in democratic nations so that people can trade with one another and not focus on party affliation. Socialist and capitalist gasoline burns the same way in your car. Liberals should buy from and sell to conservatives and vice versa. Trading rules are claimed to be depoliticized in GATT, NAFTA and WTO. If only this were true, there would not have been so much initial and continued disagreement over these agreements and resulting institutions across the globe.

A more potent feature of depoliticization is to kick globalizing corporations out of politics completely in all nations. The move to politicize large corporations and inject them into lobbying, legislation and governors' and presidents' offices is nothing more than another cold war hangover, an anachonistic practice that must be stopped for many reasons previously outlined. Automakers should make cars; airplane makers should make airplanes; governors should govern. Business ought to consider how much damage it creates in the body politic when it uses corporate assets to attain political goals. They and their surrogates in Congress complain ever so loudly when union dues are used for political purposes, never even giving a passing thought to shareholder anger at the use of corporate dollars to achieve political goals that shareholders may find incompatible with their own independent political views. Corporate money is not to be spent legally as if it is the private piggy bank of the CEOs and the boards of directors. Corporate spending on political goals has nothing to do with business in most cases; it is a total wasting of assets belonging to shareholders. Each act, each dollar spent on politics invites a counterreaction to the point where some are now advocating very strong measures to depoliticize corporate life—especially in international trade. There is no end to the actions citizens can take in a democracy to reassert their sovereign authority over corporations. Richard Grossman, the co-director of the Program on Corporations, Law and Democracy, spoke in 1996 of the basic need to "revoke the corporation" in all of its current senses and to start over:

We plan to accomplish these goals by state corporation codes, by rewriting corporate charters, by revoking charters, by forbidding corporations from owning other corporations, by limiting corporate capitalization and holding, by banning corporations entirely from participating in elections, in our lawmaking, in our education, by ending the absurdity of corporate personhood. (Grossman, 1996)

Even so great an advocate of big corporations as Peter Drucker is deeply disturbed by the too high salaries paid to CEOs of globalizing corporations, particularly the very largest. In March of 1997, at the age of 87, Peter Drucker was quoted in *Fortune* with this startlingly critical observation:

It disgusts Drucker that some of the media glorify people who get huge bonuses after laying off thousands of workers. Few executives, he says, can even imagine the hatred, contempt and fury that has been created—not primarily among blue-collar workers who have never had an exalted opinion of the "bosses"—but among middle management and professional people. [Drucker continued] I don't know what form it will take, but the envy developing from their enormous wealth will cause trouble. (*Fortune*, March 1997)

It is not solely the bad judgments of boards of directors in awarding multimillion-dollar salaries and bonuses and stock options and a myriad of other corporate perquisites, but equally bad judgment of CEOs in accepting such lavish and unwarranted payments that accumulate over time into grotequesly wasteful corporate expense and wasting of assets. Sometimes it is merely one degree off from theft. And the creation of class warfare by such actions is a sad commentary on the judgment of the CEOs as a group in today's world. Many of them ought to get out of the way and retire or take up another line of work or philanthropy. Depoliticization of business becomes even more potent a need in such circumstances of rank greediness (Hacker, 1997).

Transparency

The goal should be to open up globalizing corporate operations to more complete public scrutiny and it should increase with greater globalization. Internet and Freedom of Information Acts could be a godsend device here. Openness is a hallmark of the U.S. Securities and Exchange Commission (SEC) and its controls over the stock market. Freedom of Information Acts are a boon to democracy. Openness is so great that foreign companies from Europe are finding it very distressing to reveal matters they do not tell the public in Europe. International trade needs the truth to survive and transparency and freedom of information are clearly a way to achieve more complete public control that could be coordinated among national regulators, prosecutors and investigators, should cross-border controls need to be exercized. We should examine the transfer of the UN Truth Commission in El Salvador technique of study ''whose final report effectively forced or precluded from public office every single person it accused of a serious violation of human rights'' (Brower, 1997). Such a policy would enhance all cross-border relations of nations in regulating international commerce and globalizing corporations.

Sovereignty

In Chapters 3 and 4 of this book the idea of popular sovereignty was examined in some depth. The negative impact of globalizing corporations on national sovereignty was noted in many ways. It is clear that rules of international trade must be redesigned to maximize respect for, and conformity to, the sovereign authority of nations—all nations. The role of the nations as sovereign authority on behalf of the people is designed to get in the way of globalizing corporations to make certain no corporation does anything to impinge adversely on the people or place them in harm's way or violate their laws or sensibilities. While more controversial but of equal importance, nations ought to get in the way of regional authorities like the European Union when they attempt to usurp sovereign authority of the people of a nation. Whether it be a globalizing corporation, a regional authority or the United Nations itself—none of them should interfere with the sovereignty of the people, much as they may wish to supersede nations. This is the only way that 2,500 years of struggle to achieve a democracy by the people will be protected ultimately and kept alive continually over long periods of time. Fake allegiance (prompted by false advertising) to globalizing corporations, to regional authorities or to the UN is not a secure foundation for law and order in national or international affairs. The UN charter is clear on this.

For those who may think the United States is understanding clearly what ''We the People'' means in the national constitution because of its 200-hundred-year focus on constitutional order, there should be further reflection caused by the case of *U.S. Term Limits Inc. v. Thornton*, 115 S.Ct. 1842 (1995). The Supreme Court of the United States appears to have four members who mistakenly think sovereignty is found in the people of each state in the union, not in the people as a whole. It is as if the thoughts of the southerner Calhoun from South Carolina had new life breathed into them long after the Civil War. Since this matter has been analyzed at some length in Chapter 3 it is only necessary here to recall that examination and refer to it. It is amazing how obtuse the Justices seem to be to historical learning (Cates, 1996). Or perhaps there is an agenda that needs to be worked out in historical terms to accomplish some other goals yet to be announced from an agendaless institution.

Regulatory Capitalism

In Chapter 5 the idea of regulatory capitalism was formulated and explored. The idea is that the United States has designed a 200-year-old regulated capitalistic order for domestic and foreign commerce. The domestic side among the 50 states is well developed while the power for the international side for foreign commerce found in Article One, Section 8 of the U.S. Constitution is anemic, insipid and sickly in nature. That nature is by design, not accident. The OTA study reviewed earlier in this chapter said the same thing much more elegantly. Much of the current debate over international trade in NAFTA, GATT and WTO centers upon this asymmetrically distorted and incompletely developed national power. Regulatory capitalism certainly includes the ideas of extraterritoriality mentioned in this chapter. But unfortunately, regulatory capitalism fails to offer international protection for labor standards, environmental standards, and health, safety and consumer protections in international trade agreements and treaties. Both Chapters 6 and 7 explored the implications of the lack of protection for U.S. citizens. What we find is that compact discs get more protection than human beings who work and need adequate protection, according to U.S. Representative David Bonior. Property rights are elevated to a greater importance than human rights. Can this stand for long in a democracy?

From the standpoint of the sovereign powers of the people in a constitutional democracy premised upon egalitarian norms generated by co-equal human being citizens operating with popular sovereignty, there is clearly a subordinate role for state-chartered globalizing corporations in such a regulated capitalistic order. A subordinate role is all that is left for the *Fortune* 500 corporations, their CEOs and the people who work for them. The same is true of the subordinate place for foreign corporations being hosted in the United States. The same is true of business as a whole, it is subordinate to the citizens of the nation. The law and order expressed in the regulated capitalistic system, rather fully expressed in the last 200 years, shows no change of course on this issue. The multinational corporation is a myth (Doremus, Keller, Pauly and Reich, 1998). Even the last fifteen years of concerted ''deregulation'' and ''privatization'' are mere wisps of wind in the general course the nation has taken and those efforts of business could never change the fundamental position of the American nation. It is painfully obvious that trade laws for regulation of international commerce must be expanded vigorously by all nations working in concert. The United States must work hardest of all nations to develop symmetry and balance so that its regulated capitalistic order domestically developed becomes the norm for its international regulation of the capitalistic order. Americans do not want strong internal controls and weak external controls of business—they want balance and strength in both sectors. Nor does strength suggest blockage of German, Japanese or other businesses. Some argue that a new Bretton Woods–style international treaty control of capital flows, currency controls and other regulations is needed by nation-states before another monetary global chaos erupts (Block, 1977; Woodrow Wilson Conference, 1998).

Taxation

Immediate and far-reaching reform is needed by nations in the field of taxation of international commerce. This book identified transfer pricing schemes as the worst source of tax evasion and tax avoidance games played by globalizing corporations on the people of nations. Ask any tax official in any nation—it is a joke being played on citizens who pay taxes in every nation. Global law and order in the tax field needs a flaming rebirth just as soon as the fires can be lit. Global trade without taxes being paid is as close to national robbery and burglary as one can get. Host nations finding their guests defrauding them on taxes ought to get strong and tough remedies like kicking the globalizing corporations out of the nations forever; and blacklisting them to boot may be deserved, so that they are in no position to harm other nation's citizens. Equal treatment would mean that both domestic and foreign corporations would get the same treatment, a matter that seems only just. Nations have to be ready to dissolve tax cheaters by legal means, killing their corporate charters by dissolution involuntarily. And there is no doubt that trade liberalization found in the proposed Multilateral Agreement on Investment is valid only if tax reform of international business is a part of the change at the same time. One should never proceed without the other.

To stop tax cheating in the United States, Senator Byron Dorgan of North Dakota, who was a state tax official and who has pursued this matter for years, has attacked the arm's length tax approach and Section 482 of the U.S. Internal Revenue Code for being "hopelessly obsolete and in my judgment misguided." In April of 1995, the U.S. General Accounting Office reported on international taxation and transfer payments in a study that offered no clear evidence of transfer price abuses in the narrow sample of corporate tax returns from 1987 to 1991. However, it was found by clear evidence that no U.S. income taxes were paid by a higher percentage of large foreign-controlled companies and even domestic companies in that period (U.S. GAO, 1995).

The most obvious answer to keep tax revenues from drying up completely from globalizing corporations is found in the state of California's worldwide formulary apportionment of taxes that puts an end to transfer pricing (U.S. GAO, 1995). Taxes are calculated on a formula that is clear and respecfully fair. By contrast, the federal tax system is poorly administered, globalizing corporations are given an opportunity to argue about everything and anything to delay paying taxes, and income wealth is too often not taxed at all. All of this should encourage nations to explore the California system of taxation apportionment by formula. The more that nations would tax in this manner, the sooner the Internet could offer to the world both the weather and the taxes paid to each nation by every globalizing corporation. Since all of this data is public in nature, no national tax authorities would ever need to wonder what the hosted globalizing corporations paid in reality on a real-time basis. The citizens would be well armed, too. Not a bad future state of affairs given the current state.

Due Process

Protection of dissent is the main reason for free speech rights that are exercised by whistleblowers who work in globalizing corporations. They spot something wrong and they let the world know about it. To assure these honest people some due process, there is a need to protect them under a global treaty designed to protect the people and the truth. A treaty among nations would strengthen the relationship of workers to corporations trying to cover up wrongdoing. A UN-funded regime of officers who could provide a safe haven and assure procedural protections for whistleblowers is vital to the citizens of nations. An educational program about such a treaty would let workers know of the protections. To smoke out illegal and harmful corporate behaviors from the inside requires national and international attention because this criminality is happening everywhere on earth now. Trade liberalization of any kind should be conditioned upon moving forward the procedural and other safeguards whistleblowers need when they risk their lives and reputations for people in their nation and in other nations. The global impact of whistleblowing activity is no less important than the global impact of human rights activists who have developed a similar form of protection with safe houses in various nations. The risks whistleblowers take should be borne by all of the world, not just the single person. This is fairness at work on a global basis—the building of a humane global society and strengthening of ties among workers in the world by explicit treaty posted in every business place.

To wrap up this part of Chapter 10, consider the nine areas of concern just covered to be merely a stimulative list of national trends and ideas that deserve serious consideration by nations that wish to provide greater measures of law and order and justice in international commerce by their own globalizing corporations to keep them in line. These must be coordinated with other nations' efforts in structuring, confining and checking the visiting globalizing corporations they are hosting. Vast new areas of global cooperation among nations must be opened up and pursued with vigor and renewed energy. That energy will help nations, people, workers and, yes, even globalizing corporations will be helped because the rotten apples of business will be culled out on an international basis. Trust in business honesty may even rise justifiably in that future world.

AN ANSWER TO THE MOST IMPORTANT ISSUES: DIRECTING WEALTH INVESTMENTS IN COMMUNITIES IN A WORLD SOCIETY: WHOSE JOB IS IT TO DIRECT?

> Foreign direct investment (FDI) continues to be a driving force of the globalization process that characterizes the modern world economy. In 1996, the global FDI stock was valued at $3.2 trillion.
>
> Rubens Ricupero, Secretary-General of the United Nations
> Conference on Trade and Development, July 1997

By failing to raise the fundamental question of whose job it is to direct the wealth of the world into one investment or another, most people probably assume that the director is the owner of the wealth. Capitalism is based upon private property and the owner of that property can decide what to do with his or her own property. If Ted Turner wants to give the UN a billion-dollar gift, who's to challenge him? In other words, what is the question? It would seem on its face to be an absurdity being raised.

Vast wealth lies in the control of the largest 750 giant globalizing corporations. It is in the multitrillion dollar range. For the CEOs of the corporations, however, none are the sole owners of the corporate wealth, not even Bill Gates at Microsoft with his corporate share that was being valued in 1998 at $45 billion and rising rapidly. Share ownership is distributed and so are voting rights and protections.

The more exact question is—what is the relationship of the CEO to the wealth of GE or the CEO of any of the 749 other giant corporations? Their role is more like that of a trustee than any other role—to protect and preserve the assets and hopefully to make a profit or at least break even or not suffer losses. A trustee needs to work for beneficiaries who are the beneficial shareholders. Identifiable are 241 groups and individuals holding $1.1 trillion in net worth (*Forbes*, 10/6/97). These were the most wealthy human beings on earth in 1997, but there are mutual funds and pension funds with trillions in shares that millions of people own. All have a stake in the corporate wealth. Due to size, GE has enormous spare financial reserves to place billions of dollars wherever it chooses. As reported in Chapter 6 of this book, GE has taken $35 billion spare dollars and invested it in Europe and invested $150 million in China. Another $40 billion is planned for Asia in 1998. By what right does GE invest such sums anywhere it wants on earth without review by public authority represented by the sovereign people of the United States? Where is GE charter authority in the charter it has from a state? And who granted the GE charter? And what is their global authority? Where is the power of the people in the Constitution of the United States in all of this?

The slender reed of authority for the CEOs of major globalizing corporations is tenuous at best. In 1996, when President Clinton challenged DuPont's subsidiary Conoco in its attempted trade and investment in Iran, with whom the United States restricts trade by law, DuPont and Conoco backed off right away from the Iranian deal. The Helms-Burton Act, though challenged by many nations, does itself challenge trade and investment in Cuba by any corporation and its officers. So, let us not assume a thoughtless stance that corporations can do whatever they wish with their assets. Free enterprise is not that free and it never has been. That is the first falsehood of unlimited power; to expose the reality is that the power of a CEO is a limited power of investment subject to many restrictions and conditions that are both public and private in nature. However, many CEOs give the impression that they need no approval beyond the board of directors to invest as they please. This is a fatal flaw in thinking by many corporate leaders.

Looking back in this book, the question of investment authority of globalizing corporations in foreign nations was highlighted by noting the $330 billion in profits of the *Fortune* 500 in 1997 that shows the vast sums of wealth to direct in the United States and elsewhere. The 1997 UN report shows that the United States was by far the largest FDI recipient and investor abroad. The source of $85 billion invested from outside the nation into the United States matches what it invested abroad—$85 billion in investment going out of the nation in 1996 (UN, 1997: xix). No other nation experienced such levels or flows of investments in 1996. To recapitulate, in Chapter 2 of this book both Ford and Boeing investment practices were reviewed. Investment choices emerged as the most important of issues. Chapter 6 makes clear how much foreign direct investment has become a significant feature of global investment. The 1997 UN report reinforces that importance. In 1998 there was a downswing in global capital flows and a change in direction.

Controls over investment is an immense topic. First, we should look at the field with an overview. Next, the Multilateral Agreement on Investment (MAI) should be studied. And finally, we should conclude with advice on investment strategies for nations. This next few years will be more important than ever for at least one potential reason. The OECD, a 29-member, Paris-based group of nations announced its intentions to offer a proposed agreement for mutual consideration of the nations. They proposed to finalize terms by May of 1998 (WSJ, Bray, 5/27/97) but that was deferred for a second time. On April 29, 1998, OECD decided to create a ''period of reflection on the MAI proposal until October 1998 (WP, Swardson, 4/29/98: C13). If granted fast track authority, this or the next president of the United States may be proposing an up or down vote on the complex MAI proposal. The public had better get well prepared to understand the issues and to direct their Congress to vote the way they wish. Hopefully, this book will help citizens in many nations to make a sound judgment.

Whose Job Is It to Direct Wealth?

Directing wealth of a society is a job for public authority which is primarily expressed as tax systems, as public debt, and as public goals to achieve. Such goals are found in the national constitutions and implementing legislation. In the U.S. Constitution the commerce clause regulates trade among the 50 states, with foreign nations and with American Indian tribes. This is the grand regulator of them all for the United States. It must not be overlooked. Once the government of the people is established in a democracy and society is functioning, there is room for further direction of wealth by private means by individuals, globalizing corporations, other businesses, religions, educational organizations and many other organizations. The primacy of the nation-state is a clear thesis of this book. Public law and order precedes all other needs, especially private needs that must be subordinated to the greater good of the whole society. Even those whose wealth is calculated in the billions of dollars are subject to this communal power because they only have such wealth recognized by a community that respects them when the respect is mutual. A band of pirates quickly would put a short end to such wealth accumulations.

Within the context of public control of the economy lie the many questions of control over the investments by domestic and foreign globalizing corporations. Decisions by public authority to tax, to control currency, to regulate banking, to protect shareholders, to control interstate and foreign commerce and to control many other matters—such as bankruptcy laws for defunct businesses—are important, but are not the prime focus here. The control of investments of wealth is a narrower set of questions and issues. The subject to be pursued does not include dispositions of property on death which involves the entire probate system of controls over private property by state, federal and local authorities.

First, let us examine dispassionately the facts of wealth investment, to answer the question: How big a task is direction of wealth? One of the largest numbers to be used in this book, as an indicator only, is the 1994 gross domestic product of 40 large nations—$27.8 trillion. For another 140 nations the figure would be much larger. Woven within that figure is the work of most of the globalizing corporations identified in the appendix of this book. The gross domestic product of the United State in 1995 was $7.2 trillion. The U.S. direct investment position abroad in all countries was $612 billion in 1994. The largest single nation in the list of invested places for the United States was the United Kingdom at $102 billion. U.S. assets abroad rose cumulatively from $936 billion in 1980 to $2.47 trillion by 1994. Foreign assets in the United States were $543 billion in 1980 rising to $3.1 trillion by 1994. This fifteen-year rise is 164% for assets abroad, 518% rise in foreign-owned assets in the United States. The picture is simple—a lot more wealth came into the United States than left it during that period. Foreign direct investment is part of that increase in wealth in the United States but not by U.S. citizens, by foreign interests instead.

International capital markets are studied by the International Monetary Fund (IMF). The 1994 capital flow to developing countries was $125 billion (IMF, 1995: 3). There were many national restrictions on capital flows in and out of nations, clear evidence that nations are vitally concerned with investment practices of any kind crossing borders. One large flow IMF noted was derivative contracts that are exchange-traded, including interest rate futures and options, currency futures and options, and stock-market indexed futures and options. Globally this trading grew from $.6 trillion in 1986 to $8.8 trillion in 1994. This is largely casino capitalism or unregulated trading and it is linked to the Barings Bank scandal reviewed in Chapter 6 of this book (IMF, 1995: 17, 138; Millman, 1995).

Finally, by way of general background, the IMF noted that institutional investors are a very rapidly growing part of capital markets. This includes the 300 largest U.S. institutional investors' assets which rose from $535 billion in 1975 to $7.2 trillion in 1993. Five major industrial nations in their pension funds, insurance companies, and mutual funds had close to $13 trillion in assets in 1993. The global equity market capitalization in 1993 was $14.1 trillion. Government debt in the seven largest industrialized nations was $9 trillion. What should all of this tell you? The world is now quite rich and getting richer by the minute so the question is not wealth creation, but wealth distribution, which is a governing problem, not a problem for private businesses. Next, what does the multinational corporation have to do with all of this?

Raymond Vernon, the well-recognized expert on multinationals, whose work has been mentioned numerous times in this book, suggested that by the 1980s almost every major U.S. industrial enterprise and banking institution was organized on a multinational basis with subsidiaries and affliates all over the world. This development spurred the growth of foreign direct investment. Oligopoly conditions helped to spread the MNCs, and the sheer size, special technological capabilites, and geographical spread of oil and metals were further growth factors. But Vernon identified ''the obsolescing bargain'' of foreign investment. For example, oil exporting nations after a while needed no capital since they exported oil and capital; they had easy access to technical help, but did need access to channels of distribution.

Most significantly, Vernon thought attitudes and interests of governments were the key point of concern for multinationals. That is, nations would invite MNCs into the nation knowing that the MNC had global concerns and could not devote all of its resources to one nation. Furthermore, U.S. MNCs would never lose their U.S. nature and U.S. controls, nor do other nations let go of their MNCs. He noted the very poorly conceived controls over the MNCs except for some of the bilateral tax agreements. As we have seen throughout this book the conditions have not changed much in the last few decades. And under weak controls, the MNCs have become even more complex and hard to understand with vast numbers of subsidiary corporations, alliances, joint ventures to both muddy up the water of international investment and to share risks of several kinds that vary by nation and industry over time. Let us look at the risks in a little more detail.

The risks of foreign direct investment are from two distinct sources. One is business decisions and one is governmental risk. The business risks are not relevant here, like not gauging competition accurately. Political risks from nations comes in five versions from a host nation receiving investment capital:

1. Expropriation, nationalization and confiscation of the corporate business,

2. De facto expropriation by a series of actions designed to get rid of the foreign corporation, or destroy it, or weaken it through heavy taxation,

3. Currency risk where profits cannot be remitted to the parent company in the home nation,

4. Political violence and disruption, and

5. Breach of contract (Comeaux and Kinsella, 1996).

Nationalizations of foreign direct investments were many: Soviet Union (1917), Brazil and Mexico (1930s), China, Bulgaria, Czechoslovakia, Hungary and Poland (1940s), Cuba, Bolivia and Eygpt (1950s). Middle Eastern decolonization meant national authority over oil fields. Up to the 1970s expropriations continued, but then began to taper off.

In the 1980–1998 period the flows of direct investment, even into Cuba which seized about $2 billion in private assets, is rising. Even *Forbes* included Fidel Castro among the world's richest capitalists with a net worth of $1.4 billion in 1997. Whether the Commandante would agree is open to question. No one can doubt the change in Russia, China, India and other nations toward investment, and even state-owned MNCs have invited capital investment from other sources. Oil businesses and their investment surrogates are scouring the earth in nations that at one time would have shot them for such subversive activity, or what was viewed as such capitalistic and parasitic investments (Comeaux and Kinsella, 1996: xxiv).

The dramatic fifteen-year reversal is a product of the end of the cold war, competition for capital in developing nations, liberalizing of investment codes, embracing of foreign direct investment, signing of bilateral treaties, and other factors such as peace. Most of the investment is east and west in the Northern Hemisphere of the earth; it is not so much north-south on the globe, and Africa remains a Dark Continent devoid of any significant investment. So there is significant change underway in several different directions all at once. Next, how do nations control investments into them?

The framework for control of foreign investment is most effective under the laws of the host nation that is receiving the investment (Folsom and Gordon, 1995: 577). The home nation of the MNC and various organizations may play a role, especially when foreign investment is insured by the World Bank or by national federal agencies like the Overseas Private Investment Corporation (OPIC) in the United States. Nations condition entry, operations and exit from the nation by restricting the permissions given in permits. Controls come in many forms including ownership requirements, acquisitions of types of assets, limits on management, standards of performance, transfer controls over movement of capital and movement of earnings and some nations have foreign investment review committees such as the United States (Folsom and Gordon, 1995: 588). Regional or global trade agreements like NAFTA and GATT included "trade-related aspects of investment" that covered matters for labor, environment and special property protections for intellectual property recognized in the United States and many other nations. Bilateral agreements in the field of taxing international commerce are still a very strong practice.

The control of foreign investment is complicated a bit more by a few other controls over investments and trade of goods and services. Most of these controls have been around forever or at least as long as the nation's existence and are well-known: customs taxes, tariffs, duty free imports, anti-dumping duties, subsidies and countervailing duties, import controls, export licenses, foreign corrupt practices, boycott provisions, licensing controls and other matters. The body of law is not large, but it articulates national interest in international trade and limitedly, an interest in investment. What troubles most people who look from the outside at foreign investment?

The most troublesome part of the lack of control over foreign investment is the very obvious lack of adequate investment directed toward the bulk of the world's population. No one could argue reasonably that $125 billion is adequate for 4.5 billion people. It would be an insult to the intelligence of everyone on earth to do so. Here are the refugees—some 23 million in 1998 without a place to call home. Here are sickness and starvation and war. Here there is need calling out for help from investors. Where are they? Where is the Marshall Plan for them? The disaffection is expressed by Richard Falk, a noted international law scholar from Princeton University, who believes there is a terrible investment imbalance:

At the very core of this system is the effort of the G-7 states to establish economic policy for the world as a whole—an arrogant undertaking, considering that 80% of humanity is excluded from the process, and that it is the peoples of the South who are being victimized by current operating practices. (Falk in Report of the International People's Tribunal to judge the G-7, Tokyo, July 1993)

The same type of disaffection for investment practices of the rich nations and rich globalizing corporations was expressed by Catherine Caufield in her *Masters of Illusion* (1996). Along with a number of critics, Caufield asked whether the third of a trillion dollars lent since 1946 by the World Bank has helped the poor of the world? The answer is tragic. The poor have not benefitted, but have paid dearly for such investments. Who profits from the World Bank are its bureaucracy, the heads of government, well-connected contractors, exporters, consultants and middlemen in rich countries. The rich in the host nation become richer than ever. The donors to the World Bank, the taxpayers of the rich nations, are the middle class or poor who pay taxes for distribution to rich in poor countries (Caufield, 1996: 338). This borders on insanity in world affairs. As some say, 50 years of this is certainly enough, regardless of the reform underway that is so highly idiosyncratic with the changing leaders and their whims.

There is not much doubt that there is justifiable and growing unhappiness with the World Bank and the IMF (Danaher, 1996). New investment controls by nations could change this investment climate overnight from big dams to large solar projects or methane combinations projects to boost local disconnected energy systems for the billions who need help to attain more power, new water systems, new health systems, and better communication systems. More investment and better policies are needed for this flow of investment. But there is a fifteen-year-old, newer disaffection in the way globalizing corporations direct investment capital flowing from industrial nations to newly developing nations like Mexico, Malaysia and South Korea. It is this investment flow of capital and its control that is the precise concern next. The problems are similar to the capital flow to the poorest nations, but the consequences again reverberate back into the donor population, the nation that is the source of the capital. Who should control investment practices of globalizing corporations? Why must they do so?

More investment controls by home nations over the foreign direct investments by globalizing corporations made outside the home nation is the precise zone of capital investment that is the subject of the central question that is ending this book—who should direct investment practices of globalizing corporations? The principal argument is that home nations must become more responsible to their citizens to review exactly every investment made by any corporation and approve of investments made outside of the nation, even into alliances, joint ventures and any type of subsidiary corporation. Host nations must be much more deeply involved in each investment action; not just in counting totals invested, not just in begging for corporate information, and not just in after-the-fact discovery that $1 billion in investment capital just left your boundaries. There must be a completely new approach to regulation of capital investment by every nation on earth working in concert. The effort is not to stop investments that the public approves; these would go ahead. It is to stop those which the public disapproves and to modify many investments to comply with the public interest of home and host nation jointly. The role of the nations must be injected into the capital investment process with renewed vigor and with not the slightest hint of apology or regret. This is exactly where the public interest lies now and in the long-run future. Too few minds have been involved in the investment of capital, too few interests taken into consideration. The World Bank example illustrates how things must change for them. So also must things change for the 750 globalizing corporations listed in the appendix of this book. Each of them must bend every effort to stop the old secretive way of moving capital and instead ventilate, air out, let sunshine into the musty investment process, yes, even democratize it and make it a lively and noisy market for the demos. The people do not need any of the stuffed-shirt merger and acquisition types, legislators, bankers, and diplomats and all of their hangers-on to accomplish this wider public interest goal. There are talents abounding on the planet for these capital investment judgments and they do not exist just inside banks, investment firms or corporate headquarters of giant corporations. The *Forbes* 241 wealthiest individuals and families certainly do not have all of the talent to make these investments. Some of their judgments are sadly short-sighted and deficient. And none of the managers of funds of all types is capable of wisely announcing where capital shall be invested. The decision matrix must be widely spread out to many greater sectors of people all over the globe. This change could possibly help to keep peace more than any other thing we could do in the public affairs of the world. What do we face in making this transformation of capital investment practices by democratizing it?

There are but two control points. The home nation and the host nation in investments of capital are the two control points; all of the rest are minor and easily evaded by crafty lawyers and business people. The guardians of the public interest rest in both nations and they must work together. Home nation control over the parent corporations and host nation control over the subsidiary corporations that is jointly exercised and well coordinated will keep all alliances, joint ventures and other forms of international business collaboration in public view at all times. Heightened international cooperation is the soundest answer. More treaties are needed, not fewer. Henry Kaufman, an American investment expert, argued for greater financial controls (WP, Kaufman, 1/28/98).

One attitude must be identified and rejected as harmful to international cooperation. Up to 1979, there was a yearning built up for almost two decades that pleaded for a peculiar type of corporation—an *anational corporation*. This is mentioned in Chapter 2 and Appendix B of this book. Corporate officials from many corporations asked for something like the anational corporation on the international scene—a corporation not answerable to any nation. It fell on deaf ears inside nations. In the United States corporate officials from Dow Chemical Company, General Motors, the National Association of Manufacturers, Pfizer, Inc., Citicorp, IBM, Ford, Caterpillar Tractor Co., Merck and Co., Nestle, Ronson and Union Carbide and many others voiced such a desire. The 1973 U.S. Congress heard much of this complaining attitude (Munkirs, 1985: 188–216).

What has been happening is a transformation of American corporate capitalism from highly decentralized and smaller businesses to a centralized planning private sector, according to Munkirs (Munkirs, 1985). This meant that industrial policy was thought to come from the globalizing corporations, not from governments. Investment of capital was thought to be a matter for concern exclusively of private businesses. In the *anational* corporation a transnational firm would be totally free from control by any other institution-nations, and anyone else. They would invest wherever and whenever they wished. This is the cosmocorp referred to before—the supposed utopian wave of the future. The future has come and gone and we still have the same old nations and the same old corporations. The anational idea has died except for an occasional hiccup from some corporate official about the company belonging to the world. We now know that an anational corporation would have become a very dangerous actor on the international scene. There is a groundswell of new understanding that corporations are deeply embedded in their home nations. There is no corporate life in space outside of nations. Responsibility lies with nations alone to control globalizing corporations. A study confirms the myth of the global corporation (Doremus, Keller, Pauly and Reich, 1998).

Nations that do not take seriously their responsibility to direct and control capital investment invite potential disaster. They are like the tax haven nations that deserve what they are likely to get in the future as their destructive, crime and drug-ridden, money-laundering and sleazy actions are made so obvious to the world. Cold cash of rational nations will drive the ''hot money'' out of existence in the next few decades, if that long. Even worse is in store for lax nations. The worst condition is not easy to express and many authors approach it in different ways. The central fear is a rebirth of facism arising in a chaotic global economic mess created by business. Such a mess would very probably reflect a reinvention of archaic capital investment practices aloof from the democracies in a variety of more totalitarian forms of unjust states. From this tailspin democracies might never fully recover as the world would head into totalitarian darkness once again.

Corporate Investment Controls by Nations—The U.S. Experience

Resistance to government controls of capital investment is likely to be great and biased. Let us take a look at the experience of the United States in the two decades from 1960 to 1980. Under conditions of a full cold war with a nuclear stand-off between the United States and the Soviet Union, and when the Cuban missile crisis had yet to flower in October of 1963, and the Kennedy assassination yet to unfold, and the Vietnam War and the Civil Rights revolution were yet to happen, there came a need to control capital flows for many reasons. James P. Hawley, an American scholar, in 1987 wrote a wisely uncommon perspective on these two decades titled *Dollars and Borders: U.S. Government Attempts to Restrict Capital Flows, 1960–1980* (1987). As the title suggests, the United States tried, but failed to develop controls over capital movement in:

1. The 1962 Revenue Act
2. The Interest Equalization Tax Act—1963–1971
3. The Voluntary Capital Control Programs—1965–1967
4. The Mandatory Capital Control Programs—1968–1971
5. Eurocurrency Controls—1979–1980.

A nation-state, the United States of America, tried to control and restrict international movements of capital through initiatives of four presidents. Acrimonious conflict developed between the four administrations on one side, and the U.S.–based multinational corporations and the banks on the other side. Hawley believed that the Eurodollar grew out of the efforts to control capital in the United States. The social and political character of capitalists is brought into the equation along with their economic practices. This research reveals a very illuminating side to American corporate capitalism that is not unique. Similar evidence accumulated during the Second World War about American business attitudes (Sutherland, 1983). Hawley predicted: "In the future, there is little doubt that we will again witness a variety of attempts by governments to control and re-regulate increasingly integrated international capital markets and institutions" (Hawley, 1987: 4). The first example to come to mind is Senator Jeff Bingaman's 1996 legislative proposals, then Senator Byron Dorgan's attack on transfer pricing fraud and finally, many senators' attacks on corporate welfare. This book itself falls within Hawley's prediction. Fights over NAFTA and GATT and "fast track" are part of it with very heavy lifting by leaders of the U.S. House of Representatives Richard Gephardt and David Bonior. Continued struggle in this field is assured.

After some sparring, the question of direct investment versus exporting was left in an inconclusive posture (Hawley, 1987: 32–33). Big business had its liturgy which read, "The business goose that laid the golden egg of foreign

investment may die if one imposes capital export controls'' (Hawley, 1987: 43).
"Jawboning" by the Johnson administration was called "voluntary capital controls." A Presidential Executive Order No.11–387 imposed controls over capital
export under authority of Section 5(b) of the Trading With the Enemy Act of
1917. On January 1, 1968 there was an attempt at mandatory control (Hawley,
1987: 90). The controls failed eventually; and so it was the same with all of the
other attempts. Hawley's book tried to understand why this strange result occurred, a stand-off.

Hawley's conclusion is that the state must protect capitalism from itself. "My
work, which supports Polyani's thesis, suggests that contemporary state monetary policy tends toward growing fragmentation and is increasingly susceptible
to pressures for massive deregulation, which, if successful, threaten the stability
of the global economic system" (Hawley, 1985: 170). Consider the massive
further deregulation by the MAI being proposed for 1998 or later by the OECD,
and what it could bring to the world. This proposal is explored in a few pages
in more depth.

Hawley made a number of wise observations from his research. One of the
most *profound* for today's world is his belief that the nation-state must be autonomous from globalizing corporations and from transnational capital. The
nation-state is embedded in a much larger web of social and legal and economic
and political concerns than any globalizing corporation, no matter how big the
corporation. Hawley argued that the state mediates between larger social, political and economic interests than any globalizing corporation. And, as Hawley
believed, the interests among those in international capital formation are complex and contradictory themselves. "This contributes to the state's capacity, and
indeed sometimes its necessity, to operate independently of capital" (Hawley,
1987: 145). The state must stiff-arm some powerful economic interests who will
never get what they want from the government. Separation of government and
corporations is important to the future existence of corporations, noted at the
outset of this book.

Capital controls like those examined by Hawley are expressions of national
economic sovereignty of the people of a nation, a frank recognition of dual
sources of independent leadership (Lindblom, 1977: 178–194). A priority existed in the mind of President Abraham Lincoln:

Labor is prior to, and independent of, capital. Capital is only the fruit of labor, and could
never have existed if labor had not first existed. Labor is the superior of capital, and
deserves much the higher consideration. (Quoted by President Theodore Roosevelt on
August 31, 1910 in a speech titled "The New Nationalism," in Osawatomie, Kansas.)

And business interests are not monolithic. Business interests represent contradictory interests in both growth and stability (Hawley, 1987: 150). Profit is
not a unitary idea; accounting conventions vary and disagreements over which
convention to follow illustrate this. The size of globalizing corporations and

each corporation's inherent complexity does not yield a single view of what is best for that firm. Internal firm coherence and external firm class cohesiveness with other firms are not a given state of affairs equal to "business interests." Hawley points to the great mediating tasks of the state among ideologies of big and small business, among dying and growing businesses, between old and new products, among geographical differences of markets in addition to mediation with business and the rest of the world, both inside the nation and outside of the nation. No global corporation is capable of taking on and profiting from the immense role of the nation-state. Often the tasks that need doing are thankless jobs and voters are often fickle.

As Hawley summarized:

The capital controls in this study were responses to what state officials perceived as serious monetary disorder after 1960, even though the existence of a monetary crisis was barely recognized by many banks and corporate managers. Such action meant sacrificing what state managers saw as the short-run interests of the TNCs and TNBs [transnational banks] by restricting capital outflow in order to protect the ability of the state to pursue its foreign and domestic politics. . . . The history of the five capital controls to deal with the payment deficit illustrates that state intervention leads to financial innovation. (Hawley, 1987: 157)

The nation-states today from Canada, the United States and Britain to France are tending toward more separation from the corporate free trade ideology. Even Indonesia had the temerity to think of a currency control board, raising the ire of the IMF and others in 1998. The popular votes in recent elections illustrate the very different direction desired by the people. The leaders of the nations are responding and must respond to the people to stay in power.

Part of the mediating process with global capital will be capital controls of nations (maybe a new Bretton Woods–type of control) reinserted into the public equation of control. This may set off a further search in business to escape controls. This may then trigger another search by nations for more than capital controls, perhaps even another round of expropriations in the decades ahead, if Hawley is correct that capital and the state are in a symbiotic relationship. But symbiosis is one view and another is superior-subordinate. The state is superior to the corporation, its creature. These two may alternate over time, waxing and waning. When capitalism of any variety produces 12%+ unemployment, when downsizing of longtime employees to shift their work globally to cheaper labor occurs, when capitalism demands a lesser welfare state along with a borderless world coupled with selling off public property at cheap prices to make a few rich, then the state will most certainly become a candidate for demagogues, and facism could reveal itself when the markets fail (Greider, 1997: 53, 363, 364, 385–386). The world has seen this condition before, in the 1930s.

Multilateral Agreement on Investment—OECD, 1998 or 1999 or Whenever

The proposed Multilateral Agreement on Investment (MAI) is under study and negotiation in Paris, France at the OECD, the 29-member Organization for Economic Cooperation and Development. The proposal is designed to protect investors' financial investments in 29 nations. To do this, MAI must tie up governments and stop them from doing what the people may want for five years at a minimum and 20 years in some cases. MAI is cleverly designed and extremely lethal to democracies and the ordinary people in them. It was under secretive negotiation from 1995 to late 1997 and early 1998. Few people even realize the dangers of the MAI, thus this explanation and commentary. The MAI proposal is not regulated capitalism as defined in this book, it is regulated government, as Tony Clarke of Canada wrote:

The MAI is designed to establish a whole new set of global rules for investment that will grant transnational corporations (TNCs) the unrestricted "right" and "freedom" to buy, sell, and move their operations whenever and wherever they want around the world, unfettered by government intervention or regulation. (Clarke, 1997: 260) (See also Clarke and Barlow, 1997 and 1998)

From the data already explored in this and previous chapters, the fact is that no one needs an agreement on investments to encourage a global flow of capital investment funds; $129 Billion of global investment to the developing world was doing quite well, thank you, in 1996, according to the UN. The solution to protection of investments lies in treating people well so they do not seek nationalization of businesses. Further "liberalization" of investment rules plunders the political powers of the people and labor. The MAI is corporate political rule not trade-related in any reasonable way. The MAI is classical economics gone wild, the specific disease is megalomania, a delusion of greatness or delusion of wealth. To imagine any nation calling itself a self-respecting democracy that would wish to sign this MAI proposal is almost beyond credibility. The MAI effort is exactly the opposite of the capital controls proposed in this book, and it suffers from narrow self-centeredness that does not seek greater responsiblility toward the public by business. The MAI will stimulate more casino capitalism. The MAI is exceptionally unwise public policy for any democracy of sovereign citizens who wish to rule their own lives and nations.

Secrecy itself by the OECD is anti-democratic behavior. What has been learned by a few about the MAI is that since 1995 this agreement has been under review by businesses and a few government agents, but nothing is available to the public (including this author who tried to obtain a copy of the proposal draft directly from OECD and the U.S. State Department). Only bits of secondary information here and there could be found until a secret draft of the MAI was found and placed on the Internet for the world to see. And the Internet copy is dated at this writing. Is this any way to treat the world's citizens? Is this any way to treat a subject of such fundamental importance? Who needs an OECD at all? This all appears to be the trailing part of the free trade ideology that was described before in this chapter. It appears to be more of the secrecy that haunted the NAFTA and GATT negotiations and it is linked to the late 1997 fast-track debates, where no one will say MAI will be fast-tracked for the 750 largest corporations in the appendix of this book. This logic is emerging as the justification for secrecy in a democratic society. How could the president of the United States allow U.S. federal agents to take part in a massive anti-democratic change in the investment rules for 29 nations to limit the power of U.S. citizens? How could the president of the United States belittle popular sovereignty in this manner? And what will other leaders do in Britain, France, Germany, Japan and many other nations?

Let us ask whether it is in the interest of the sovereign people of the United States and any other nation to:

1. Grant businesses and investors an unlimited absolute right to buy, sell or move assets and people anywhere in the world at anytime,

2. Reduce responsibility of transnational corporations to the public to zero,

3. Prohibit states and cities from regulating the health and safety of commerce and from conditioning local investment in foreign firms with joint-local and foreign leadership and managers,

4. Strike down federal, state and local laws that require government-subsidized businesses to reinvest in the community, offer living wages and other benefits,

5. Freeze the government for 20 years by international agreement to suit investors with very odd controls on the populace called "standstills" or "rollbacks" or other such weird limits on sovereign, independent and free people who have only so far agreed to a national constitution.

Renato Ruggiero, the director general of the WTO, is reported to have been enthusiastically in favor of the proposed MAI: "We are writing the Constitution of a single global economy" (Marjorie Kelly, *Star Tribune* editorial, 2/24/97). Who in the United States asked him for this result? Why is there no news about this constitutional reform movement? Was the U.S. constitutional amending section changed when I was not looking? Someone must be living in a Geneva, Switzerland dream world, minding clouds as David Korten suggested that some of the people do at such high altitudes. It is some evidence of arrogant, ignorant or delusionary thinking of anti-democratic origin. For democrats this is dangerous thinking at high places.

One of the bits of information the OECD released in February of 1997 was a report on the "state of play" discussion of the MAI. Those "in the know" about the "state of play" included the following:

• Deputy Secretary of the OECD, Paris
• Senior Trade and Investment Negotiator, Canada
• Chief Negotiator for the MAI, Austria
• Department Head, Fed. Min. of Econ., Germany
• Department Head, Bureau of Glob. Monet. Aff., France
• Head, Invest. Div., Min. of Econ., Netherlands
• Department Perm. Rep. to OECD, Sweden
• Chair, Expert Group, Disp. Sett., Switzerland
• Director, New Trade Issues, United Kingdom

These could be called fairly the faceless, nameless bureaucrats of the international trade world, wonderful humans though they be in reality. They are the
founding fathers of the new world economic order apparently drafting a constitution for 5.5 billion people without talking to them, and while being rather
secretive about the rather large job that has been assigned to them by *who knows*.
What in the world is this type of behavior? How can something so earthshaking
be done so secretly and with such affrontery to the people in democracies without elected, responsible officials in every nation having to account to the people
for this type of behavior apparently done in the name of the people? There is a
major puzzle unfolding here.

Who else is "in the know" about the "state of play" of this mysterious MAI
proposal? Those listed by the OECD include:

• Business and Industry Advisory Committee to the OECD—"regularly consulted"
• Keidanren—Japanese business organization
• European-American Chamber of Commerce
• United States Council for International Business (United States affliate of the Inter-
  national Chamber of Commerce)
• Coalition of service industries—"strongly supports"

OECD ministers targeted May of 1997 for the initial release. Then, it was
slipped a year to May 19, 1998. Rumor had it that the date would slip again,
and as we knew by April 29, 1998, OECD deferred the date to October 1998.
The politics of this MAI effort is sadly lacking in democratic legitimacy in the
eyes of this beholder (Clarke and Barlow, 1997).

In conclusion, the MAI is viewed as a set of rules to restrict what governments
may do to regulate international investment and corporate actions. The obvious
effect of such rules is to reduce popular sovereignty and to protect and expand
corporate political power besides "guaranteeing" a stable investment climate:
elimination of capital controls by states to stop repatriation of profits, ensuring
market access inside nations on a "national treatment" basis regardless of what

citizens may wish, and for whoever signs such a treaty—little or no national capital controls such as those reviewed by Hawley, discussed in this chapter. And most devastating is the MAI's abandonment of a crucial governance principle: there should be a completely autonomous role for the nation-state separate from business. This principle is just ripped out of 29 national constitutions as if it meant nothing. How could this possibly be good public policy for nations or for people? Why must business be placed in charge of society? What justification is there for such an inversion of power? The six "American Keiretsus"—Microsoft, Disney ABC, Time Warner, GE/NBC, TCI, New Corporation (Murdock) co-opt competition and mass media so that citizens will never be enlightened about the MAI and its golden pathway to their corporate global dominance (Aluetta, 1997).

What would be the effects of such a proposed MAI agreement? There would be a disaster for nations signing such an agreement. Facism may raise its ugly head again and demonstrate that amnesia is a global disease suffered most acutely by those in international trade. The disaster called WTO and NAFTA headed by trade crusaders with their free trade ideology could well project harms worldwide. Take the NAFTA experience as an indicator of a world class business tragedy lurking in the MAI: imagine a world where 90% of the business promises are *not* kept, where job losses are measured by 480%, where Allied Signal, General Electric, Johnson and Johnson, Kimberly-Clark, Lucent Technologies, Mattel, Procter & Gamble, Siemens, Whirlpool, Xerox and Zenith laid off workers due to NAFTA, and finally where workers in 1,400 firms in 48 states filed for assistance due to NAFTA impacts. NAFTA job losses are a half a million (Public Citizen, February 1997). One could hardly imagine conditions more favorable for political revolution if projected into smaller economies of the world. Revolution breeds multiple nations: anarchy, tyrants and much more.

Where free markets exist in various nations does there have to be political freedom for business as well? I do not think so. Neither does Nobel Prize–winner economist Milton Friedman, who answered the question this way: "Obviously not, because Hong Kong has had no political freedom, and it had the freest market in the world" (WSJ, Friedman, 2/12/97: A-16). The disjunction between political freedom and economic freedom is both real and active in Hong Kong since the Chinese took over. But could we conclude that there is no connection at all between political freedom and economic freedom based upon the Hong Kong example? Could the reverse exist—no economic freedom at all (like the United States during World War II from 1940 to 1945) and great civic and political liberties becoming the pride of the nation fighting the Japanese, Italian and Nazi regime of Germany? Yes, this actually existed in the United States, but the condition was temporary. Kenneth Lewis, a retired shipping company executive and member of the Presidential Commission on United States-Pacific Trade and Investment Policy, recently wrote: "Would our present policies, for instance, prohibit trading with a country like a Nazi Germany if it wanted to sell us low-priced goods that would make profits for our companies

and provide low-cost goods for our consumers? Sadly, I don't think they would''
(NYT, Lewis, 7/13/97). This future trade projection may be why Lewis surprised
himself dissenting from a trade report to the president on the United States. The
trade deficits with the Far East as a whole do require rethinking. Before the
commission experience, the view Lewis held was that trade was an unqualified
good for the United States; now he wonders, after 30 years of international trade
experience and over 100 trips to the Asia-Pacific region. There is no better way
to end this inquiry than to think seriously about why this American business
man, Kenneth Lewis, from Portland, Oregon, took the road of dissenting, and
to let him speak in his own words:

I participated in the statement of dissent because I believe a significant national dialogue
is needed. It should be conducted through Congressional hearings, and trade results
should be monitored by a permanent commission, charged with developing plans to end
in the next 10 years our huge and continuing trade deficits. Full discussion is needed on
questions like: What is the purpose of our trade policy and and what do we want our
domestic economy to look like? Who gains and who loses, and to what extent, from the
increases in exports and the greater increases in imports? Do American workers benefit,
or only consumers and investors? What conditions must exist—concerning human rights,
workers' rights or environmental protections—for us to allow other nations' goods to
enter our country? Are there other limits to impose? (NYT, Lewis, 7/13/97)

If Kenneth Lewis was open-minded and objective (as I believe he was) and he
still was having second thoughts on free trade after such great experience, perhaps we should listen to him very carefully and follow his advice to reassess
the national policies toward trade and appoint such a commission with broad
labor, management, educational and other interests from small and large business
including *all* interests. Trade policy is too important to be left to the experts—it
is central to globalization, globalizing corporations and democratic nations with
their own important bosses—the sovereign citizens of each nation.

As this book opened, so it closes by connecting the dots right down to a call
for a review of trade policies in America. The review by ordinary people in
nation after nation will find democracy pushed to one side by aggressive globalizing corporations and their CEOs who want to set global policy for nations.
The subordination of large global corporations to the people and their sovereign
power in a democracy will set the appropriate tone for corporate nation-state
relations in the twenty-first century. Democracy at its best requires absolute
subordination of corporations. No more tails wagging dogs.

List of Globalizing Corporations and Organizations

The following list of globalizing corporations and organizations is constructed from four sources:

1. London *Financial Times*, 1997.
2. *Fortune*, Global 500, 1997.
3. *Forbes*, Foreign 500, 1997.
4. Variety of other sources including United Nations and Hoover listings.

The presence of a dot symbol to the right of the name indicates presence on a particular listing of the first three lists. Absence of a dot symbol means that particular list did not include the corporation or organization. Those with no dot symbols to the right are based upon a variety of other sources, including United Nations and Hoover listings, and they do not appear in the first three lists. The total number listed is 772 corporations and organizations.

Some minor fluidity in this list arises over time due to mergers, acquisitions and failures, but it is a list grounded in substantial research intended to present relative permanence of organizational existence regardless of superficial ''make overs'' for image purposes.

Globalizing Company	Nation	Financial Times, 1997	Fortune Global 500, 1997	Forbes Foreign 500, 199

A

Globalizing Company	Nation	Financial Times, 1997	Fortune Global 500, 1997	Forbes Foreign 500, 199
Aachener & Münchener	Germany		•	•
ABB Asea Brown Boveri	Switzerland	•	•	•
Abbey National	Britain	•	•	•
Abbott Laboratories	U.S.	•	•	
ABN Amro Holding	Netherlands	•	•	•
Accor	France			•
Aegon	Netherlands	•	•	•
Aerospatiale	France		•	
Aetna Life & Casualty	U.S.	•	•	
Aflac	U.S.			

Globalizing Company	Nation	Financial Times, 1997	Fortune Global 500, 1997	Forbes Foreign 500, 199
Air France Group	France			
Aisin Seiki	Japan			•
Akzo Nobel	Netherlands	•	•	•
Albertson's	U.S.	•	•	
Alcan Aluminum	Canada			•
Alcatel Alsthom	France	•	•	•
Alco Standard	U.S.			
Alcoa	U.S.		•	
All Nippon Airways	Japan	•	•	•
Allianz Worldwide	Germany	•	•	•

Globalizing Company	Nation	Financial Times, 1997	Fortune Global 500, 1997	Forbes Foreign 500, 199
Allied Domecq	Britain	•		•
Allied Signal	U.S.	•	•	
Allstate Corp.	U.S.	•	•	
Amdahl	U.S.			
Amerada Hess	U.S.			
American Brands	U.S.	•		
American Express	U.S.	•	•	
American Home Products	U.S.	•	•	
American International Group	U.S.	•	•	
American President	U.S.			

Globalizing Company	Nation	Financial Times, 1997	Fortune Global 500, 1997	Forbes Foreign 500, 199
American Standard	U.S.			
American Stores	U.S.		•	
Ameritech	U.S.	•	•	
Amgen Inc.	U.S.	•		
Amoco	U.S.		•	
AMP	U.S.			
AMR Corp.	U.S.	•	•	
Anheuser-Busch	U.S.		•	
Apple Computer	U.S.		•	
Aramark	U.S.			

Globalizing Company	Nation	Financial Times, 1997	Fortune Global 500, 1997	Forbes Foreign 500, 199
Archer Daniels Midland	U.S.		•	
Argyll Group	Britain			
Armstrong World Industries	U.S.			
Arthur Anderson and Co.	U.S.			

Globalizing Company	Nation	Financial Times, 1997	Fortune Global 500, 1997	Forbes Foreign 500, 1997
Asahi Bank	Japan	•	•	•
Asahi Chemical Industry	Japan	•	•	•
Asahi Glass	Japan	•	•	•
Asahi Mutual Life Insurance	Japan		•	
Ashland	U.S.		•	
Asko Deutsches Kaufhaus	Germany			
Assicurazioni Generali	Italy		•	
Assurances Générales de France	France		•	
Ast Research	U.S.			
AT&T Corp.	U.S.	•	•	
Atlantic Richfield	U.S.	•		
Automatic Data Processing	U.S.	•		
Avis	U.S.			
Avon Products	U.S.			
AXA	France	•	•	•

B

Globalizing Company	Nation	Financial Times, 1997	Fortune Global 500, 1997	Forbes Foreign 500, 1997
B. A. T. Industries	Britain	•		•
Baker Hughes	U.S.			
Banc One Corp.	U.S.		•	
Banca Commerciale Italiana	Italy		•	•
Banca Nazionale Del Lavoro	Italy		•	
Banco Bilbao Vizcaya	Spain	•	•	•
Banco Central Hispanoamericano	Spain			•
Banco de Santander	Spain	•		
Banco do Brasil	Brazil		•	•
Bank of Boston	U.S.	•		
Bank of China	China		•	
Bank of Montreal	Canada	•	•	•
Bank of New York	U.S.			
Bank of Tokyo-Mitsubishi	Japan	•	•	•
BankAmerica Corp.	U.S.		•	
Bankers Trust New York Corp.	U.S.		•	
Banque Nationale de Paris	France	•	•	
Barclays Bank	Britain	•	•	•
BASF Group	Germany	•	•	•
Bass	Britain	•		
Baxter International	U.S.	•		
Bayer Group	Germany	•	•	•
Bayerische Landesbank	Germany		•	
Bayerische Vereinsbank	Germany	•	•	•
BCE	Canada	•	•	•
Bear Stearns	U.S.			
Bechtel Group	U.S.			
Becton Dickinson	U.S.			
Bell Atlantic Corp.	U.S.	•	•	

Globalizing Company	Nation	Financial Times, 1997	Fortune Global 500, 1997	Forbes Foreign 500, 199
Bellsouth Corp.	U.S.	•	•	

Benneton Group	Italy			
Bertelsmann	Germany		•	
Black & Decker	U.S.			
BMW-Bayerische Motor	Germany		•	
Bodyshop	Britain			
Boeing Co.	U.S.	•	•	
Bombardier	Canada		•	
Boots Company	Britain	•		•
Borden	U.S.			
Bouygues Group	France	•	•	

Bridgestone Corp.	Japan	•	•	•
Bristol-Myers Squibb	U.S.	•	•	
British Aerospace	Britain	•	•	•
British Airways	Britain	•	•	•
British Gas	Britain	•		
British Petroleum	Britain	•	•	•
British Post Office	Britain	•		
British Telecommunications	Britain	•	•	
Broken Hill Proprietary	Australia	•	•	
Browning-Ferris Industries	U.S.			

Brunswick	U.S.			
BT	Britain	•	•	
BTR	Britain	•	•	•

C

Cable & Wireless	Britain	•	•	•
Cadbury Schweppes	Britain	•		•
Caltex	U.S.			
Campbell Soup Co.	U.S.	•		
Canadian Imperial Bank	Canada	•	•	•
Canadian Pacific	Canada	•	•	•
Canal +	France			
Canon, Inc.	Japan	•	•	•
Cargill	U.S.			
Cariplo	Italy		•	

Carlsberg A/S	Denmark			
Carlson	U.S.			
Carnival	U.S.			
Carrefour Group	France	•		•
Case	U.S.			
Casio Computer	Japan			
Caterpillar	U.S.	•	•	

Globalizing Company	Nation	Financial Times, 1997	Fortune Global 500, 1997	Forbes Foreign 500, 1997
Cea-Industrie	France	•		
Central Japan Railway	Japan	•		
Champion International	U.S.			
Chase Manhattan Corp.	U.S.	•	•	
Chevron	U.S.	•	•	
Chinese Petroleum	Taiwan		•	
Chiquita Brands International	U.S.			
Chiyoda Mutual Life Insurance	Japan		•	
Chrysler	U.S.	•	•	
Chubu Electric Power	Japan	•	•	•
Chugoku Electric Power	Japan	•	•	•
Cie de Suez	France		•	
Cie Financi	France			
Cie Générale des Eaux	France		•	
Cifra	Mexico			
Cigna Corp.	U.S.	•	•	
Circle K	U.S.			
Citicorp	U.S.	•	•	
Clorox	U.S.			
CNP Assurances	France		•	
Coastal	U.S.	•	•	
Coca-Cola	U.S.	•	•	
Cofco	China		•	
Coles Myer	Australia		•	•
Colgate-Palmolive	U.S.	•		
Columbia/HCA Healthcare	U.S.	•	•	
Commercial Union	Britain		•	•
Commerzbank	Germany	•	•	•
Compagnie des Machines Bull	France			
Compaq Computer	U.S.	•	•	
Computer Associates	U.S.	•		
Conagra	U.S.	•	•	
Conner Peripherals	U.S.			
Consolidated Freightways	U.S.			
Continental	U.S.			
Continental Airlines	U.S.			
Cooper Industries	U.S.			
Coopers & Lybrand	U.S.			
Corning	U.S.	•		
Cosmo Oil	Japan		•	•
CPC International	U.S.	•	•	
Crédit Agricole	France		•	
Crédit Lyonnais Group	France		•	•
Crown Cork & Seal	U.S.			

Globalizing Company	Nation	Financial Times, 1997	Fortune Global 500, 1997	Forbes Foreign 500, 199⬤
CS Holding	Switzerland	•		
CSX Corp.	U.S.	•	•	
Cummins Engine	U.S.			
Cyprus Amax Minerals	U.S.			

D

Globalizing Company	Nation	Financial Times, 1997	Fortune Global 500, 1997	Forbes Foreign 500, 199⬤
Daewoo	South Korea		•	•
Dai Nippon Printing	Japan	•	•	•
Daido Life Insurance	Japan		•	
Daiei	Japan	•	•	•
Daihatsu Motor	Japan			•
Daihyaku Mutual Life Insurance	Japan			
Dai-Ichi Kangyo Bank	Japan	•	•	•
Dai-Ichi Mutual Life Insurance	Japan		•	
Daimler-Benz	Germany	•	•	•
Dainippon Ink & Chemicals	Japan			•

Globalizing Company	Nation	Financial Times, 1997	Fortune Global 500, 1997	Forbes Foreign 500, 199⬤
Daiwa Bank	Japan	•		•
Daiwa House Industry	Japan	•	•	•
Dana	U.S.			
Danone Group	France	•		•
Dayton Hudson	U.S.	•	•	
Deere	U.S.	•	•	
Degussa	Germany		•	•
Delhaize Le Lion Group	Belgium		•	•
Dell Computer	U.S.	•		
Deloitte & Touche	U.S.			

Globalizing Company	Nation	Financial Times, 1997	Fortune Global 500, 1997	Forbes Foreign 500, 199⬤
Delta Air Lines	U.S.		•	
Dentsu	Japan		•	
Deutsche Bahn	Germany		•	
Deutsche Bank	Germany	•	•	•
Deutsche Genossenschaftsbank	Germany			
Deutsche Post	Germany	•		
Deutsche Telekom	Germany		•	•
Dial	U.S.			
Digital Equipment	U.S.		•	
Docks de France	France			

Globalizing Company	Nation	Financial Times, 1997	Fortune Global 500, 1997	Forbes Foreign 500, 199⬤
Dole Food	U.S.			
Domino's Pizza	U.S.			
Dow Chemical	U.S.	•	•	
Dow Jones & Co.	U.S.			
Dresdner Bank	Germany	•	•	•
Dresser Industries	U.S.			
Du Pont (E.I.) de Nemours	U.S.	•	•	
Dun & Bradstreet	U.S.	•		

Globalizing Company	Nation	Financial Times, 1997	Fortune Global 500, 1997	Forbes Foreign 500, 1997
E				
East Japan Railway	Japan	•	•	•
Eastman Chemical	U.S.			
Eastman Kodak	U.S.	•	•	
Eaton	U.S.			
Edeka Zentrale	Germany		•	
Électricité de France	France		•	
Electrolux	Sweden		•	•
Electronic Data Systems	U.S.	•		
Elf Aquitaine	France	•	•	•
Eli Lilly	U.S.			
Emerson Electric	U.S.	•	•	
Enel	Italy		•	
Eni	Italy	•	•	•
Enron	U.S.	•	•	
Equifax	U.S.			
Ericsson, L. M.	Sweden	•	•	•
Ernst & Young	U.S.			
Espirito Santo Financial Holdings	Portugal			
Esterreichische Pos	Austria			
Evergreen Group	Taiwan			
Exxon	U.S.	•	•	
F				
Farmland Industries	U.S.		•	
Federal Express	U.S.		•	
Federal Home Loan Mortgage	U.S.	•	•	
Federal National Mortgage Assur.	U.S.	•		
Federated Department Stores	U.S.	•	•	
Ferruzzi Finanziaria	Italy			
Fiat	Italy	•	•	•
First Chicago NBD Corp.	U.S.	•	•	
First Data	U.S.	•		
First Union Corp.	U.S.	•	•	
Fleming	U.S.		•	
Fletcher Challenge	New Zealand			•
Fluor	U.S.		•	
FMC	U.S.			
Ford Motor	U.S.	•	•	
Formosa Plastics	Taiwan			
Fortis	Belgium/Nether.	•	•	•
Foster's Brewing Group	Australia			
France Télécom	France		•	
Franz Haniel	Germany			
Fried, Krupp	Germany			

Globalizing Company	Nation	Financial Times, 1997	Fortune Global 500, 1997	Forbes Foreign 500, 1997
Fruit of the Loom	U.S.			
Fuji Bank	Japan	•	•	•
Fuji Electric	Japan			•
Fuji Heavy Industries	Japan		•	•
Fuji Photo Film	Japan	•	•	•
Fujitsu	Japan	•	•	•
Fukoku Mutual Life Insurance	Japan		•	

G

GAN	France		•	•
Gateway 2000	U.S.			
Gaz de France	France		•	
General Accident	Britain		•	•
General Electric Co.	U.S.	•	•	•
General Mills	U.S.	•		
General Motors	U.S.	•	•	
General RE Corp.	U.S.	•		
Générale Bank	Belgium		•	•
Generitech	U.S.			

George Weston	Canada			
Georgia-Pacific	U.S.	•	•	
Gillette	U.S.	•	•	
Glaxo Wellcome	Britain	•	•	•
Goldman Sachs Group	U.S.			
Goodyear Tire & Rubber	U.S.	•	•	
Grand Metropolitan	Britain		•	•
Great Atlantic & Pacific Tea	U.S.		•	
Groupe Casino	France		•	
Groupe Pinault-Printemps	France			

GTE	U.S.	•	•	
Guinness PLC	Britain	•		•

H

H.J. Heinz	U.S.			
H&R Block	U.S.			
Halifax Building Society	Britain		•	
Halliburton	U.S.			
Hallmark	U.S.			
Hanson	Britain	•		
Harley Davidson	U.S.			
Harris	U.S.			
Hasbro	U.S.			
Hearst	U.S.			

Heineken	Netherlands	•		•

Globalizing Company	Nation	Financial Times, 1997	Fortune Global 500, 1997	Forbes Foreign 500, 1997
Henkel Group	Germany		•	•
Hercules	U.S.			
Hershey Foods	U.S.	•		
Hewlett-Packard	U.S.	•	•	
Hilton Hotel	U.S.			
Hitachi	Japan	•	•	•
Hoechst Group	Germany	•	•	•
Home Depot	U.S.	•	•	
Honda Motor	Japan	•	•	•
Honeywell	U.S.	•		
Hong Kong Telecommunications	Hong Kong	•		
Hopewell Holiday	Hong Kong			
Hormel Foods	U.S.			
Household International	U.S.	•		
HSBC Holdings	Britain	•	•	•
Hudson Bay Company	Canada			
Hughes Electronics	U.S.			
Huthinson Whampoa	Hong Kong			•
Hyatt	U.S.			
Hypo-Bank Group	Germany		•	
Hyundai Group	South Korea		•	•

I

Globalizing Company	Nation	Financial Times, 1997	Fortune Global 500, 1997	Forbes Foreign 500, 1997
IBP	U.S.		•	
Idemitsu Kosan	Japan		•	
Illinois Tool Works	U.S.	•		
Imperial Chemical Industries	Britain	•	•	•
Imperial Oil	Canada	•		•
Inchcape	Britain		•	•
Inco	Canada			
Indian Oil	India		•	
Industrial Bank of Japan	Japan	•	•	•
ING Group	Netherlands	•	•	•
Ingersoll-Rand	U.S.			
INI	Spain			
Intel	U.S.	•	•	
Intl. Business Machines	U.S.	•	•	
International Paper	U.S.	•	•	
IRI	Italy		•	
Ishikawajima-Harima Heavy Inds.	Japan		•	•
Istituto Banc. San Paolo Di Torino	Italy		•	
Isuzu Motors	Japan		•	•
Ito-Yokado	Japan	•	•	•
Itochu	Japan	•	•	•

Globalizing Company	Nation	Financial Times, 1997	Fortune Global 500, 1997	Forbes Foreign 500, 1997
ITT	U.S.			
ITT Hartford Group	U.S.	•		

J

J.C. Penney	U.S.			
J.P. Morgan & Co.	U.S.			
James River	U.S.			
Japan Airlines	Japan	•	•	•
Japan Energy	Japan		•	•
Japan Postal Service	Japan		•	
Japan Tobacco	Japan		•	•
Japan Travel Bureau	Japan		•	
Jardine Matheson	Hong Kong		•	•
John Hancock Mutual Life	U.S.			

John Labatt	Canada			
Johnson & Johnson	U.S.	•	•	
Johnson Controls	U.S.		•	
Jusco	Japan	•	•	•

K

Kajima	Japan	•	•	•
Kanematsu	Japan		•	•
Kansai Electric Power	Japan	•	•	•
Kao Corporation	Japan	•		•
Karstadt	Germany		•	•
Kaufhof	Germany			
Kawasaki Heavy Industries	Japan	•	•	•
Kawasaki Steel	Japan	•	•	•
Kawasho	Japan		•	•
Kellogg	U.S.	•		

Kelly Services	U.S.			
Kerr-McGee	U.S.			
Kimberly-Clark	U.S.	•	•	
King Ranch	U.S.			
Kinki Nippon Railway	Japan	•		•
Kirin Brewery	Japan	•		•
KLM Royal Dutch Airlines	Netherlands			•
K-Mart	U.S.		•	
Knight-Ridder	U.S.			
Kobe Steel	Japan	•	•	•

Koç Holding	Turkey		•	•
Koch	U.S.			
Komatsu	Japan	•	•	
Koninklijke Ahold	Netherlands		•	•

Globalizing Company	Nation	Financial Times, 1997	Fortune Global 500, 1997	Forbes Foreign 500, 1997
Koor Industries	Israel			
Korea Electric Power	South Korea	•	•	•
KPMG	Netherlands			
KPMG	U.S.			
Kroger	U.S.		•	
Kubota	Japan	•	•	•
Kumagai Gumi	Japan		•	•
Kyocera	Japan	•		•
Kyoei Life Insurance	Japan		•	
Kyushu Electric Power	Japan	•	•	•

L

Globalizing Company	Nation	Financial Times, 1997	Fortune Global 500, 1997	Forbes Foreign 500, 1997
Ladbroke Group	Britain			•
Lagardère Groupe	France		•	•
Lehman Brothers	U.S.		•	
Levi Strauss Associates	U.S.			
Liberty Mutual Insurance Group	U.S.		•	
Litton Industries	U.S.			
Liz Claiborne	U.S.			
Lloyds Bank	Britain			
Lockheed Martin	U.S.	•	•	
Loews	U.S.	•	•	
Lon Rito Plc	Britain			
Long-Term Credit Bank of Japan	Japan	•	•	•
Loral	U.S.			
L'Oreal	France	•	•	•
LTV	U.S.			
Lufthansa Group	Germany		•	
LVMH Moet Hennessy Louis Vit.	France	•		•
Lyondell Petrochemical	U.S.			
Lyonnaise des Eaux	France		•	•

M

Globalizing Company	Nation	Financial Times, 1997	Fortune Global 500, 1997	Forbes Foreign 500, 1997
MacMillan Bloedel	Canada			
MAN	Germany		•	•
Mannesmann	Germany	•	•	•
Manpower	U.S.			
Manville	U.S.			
Mapco	U.S.			
Marks & Spencer	Britain	•	•	•
Marriott International	U.S.	•	•	
Mars	U.S.			
Marsh & McLennan	U.S.	•		
Martin Marietta	U.S.			

Globalizing Company	Nation	Financial Times, 1997	Fortune Global 500, 1997	Forbes Foreign 500, 1997
Marubeni	Japan	•	•	
Maruha	Japan			•
Masco	U.S.			
Matsushita Electric Industrial	Japan	•	•	•
Matsushita Electric Works	Japan	•	•	•
Mattel	U.S.	•		
May Department Stores	U.S.	•	•	
Maytag	U.S.			
Mazda Motor	Japan		•	•
McDermott	U.S.			
McDonald's	U.S.	•	•	
McDonnell Douglas	U.S.	•	•	
McGraw-Hill	U.S.			
MCI Communications	U.S.	•	•	
McKesson	U.S.	•		
McKinsey & Co.	U.S.			
Mead	U.S.			
Meiji Mutual Life Insurance	Japan		•	•
Mellon Bank Corp.	U.S.	•		
Melville	U.S.			
Merck	U.S.	•	•	
Merisel	U.S.			
Merrill Lynch	U.S.	•	•	
Metallgesellschaft	Germany		•	•
Metropolitan Life Insurance	U.S.		•	
Michelin	France		•	•
Microsoft	U.S.	•		
Migros	Switzerland		•	
Minnesota Mining & Manufac.	U.S.	•	•	
Minolta	Japan			
Mitsubishi Group	Japan	•	•	•
Mitsui Group	Japan	•	•	•
Mitsukoshi	Japan		•	•
Mobil	U.S.	•	•	
Molson Companies	Canada			
Monsanto	U.S.	•	•	
Monte dei Paschi di Siena	Italy			
Moore	Canada			
Morgan Stanley Group	U.S.	•	•	
Morton International	U.S.			
Motorola	U.S.	•	•	
Münchener Rück	Germany	•	•	•

Globalizing Company	Nation	Financial Times, 1997	Fortune Global 500, 1997	Forbes Foreign 500, 1997
N				
National Semiconductor	U.S.			
National Westminster Bank	Britain	•	•	•
NationsBank	U.S.	•	•	
Nationwide Insurance Enterprise	U.S.		•	
Navistar International	U.S.			
NEC	Japan	•	•	•
Neste	Finland			•
Nestlé	Switzerland	•	•	•
New Oji Paper	Japan			
New York Life Insurance	U.S.		•	
New York Times	U.S.			
News Corp.	Australia	•	•	•
Nichii	Japan			
Nichimen	Japan		•	•
Nike	U.S.	•		
Nintendo	Japan	•		
Nippon Credit Bank	Japan		•	•
Nippon Dantai Life Insurance	Japan		•	
Nippondenso	Japan			
Nippon Express	Japan	•	•	•
Nippon Life Insurance	Japan		•	
Nippon Oil	Japan	•	•	•
Nippon Paper Industries	Japan		•	•
Nippon Steel	Japan	•	•	•
Nippon Telegraph & Telephone	Japan	•	•	•
Nippon Yusen	Japan			•
Nissan Motor	Japan	•	•	•
Nissho Iwai	Japan		•	•
Nittetsu Shoji	Japan		•	•
NKK	Japan	•	•	•
Nomura Securities	Japan	•		•
Norinchukin Bank	Japan		•	
Norsk Hydro	Norway	•	•	•
Northern Telecom	Canada	•		
Northwest Airlines	U.S.		•	
Northwestern Mutual Life Insur.	U.S.		•	
Novartis	Switzerland		•	•
Novell	U.S.			
Novo Nordisk	Denmark			
Nucor	U.S.			
NYNEX	U.S.	•	•	
O				
Obayashi	Japan		•	•

Globalizing Company	Nation	Financial Times, 1997	Fortune Global 500, 1997	Forbes Foreign 500, 199'
Occidental Petroleum	U.S.	•	•	
Ogde	U.S.			
Oki Electric	Japan			•
Olivetti Group	Italy			•
Oracle	U.S.	•		
Otto Versand	Germany			•
Owens-Corning Fiberglas	U.S.			
Owens-Illinois	U.S.			

P

Globalizing Company	Nation	Financial Times, 1997	Fortune Global 500, 1997	Forbes Foreign 500, 199'
Paccar	U.S.			
Pacific Dunlop	Australia			
Pacific Gas & Electric	U.S.	•		
Pacific Telesis Group	U.S.	•	•	
Packard Bell Electronics	U.S.			
Paine Webber Group	U.S.			
Panhandle Eastern	U.S.			
PDVSA	Venezuela		•	
Pearson	Britain			
Péchiney	France		•	•

Peninsular & Oriental	Britain		•	•
Pennzoil	U.S.			
Pepsico	U.S.	•	•	
PetroFina	Belgium	•	•	•
Petroleo Brasileiro	Brazil			
Petroleos de Venezuela	Venezuela			
Petroleos Mexicanos	Mexico			
Peugeot	France		•	•
Pfizer	U.S.	•	•	
Phelps Dodge	U.S.			

Philip Morris	U.S.	•	•	
Philips Electronics	Netherlands	•	•	•
Phillips Petroleum	U.S.	•	•	
Pioneer Electronic	Japan			•
Pirelli Group	Italy			•
Pitney Bowes	U.S.	•		
Pohang Iron & Steel	South Korea		•	•
Polaroid	U.S.			
PPG Industries	U.S.	•		
Premark International	U.S.			

Preussag	Germany		•	•
Price Waterhouse	Britain			
Price Waterhouse	U.S.			
Price/Costco	U.S.			
Principal Mutual Life Insurance	U.S.			
Procter & Gamble	U.S.	•	•	

Globalizing Company	Nation	Financial Times, 1997	Fortune Global 500, 1997	Forbes Foreign 500, 1997
Promodès Group	France		•	•
Prudential	Britain		•	•
Prudential Insur. Co. of America	U.S.	•	•	
PSA Peugeot Citroen	France		•	•
PTT Suisses	Switzerland		•	
Publix Super Markets	U.S.		•	

Q

Qantas Airways	Australia			•
Quaker Oats	U.S.			
Quantum	U.S.			
Quebecor	Canada			
Quelle Group	Germany			

R

R.R. Donnelley & Sons	U.S.			
Rabobank	Netherlands		•	
Ralston Purina	U.S.	•		
Rank Organisation	Britain			
Raytheon	U.S.	•	•	
Reader's Digest Association	U.S.			
Reckitt and Colman	Britain			
Reebok	U.S.			
Reed Elsevier	Britain	•		•
Renault	France		•	
Repsol	Spain	•	•	•
Reuters Holdings	Britain	•		
Reynolds Metals	U.S.			
Rhône-Poulenc	France	•	•	•
Ricoh	Japan	•	•	•
RJR Nabisco Holdings	U.S.	•	•	
Roadway Services	U.S.			
Robert Bosch	Germany			
Roche Holding	Switzerland	•	•	•
Rockwell International	U.S.	•	•	
Rogers Communications	Canada			
Rolls-Royce	Britain			•
Royal Ahold	Netherlands			
Royal Bank of Canada	Canada		•	•
Royal Dutch/Shell Group	Britain/Nether.	•	•	•
Royal Insurance Holdings	Britain			
Royal PTT Nederland	Netherlands		•	
RTZ	Britain	•		
Rubbermaid	U.S.			

Globalizing Company	Nation	Financial Times, 1997	Fortune Global 500, 1997	Forbes Foreign 500, 199[
Ruhrkohle	Germany			
RWE Group	Germany	•	•	•
Ryder System	U.S.			

S

S.C. Johnson & Sons	U.S.			
Saab-Scania Holdings Group	Sweden			
Saatchi and Saatchi	Britain			
Safeway	U.S.	•	•	
Sainsbury (J.)	Britain		•	•
Saint-Gobain	France	•	•	•
Sakura Bank	Japan	•	•	•
Salomon	U.S.			
Samsung Electronics	South Korea		•	•
San Miguel	Philippines			

Sanwa Bank	Japan	•	•	•
Sanyo Electric	Japan	•	•	•
Sara Lee	U.S.	•	•	
SBC Communications	U.S.	•	•	
Scandinavian Airlines System	Sweden			
Scecorp	U.S.			
Schering-Plough	U.S.	•		
Schlumberger	U.S.			
Schneider	France			•
SCI Systems	U.S.			

Scitex	Israel			
Scott Paper	U.S.			
Seagate Technology	U.S.			
Sears Roebuck	U.S.	•	•	
Sega Enterprises	Japan			
Seiko	Japan			
Seiyu	Japan		•	•
Sekisui Chemical	Japan		•	•
Sekisui House	Japan	•	•	•
Shanghai Petrochemical	China			

Sharp	Japan	•	•	•
Sherwin-Williams	U.S.			
Shimizu	Japan	•	•	•
Shiseido	Japan			•
Shoko Chukin Bank	Japan			
Showa Shell Sekiyu	Japan		•	
SHV Holdings	Netherlands		•	
Siemens	Germany	•	•	•
Silicon Graphics	U.S.			

298

Globalizing Company	Nation	Financial Times, 1997	Fortune Global 500, 1997	Forbes Foreign 500, 1997
Sime Darby Berhad	Malaysia	•		
Singapore Airlines	Singapore	•		•
Sinochem	China		•	
SmithKline Beecham	Britain	•	•	•
SNCF	France	•		
Snow Brand Milk Products	Japan		•	•
Sony	Japan	•	•	•
Southern	U.S.	•	•	
Southland	U.S.			
SPAR Handels	Germany			•
Spiegel	U.S.			
Springs Industries	U.S.			
Sprint	U.S.	•	•	
Ssangyong	South Korea		•	•
Standard Life Assurance	Britain		•	
Stanley Works	U.S.			
State Farm Group	U.S.		•	
Statoil	Norway		•	
STET	Italy	•		•
Stone Container	U.S.			
Storage Technology	U.S.			
Sumikin Bussan	Japan		•	•
Sumitomo	Japan	•	•	•
Sun	U.S.		•	
Sun Microsystems	U.S.	•		
Sunkyong	South Korea		•	•
Suntory	Japan			
Supervalu	U.S.		•	
Suzuki Motor	Japan		•	•
Swire Pacific	Hong Kong	•	•	•
Swiss Bank	Switzerland	•	•	•
Swiss Life Ins. & Pension	Switzerland		•	
Swiss Reinsurance	Switzerland	•	•	•
Sysco	U.S.		•	

T

Globalizing Company	Nation	Financial Times, 1997	Fortune Global 500, 1997	Forbes Foreign 500, 1997
Taisei	Japan		•	•
Taiwan Power	Taiwan			
Taiyo Mutual Life Insurance	Japan		•	
Takashimaya	Japan		•	•
Takenaka	Japan		•	
Tandy	U.S.			
Tata Enterprises	India			
Tata and Lyle	Britain			

Globalizing Company	Nation	Financial Times, 1997	Fortune Global 500, 1997	Forbes Foreign 500, 19
Teachers Insur. & Annuity Assoc.	U.S.		•	
Telefónica de España	Spain	•	•	•
Teléfonos de Chile, Companie de	Chile			
Teléfonos de México	Mexico	•		•
Teleglobe	Canada			
Tenneco	U.S.	•	•	
Tesco	Britain	•	•	•
Texaco	U.S.	•	•	
Texas Instruments	U.S.	•	•	
Textron	U.S.	•	•	
Thomson Corp.	Canada	•		•
Thomson-CSF	France			•
Thorn Emi	Britain			
Thyssen	Germany		•	•
Time Warner	U.S.	•	•	
TJX	U.S.			
Toho Mutual Life Insurance	Japan		•	
Tohoku Electric Power	Japan		•	•
Tokai Bank	Japan	•	•	•
Tokio Marine & Fire Insurance	Japan	•	•	•
Tokyo Electric Power	Japan	•	•	•
Tokyo Gas	Japan	•	•	
Tomen	Japan		•	•
Toppan Printing	Japan	•	•	•
Toray Industries	Japan	•	•	•
Toronto-Dominion Bank	Canada			•
Toshiba	Japan	•	•	•
Toshoku	Japan			•
Total	France	•	•	•
Toyo Seikan Kaisha	Japan			•
Toyota Motor	Japan	•	•	•
Toyota Tsusho	Japan		•	•
Toys "R" Us	U.S.		•	
Tractebel	Belgium			•
Trans World Airlines	U.S.			
Transamerica	U.S.			
Travelers	U.S.	•	•	
TRW	U.S.		•	
Turner	U.S.			
Turner Broadcasting	U.S.			
Tyco International	U.S.			
Tyson Foods	U.S.			

U

| U.S. Postal Service | U.S. | | • | |

Globalizing Company	Nation	Financial Times, 1997	Fortune Global 500, 1997	Forbes Foreign 500, 1997
UAL	U.S.		•	
Unilever	Britain/Nether.		•	•
Union Bank of Switzerland	Switzerland	•	•	•
Union Carbide	U.S.			
Union des Assur. de Paris	France		•	
Union Pacific	U.S.	•	•	
Unisys	U.S.			
United Parcel Service	U.S.		•	
United Services Automobile Assoc.	U.S.			
United Technologies	U.S.	•	•	
Universal	U.S.			
Unocal	U.S.	•		
UNY	Japan			•
Upjohn	U.S.			
US West	U.S.		•	
USAir Group	U.S.			
Usinor-Sacilor	France			•
USX	U.S.		•	

V

Globalizing Company	Nation	Financial Times, 1997	Fortune Global 500, 1997	Forbes Foreign 500, 1997
VEBA Group	Germany	•	•	•
Vendex International	Netherlands			•
Verenigd Bezit Vnu	Netherlands			
VF	U.S.			
Viacom	U.S.	•	•	
VIAG Group	Germany	•	•	•
Vickers	Britain			
Virgin Group	Britain			
Volkswagen	Germany	•	•	•
Volvo	Sweden	•	•	•

W

Globalizing Company	Nation	Financial Times, 1997	Fortune Global 500, 1997	Forbes Foreign 500, 1997
W. Wrigley	U.S.			
W.R. Grace	U.S.			
Walgreen	U.S.	•	•	
Wal-Mart Stores	U.S.	•	•	
Walt Disney	U.S.			
Warner-Lambert	U.S.	•		
Washington Post	U.S.			
Waterford Wedgwood	Ireland			
West Japan Railway	Japan		•	•
Westdeutsche Landesbank	Germany		•	
Westinghouse Electric	U.S.	•	•	
Weyerhaeuser	U.S.	•	•	
Whirlpool	U.S.			

Globalizing Company	Nation	Financial Times, 1997	Fortune Global 500, 1997	Forbes Foreign 500, 19
Whitman	U.S.			
Winn-Dixie Stores	U.S.			
Winterthur Group	Switzerland		•	•
WMX Technologies	U.S.	•		
Woolworth	U.S.		•	

X

Xerox	U.S.	•	•	

Y

Yamaha Corp.	Japan			•
Yasuda Fire & Marine Insurance	Japan		•	•
Yasuda Mutual Life Insurance	Japan		•	
Yellow	U.S.			
Young & Rubicam	U.S.			
YPF Sociedad Anonima	Argentina			•

Z

Zambia Consol. Copper Mines	Zambia			
Zenith Electronics	U.S.			
Zurich Insurance	Switzerland	•	•	•

Appendix B

Global Corporate Data

This appendix recognizes one of the chief problems faced when trying to understand the giant, globalizing corporations of America and the rest of the world. The swarm of issues and the storms (political, social, legal and economic) over the activities of multinational corporations in the last 40 years are confusing to everyone—in businesses and in the community.

Speaking truth to power asks first, "What is power in corporate form?" The illusions, delusions and deliriums must be cast aside to get at the truth. What in an empirical sense is the globalizing giant corporation? And whatever it may be as a unit of analysis, how does the unit of analysis relate to the swarms of issues that surround all corporations? We must, to get at the truth, narrow our interest from the whole economy, then to corporations (4 million in the United States) and then to giants of U.S. corporations (1,000 plus) and finally to 150 super giants and numerous near-giant globalizers. Then add in 600 plus foreign (non–U.S.) corporate or similar enterprises. The task is formidable. The subject of this inquiry is elusive.

THE FACTS

This appendix has one aim: it will examine some of the empirical realities that underlie the idea of globalizing corporations. The empirical reality could take several directions. The direction selected for this book will be examined so that the reader is sure of what a globalizing corporation really is. The corporations have names and officers.

Empirical Realities of Globalizing Corporations

One must know what a globalizing corporation is before one could hope to think about it in any productive manner. Who really knows the most about these corporations? The investment analysts, especially for pension funds, who guide their clients in acquisition of good common stock and solid bonds issued by such globalizing corporations are knowledgeable. The two critical questions for investment analysts are: Will the corporation's stock increase in value over time and pay some dividends and will the corporation successfully pay back its debt? Answering these questions requires great knowledge of a corporation—its industry, its market strengths and weaknesses, and its management and prospects for the future. Both domestic and foreign aspects are important for globalizing corporations. The bottom line of profitability pervades all discussions from this perspective. Another extremely knowledgeable group is the directing CEO, Board of Directors and top managers who can see inside the corporation as an operating unit in its markets. Academics in business schools follow corporations as such and they are very knowledgeable. Lawyers who practice corporate law are very knowledgeable, as are their teaching colleagues in law schools. Economists who focus upon corporation activity, sociologists who study organizational activity in corporations and a few others in government regulatory agencies, labor unions, chambers of commerce, for example, have some deep insights into the creature we are calling a globalizing corporation.

How difficult it is for anyone to get a broad grasp and deep understanding of the globalizing corporation as a unit of analysis is obvious. The task is so daunting it is usually the most formidable obstacle in studying giant corporations; and this study is no exception. Since 1991, with some increased attentiveness, and long before that just the monitoring of giant corporations since the late 1950s, there is a shade pulled down over corporate operations that may give one a glimpse of reality, but the glimpse is a mere foggy snapshot of the real world—standing still in time and usually dated rather rapidly. This ambiguity increases the risks of misunderstanding important giant institutions at work globally night and day.

Let me use some examples. Janet Lowe's focus on 25 of the largest corporations in the world in 1990 reveals a business journalist's dilemmas. In *The Secret Empire* (1992), Lowe chose Nestlé, Matshushita Electric, Daimler-Benz, Philip Morris and Bristol Myers-Squibb, among others because of size and prominence, but 25 companies is a very small and inadequate number compared with the 700 or so identified here in this book. Perhaps time and money constraints held back a bigger sample size. She does identify the 25 companies by name, date of founding, latest assets, sales, industry and brand name, the latter tag helping one grasp what corporate entity is associated with what products or services. She called these corporations the ''meganationals,'' and her analysis is very high quality, regardless of the small sample.

By contrast, John H. Dunning, in *Multinational Enterprises and the Global Economy* (1993), in a most scholarly manner—typical of an academic—attempted to grasp the 1988 reality of finding 17,500 to 20,000 ''enterprises'' with foreign affiliates numbering 120,000 to 125,000. His MNEs (multi-national enterprises) had assets from $9 to $10 trillion, with foreign affiliates worth $3 trillion of that total. Sales of this universe were $13.5 trillion with $4–4.5 trillion in foreign affiliates. Some 50 million to 55 million people worked for these MNEs. Of that total number of workers, "foreign" to the home companies were 14 million to 15 million employed by foreign affiliates. Dunning's net is certainly cast very wide, although he wrote: "However, the largest 300 MNEs are thought to account for 70% of the total foreign direct investment stake" (Dunning, 1993: 15).

And, as you may suspect, the UN published a rather broad view of international activities of corporations in its *World Investment Report 1995* (1995). The report began: "International production by TNCs—now some 40,000 parent firms and some 250,000 foreign affiliates—increasingly influences the size and nature of cross-border transactions. In the process, it shapes the nature of the world economy" (UN, 1995: 1). To grasp something so fluid and immense, the UN report said there are two generally accepted "proxy-indicators" of international production:

• Outward Foreign Direct Investment: $2.6 trillion (1995)

• Global Sales of Foreign Affiliates: $5.2 trillion (1992)

The reality facing Lowe, a single reporter; Dunning, a scholar with more resources; or the United Nations with the full-time, scholarly staff results in estimating and guessing, at all levels and types of analyses. This reality is inescapable in the type of analytical study used here, because it is inherently complex and *no one knows the full picture*. Nor will we ever know it all. This is not unlike what we know and do not know about hurricanes. Yes, we get precise readings of wind speed at a certain time, date and altitude, and we get directions and wobbles in course taken. We now get a satellite view frequently. It is the same in the corporate business—we dip in periodically and infer from samples just what is going on. The main inference to be taken from Lowe, Dunning and the UN is that an enormous amount of cross-border activity is taking place and the trend is clearly upward in volume. This is well-known as a suspected reality by thousands of people, maybe tens of thousands across the globe. Exactly what is going on remains a mystery as deep as the inside of a hurricane. Glimpses are all that we really know of each (United States Congress, Office of Technology Assessment, September 1993; Greider, 1997).

The flavor for knowing multinational corporations has a great diversity to it and this, too, is worth exploring because insight is gained from such literature. There are the investors' services with a company-by-company reality such as the Dun and Bradstreet Series, some of which are used in this book. Moody's is another service, and there are others. Smaller and more compact are Hoover's handbooks and studies like Philip Mattera's *World Class Business* (1992).

There is a core class of literature that begins with the empirical work found in Adolph Berle, Jr., and Gardiner Means, *The Modern Corporation and Private*

Property (1932). An update in part is Phillip I. Blumberg's *The Megacorpora-tion in American Society* (1975) and Ralph Nader et al., *Taming the Giant Corporation* (1976). A mix of economic data and public policy analysis is found in works like Walter Adams and James W. Brock's, *The Bigness Complex* (1986). More historical and political and policy-oriented but less empirical is Scott R. Bowman's *The Modern Corporation and American Political Thought* (1996) and Ralph Estes', *Tyranny of the Bottom Line* (1996). David Korten's *When Corporations Rule the World* (1995) follows this pattern. Transfixed in every author is a vision of a globalizing corporation. And there was such a vision in 1997 by William Greider, in *One World, Ready or Not*, and Edward H. Graham's *The Global Corporations and National Governments* (1996).

To illustrate the diversity even further, one cannot ignore a more company-focused analysis which is displayed by a class of books providing exceptionally detailed insight into a single corporation family's activities over a long period of time. There are many of these about IBM, DuPont, and Coca-Cola and General Motors. A good recent example is by Mark Pendergrast, *For God, Country and Coca-Cola* (1993). Another in this line but with a mixture of policy analysis is *Global Dreams* (1994) by Richard J. Barnet and John Cavanagh. Barnet's work goes back to *Global Reach* (1974) with Ronald A. Mueller.

Many economists in the last 100 years have devoted great attention to corporations—John Kenneth Galbraith, to mention one of the more prominent, in addition to Walter Adams and James Brock, mentioned above. Martin L. Lindahl and William A. Carter, in 1959, offered the third edition of *Corporate Concen-tration and Public Policy*. This opened a window to a vast literature on antitrust analysis of industrial monopoly and oligopoly of the automobile, petroleum, sulphur, iron and steel, glass container, shoe machinery, aluminum and tobacco products industries in the United States. While not so significant at this time, this empirical work was then and remains today a significant resource going all the way back to the trust era in the 1880s and 1890s in America. The federal antitrust division of the U.S. Justice Department, the Federal Trade Commission, the Interstate Commerce Commission (now abolished), the Food and Drug Ad-ministration all offered empirical work along with the Commerce Department's Bureau of Economic Analysis, which has relevant data that we examined in Chapter 6 relating to foreign direct investment issues and globalizing corpora-tions. Congress many times, through hearings, has generated data of interest to those studying multinational corporations.

Historians have helped to explore the course taken by American corpora-tions—two are fine examples of a wide literature—Mira Wilkins' *The Maturing of Multinational Enterprise* (1974) and Martin J. Sklar's *The Corporate Recon-struction of American Capitalism* (1988). These are empirical in a historical sense and very carefully crafted representations of the past.

There are other works that are empirical and these deserve special mention here because they are significant in themselves. As already mentioned, Raymond Vernon, in *Sovereignty at Bay* (1971), based the book on Harvard University's

Multinational Enterprise Project that began in 1965. Key characteristics of 187 U.S.–controlled multinational enterprises were examined in some depth. In defining his target he spoke of a parent and cluster of subsidiaries. Vernon mentioned size of sales—must be over $100 million in annual sales, not mere exporters or licensers of technology and certainly geographic global spread, not merely in one or two nations. These were significant limits. Vernon was explicit:

For instance, during 1967, 180 enterprises on the *Fortune* list had manufacturing subsidiaries in six or more countries, and this group alone accounted for more than 2,000 of the 2,500 "subsidiary countries" of the entire *Fortune* group; these 180 accordingly seemed presumptively entitled to the "multinational enterprise" label. (Vernon, 1971: 11)

The careful assessment by Vernon set a standard for this inquiry and guided my judgment in evaluating empirical data. What the "sovereignty at bay" model meant to others was explored by Robert Gilpin in *U.S. Power and the Multinational Corporation* (1975: 220–228) (see also Kindleberger, 1984).

Finally, in this perspective toward empirical data on globalizing corporations in democratic nations—it is important to keep in mind a peculiar "multinational corporation." Jean-Pierre Anastassopoulos, George Blanc and Pierre Dussauge, in *State-Owned Multinationals* (1987), offered the paradox of a business corporation that is state-owned, and the implications of this paradox. Airbus is a well-known manufacturer in Europe of globally sold aircraft also used in the United States. Airbus was a consortium of four nations as owners. Other state-owned companies were Renault, which was owned by France, and Keppel Shipyard was 70% owned by Singapore. Embraer was controlled by the Brazilian government and there were many more (Anastassopoloulos et al., 1987: 2–4).

Big Trends

What are the big trends that would help you the reader to focus on where the multinational corporation fits into the world of business and society as a whole? Think, first and foremost, that most businesses are small businesses. This fact is mostly false for globalizing corporations that are very large. The base of the triangle-shaped pyramid in the United States is 5,354,000 businesses with 20 or fewer employees. Exclude those tiny ones in this book. Next are 684,000 businesses with 20 to 99 employees—exclude those as well. There are 122,000 businesses with 100 to 499 employees—discard these from your concern in reading this book. Finally, there are 10,000 businesses with 500 to 1,000 employees—forget these as well. The very tip of the triangle concerns us here—about 6,000 businesses with 1,000 or more employees.

Now, some further narrowing is needed to go from 6,000 U.S. businesses to about 750 corporations worldwide. Please note that the *Fortune* 500 is only 500 corporations so it is already narrow but very large in organizational size. Much of the *Fortune* 500 consisted of corporations with sales of $5 billion a year or less, but this is large by any global standard. Only 150 or so of the *Fortune* 500 have globally noticeable sales over $10 billion a year. But, the *Fortune* 500 includes just American home-based companies—and some of these could not begin to qualify as multinationals in Raymond Vernon's classical definition given above. And what is missing above the *Fortune* 500 are the European and Asian large business companies—those will be included here. *Fortune* is evolving continuously a new Global 500.

Big Picture Data for the United States

Add some other big picture empirical realities from the United States to this analysis. This perspective is justified because the United States is home base for at least 150 of the 500 global companies in the *Fortune* Global 500. Japan is home base for about another 150 companies. That is, three-fifths or 60% of the Global 500 are home-based in just two nations. The other 40% of the *Fortune* Global 500 companies (200) are in Europe, South America, Australia, Africa and Asia. Thus, the American perspective is important on a global scale.

Rolf Anderson, "Atlas of the American Economy" (1994), opened the relevant big picture that is composed of smaller bits of data and he does highlight most of the following 1990–1993 items:

1. *Fortune* 500 employment is declining (16.1 to 11 million in *Fortune* 500 from 1980 to 1994 because, until 1995 reports, the group was only manufacturing industrial giants like General Motors). Manufacturing in the United States is downsizing and downward sliding in all measures.

2. Four decades—1950 to 1990—have seen the labor force go from 60 million in 1950 to over 120 million in the 1990s—a doubling in just under a half century (1950–2000).

3. The United States has a 1995 population estimated at 260 million which is 5% of the world's population of 5.5 billion people. The United States produces about 25% of the global economic output but this share is declining.

4. Exports and imports were about 20% of the GDP in 1990. From the 1960 level at about $25 billion, the rise of exports and imports in 1990 was $550 billion exports and $600 billion imports. We are into cross-border trading much more today.

5. The leading export is aerospace products—jetliners. Two-thirds of exports are traded by multinational companies such as Boeing. Called "intrafirm trade," the exports and imports travel inside the corporations and subsidiaries but move across national boundaries.

6. Leading imports are oil and autos. The United States consumes 16.7 million barrels of petroleum products per day (25% of global production). The United States produces 7.4 million barrels of crude oil per day. The balance of 9.3 m/b/d crosses our borders every day as an import. Half the nation's 15,000 independent oil companies ceased business from 1986 to 1992, creating much greater concentration in the six

largest companies. In 1992, the United States imported $50 billion in oil and $46 billion in autos.

7. Transfers between parent companies in the United States and their foreign affiliates is 25% of all exports and 15% of all imports. These were not genuine arm's-length wholesale or retail transactions. The same are the transfers from U.S. subsidiaries of foreign parent corporations.

8. In 1992, foreign direct investment into the United States by foreign investors was $521 billion—a record.

9. Foreign investors hold more than $2.5 trillion in U.S. assets while U.S. assets abroad are just over $2 trillion.

10. In 1990, global international trade (goods, services and investments) was $3.4 trillion among nations to be contrasted with $1 trillion a day for foreign exchange, financial markets or $250 trillion a year.

11. The United States trades mostly with Canada, then Japan, then Mexico in both imports and exports. The United States trades with a wide array of other countries at lesser levels.

The Globalizing 700 Corporate Types: Mid-1990s

The globalizing corporations of this book come from all over the world. The purpose of this part of this appendix is to offer as clear a picture as possible of these globalizers. In Appendix A, there is an alphabetical list of globalizing corporations of the world. For readers interested in whether or not a particular corporation is deemed a globalizing corporation, please refer that list.

The criteria for including a globalizing corporation in this book were these:

1. Percent of foreign sales or revenues and percent of global employees deemed ''foreign'' that exceeded 20% of the total for a given year.

2. Presence of majority-owned subsidiary corporations, branches of parent corporation or other indicators of activity in broad sections of the world—such as Europe, or North America, for example.

3. Inclusion in lists of major studies of globalizing corporations, for example, UN and Mattera's list and others.

4. Other descriptive indicators of globalization focused in reports about the corporation from a variety of sources.

Variety

From a practical standpoint, there is no question about the globalizing character of a large number of corporations recognized by the *World Investment Report of the United Nations* (UN, 1995). The list of 100 in Table B-1 was published in the 1995 report (ranked by foreign assets, 1993). Dunning ranked 46 of the world largest industrial companies in 1989 by net sales in U.S. dollars. The global sales ranged from $123 billion for General Motors to $20 billion for

Table B-1
100 Largest Global Corporations

U.S. Corporations	Non-U.S. Corporations
1. Exxon - M	1. Royal Dutch Shell
2. IBM - M	2. Toyota - J - M
3. General Motors - M	3. Hitachi - J - M
4. General Electric - M	4. SONY - J - M
5. Ford - M	5. Mitsubishi - J - M
6. Mobil - M	6. Nestlé - Swiss - M
7. DuPont - M	7. Nissan Motors - J - M
8. Philip Morris - M	8. Matsushita Electric - J - M
9. Chevron - M	9. Elf Aquitaine - France - M
10. Xerox	10. Asea Brown Boveri - Swiss - M
11. Dow Chemical	11. Phillips Electronics - Neth. - M
12. Procter & Gamble - M	12. British Petroleum - UK - M
13. Texaco	13. Hanon - UK
14. Amoco	14. Siemens - Germany - M
15. Hewlett-Packard - M	15. Unilever - Neth/UK - M
16. ITT	16. Mitsui - J
17. Eastman Kodak - M	17. Alcatel Alsthom - France - M
18. Pepsico	18. B.A.T. Industries - UK
19. AT&T - M	19. Volkswagen - Germany - M
20. Digital Equipment	20. Nissho Iwai - J
21. Chrysler	21. Ciba-Geigy - Swiss - M
22. GTE	22. Hoechst - Germany - M
23. McDonald's - M	23. Veba - Germany
24. ALCOA	24. Sumitomo - J - M
25. Johnson & Johnson - M	25. Renault - France
26. Atlantic Richfield	26. Itochi Corp. - J

Table B-1 (continued)

U.S. Corporations	Non-U.S. Corporations
27. Sara Lee	27. Daimler-Benz - Germany - M
28. Minnesota Mining - M	28. BASF - Germany - M
29. Motorola, Inc. - M	29. Saint Gobain - France
30. United Technologies - M	30. Michelin - France - M
31. International Paper - M	31. Marubeni - J
32. RJR Nabisco - M	32. Bayer - Germany - M
	33. Toshiba - J - M
	34. Volvo - Sweden
	35. Lyonnaise des Eaux - France
	36. Honda - J
	37. Sharp Corp. - J
	38. Fujitsu Ltd. - J - M
	39. Ferruzzi-Montedison - Italy
	40. Electrolux - Sweden - M
	41. Nippon Steel - J
	42. ENI - Italy
	43. Thompson Corp. - Canada - M
	44. Glaxo Holdings - UK - M
	45. Holderbank - Swiss
	46. Grand Metropolitan - UK - M
	47. NEC Corp. - J - M
	48. Seagrams - Canada - M
	49. Total - France
	50. Robert Bosch - Germany
	51. Bridgeston - J - M
	52. MNA AG - Germany

Table B-1 (continued)

U.S. Corporations	Non-U.S. Corporations
	53. Sanyo Electronics - J
	54. Canon, Inc. - J
	55. Solvay - Belgium
	56. Roche Holdings - Swiss - M
	57. Mannuesmann - Germany
	58. Freid Krupp AG - Germany Hoesch-Krupp
	59. Alcan Aluminum - Canada
	60. Cable & Wireless - UK - M
	61. BHP - Australia
	62. Stora - Sweden
	63. Fletcher Challenge - New Zealand
	64. Thomson - France
	65. Fiat - Italy - M
	66. Pechineg - France
	67. RTZ - UK - M
	68. Kobe Steel - J

The letter "M" indicates the company was also included in Mattera's listing of 100 principal global corporations (Mattera, 1992). J means Japan.

Occidental Petroleum. Fifteen of the corporations were U.S., 31 were non–U.S. The percent of foreign sales ranged from 6.4% foreign to 98.1% foreign (Nestle) (Dunning, 1993: 47). Dunning listed 21 service companies, the largest in 1989, ranked by employment. There were 11 U.S. corporations and 10 non–U.S. corporations (Dunning, 1993: 48). Finally, Dunning listed 21 state-owned multinational corporations, all non–U.S. corporations.

Corporate History

Globalizing companies are companies with founding mostly from 1861 to 1940. In the data from *Fortune* Top 50 (Hoover; Mattera; Lowe) there were

Table B-2
Founding Dates of Multinational Corporations

Decade of Founding	No. U.S. Cos.*	No. Non-U.S. Cos.
1861-1870	4	8
1871-1880	5	5
1881-1890	5	4
1891-1900	5	7
1901-1910	7	4
1911-1920	7	1
1921-1930	6	6
1931-1940	3	5
Total	42	40

*About 17 of the United States corporations out of the *Fortune* 50 list are marginal globalizers—insurance companies, retail chains and similar types. Thus, the list may overstate U.S. companies.

only nine globilizers created before 1861—DuPont (1802), Ciba-Geigy (1758) and Procter and Gamble (1837) are examples. By decade, from 1861 onward, Table B-2 illustrates the march of corporation founding of globalizing corporations that is amazing.

The message is clear from this data. Globalizing corporations are "stayers" in the game of perpetuity whether in the United States or elsewhere. The globalizers are voracious buyers of other companies—like General Electric and Daimler-Benz. Merger activity and acquisitions of the 25 globalizing corporations Lowe studied revealed 116 major transactions from 1986 to 1991. The same trend continues to 1999. This pattern of growth repeats itself periodically when treasuries of global giants are particularly fat with cash and liquid assets. The strategies of survival and control are many over time. This is global capitalism.

Fortune 500—Global 500

The *Fortune* 500 are U.S. companies and the *Fortune* Global 500 are a mix of U.S. companies and others (about 350) from around the world. In 1995 the types of corporations *Fortune* expanded to include were many non-industrial, non-manufacturing corporations—retail companies, banks, service and insurance firms. These two overlapping listings are a good initial indicator of globalization. Here, there will be only a brief commentary on the general character of each

Table B-3
Comparison of *Fortune* 500 and *Fortune* Global 500

	1995 *Fortune* U.S. Corporation *Fortune* 500 (4/29/96)	*Fortune* Global 500 in 1995 (8/5/96)
Revenues*	$4,690	$11,378
Profits*	$244	$323
Assets*	$10,491	$32,136
Employees	20,205,263	35,119,851

*Financial data in billions of dollars.

list and how the lists relate to one another. The numbers are overwhelming in every aspect of operation due to sheer size of the corporations. A patient examination of the *Fortune* 500 reporting since 1954 reveals a degree of consistent focus on the largest American industrial manufacturing companies. For 45 years, this listing is an acknowledged "prestige" listing that corporations favor and on which they would like to be included. This enhances the cooperation of publisher to source and increases the long-term consistency and validity of the report (see Table B-3).

The question is: How much of the Global 500 is represented by U.S. home-based companies? Of 500 companies globalized, 153 are U.S.–based or 30.6%. Just slightly under one-third of the companies are U.S. home-based for this particular listing of globalizers.

See Figure B-1 from the 1993 Office of Technology Assessment report for significant downward U.S. trends noted in text and graphs.

Keep in mind how different these two are—the U.S. *Fortune* 500 and the *Fortune* Global 500. (Table B-4 lists the Global 500 corporations by country.) In 1995, the U.S. *Fortune* 500 companies had revenues that ranged from a high of $168.8 billion for General Motors to a low of $2.4 billion for Advanced Micro Systems. More than half (268) the companies were like Advanced Micro Systems with revenues from $5 billion down to $2 billion. There were 355 U.S. corporations in the U.S. *Fortune* 500 list with revenues of $8.9 billion or less. That is, 71% of the U.S. *Fortune* 500 companies have revenues from $2 to $8 billion. That leaves 29% of the U.S. *Fortune* 500 or 145 companies in the "nearing giant" list—revenues from $9 billion a year to $168 billion. Many of these are globalizing corporations as well.

Fortune 500 is to be called "F-500." *Fortune* Global 500 is to be called "G-500." It turns out that with a few exceptions noted below, the top F-500 equals the U.S. part of the G-500. The exceptions are (1) the United States Postal Service with $54 billion in revenues and $1.7 billion in profit is included in G-500 and not in F-500; (2) Federal National Mortgage Association is included on both lists; (3) Great Atlantic and Pacific Tea is 127 on the G-500 list, but

Figure B-1
Office of Technology Assessment Report—U.S. Downward Trends

The International Fortune 500: Steady Erosion of U.S. Dominance

Since 1966 there has been a steady erosion in the percentage of the international Fortune 500 firms based in the United States. As figure 1-6 demonstrates, in 1966 the United States accounted for 61 percent (304) of these firms. In 1991, only 31 percent (157) of the 500 largest manufacturing firms were based in the United States. In comparison, firms based in Europe grew from 28 percent (139) in 1966 to 34 percent (168) in 1991. In the same period, firms based in Japan grew rapidly from 7 percent (37) in 1966 to 24 percent (119) in 1991.

Figure 1-7 shows that in 1966, U.S.-based firms in the Fortune 500 International had sales of $299 billion, or roughly 67 percent of the $441 billion in total sales of the International Fortune 500. Firms based in Japan accounted for less than 5 percent ($21 billion) and firms based in Europe accounted for 25 percent ($111 billion). In comparison, in 1991 total sales of the International Fortune 500 were $5,188 billion. U.S.-based firms accounted for 34 percent ($1,785 billion). Firms based in Japan accounted for 21 percent ($1,097 billion) and firms based in Europe accounted for 36 percent ($1,901 billion), exceeding sales of U.S.-based MNEs.

Overall employment of the International Fortune 500 grew from 21 million in 1966 to 26 million in 1991. Most of this growth took place in the period 1966-1971. Figure 2-C-1 shows that U.S.-based firms increased their employment by 1.5 million workers between 1966 and 1971. Between 1971 and 1991, U.S.-based firms shed 3.2 million workers. In comparison, employment for firms based in Japan has grown from 1.2 million to 3.5 million. Other Asian-based firms saw their employment grow from 0 to 581,000 during this period. Between 1966 and 1971, employment for firms based in Europe grew from 8.1 million to 10.3 million. It has remained relatively stable since. Firms based outside Asia, Europe, and North America saw employment grow from 271,000 to 1.9 million.

Figure 2-C-1—Employment by International Fortune 500 Firms by Region of Origin, 1966-1991

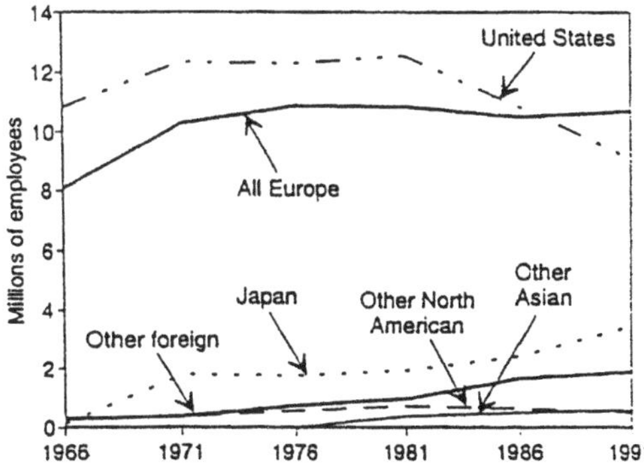

SOURCE: OTA data base compiled from annual reports, Fortune 500 International, and Standard and Poor's Register.

Figure B-1 (continued)

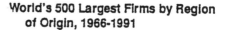

World's 500 Largest Firms by Region of Origin, 1966-1991

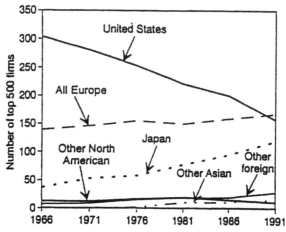

NOTE: Firms are ranked by sales as listed in the International Fortune 500. Some analysts suggest that this figure would be less dramatic if adjusted for exchange rate fluctuations.

SOURCE: OTA database compiled from annual reports, Fortune 500 International, and Standard and Poor's Register.

Sales of World's 500 Largest Firms by Region of Origin, 1966-1991

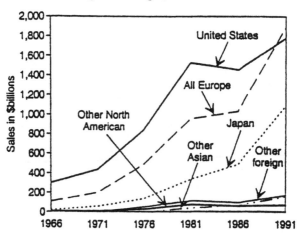

NOTE: Sales are calculated in nominal dollars. Some analysts suggest that this figure would be less dramatic if adjusted for exchange rate fluctuations.

SOURCE: OTA database compiled from annual reports, Fortune 500 International, and Standard and Poor's Register.

Table B-4
List of Global 500 Corporations by Country

Country	Number	Country	Number
Australia	3	Japan	149
Austria	1	Mexico	2
Belgium	4	Netherlands	8
Belgium/Netherlands	1	Netherlands Antilles	1
Brazil	2	Norway	2
Britain	33	South Korea	8
Britain/Netherlands	2	Spain	6
Canada	5	Sweden	3
China	3	Switzerland	14
Finland	1	Taiwan	2
France	40	Turkey	1
Germany	44	United States	151
Hong Kong	1	Venezuela	1
India	1	Total	500
Italy	11		

Source: Fortune, August 5, 1996.

does not appear in the F-500 list; (4) the Federal Home Loan Mortgage (137) on G-500 appears in both lists with different data and this is true of American Express and McKesson. Otherwise, this formula prevails: U.S. F-500 from 1 to number 151 in revenues appeared as globalizing *Fortune* G-500 companies. This is the judgment of the *Fortune* editors who constructed the list. That judgment does not square with this book which selects a different basis using different criteria. For example, Wal-Mart Stores is not a full-fledged globalizer, because so far its life is entirely domestic inside the United States even though it recently started Latin American and Canadian operations. Wal-Mart may well become a more complete globalizer soon. On balance, Wal-Mart Stores is in Appendix A. This example illustrates how careful one must be in assuming that some globalizing traits, though minor, may not necessarily make a company a globalizer with significant international business.

Another way to view globalizers is to see who is on the *Fortune* G-500 list from other nations. Table B-5 explores this dimension of globalization.

Let's look at globalizing another way through the *Fortune* G-500 (see Table B-6).

A continuation of this table to the lowest levels is as follows:

Five Companies

• Belgium

Four Companies

• Australia

• Brazil

Three Companies

• Sweden

Two Companies

• Britain/Netherlands

• China

• Finland

• Norway

One Company

• Belgium/Netherlands

• Hong Kong

• India

• Mexico

• Netherlands Antilles

• Taiwan

• Turkey

• Venezuela

This last analysis shows a distribution of globalizing corporations highly skewed to only five nations—308 of 500 in the United States, Japan, France, Germany and Britain. Another six nations have 60 corporations. So eleven nations have 368 of 500 or 73.6% of the giant globalizing corporations. Finally, there are fourteen nations with one to four corporations.

If eleven nations are the home base of 73.6% of the globalizing corporations (*Fortune* G-500) in the world, what is the population of these home nations? The world population in 1994 was 5.6 billion people. The eleven nations are in two population groups—the top four with 582.7 million and the next six nations with 192.8 million or a total of 775.5 million or three-fourths of a billion people

Table B-5
Distribution of Globalizing Corporations by Nation

Nation	No. of Companies	Revenue Range (billions U.S. dollars)
1. Australia	4	9.0 - 13.7
2. Belgium	5	9.2 - 12.6
3. Belgium/Netherlands	1	22.6
4. Brazil	4	8.8 - 18.5
5. Britain	32	9.0 - 56.9
6. Britain/Netherlands	2	49.7 - 109.8
7. Canada	6	8.9 - 17.9
8. China	2	12.3 - 19.2
9. Finland	2	9.1 - 10.0
10. France	42	8.9 - 43.6
11. Germany	40	9.6 - 72.2
12. Hong Kong	1	10.6
13. India	1	12.8
14. Italy	12	10.1 - 46.4
15. Japan	141	8.9 - 184.3
16. Mexico	1	22.3
17. Netherlands	8	12.1 - 40.1
18. Netherlands Antilles	1	16.1
19. Norway	2	12.5 - 13.6
20. South Korea	12	11.1 - 51.2
21. Spain	6	9.0 - 17.1
22. Sweden	3	13.9 - 24.0
23. Switzerland	16	8.9 - 56.4
24. Taiwan	1	9.6
25. Turkey	1	11.5
26. United States	153	8.8 - 168.8
27. Venezuela	1	26.0

Table B-6
Distribution of Globalizing Corporations by Nations (Concentrated)

Nation	Number of Companies	1994 Population Est.*
1. United States	153	260.7
2. Japan	141	125.1
3. France	42	57.8
4. Germany	40	81.0
5. Britain	32	58.1 (U.K.)
Totals	308	582.7
1. Switzerland	16	7.0
2. South Korea	12	45.0
3. Italy	12	58.1
4. Netherlands	8	15.3
5. Canada	6	28.1
6. Spain	6	39.3
Totals	60	192.8

Source: U.S. Department of Commerce, *World Population* profile, 1994: Tables 3 & 4.

or 13.7% of the world's population of 5.6 billion. What is the major inference one can draw from this?

The major inference is that 86.3% of the world's 5.6 billion people are not in the home nations of three-fourths of the largest globalizing corporations on earth. The developing world has an estimated 4.4 billion people. China has 1.1 billion people; India has 919 million and together they have about half the developing world population. China (2) and India (1) have three globalizing corporations in the *Fortune* G-500 list. This data reveals an enormously skewed distribution of *Fortune* G-500 across the globe. What the implications are for this warped distribution are not at all puzzling. Eleven nations have major obligations toward the other nations of the world. The roster of nations of the UN was 185 members in September 1995. Eleven nations are obligated to 174 other nations and to 86.3% of the world's population. The nature of the obligation can only be imagined if there is such a theory as a world society. Since the creation of the UN in 1945, a world society seems increasingly possible.

The Lure of Delaware

About 273 of the *Fortune* 500 are incorporated in the state of Delaware, or 54.6%. A further refinement shows that of the 151 *Fortune* Global 500 from the United States—84 or 55.6% are incorporated in Delaware. The popularity of Delaware remains high with globalizing corporations in the United States due to the relative absence of legal controls over corporate affairs by the state.

Foreign Sales

Based upon a special analysis made up of the top *Fortune* 50 corporations, there is a striking lack of consistent globalization. At least 23 of the top 50 had foreign sales in 1992 of 21% to 79%. Except for three companies (Boeing, Xerox and AMR), the top 23 were loaded with 1,619 foreign subsidiary corporations in 1994. Eight companies had no foreign sales in 1992, nine companies had under 17% foreign sales.

Thus, highly globalized are 23 of the largest U.S. corporations; moderate globalization is part of the picture and *no* global sales is part of the scene for very large corporations. This is another fact that must be taken into account because other indicators show such variation where one could anticipate uniformity. This data helps to clarify the idea of globalization as a part of revenue production. There is great variation.

Subsidiaries—Domestic and Foreign Corporations

The structure of large corporations is important. In a review of 1995 data for the top *Fortune* 50 corporations, there were found about 6,400 corporations woven together into 50 corporate families. There were 3,680 separate domestic subsidiary corporations in this group and 2,670 foreign subsidiary corporations in this group—or a 57% to 41% split. The presence of so many other corporations, both domestic and foreign-owned and controlled by these 50 giant corporations, does *not* include divisions and branches of such companies that do not have a separate corporate existence. There are also in some corporations both branches and divisions of the parent corporation and then as many as eight levels of subsidiary corporations owned and controlled by the parents—the 50 parents, or as they are described, "ultimate parents." (Dun and Bradstreet, America's Corporate Families, 1995). The entire corporate universe is 11,000 U.S. parents that control 76,000 subsidiary corporations, divisions, and branches. There are 2,900 U.S. parents with 21,000 foreign subsidiaries and 2,800 foreign parents with 11,000 U.S. subsidiaries. This is a strikingly interwoven network of corporations about which too little is known.

After examining the data, this conclusion emerges: The top 50 corporations of the *Fortune* 500 owned 51% (or more) of more than 3,500 domestic subsidiary corporations and 2,500 foreign subsidiary corporations that equal 6,000 total corporations. In other words, the work of just 50 top U.S. globalizing corporations is expressed through 6,000 other corporations. This data sample says nothing about a larger universe of a thousand other large corporations with their domestic and foreign hordes of subsidiary corporations. It is clear that globalization is expressed through very large subsidiaries of foreign corporations in the United States. Japanese transplant factories for auto production are one example. *Fortune* noted, in August 1996, the presence of the top 25 U.S. subsidiaries of global parents with home base located outside the United States (*Fortune*, August 5, 1996: 108). The revenues of these 25 U.S. subsidiaries were $250.5 billion in 1995 with 438,245 employed in the United States by these 25 subsidiaries. The parent corporations were from Japan (11), Germany (5), and a scattering—Shell Oil, Royal Dutch from Britain/Netherlands; BP from Britain; Citgo from PDUSA of Venezuela; Unilever US from Britain and Netherlands; Food Lion, Delhaize of Belgium; Nestlé of Switzerland; AXA of France; Philips Electronics of the Netherlands and Seagrams of Canada. The Seagrams Canada parent corporation received 80.9% of its revenues from the United States, Food Lion provides 64.6% of Delhaize revenues for Belgium. Eight foreign parents earned in the United States from 25.5% (Bayer) to 42.3% for Honda of Japan. Sixteen parent corporations earned 5.4% to 24% of their revenues in the United States There is little doubt of the major impact on the American economy by operations of this size in U.S. subsidiaries of foreign parents.

A Clearer View of Globalizing Corporations

So far, the U.S. vision of a globalizing corporation should be as follows:

1. Almost every large corporation with sales or revenues of at least $8 billion a year.
2. If a U.S. company—more often than not incorporated in the state of Delaware.
3. Probably a parent, "ultimate parent" of a large number, perhaps hundreds of subsidiary corporations—domestic and foreign.
4. Probably founded from 1861 to 1940.
5. Had foreign sales of about 40% to 60% of its sales globally.
6. Operated in more than a half dozen nations to as many as 120 nations.
7. Employed quite a few workers in other nations.
8. If a U.S. globalizer, probably one of top 150 companies in revenue according to *Fortune* standards.
9. Probably existed as a home ultimate parent corporation in one of eleven nations within the Northern Hemisphere, in the United States, Japan or Europe.
10. As asset collectors, in a selected group of 15 of the top 50 of the *Fortune* 500, the number of billion-dollar asset companies were in 1937 (4), in 1947 (7), in 1957 (10) and in 1994 (15). All of the 15 corporations in 1994 were holding assets from a low of $13.8 billion to a high of $198 billion. As repositories of wealth, nothing could beat them. This may be true of foreign parents.

There are just two final characteristics that will be explored to round out a clearer picture of the globalizing corporation—employment and distribution by civilization.

Table B-7
Percent Foreign Employment—1993

60-69%	50-59%	40-49%	30-39%	20-29%	10-19%
Digital Eq.	Alcoa	Eastman	Pepsico	ITT	Amoco
Exxon	Johnson &	Kodak	General	AT&T	
	Johnson	Motorola	Motors	Chrysler	
	Sara Lee	Philip Morris	DuPont	GTE	
	IBM	Dow	Texaco	Atlantic	
	Ford	Chemical	Hewlett-	Richfield	
	Proctor &	RJR Nabisco	Packard	Minn. M&	
	Gamble	Mobil		Mfg.	
	United Tech.			General	
				Electric	
				Chevron	
				Xerox	
				Int'l Paper	

Globalizing Employers: Foreign Employment

Thirty-one American globalizing companies (in the UN report on world investment) had anywhere from 17.1% to 63.8% foreign employees in 1993. This translated to 4.6 million total employees in 1993 in these 31 companies, of which 38.5% or 1.7 million were foreign, while 2.8 million were domestic U.S. employees—61.3%. The percent of foreign employment for the top globalizing corporations is shown in Table B-7.

The 60% domestic–40% foreign is basic to a globalizer with variations—always with variations.

Globalizing Corporations by Civilization

Finally, a clearer understanding of the globalizing corporations could be viewed by civilization. The justification for this arises from an interesting assertion by Samuel P. Huntington of Harvard University that (and it was just an assertion):

It is my hypothesis that the fundamental source of conflict in this new world will not be primarily ideological or primarily economic. The great divisions among humankind and the dominating source of conflict will be cultural. Nation states will remain the most powerful actors in world affairs, but the principal conflicts of global politics will occur between nations and groups of different civilizations. The clash of civilizations will dominate global politics. The fault lines between civilizations will be the battle lines of the future. (Huntington, 1993: 22–49 at 22; Huntington, 1996)

How do globalizing corporations distribute by civilization? Table B-8 shows the distribution using the *Fortune*, July 25, 1994 list of 500 of the world's largest corporations with $2.7 trillion in revenues.

Table B-8
Distribution of Globalizing Corporations by Civilization

Civilization	No. of Companies
Western	327
Japanese	141
	Subtotal: 468
Confucian	14
Islamic	4
Hindu	3
Slavic/Orthodox	0
Latin American	7
African	4
	Subtotal: 32

The civilizations are taken from Huntington as a given, although it is well-known that there are disputes over this typology. Although Hedley Bull's world society view appears to have little relevance to Huntington, that is certainly a different perspective. At least this distribution highlights where Western capitalism in corporate capitalistic form predominates. This fact of corporate distribution adds to the potentials for conflict that Huntington thinks are inevitable based on other factors.

Crumbs Are Not Bread

The difference between the crumbs and the bread is this:

Ninety-eight percent of all companies in the United States account for only about 25 percent of the business in this country; the remaining 2 percent account for nearly 75 percent. The top 500 industrial corporations, which represent only one-tenth of one percent of this elite 2 percent, control over two-thirds of the business resources, employ two-thirds of the industrial workers, account for 60 percent of the sales, and collect 70 percent of the profits. (Schwartz, 1987: 3)

The bread of American business (75%) is in just 1/10 of 1% of the elite top industrial corporations. The crumbs (25%) are for the rest of business. These globalizing giant corporations are listed in Appendix A. The data upon which the quoted statement rests was found in IRS, congressional and other records from 1970 to 1985. Is the statement true in 1999? Yes, the facts are about the same a decade or so later.

Selected Bibliography

BOOKS AND SUBSTANTIAL REPORTS

Accordino, John J. *The United States in the Global Economy*. Chicago: American Library Association, 1992.

Adams, Walter and James W. Brock. *Antitrust Economics on Trial: A Dialogue on the New Laissez-Faire*. Princeton, NJ: Princeton University Press, 1991.

———. *Dangerous Pursuits: Mergers and Acquisitions in the Age of Wall Street*. New York: Pantheon Books, 1989.

———. *The Bigness Complex: Industry, Labor and Government in the American Economy*. New York: Pantheon Books, 1986.

Albert, Michel. *Capitalism vs. Capitalism: How America's Obsession with Individual Achievement and Short-term Profit Has Led It to the Brink of Collapse*. New York: Four Walls Eight Windows, 1993.

Alexander, Titus. *Unraveling Global Apartheid: An Overview of World Politics*. Cambridge, UK: Polity Press, 1996.

Alston, Philip, Stephen Parker and Jolen Seymour (Editors). *Children's Rights and the Law*. Oxford, UK: Clarendon Press, 1992.

Alvares, Claude (Editor). *Unwanted Guest: Goans vs. DuPont*. Goa, India: The Other India Press, 1991.

American Law Institute. *Principles of Corporate Governance: Analyses and Recommendations*, Vol. 1. St. Paul, MN: American Law Institute Publishers, 1994.

American University. "Conference on Changing Notions of Sovereignty and Private Actors in International Law." *Conference Proceedings*. Washington, DC: Washington College of Law, American University, March 25–26, 1993.

Anastassopoulos, Jean-Pierre, Georges Blanc and Pierre Dussauge. *State-Owned Multinationals*. Chichester, UK: John Wiley and Sons, 1987.

Anderson, Rolf. "Atlas of the American Economy." *Congressional Quarterly*, Washington, DC, 1994.

Arnold, N. Scott. *The Philosophy and Economics of Market Socialism: A Critical Study.* New York: Oxford University Press, 1994.

Arnold, Thurman W. *The Folklore of Capitalism.* New Haven, CT: Yale University Press, 1937.

Athanasiou, Tom. *Divided Planet: The Ecology of Rich and Poor.* Boston: Little, Brown and Co., 1996.

Atkins, Richard D. (Editor). *The Alleged Transnational Criminal: The Second Biennial International Criminal Law Seminar.* The Hague, The Netherlands: Martinus Nijhoff, 1995.

Bailey, David, George Harte and Roger Sugden. *Making Transnationals Accountable— A Significant Step for Britain.* London: Routledge, 1994.

————. *Transnationals and Governments. Recent Policies in Japan, France, Germany, the United States and Britain.* London: Routledge, 1994.

Bairoch, Paul. *Economics and World History: Myths and Paradoxes.* Chicago: University of Chicago Press, 1993.

Barlett, Donald L. and James B. Steele. *America: Who Really Pays the Taxes?* New York: Simon & Schuster, 1994.

Barlow, Maude and Tony Clarke. *MAI and the Threat to American Freedom.* Toronto, Canada: Stoddart Publishing, 1998.

Barnet, Richard J. and John Cavanagh. *Global Dreams: Imperial Corporations and the New World Order.* New York: Simon & Schuster, 1994.

Barnet, Richard J. and Ronald E. Müller. *Global Reach: The Power of the Multinational Corporations.* New York: Simon & Schuster, 1974.

Barnett, Harold C. *Toxic Debts and the Superfund Dilemma.* Chapel Hill: University of North Carolina Press, 1994.

Barzun, Jacques. *The Culture We Deserve.* Middletown, CT: Wesleyan University Press, 1989.

Batra, Ravi. *The Great American Deception.* New York: John Wiley & Sons, 1996.

————. *The Myth of Free Trade.* New York: Charles Scribner's Sons, 1993.

Beer, Samuel H. *To Make a Nation: The Rediscovery of American Federalism.* Cambridge, MA: Harvard University Press, 1993.

Bell, Daniel. *The Cultural Contradictions of Capitalism.* 20th Anniversary Edition. New York: Basic Books, 1996.

Bello, Walden. *Dark Victory. The United States, Structural Adjustment, and Global Poverty.* London: Pluto Press, 1994.

Berger, Peter L. *The Capitalist Revolution.* New York: Basic Books, 1986.

Berger, Peter L. (Editor). *The Capitalist Spirit: Toward a Religious Ethic of Wealth Creation.* San Francisco, CA: Institute for Contemporary Studies, 1990.

Berk, Gerald. *Alternative Tracks. The Constitution of American Industrial Order, 1865– 1917.* Baltimore, MD: Johns Hopkins University Press, 1994.

Berle, Adolf A. *Power without Property: A New Development in American Political Economy.* New York: Harcourt, Brace and World, 1959.

Berle, Adolf A., Jr., and Gardiner C. Means. *The Modern Corporation and Private Property.* New Brunswick, NJ: Transaction Publishers, 1991 (originally published in 1932).

Berlin, Isaiah. *The Sense of Reality. Studies and Ideas and Their History.* New York: Farrar, Straus and Giroux, 1997.

Bernstein, Michael A. and David E. Adler (Editors). *Understanding American Economic Decline*. Cambridge, UK: Cambridge University Press, 1994.

Bhagwati, Jagdish and Robert E. Hudec (Editors). *Fair Trade and Harmonization: Prerequisites for Free Trade?* Vol. 1, Economic Analysis. Vol. 2, Legal Analysis. Cambridge, MA: The MIT Press, 1996.

Bhala, Raj K. *Foreign Bank Regulation after BCCI*. Durham, NC: Carolina Academic Press, 1994.

Bialos, Jeffrey P. and Gregory Husisian. *The Foreign Corrupt Practices Act: Coping with Corruption in Transitional Economics*. Dobbs Ferry, NY: Oceana Publications, 1997.

Bill, James A. *George Ball: Behind the Scenes in U.S. Foreign Policy*. New Haven, CT: Yale University Press, 1997.

Birnbaum, Jeffrey H. *The Lobbyists: How Influence Peddlers Work Their Way in Washington*. New York: Random House, 1992.

Blair, Margaret M. *Ownership and Control: Rethinking Corporate Governance for the Twenty-First Century*. Washington, DC: The Brookings Institution, 1995.

Blankenship, Michael B. (Editor). *Understanding Corporate Criminality*. New York: Garland, 1993.

Blasi, Joseph R. *Employee Ownership: Revolution or Ripoff?* Cambridge, MA: Ballinger Publishing Co., 1988.

Blasi, Joseph R., Maya Kroumova and Douglas Kruse. *Kremlin Capitalism: The Privatization of the Russian Economy*. Ithaca, NY: ILR Press of Cornell University Press, 1997.

Blasi, Joseph R., and Douglas L. Kruse. *The New Owners: The Mass Emergence of Employer Ownership in Public Companies and What It Means to American Business*. New York: HarperBusiness, 1991.

Block, Fred L. *The Origins of International Economic Disorder: A Study of United States International Monetary Policy from World War II to the Present*. Berkeley: University of California Press, 1977.

Bluestone, Barry and Irving Bluestone. *Negotiating the Future: A Labor Perspective on American Business*. New York: Basic Books, 1992.

Bluestone, Barry and Bennett Harrison. *The Deindustrialization of America: Plant Closing, Community Abandonment and Dismantling of Basic Industry*. New York: Basic Books, 1982.

Blumberg, Phillip I. *The Megacorporation in American Society: The Scope of Corporate Power*. Englewood Cliffs, NJ: Prentice-Hall, 1975.

———. *The Multinational Challenge to Corporation Law: The Search for a New Corporate Personality*. New York: Oxford University Press, 1993.

Blumberg, Phillip I., Kurt A. Strasser and Linda Evans. *The Law of Corporate Groups*. Boston: Little, Brown and Co., Vol. 1 to Vol. 6, published various times from 1983–1996 with supplements.

Bodin, Jean. *On Sovereignty* (edited and translated by J. H. Franklin). Cambridge, MA: Cambridge University Press, 1992.

Bonsignore, John J. *Law and Multinationals: An Introduction to Law and Political Economy*. Englewood Cliffs, NJ: Prentice-Hall, 1994.

Booth, Douglas E. *Valuing Nature: The Decline and Preservation of Old-Growth Forests*. Lanham, MD: Rowman and Littlefield, 1993.

Bowman, Scott R. *The Modern Corporation and American Political Thought: Law, Power and Ideology.* University Park: Pennsylvania State University Press, 1996.

Boyer, Robert and Daniel Drache (Editors). *States against Markets: The Limits of Globalization.* New York and London: Routledge, 1996.

Boyer, William H. *America's Future: Transition to the 21st Century.* New York: Praeger, 1984.

Bradshaw, Thorton and David Vogel (Editors). *Corporations and Their Critics.* New York: McGraw-Hill, 1981.

Brand, Donald R. *Corporatism and the Rule of Law: A Study of the National Recovery Administration.* Ithaca, NY: Cornell University Press, 1988.

Brandeis, Louis D. *The Curse of Bigness.* Port Washington, NY: Kennikat Press, 1965.

———. *The Curse of Bigness* (edited by Osmond K. Fraenkel). New York: Viking Press, 1934.

Braudel, Fernand. *The Perspective of the World: Civilization and Capitalism, 15th–18th Century,* Vols. I, II, and III. Berkeley: University of California Press (original French publication 1979; English ed. 1992).

Brecher, Jeremy, J. B. Childs and J. Cutler. *Global Visions.* Boston: South End Press, 1993.

Brickey, Kathleen F. *Corporate and White Collar Crime. Cases and Materials.* Boston: Little, Brown and Co., 1990.

Brock, James W. and Kenneth G. Elzinga (Editors). *Antitrust, the Market, and the State: The Contributions of Walter Adams.* Armonk, NY: M. E. Sharpe, 1991.

Brody, David. *In Labor's Cause. Main Themes on the History of the American Worker.* New York: Oxford University Press, 1993.

Brown, Lester R. *Who Will Feed China?* New York: W. W. Norton & Co., 1995.

Brown, Lester R., Christopher Flavin and Hilary French. *State of the World.* New York: W. W. Norton and Co., 1996 and 1997.

Bryant, Bunyon (Editor). *Environmental Justice.* Washington, DC: Island Press, 1995.

Bryant, Keith L. and Henry C. Dethloff. *A History of American Business.* 2nd ed. Englewood Cliffs, NJ: Prentice-Hall, 1990.

Brzezinski, Zbigniew. *Out of Control: Global Turmoil on the Eve of the 21st Century.* New York: Macmillan Publishing, 1993.

Buchanan, Patrick J. *The Great Betrayal.* Boston: Little, Brown and Co., 1998.

Buchholz, Rogene A. *Business Environment and Public Policy.* 3rd ed. Englewood Cliffs, NJ: Prentice-Hall, 1989.

Bull, Hedley. *The Anarchical Society: A Study of Order in World Politics.* 2nd ed. New York: Columbia University Press, 1995.

Bull, Hedley, Benedict Kingsbury and Adam Roberts. *Hugo Grotius and International Relations.* Oxford, UK: Clarendon Press, 1992.

Burger, Joanna. *Oil Spills.* New Brunswick, NJ: Rutgers University Press, 1997.

Burtless, Gary, Robert Z. Lawrence, Robert E. Litan and Robert J. Shapiro. *Globaphobia: Confronting Fears about Open Trade.* Washington, DC: The Brookings Institution, 1998.

Burton, Theodore E. *Corporations and the State.* New York: D. Appleton and Co., 1911.

Calavita, Kitty, Henry N. Pontell and Robert H. Tillman. *Fraud and Politics in the Savings and Loan Crisis.* Berkeley: University of California Press, 1997.

Cameron, Stevie. *On the Take: Crime, Corruption and Greed in the Mulroney Years.* Toronto, Canada: McClelland-Bantam, 1995.

Camilleri, Joseph A. and Jim Falk. *The End of Sovereignty? The Politics of a Shrinking and Fragmentary World.* Hants, UK: Edward Elgar, 1992.

Campbell, C. J. *The Coming Oil Crisis.* Brentwood, Essex, UK: Multi-Science Publishing Co., 1988.

Campbell, C. J. *The Golden Century of Oil 1950–2050: The Depletion of a Resource.* Dordrecht, Netherlands: Kluwer Academic Publishers, 1991.

Carpenter, Donna S. and John Feloni. *The Fall of the House of Hutton.* New York: Henry Holt and Co., 1989.

Carrere, Ricardo and Larry Lohmann. *Pulping the South: Industrial Tree Plantations and the World Paper Economy.* London: Zed Books, 1996.

Carson, Rachel L. *Silent Spring.* Boston: Houghton Mifflin Co., 1962.

Caufield, Catherine. *Masters of Illusion: The World Bank and the Poverty of Nations.* New York: Henry Holt and Co., 1996.

Cavanagh, John, John Gershman, Karen Baker and Gretchen Helmke (Editors). *Trading Freedom.* San Francisco: Institute for Food and Development Policy, 1992.

Chandler, Alfred D., Jr. *Scale and Scope. The Dynamics of Industrial Capitalism.* Cambridge, MA: Harvard University Press, 1990.

———. *The Visible Hand: The Managerial Revolution in American Business.* Cambridge, MA: Harvard University Press, 1977.

Charkham, Jonathan P. *Keeping Good Company: A Study of Corporate Governance in Five Countries.* Oxford, UK: Clarendon Press, 1994.

Chayes, Abraham and Antonia H. Chayes. *The New Sovereignty: Compliance with International Regulatory Agreements.* Cambridge, MA: Harvard University Press, 1995.

Chesterton, G. K. *St. Frances of Assisi.* New York: Doubleday, 1990.

Chomsky, Noam. *World Orders Old and New.* New York: Columbia University Press, 1994.

Chouhan, T. R. et al. *Bhopal: The Inside Story.* New York: Apex Press, 1994.

Clarke, Tony. *Silent Coup: Confronting the Big Business Takeover of Canada.* Ottawa, Canada: Canadian Center for Policy Alternatives; Toronto, Canada: James Lorimer & Co., 1997.

Clarke, Tony and Maude Barlow. *MAI, The Multinational Agreement on Investment and the Threat to Canadian Sovereignty.* Toronto, Canada: Stoddart Publishing Co., 1997.

Cleveland, Harlan. *Birth of a New World Order.* San Francisco: Jossey-Bass, 1993.

Clinard, Marshall B. *Corporate Corruption: The Abuse of Power.* New York: Praeger Publishers, 1990.

Clinard, Marshall B. and Peter C. Yeager. *Corporate Crime.* New York: The Free Press, 1980.

Cohen, Joel E. *How Many People Can the Earth Support?* New York: W. W. Norton & Co., 1995.

Cohen, Stephen D., Joel R. Paul and Robert A. Blecker. *Fundamentals of U.S. Foreign Trade Policy.* Boulder, CO: Westview Press, 1996.

Colas, Bernard (Editor). *Global Economic Cooperation: A Guide to Agreements and Organizations.* 2nd ed. Tokyo: United Nations University Press, 1994.

Colborn, Theo, Dianne Dumanoski and John P. Myers. *Our Stolen Future.* New York: Penguin Books, 1996.

Comeaux, Paul E. and N. Stephan Kinsella. *Protecting Foreign Investment under International Law*. Dobbs Ferry, NY: Oceana Publications, 1997.

Conybeare, John A. C. *Trade Wars: The Theory and Practice of International Commercial Rivalry*. New York: Columbia University Press, 1987.

Copetas, A. Craig. *Metal Men*. New York: G. P. Putnam's Sons, 1985.

Corbridge, Stuart, Nigel Thrift and Ron Martin (Editors). *Money, Power and Space*. Oxford, UK: Blackwell, 1994.

Cowling, Keith and Roger Sugden. *Beyond Capitalism: Towards a New World Economic Order*. New York: St. Martin's Press, 1994.

Cruver, Donald R. *Complying with the Foreign Corrupt Practices Act: A Guide for United States Firms Doing Business in the International Marketplace*. Chicago: American Bar Association, 1994.

Curtler, Hugh. *Shame, Responsibility and the Corporation*. New York: Haven Publications, 1986.

Daly, Herman E. *Beyond Growth: The Economics of Sustainable Development*. Boston: Beacon Press, 1996.

Daly, Herman E. *Steady-State Economics*. 2nd ed. Washington, DC: Island Press, 1991.

Daly, Herman E., and John B. Cobb, Jr. *For the Common Good*. Boston: Beacon Press, 1998.

Danaher, Kevin. *Corporations Are Gonna Get Your Mama: Globalization and the Downsizing of the American Dream*. Monroe, ME: Common Courage Press, 1996.

D'Aprix, Roger M. *In Search of a Corporate Soul*. New York: Amazon, 1976.

Davidson, James Dale and Lord William Rees-Mogg. *The Sovereign Individual*. New York: Simon & Schuster, 1997.

Defoe, Daniel (1661–1731). *A General History of the Robberies and Murders of the Most Notorious Pyrates*. New York: Garland Publishing, 1972.

DeGeorge, Richard T. *Competing with Integrity in International Business*. New York: Oxford University Press, 1993.

DeJouvenel, Bertrand. *Sovereignty. An Inquiry into the Political Good*. Chicago: University of Chicago Press, 1957.

Dembo, David, Ward Morehouse and Lucinda Wykle. *Abuse of Power: Social Performance of Multinational Corporations: The Case of Union Carbide*. New York: New Horizons Press, 1990.

Destler, I. M. *American Trade Politics*. 2nd ed. Washington, DC: Institute for International Economics, 1992.

Doernberg, Richard L. *International Taxation*. St. Paul, MN: West Publishing Co., 1989.

Doremus, Paul N., William W. Keller, Louis W. Pauly and Simon Reich. *The Myth of the Global Corporation*. Princeton, NJ: Princeton University Press, 1998.

Dowd, Douglas. *The Waste of Nations: Dysfunction in the World Economy*. Boulder, CO: Westview Press, 1989.

———. *U.S. Capitalist Development Since 1976: Of, by and for Which People?* Armonk, NY: M. E. Sharpe, 1993.

Dowie, Mark. *Losing Ground: American Environmentalism at the Close of the 20th Century*. Cambridge, MA: MIT Press, 1995.

Drucker, Peter F. *Concept of the Corporation*. New York: John Day Co., 1972.

———. *Post-Capitalist Society*. New York: HarperCollins, 1993.

Dryden, Steve. *Trade Warriors: USTR and the American Crusade for Tree Trade*. New York: Oxford University Press, 1995.

Duchrow, Ulrich. *Alernatives to Global Capitalism: Drawn from Biblical History, Designed for Political Action*. Utrecht, Netherlands: International Books with Kairos Europa, 1995.

Dugger, William M. *Underground Economics: A Decade of Institutionalist Dissent*. Armonk, NY: M. E. Sharpe, 1992.

Dun and Bradstreet. *America's Corporate Families*. London: Dun & Bradstreet, 1995.

Dunlap, Albert J. *Mean Business. How I Save Bad Companies and Make Good Companies Great*. New York: Time Business, 1996.

Dunning, John H. *Multinational Enterprises and the Global Economy*. Reading, MA: Addison-Wesley Publishing Co., 1993.

Durning, Alan. *How Much Is Enough? The Consumer Society and the Future of the Earth*. New York: W. W. Norton & Co., 1992.

Ebbe, Ob. N. Ignatius (Editor). *Comparative and International Criminal Justice Systems: Policing, Judiciary and Corrections*. Boston: Butterworth-Heinmann, 1996.

Eckes, Alfred E., Jr. *Opening America's Market: U.S. Foreign Trade Policy Since 1776*. Chapel Hill: University of North Carolina Press, 1995.

Ehrenberg, Ronald G. *Labor Markets and Integrating National Economies*. Washington, DC: The Brookings Institution, 1994.

Eichengreen, Barry. *Globalizing Capital: A History of the International Monetary System*. Princeton, NJ: Princeton University Press, 1996.

Elfstrom, Gerard. *Moral Issues and Multinational Corporations*. New York: St. Martin's Press, 1991.

Elliott, Kimberly Ann (Editor). *Corruption and the Global Economy*. Washington, DC: Institute for International Economics, 1997.

Encarnation, Dennis J. *Dislodging Multinationals: India's Strategy in Comparative Perspective*. Ithaca, NY: Cornell University Press, 1989.

―――. *Rivals Beyond Trade. America Versus Japan in Global Competition*. Ithaca, NY: Cornell University Press, 1992.

Ernst, Morris L. *Too Big*. Boston: Little, Brown and Co., 1940.

Estes, Ralph. *Tyranny of the Bottom Line: Why Corporations Make Good People Do Bad Things*. San Francisco, CA: Berrett-Koehler Publishers, 1996.

Etzioni, Amitai. *Capital Corruption: The New Attack on American Democracy*. New Brunswick, NJ: Transaction Books, 1988.

Evans, Peter. *Embedded Autonomy: States and Industrial Transformation*. Princeton, NJ: Princeton University Press, 1995.

Fagin, Dan and Marianne Lavelle. *Toxic Deception*. Secaucus, NJ: Carol Publishing Group, 1996.

Falk, Richard. *On Humane Governance: Toward a New Global Politics*. University Park: Pennsylvania State University Press, 1995.

Falk, Richard A. *Revitalizing International Law*. Ames: Iowa University Press, 1989.

Ferguson, Karen and Kate Blackwell. *Pensions in Crisis*. New York: Arcade Publishing, 1995.

Fisse, Brent and John Braithwaite. *Corporations, Crime and Accountability*. New York: Cambridge University Press, 1993.

Fligstein, Neil. *The Transformation of Corporate Control*. Cambridge, MA: Harvard University Press, 1990.

Folsom, Ralph H. and Michael W. Gordon. *International Business Transactions*. St. Paul, MN: West Publishing Co., 1995.

Fowler, Michael R. and Julie M. Bunck. *Law, Power and the Sovereign State: The Evolution and Application of the Concept of Sovereignty.* University Park: Pennsylvania State University Press, 1995.

Frantz, Douglas and David McKean. *Friends in High Places: The Rise and Fall of Clark Clifford.* Boston: Little, Brown and Co., 1995.

French, Peter A. *Collective and Corporate Responsibility.* New York: Columbia University Press, 1984.

French, Peter A., Jeffrey Nesteruk and David T. Risser with J. M. Abbarno. *Corporations in the Moral Community.* Fort Worth, TX: Harcourt Brace Jovanovich College Publishers, 1992.

Fried, Edward R. and Philip H. Trezise. *Oil Security.* Washington, DC: The Brookings Institution, 1993.

Friedman, George and Meredith Lebard. *The Coming War with Japan.* New York: St. Martin's Press, 1991.

Galambos, Louis and Joseph Pratt. *The Rise of the Corporate Commonwealth: U.S. Business and Public Policy in the Twentieth Century.* New York: Basic Books, 1988.

Galbraith, John K. *The Good Society: The Humane Agenda.* Boston: Houghton Mifflin Co., 1996.

———. *The New Industrial State.* Boston: Houghton Mifflin Co., 1967.

Garrett, Laurie. *The Coming Plague.* New York: Penguin Books, 1994.

Garten, Jeffrey E. *The Big Ten.* New York: Basic Books, 1997.

Geis, Gilbert. "White Collar Crime: The Heavy Electrical Equipment Antitrust Cases of 1961." In *Criminal Behavior Systems: A Typology,* edited by Marshall B. Unard and Richard Quinney. New York: Holt, Rinehart & Winston, 1967.

Geis, Gilbert, Robert F. Meier and Lawrence M. Salinger. *White Collar Crime.* 3rd ed. New York: Free Press, 1995.

Gelbspan, Ross. *The Heat Is On: The High Stakes Battle over Earth's Threatened Climate.* Reading, MA: Addison-Wesley Publishing Co., Inc., 1997.

Genzherger, Christine et al. *China Business.* San Rafael, CA: World Trade Press, 1995.

George, Susan and Fabrizio Sabelli. *Faith and Credit: The World Bank's Secular Empire.* London: Penguin Books, 1994.

Gerlach, Michael L. *Alliance Capitalism: The Social Organization of Japanese Business.* Berkeley: University of California Press, 1992.

Gershuny, Jonathan. *After Industrial Society? The Emerging Self-Service Economy.* Atlantic Highlands, NJ: Humanities Press, 1978.

Gill, William J. *Trade Wars against America: A History of United States Trade and Monetary Policy.* New York: Praeger, 1990.

Gilpin, Robert. *U.S. Power and the Multinational Corporation: The Political Economy of Foreign Direct Investment.* New York: Basic Books, 1975.

Gladwin, Thomas N. *Environment, Planning and the Multinational Corporation.* Greenwich, CT: JAI Press, 1977.

Gladwin, Thomas N. and Ingo Walter. *Multinationals under Fire: Lessons in Management of Conflict.* New York: John Wiley and Sons, 1980.

Glasmeier, Amy K. and Marie Howland. *From Combines to Computers: Rural Services and Development in the Age of Informational Technology.* Albany: State University of New York Press, 1995.

Goldsmith, James. *The Trap.* New York: Carroll & Gray Publishers, 1993.

Goodrich, Carter (Editor). *The Government and the Economy, 1783–1861.* Indianapolis, IN: Bobbs-Merrill Co., 1967.

Gomes-Casseres, Benjamin. *The Alliance Revolution: The New Shape of Business Rivalry.* Cambridge, MA: Harvard University Press, 1996.

Goodwyn, Lawrence. *The Populist Moment: A Short History of the Agrarian Revolt in America.* New York: Oxford University Press, 1978.

Gordon, David M. *Fat and Mean: The Corporate Squeeze of Working Americans and the Myth of Managerial "Downsizing."* New York: Simon & Schuster, 1996.

Gordon, Sara L. *The United States and Global Capital Shortages: The Problem and Possible Solutions.* Westport, CT: Quorum Books, 1995.

Gottlieb, Roger S. (Editor). *The Sacred Earth.* New York: Routledge, 1996.

Gould, Douglas and Andrew Willis. *The Bre-X Fraud.* Toronto, Canada: McClelland & Stewart, 1997.

Gould, Lewis L. *The Presidency of Theodore Roosevelt.* Lawrence: University Press of Kansas, 1991.

Graham, Edward M. *The Global Corporations and National Governments.* Washington, DC: Institute for International Economics, 1996.

Graham, Edward M. and Paul R. Krugman. *Foreign Direct Investment in the United States.* 3rd ed. Washington, DC: Institute for International Economics, 1995.

Graham, John W. *The U.S. Securities and Exchange Commission: A Research and Information Guide.* New York: Garland Publishing, 1993.

Gray, John. *False Dawn. The Delusions of Global Capitalism.* London: Granta Books, 1998.

Greer, Douglas F. *Industrial Organization and Public Policy.* 3rd ed. New York: Macmillan Publishing Co., 1992.

Grefe, Edward A. and Marty Linsky. *The New Corporate Activism: Harnessing the Power of Grass Roots Tactics for Your Organization.* New York: McGraw-Hill, 1995.

Greider, William. *One World, Ready or Not: The Manic Logic of Global Capitalism.* New York: Simon & Schuster, 1997.

———. *Who Will Tell the People: The Betrayal of American Democracy.* New York: Simon & Schuster, 1992.

Griffin, Stephen M. *American Constitutionalism.* Princeton, NJ: Princeton University Press, 1996.

Guéhenno, Jean-Marie. *The End of the Nation State.* Minneapolis: University of Minnesota Press, 1995.

Hacker, Andrew. *Money: Who Has How Much and Why?* New York: Scribner, 1997.

Hall, Ivan P. *Cartels of the Mind: Japan's Intellectual Closed Shop.* New York: W. W. Norton & Co., 1998.

Hamilton, Walton H. *The Politics of Industry.* New York: Alfred A. Knopf, 1957.

Hampden-Turner, Charles and Alfons Trompenaars. *The Seven Cultures of Capitalism.* New York: Bantam Doubleday Dell Publishing Group, 1993.

Hanson, Jim. *The Decline of the American Empire.* Westport, CT: Praeger, 1993.

Harrison, Bennett. *Lean and Mean.* New York: Basic Books, 1994.

Harrison, Bennett and Barry Bluestone. *The Great U-Turn: Corporate Restructuring and the Polarizing of America.* New York: Basic Books, 1988.

Harrison, E. Bruce. *Going Green: How to Communicate Your Company's Environmental Commitment.* Homewood, IL: Business One Irwin, 1993.

Hart, Vivien. *Bound by Our Constitution: Women, Workers and the Minimum Wage.* Princeton, NJ: Princeton University Press, 1994.

Hartmann, Thom. *The Last Hours of Ancient Sunlight.* Northfield, VT: Mythical Books, 1998.

Haslett, D. W. *Capitalism with Morality.* Oxford, UK: Clarendon Press, 1994.

Hathaway, Dale A. *Can Workers Have a Voice? The Politics of Deindustrialization in Pittsburgh.* University Park: Pennsylvania State University Press, 1993.

Hawken, Paul. *The Ecology of Commerce: A Declaration of Sustainability.* New York: Harper Business, 1993.

Hawley, James P. *Dollars and Borders: U.S. Government Attempts to Restrict Capital Flows, 1960–1980.* Armonk, NY: M. E. Sharpe, 1987.

Heenan, David A. *The New Corporate Frontier: The Big Move to Small Town, U.S.A.* New York: McGraw-Hill, 1991.

Heilbroner, Robert. *21st Century Capitalism.* New York: W. W. Norton & Co., 1993.

Heilbroner, Robert L. and William Milberg. *The Crisis of Vision in Modern Economic Thought.* Cambridge, UK: Cambridge University Press, 1995.

Higgins, Rosalyn. *Problems and Process: International Law and How We Use It.* Oxford, UK: Clarendon Press, 1964.

Hightower, Jim. *There's Nothing in the Middle of the Road but Yellow Stripes and Dead Armadillos.* New York: HarperCollins, 1997.

Hilz, Christoph. *The International Toxic Waste Trade.* New York: Van Nostrand Reinhold, 1992.

Hipple, F. Steb. *Multinational Companies in United States International Trade.* Westport, CT: Quorum Books, 1995.

Hoekman, Bernard M. and Michel M. Kostecki. *The Political Economy of the World Trading System: From GATT to WTO.* Oxford, UK: Oxford University Press, 1995.

Holm, Han-Henrik and Georg Sorensen. *Whose World Order? Uneven Globalization and the End of the Cold War.* Boulder, CO: Westview Press, 1995.

Hoover's Handbook of World Business 1993. Austin, TX: The Reference Press, 1993.

Hoover's Handbook of American Business 1994. Austin, TX: The Reference Press, 1993.

Hoover's Handbook of World Business 1995–1996. Austin, TX: The Reference Press, 1995.

Hoover's Handbook of American Companies 1996. Austin, TX: The Reference Press, 1995.

Hovenkemp, Herbert. *Enterprise and American Law, 1836–1937.* Cambridge, MA: Harvard University Press, 1991.

Hufbauer, Gary C. and J. J. Schott. *NAFTA. An Assessment.* Washington, DC: Institute for International Economics, 1993.

Hull, Richard W. *American Enterprise in South Africa: Historical Dimensions of Engagement and Disengagement.* New York: New York University Press, 1990.

Hunsberger, Warren S. (Editor). *Japan's Quest: The Search for International Role, Recognition and Respect.* Armonk, NY: M. E. Sharpe, 1997.

Huntington, Samuel P. *The Clash of Civilizations and the Remaking of World Order.* New York: Simon & Schuster, 1996.

Hurst, James Willard. *The Legitimacy of the Business Corporation in the Laws of the United States, 1780–1970.* Charlottesville: University Press of Virginia, 1970.

Hutchinson, Terence. *Before Adam Smith: The Emergence of Political Economy, 1662–1776.* Oxford, UK: Basil Blackwell, 1988.

Hymer, Stephen H. *The Multinational Corporation: A Radical Approach.* Cambridge, UK: Cambridge University Press, 1979.

Idris-Soven, Ahamed, Elizabeth Idris-Soven and Mary K. Vaughn. *The World as a Company Town: Multinational Corporations and Social Change.* The Hague, Netherlands: Mouton, 1978.

International Monetary Fund (IMF). *International Capital Markets.* Washington, DC: IMF, 1995.

International Petroleum Encyclopedia. Tulsa, OK: Permwell Publishing Co., 1995.

Irwin, Douglas A. *Against the Tide: An Intellectual History of Free Trade.* Princeton, NJ: Princeton University Press, 1996.

Jacobs, Michael T. *Short-Term America: The Causes and Cures of Business Myopia.* Boston: Harvard Business School Press, 1991.

Jacoby, Neil H. *Corporate Power and Social Responsibility: A Blueprint for the Future.* New York: Macmillan Publishing Co., 1973.

Jacoby, Neil H., Peter Nehemkis and Richard Ells. *Bribery and Extortion in World Business.* New York: Macmillan Publishing Co., 1977.

James, William. *Writings 1878–1899* (Selected Essay—The Knowing of Things Together, 1894). New York: Library of America, Literary Classics of the United States, 1992.

Jeannet, Jean-Pierre and Hubert D. Hennessey. *Global Marketing Strategies.* 2nd ed. Boston: Houghton Mifflin Co., 1992.

Jingsheng, Wei. *The Courage to Stand Alone: Letters from Prison and Other Writings,* translated and edited by Kristina M. Torgeson. New York: Penguin Group, 1997.

Johnson, Bryan T., Kim R. Holmes and Melanie Kirkpatrick. *1998 Index of Economic Freedom.* Washington, DC: Heritage Foundation, New York: Wall Street Journal, 1998.

Josephson, Matthew. *The Robber Barons: The Great American Capitalists, 1861–1901.* Reprint (original 1934). New York: Harcourt Brace Jovanovich, 1962.

Kahn, Robert L. and Mayer N. Zald (Editors). *Organizations and Nation-States: New Perspectives on Conflict and Cooperation.* San Francisco: Jossey-Bass, 1990.

Kallen, Lawrence H. *Corporate Welfare. The Mega Bankruptcies of the 80's and 90's.* New York: Carol Publishing Group, 1991.

Kammen, Michael. *Sovereignty and Liberty: Constitutional Discourse in American Culture.* Madison: University of Wisconsin Press, 1988.

Kanter, Rosabeth M. *World Class: Thriving Locally in the Global Economy.* New York: Simon & Schuster, 1995.

Kapstein, Ethan B. *Governing the Global Economy: International Finance and the State.* Cambridge, MA: Harvard University Press, 1994.

Karliner, Joshua. *The Corporate Planet: Ecology and Politics in the Age of Globalization.* San Francisco: Sierra Club Books, 1997.

Kassiola, Joel Jay. *The Death of Industrial Civilization: The Limits to Economic Growth and the Repoliticalization of Advanced Industrial Society.* Albany: State University of New York Press, 1990.

Kaufman, Allen, Lawrence Zacharias and Marvin Karson. *Managers vs. Owners: The Struggle for Corporate Control in American Democracy.* New York: Oxford University Press, 1995.

Kaysen, Carl (Editor). *The American Corporation Today*. New York: Oxford University Press, 1996.

Kefauver, Estes. *In Few Hands: Monopoly Power in America*. New York: Pantheon Books, 1965.

Kennedy, Paul. *Preparing for the Twenty-First Century*. New York: Random House, 1993.

Kerry, John. *The New War: The Web of Crime that Threatens America's Society*. New York: Simon & Schuster, 1997.

Kindleberger, Charles P. *Multinational Excursions*. Cambridge, MA: MIT Press, 1984.

————. *The World Economy and National Finance in Historical Perspective*. Ann Arbor: University of Michigan Press, 1995.

Kittrie, Nicholas N. *The War against Authority*. Baltimore, MD: Johns Hopkins University Press, 1995.

Knoke, William. *Bold New World*. New York: Kodansha International, 1996.

Kolde, Endel-Jakob. *Environment of International Business*. Boston: PWS Kent Publishing Co., 1985.

Kopinak, Kathryn. *Desert Capitalism: Maquiladoras in North America's Western Industrial Corridor*. Tucson: University of Arizona Press, 1996.

Korn, Jessica. *The Power of Separation*. Princeton, NJ: Princeton University Press, 1996.

Korten, David. *When Corporations Rule the World*. San Francisco: Berret-Koehler Publishers and Kumerian Press, 1995.

Kotz, David M. *Bank Control of Large Corporations in the United States*. Berkeley: University of California Press, 1978.

Krauze, Enrique. *Mexico, Biography of Power: A History of Modern Mexico, 1810–1996*. New York: HarperCollins, 1997.

Kroll, John A. *Closure in International Politics*. Boulder, CO: Westview Press, 1995.

Krueger, Anne O. (Editor). *The Political Economy of American Trade*. Chicago: University of Chicago Press, 1996.

Krugman, Paul R. *Peddling Prosperity*. New York: W. W. Norton & Co., 1994.

————. *The Age of Diminished Expectations: U.S. Economic Policy in the 1990's*. Cambridge, MA: MIT Press, 1994.

Krugman, Paul R. (Editor). *Strategic Trade Policy and the New International Economics*. Cambridge, MA: MIT Press, 1986.

Kuhn, James and Donald W. Shriver, Jr. *Beyond Success: Corporations and Their Critics in the 1990's*. New York: Oxford University Press, 1991.

Küng, Hans. *A Global Ethic for Global Politics and Economics*. New York: Oxford University Press, 1998.

Kuttner, Robert. *Everything for Sale: The Virtues and Limits of Markets*. New York: Alfred A. Knopf, 1997.

Kyi, Aung San Suu. *Freedom from Fear*. Rev. ed. London: Penguin Books, 1995.

Laidler, Harry W. *Concentration of Control in American Industry*. New York: Thomas Crowell Co., 1931.

Lang, Tim and Colin Hines. *The New Protectionism: Protecting the Future against Free Trade*. New York: The New Press, 1993.

Lapham, Lewis H. *Waiting for the Barbarians*. London: Verso, 1997.

Lapp, Ralph E. *The Logarithmic Century*. Englewood Cliffs, NJ: Prentice-Hall, 1973.

Lawrence, Robert Z. *Single World, Divided Nations? International Trade and OECD Labor Markets*. Washington, DC: The Brookings Institution, 1996a.

Lawrence, Robert Z., Albert Bressand and Takatoshi Ito. *A Vision for the World Economy: Openness, Diversity and Cohesion*. Washington, DC: The Brookings Institution, 1996b.

Lazonick, William. *Business Organization and the Myth of the Market Economy*. Cambridge, UK: Cambridge University Press, 1991.

Leape, Jonathan, Bo Baskin and Stefan Underhill (Editors). *Business in the Shadow of Apartheid: U.S. Firms in South Africa*. Lexington, MA: Lexington Books, 1985.

Leeson, Nick. *Rogue Trader*. Boston: Little, Brown and Co., 1996.

Leiber, James B. *Friendly Takeover: How an Employee Buyout Saved a Steel Town*. New York: Viking Penguin USA, 1995.

Lind, Michael. *The Next American Nation*. New York: The Free Press, 1995.

Lindahl, Martin L. and William A. Carter. *Corporate Concentration and Public Policy*. 3rd ed. Englewood Cliffs, NJ: Prentice-Hall, 1959.

Lindblom, Charles E. *Inquiry and Change: The Troubled Attempt to Understand and Shape Society*. New Haven, CT: Yale University Press; New York: Russell Sage Foundation, 1990.

Lindblom, Charles E. *Politics and Markets: The World's Political-Economic Systems*. New York: Basic Books, 1977.

Litfin, Karen T. *Ozone Discourses: Science and Politics in Global Environmental Cooperation*. New York: Columbia University Press, 1994.

Lorsch, Jay W. with Elizabeth MacIver. *Pawns or Potentates: The Reality of America's Corporate Boards*. Boston: Harvard Business School Press, 1989.

Lowe, Janet. *The Secret Empire. How 25 Multinationals Rule the World*. Homewood, IL: Business One Irwin, 1992.

Lundberg, Ferdinand. *America's 60 Families*. New York: Vanguard Press, 1937.

Luttwak, Edward N. *The Endangered American Dream*. New York: Simon & Schuster, 1993.

Mabey, Nick, S. Hall, C. Smith and S. Gupta. *Argument in the Green-House: The International Economics of Controlling Global Warming*. London: Routledge, 1997.

Magaziner, Ira C. and Mark Patinkin. *The Silent War: Inside the Global Business Battles Shaping America's Future*. New York: Random House, 1989.

Magaziner, Ira C. and Robert B. Reich. *Minding America's Business*. New York: Harcourt Brace Journals Publishers, 1982.

Magdoff, Harry and Paul M. Sweezy. *The Deepening Crisis of U.S. Capitalism*. New York: Monthly Review Press, 1981.

Makinson, Larry. *Follow the Money Handbook*. Washington, DC: Center for Responsive Politics, 1994.

Mandel, Michael J. *The High Risk Society: Peril and Promises in the New Economy*. New York: Times Business Books, 1996.

Mander, Jerry and Edward Goldsmith (Editors). *The Case against the Global Economy and for a Turn toward the Local*. San Francisco: Sierra Club Books, 1996.

Marshall, F. Ray. *Unheard Voices: Labor and Economic Policy in a Competitive World*. New York: Basic Books, 1987.

Martin, John M. and Anne T. Romano. *Multinational Crime*. Newbury Park, CA: Sage Publications, 1992.

Mason, Edward S. *The Corporation in Modern Society*. Cambridge, MA: Harvard University Press, 1959.

Mason, Mark and Dennis Encarnation (Editors). *Does Ownership Matter? Japanese Multinationals in Europe*. Oxford, UK: Clarendon Press, 1994.

Mattera, Philip. *World Class Business: A Guide to the 100 Most Powerful Global Corporations*. New York: Henry Holt and Company, 1992.

McCormick, Brian and Kevin McCormick. *Japanese Companies—British Factories*. Hants, UK: Avebury Alderdshot, 1996.

McCraw, Thomas K. *Prophets of Regulation*. Cambridge, MA: Harvard University Press, 1984.

McLachlan, Campbell and Peter Nygh. *Transnational Tort Litigation: Jurisdictional Principles*. Oxford, UK: Clarendon Press, 1996.

McQuaid, Kim. *Uneasy Partners: Big Business in American Politics, 1945–1990*. Baltimore, MD: Johns Hopkins University Press, 1994.

Merriam, Charles E., Jr. *History of the Theory of Sovereignty since Rousseau*. New York: AMS Press, 1968.

Michie, Jonathan and John Grieve Smith (Editors). *Managing the Global Economy*. Oxford, UK: Oxford University Press, 1995.

Miller, Arthur Selwyn. *The Modern Corporate State: Private Governments and the American Constitution*. Westport, CT: Greenwood Press, 1976.

Miller, Lynn H. *Global Order: Values and Power in International Politics*. Boulder, CO: Westview Press, 1994.

Millman, Gregory J. *The Vandal's Crown: How Rebel Currency Traders Overthrew the World's Central Banks*. New York: Free Press, 1995.

Millstein, Ira M. and Salem M. Katsh. *The Limits of Corporate Power*. New York: Macmillan Publishing Co., 1981.

Mintz, Beth and Michael Schwartz. *The Power Structure of American Business*. Chicago: University of Chicago Press, 1985.

Mitchell, Lawrence E. (Editor). *Progressive Corporate Law*. Boulder, CO: Westview Press, 1995.

Mitroff, Ian I. and Harold A. Linstone. *The Unbounded Mind*. New York: Oxford University Press, 1993.

Miyashita, Kenichi and David Russell. *Keiretsu: Inside the Hidden Japanese Conglomerates*. New York: McGraw-Hill, 1994.

Mizruchi, Mark S. *The Structure of Corporate Political Action: Interfirm Relations and Their Consequences*. Cambridge, MA: Harvard University Press, 1992.

Moore, Michael. *Downsize This! Random Threats from an Unarmed American*. New York: Crown Publishers, 1996.

Moran, Theodore H. *Multinational Corporations: The Political Economy of Foreign Direct Investment*. Lexington, MA: Lexington Books, 1985.

More, Sir Thomas. *Utopia*. 10th ed. Mineola, NY: Dover Publications, 1997.

Morehouse, Ward and M. Arun Subramanian. *The Bhopal Tragedy*. New York: Council on International and Public Affairs, 1986.

Mueller, Gerhard O. W. and Freda Adler. *Outlaws of the Ocean: The Complete Book of Contemporary Crime on the High Seas*. New York: Hearst Marine Books, 1985.

Muller, Jerry Z. *Adam Smith in His Time and Ours*. New York: Free Press, 1993.

Multatuli. *Max Havelaar or the Coffee Auctions of the Dutch Trading Company*. Amherst University of Massachusetts Press, 1982.

Munkirs, John R. *The Transformation of American Capitalism: From Competitive Market*

Structures to Centralized Private Sector Planning. Armonk, NY: M. E. Sharpe, 1985.

Myers, Desaix B. *U.S. Business in South Africa. The Economic, Political and Moral Issues.* Bloomington: Indiana University Press, 1980.

Nadelmann, Ethan A. *Cops Across Borders: The Internationalization of U.S. Criminal Law Enforcement.* University Park: Pennsylvania State University Press, 1993.

Nader, Ralph, Mark Green and Joel Seligman. *Taming the Giant Corporation.* New York: W. W. Norton & Co., 1976.

Nader, Ralph and Wesley J. Smith. *No Contest: Corporate Lawyers and the Perversion of Justice in America.* New York: Random House, 1996.

Nader, Ralph et al. *The Case against Free Trade: GATT, NAFTA and the Globalization of Corporate Power.* San Francisco: Earth Island Press, 1993.

National Academy of Sciences et al. *Finding Common Ground: U.S. Export Controls in a Changed Global Environment.* Washington, DC: National Academy Press, 1991.

New York Times. The Downsizing of America. New York: Times Books, 1996.

Nusbaumer, Jacques (Editor). *Services in the Global Market.* Boston: Kluwer Academic Publishers, 1987.

O'Barr, William M. and John M. Conley. *Fortune and Folly: The Wealth and Power of Institutional Investing.* Homewood, IL: Business One Irwin, 1992.

O'Connor, Martin (Editor). *Is Capitalism Sustainable? Political Economy and the Politics of Ecology.* New York: The Guilford Press, 1994.

Ohmae, Kenichi. *The Borderless World: Management Lessons in the New Logic of the Global Marketplace.* New York: HarperCollins, 1991.

———. *The End of the Nation State: The Rise of Regional Economies.* New York: Free Press, 1995.

Pasztor, Andy. *When the Pentagon Was for Sale: Inside America's Biggest Defense Scandal.* New York: Scribner, 1995.

Pauly, Louis W. *Who Elected the Bankers? Surveillance and Control in the World Economy.* Ithaca, NY: Cornell University Press, 1997.

Pearce, Frank and Laureen Snider. *Corporate Crime: Contemporary Debate.* Toronto, Canada: University of Toronto Press, 1995.

Pearce, Frank and Michael Woodiwiss. *Global Crime Connections.* Toronto, Canada: University of Toronto Press, 1993.

Pendergrast, Mark. *For God, Country and Coca-Cola: The Unauthorized History of the Great American Soft Drink and the Company That Makes It.* New York: Charles Scribner's Sons, 1993.

Peritz, Rudolph J. R. *Competition Policy in America, 1888–1992: History, Rhetoric, Law.* New York: Oxford University Press, 1996.

Perrucci, Robert. *Japanese Auto Transplants in the Heartland: Corporatism and Community.* New York: Aldine de Gruyter, 1994.

Pertschuk, Michael. *Revolt against Regulation: The Rise and Pause of the Consumer Movement.* Berkeley: University of California Press, 1982.

Peterson, Rodney D. *Political Economy and American Capitalism.* Boston: Kluwer Academic Publishers, 1991.

Pfaff, William. *The Wrath of Nations.* New York: Simon & Schuster, 1993.

Phelan, James and Robert Pozen. *The Company State.* Ralph Nader's Study Group Report on DuPont in Delaware. New York: Grossman Publishers, 1973.

Phillips, Kevin. *Arrogant Capital*. Boston: Little, Brown and Co., 1994.

———. *The Politics of Rich and Poor*. New York: Random House, 1990.

Picciotto, Sol. *International Business Taxation: A Study in the Internationalization of Business Regulation*. New York: Quorum Books, 1992.

Pizzigati, Sam. *The Maximum Wage: A Common Sense Prescription for Revitalizing American—by Taxing the very Rich*. New York: Apex Press, 1992.

Podgor, Ellen S. *White Collar Crime*. St. Paul, MN: West Publishing Co., 1993.

Pollack, Norman. *The Human Economy: Populism, Capitalism and Democracy*. New Brunswick, NJ: Rutgers University Press, 1990.

Polyani, Karl. *The Great Transformation*. Boston: Beacon Press, 1944.

Portz, John. *The Politics of Plant Closings*. Lawrence: University Press of Kansas, 1990.

Potter, Edward E. and Judith A. Youngman. *Keeping America Competitive*. Lakewood, CO: Glenbridge Publishing, 1995.

Presser, Stephen B. *Piercing the Corporate Veil*. Deerfield, IL: Clark, Boardman, Callaghan, 1991.

Prestowitz, Clyde V., Jr. *Trading Places*. New York: Basic Books, 1988.

Quinn, James B. *Intelligent Enterprise*. New York: Free Press, 1992.

Radebaugh, Lee H. and Sidney J. Gray. *International Accounting and Multinational Enterprises*. 3rd ed. New York: John Wiley & Sons, 1993.

Raghavan, Chakravarthi. *Recolonization, GATT, the Uruguay Round and the Third World*. London, UK: Zed Books; Penang, Malaysia: Third World Network, 1990.

Reardon, John J. *America and the Multinational Corporation: The History of a Troubled Partnership*. Westport, CT: Praeger, 1992.

Reich, Charles A. *The Greening of America*. 1995 ed. New York: Crown Trade Paperbacks, 1970.

Reich, Robert B. *The Work of Nations: Preparing Ourselves for 21st Century Capitalism*. New York: Random House, 1991.

Reich, Simon. *The Fruits of Fascism: Postwar Prosperity in Historical Perspective*. Ithaca, NY: Cornell University Press, 1990.

Reinicke, Wolfgang H. *Global Public Policy: Governing without Government?* Washington, DC: The Brookings Institution Press, 1998.

Report of the International People's Tribunal To Judge the G-7, Tokyo, July 1993. *The People vs. Global Capital*. New York: Apex Press, 1994.

Resnick, Philip. *Twenty-First Century Democracy*. Montreal, Canada: McGill–Queens University Press, 1997.

Rifkin, Jeremy. *The End of Work: The Decline of the Global Labor Force and the Dawn of the Post Market Era*. New York: G. P. Putnam's Sons, 1995.

Ritzer, George. *The McDonaldization of Society*. Thousand Oaks, CA: Pine Forge Press, 1993.

Robertson, James Oliver. *America's Business*. New York: Hill and Wang, 1985.

Rodrick, Dani. *Has Globalization Gone too Far?* Washington, DC: Institute for International Economics, 1997.

Roe, Mark J. *Strong Managers, Weak Owners: The Political Roots of American Corporate Finance*. Princeton, NJ: Princeton University Press, 1994.

Rogers, Everett M. *Diffusion of Innovations*. 4th ed. New York: Free Press, 1995.

Roosevelt, Theodore. *American Ideals*. New York: G. P. Putnam's Sons, 1901.

Rose-Ackerman, Susan. *Corruption: A Study in Political Economy*. New York: Academic Press, 1978.

————. *Rethinking the Progressive Agenda: The Reform of the American Regulatory State.* New York: Free Press, 1992.

Rosow, Jerome M. *The Global Marketplace.* New York: Facts on File, 1988.

Ross, Robert J. S. and Kent C. Trachte. *Global Capitalism—The New Leviathan.* Albany, NY: State University of New York Press, 1990.

Rubner, Alex. *The Might of the Multinationals: The Rise and Fall of the Corporate Legend.* New York: Praeger, 1990.

Saari, David J. *Too Much Liberty? Perspectives on Freedom and the American Dream.* Westport, CT: Praeger, 1995.

Sachs, Wolfgang. *For Love of the Automobile: Looking Back into the History of Our Desires.* Berkeley: University of California Press, 1992.

Sakamoto, Yoshikazu (Editor). *Global Transformation: Challenges to the State System.* Tokyo, Japan: United Nations University Press, 1994.

Sally, Razeen. *States and Firms: Multinational Enterprises in Institutional Competition.* London: Routledge, 1995.

Sampson, Anthony. *Company Man: The Rise and Fall of Corporate Life.* New York: Random House, 1995.

————. *The Sovereign State of ITT.* New York: Stern and Day Publishers, 1973.

Samuels, Richard J. *"Rich Nation, Strong Army": National Security and the Technological Transformation of Japan.* Ithaca, NY: Cornell University Press, 1994.

Samuels, Warren J. and Arthur S. Miller (Editors). *Corporations and Society: Power and Responsibility.* Westport, CT: Greenwood Press, 1987.

Sassoon, Donald. *One Hundred Years of Socialism: The West European Left in the Twentieth Century.* New York: The New Press 1996.

Sauvant, Karl P. *International Transaction in Services: The Politics of Transborder Data Flows.* Boulder, CO: Westview Press, 1986.

Schilit, Howard M. *Financial Shenanigans: How to Detect Accounting Gimmicks and Fraud in Financial Reports.* New York: McGraw-Hill, 1993.

Schiller, Herbert I. *Information Inequality: The Deepening Social Crisis in America.* New York: Routledge, 1996.

Schlacter, Gail. *Corporate America: An Historical Bibliography.* Santa Barbara, CA: ABC-CLIO Information Services, 1984.

Schrau, Martin. *Speaking Freely: Former Members of Congress Talk about Money in Politics.* Washington, DC: Center for Responsive Politics, 1995.

Schumacher, E. F. *Small Is Beautiful: Economics as if People Mattered.* New York: Harper & Row, 1975.

Schwab, Klaus (Editor). *Overcoming Indifference.* New York: New York University Press, 1995.

Schwartz, Herman A. *States Versus Markets.* New York: St. Martin's Press, 1994.

Schwartz, Michael (Editor). *The Structure of Power in America: The Corporate Elite as a Ruling Class.* New York: Holmes & Meier, 1987.

Scitovsky, Tibor. *The Joyless Economy: The Psychology of Human Satisfaction.* Rev. ed. New York: Oxford University Press, 1992.

Scott, James C. *Seeing Like a State: How Certain Schemes to Improve the Human Condition Have Failed.* New Haven, CT: Yale University Press, 1998.

Scott, John. *Corporations, Classes and Capitalism.* 2nd ed. London: Hutchinson, 1985.

Seidman, Ann and Eva Seidman. *South Africa and U.S. Multinational Corporations.* Westport, CT: Lawrence Hill and Co., 1977.

Selznick, Philip. *Law, Society and Industrial Justice.* New York: Russell Sage Foundation, 1969.

———. *The Moral Commonwealth: Social Theory and the Promise of Community.* Berkeley: University of California Press, 1992.

Sen, Amartya. *On Ethics and Economics.* Oxford, UK: Basil Blackwell, 1987.

Sethi, S. Prakish, Paul Steidlmeier and Cecilia M. Falbe. *Scaling the Corporate Wall.* Englewood Cliffs, NJ: Prentice-Hall, 1991.

Sexton, Patricia C. *The War on Labor and the Left: Understanding America's Unique Conservatism.* Boulder, CO: Western Press, 1991.

Shapiro, Alan C. *Foundations of Multinational Financial Management.* 2nd ed. Englewood Cliffs, NJ: Prentice-Hall, 1994.

Shapiro, Irving S. *America's Third Revolution: Public Interest and the Private Role.* New York: Harper & Row, 1984.

Shapiro, Susan. *Wayward Capitalists: Target of the Securities and Exchange Commission.* New Haven, CT: Yale University Press, 1984.

Shelp, Ronald K. *Beyond Industrialization: The Ascendancy of the Global Service Economy.* New York: Praeger, 1981.

Sherman, Joe. *In the Rings of Saturn.* New York: Oxford University Press, 1996.

Shuman, Michael. *Towards A Global Village: International Community Development Initiatives.* London: Pluto Press, 1994.

Silk, Leonard and Mark Silk. *Making Capitalism Work.* New York: New York University Press, 1996.

Simich, Jerry L. and Rick Rilman. *Thorstein Veblen: A Reference Guide.* Boston: G. K. Hall & Co., 1985.

Simon, David R. and D. Stanley Eitzen. *Elite Deviance.* 4th ed. Boston: Allyn and Bacon, 1992.

Sinclair, Upton B. *The Jungle.* Cambridge, MA: Robert Bentley, 1905.

Sklar, Martin J. *The Corporate Reconstruction of American Capitalism, 1890–1916: The Market, the Law and Politics.* Cambridge, UK: Cambridge University Press, 1988.

Slater, Robert. *The New GE.* Homewood, IL: Business One Irwin, 1993.

Smith, Hedrick. *Rethinking America.* New York: Random House, 1995.

Sobel, Robert. *IBM vs. Japan: The Struggle for the Future.* New York: Stern and Day Publishers, 1986.

———. *The Age of Giant Corporations. A Microeconomic History of American Business, 1914–1992.* 3rd ed. Westport, CT: Praeger, 1992.

Southwest Organizing Project. *Intel Inside New Mexico: A Case Study of Environmental and Economic Injustice.* Albuquerque, NM: Southwest Organizing Project, 1995.

Soyinka, Wole.*The Open Sore of a Continent: A Personal Narrative of the Nigerian Crisis.* New York: Oxford University Press, 1996.

Spencer, Margaret P. and Ronald R. Sims. *Corporate Misconduct.* Westport, CT: Quorum Books, 1995.

Spiro, George W. *The Legal Environment of Business.* Englewood Cliffs, NJ: Prentice-Hall, 1993.

Stead, W. Edward and Jean Garner Stead. *Management for a Small Plant: Strategic Decision Making and the Environment.* Newbury Park, CA: Sage Publications, 1996.

Stein, Benjamin J. *A License to Steal: The Untold Story of Michael Milkin and the Conspiracy to Bilk the Nation.* New York: Simon & Schuster, 1992.

Steiner, Henry J., Detlev F. Vagts and Harold Hongju Koh. *Transnational Legal Problems*. 4th ed. Westbury, NY: Foundation Press, 1994.

Stevens, Mark. *Sudden Death: The Rise and Fall of E. F. Hutton*. New York: Peguin Books USA, Inc. 1989.

Stone, Christopher. *The GNAT Is Older Than Man: Global Environment and the Human Agenda*. Princeton, NJ: Princeton University Press, 1993.

———. *Where the Law Ends: The Social Control of Corporate Behavior*. New York: Harper & Row, 1975.

Stone, Julius. *Visions of World Order: Between State Power and Human Justice*. Baltimore, MD: Johns Hopkins University Press, 1984.

Stopford, John and Susan Strange with John S. Henley. *Rival States, Rival Firms: Competition for World Market Shares*. Cambridge, UK: Cambridge University Press, 1991.

Strange, Susan. *Casino Capitalism*. New York: Basil Blackwell, 1986.

Strobel, Frederick R. *Upward Dreams, Downward Mobility: The Economic Decline of the American Middle Class*. Lanham, MD: Rowman & Littlefield, 1993.

Strum, Philippa. *Brandeis: Beyond Progressivism*. Lawrence: University Press of Kansas, 1993.

———. *Brandeis on Democracy*. Lawrence: University Press of Kansas, 1995.

———. *Louis D. Brandeis, Justice for the People*. Cambridge, MA: Harvard University Press, 1984.

Sunstein, Cass R. *Free Markets and Social Justice*. New York: Oxford University Press, 1997.

Sutherland, Edwin H. *White Collar Crime: The Uncut Version*. New Haven, CT: Yale University Press, 1983.

Sweeney, John J. *America Needs a Raise*. Boston: Houghton Mifflin Co., 1996.

Taggart, James H. and Michael C. McDermott. *The Essence of International Business*. Englewood Cliffs, NJ: Prentice Hall, 1993.

Tanzi, Vito. *Taxation in an Integrating World*. Washington, DC: The Brookings Institution, 1995.

Tarbell, Ida M. *The Nationalizing of Business, 1878–1898*. New York: Macmillan Co., 1936.

Tasini, Jonathan. *The Edifice Complex: Rebuilding the American Labor Movement to Face the Global Economy*. New York: Labor Research Association, 1995.

Taylor, Graham D. and Patricia E. Sudnik. *DuPont and the International Chemical Industry*. Boston: Twayne Publishers, 1984.

Teichgraber, Richard F. *"Free Trade" and Moral Philosophy: Rethinking the Sources of Adam Smith's Wealth of Nations*. Durham, NC: Duke University Press, 1986.

Thomson, Janice. *Mercenaries, Pirates and Sovereigns: State-Building and Extraterritorial Violence in Early Modern Europe*. Princeton, NJ: Princeton University Press, 1994.

Thurow, Lester C. *The Future of Capitalism*. New York: William Morrow and Co., 1996.

Tichy, Noel M. and Stratford Sherman. *Control Your Destiny or Someone Else Will*. New York: Doubleday Publishing, 1993.

Tiffany, Paul A. *The Decline of American Steel: How Management, Labor and Government Went Wrong*. New York: Oxford University Press, 1985.

Tilman, Rick. *Thorstein Veblen and His Critics, 1891–1963*. Princeton, NJ: Princeton University Press, 1992.

Tobin, James. *Full Employment and Growth: Further Keynesian Essays on Policy*. Cheltenham, UK: Edward Elgar, 1996.

Tokar, Brian. *Earth for Sale: Reclaiming Ecology in the Age of Corporate Greenwash*. Boston: South End Press, 1997.

Tomasko, Robert M. *Downsizing: Reshaping the Corporation for the Future*. New York: Amacom, 1990.

Tonry, Michael and Albert J. Reiss, Jr. (Editors). *Beyond the Law: Crime in Complex Organizations*. Chicago: University of Chicago Press, 1993.

Truell, Peter and Larry Gurwin. *False Profits: The Inside Story of BCCI, the World's Most Corrupt Financial Empire*. Boston: Houghton Mifflin Co., 1992.

Turner, Louis. *Invisible Empires: Multinational Companies and the Modern World*. New York: Harcourt Brace Jovanovich, 1970.

Tyson, Laura D'Andrea. *Who's Bashing Whom? Trade Conflict in High-Technology Industries*. Washington, DC: Institute for International Economics, 1992.

United Nations (UN). *Commission on Transnational Corporations, Report on 17th Session*. New York: United Nations, 1991.

————. *Transnational Corporations in World Development: Trends and Prospects*. New York: United Nations, 1988.

————. *World Investment Report 1995: Transnational Corporations and Competitiveness (UNCTAD)*. New York: United Nations, 1995.

————. *World Investment Report 1997: Transnational Corporations, Market Structure and Competition Policy*. UN Conference on Trade and Development. New York: United Nations, 1997.

Ure, P. N. *The Origin of Tyranny*. New York: Russell & Russell, 1962.

Useem, Michael. *Executive Defense*. Cambridge, MA: Harvard University Press, 1993.

————. *Investor Capitalism: How Money Managers Are Changing the Face of Corporate America*. New York: Basic Books, 1996.

Utton, M. A. *The Political Economy of Big Business*. New York: St. Martin's Press, 1982.

Vernon, Raymond. *Exploring the Global Economy: Emerging Issues in Trade and Investment*. Cambridge, MA: Center for International Affairs, Harvard University and University Press of America, 1985.

————. *Sovereignty at Bay: The Multinational Spread of U.S. Enterprises*. New York: Basic Books, 1971.

————. *Storm over the Multinationals: The Real Issues*. Cambridge, MA: Harvard University Press, 1977.

Vernon, Raymond and Debora L. Spar. *Beyond Globalism: Remaking American Foreign Economic Policy*. New York: The Free Press, 1989.

Vernon, Raymond and Louis T. Wells, Jr. *Manager in the International Economy*. 5th ed. Englewood Cliffs, NJ: Prentice-Hall, 1986.

Vietor, Richard H. K. *Contrived Competition: Regulation and Deregulation in America*. Cambridge, MA: Harvard University Press, 1994.

Vile, John R. *A Companion to the United States Constitution and Its Amendments*. 2nd ed. Westport, CT: Praeger, 1997.

Vogel, David. *Kindred Strangers: The Uneasy Relationship between Politics and Business in America*. Princeton, NJ: Princeton University Press, 1996.

———. *Trading Up: Consumer and Environmental Regulation in a Global Economy.* Cambridge, MA: Harvard University Press, 1995.

Wallerstein, Immanuel. *Historical Capitalism with Capitalist Civilization.* London: Verso, 1983.

Wapner, Paul. *Environmental Activism and World Civil Politics.* Albany: State University of New York Press, 1996.

Wasserstein, Bruce. *Big Deal: The Battle for Control of America's Leading Corporations.* New York: Warner Books, 1998.

Waters, Malcolm. *Globalization.* London: Routledge, 1995.

Weidenbaum, Murray L. *Business and Government in the Global Marketplace.* 5th ed. Englewood Cliffs, NJ: Prentice-Hall, 1995.

Weir, David. *The Bhopal Syndrome.* San Francisco: Sierra Club Books, 1987.

Weiss, Edith Brown. *In Fairness to Future Generations: International Law, Patrimony and Intergenerational Equity.* Dobbs Ferry, NY: United Nations University, Tokyo, and Transnational Publishers, 1989.

Weiss, Edith Brown (Editor). *Environmental Change and International Law: New Challenges and Dimensions.* Tokyo, Japan: United Nations University Press, 1992.

Wells, Celia. *Corporations and Criminal Responsibility.* Oxford, UK: Clarendon Press, 1993.

Wells, Louis T. *Third World Multinationals: The Rise of Foreign Investment from Developing Countries.* Cambridge, MA: MIT Press, 1983.

Wilkins, Mira. *The Maturing of Multinational Enterprise: American Business Abroad from 1914 to 1970.* Cambridge, MA: Harvard University Press, 1974.

Wolff, Edward N. *Top Heavy: A Study of the Increasing Inequality of Wealth in America.* New York: Twentieth Century Fund Press, 1995.

Wood, Adrian. *North-South Trade, Employment and Inequality—Changing Fortune in a Skill-Driven World.* Oxford, UK: Oxford University Press, 1994.

Woodmansee, John. *The World of a Giant Corporation: A Report from the GE Project.* Seattle: North Country, 1975.

Wright, Lesley, and Marti Smye. *Corporate Abuse: How "Lean and Mean" Robs People and Profits.* New York: MacMillan, 1996.

Wriston, Walter B. *The Twilight of Sovereignty: How the Information Revolution Is Transforming Our World.* New York: Charles Scribner's Sons, 1992.

Wu, Yuan-li. *Economic Warfare.* Englewood Cliffs, NJ: Prentice-Hall, 1952.

Yergin, Daniel. *The Prize: The Epic Quest for Oil, Money and Power.* New York: Simon & Schuster, 1991.

Yergin, Daniel and Joseph Stanislaw. *The Commanding Heights: The Battle between Government and the Marketplace that Is Remaking the Modern World.* New York: Simon & Schuster, 1998.

Yoffie, David (Editor). *Beyond Free Trade: Firms, Governments and Global Competition.* Boston: Harvard Business School Press, 1993.

Zeitlin, Maurice. *The Large Corporation and Contemporary Classes.* New Brunswick, NJ: Rutgers University Press, 1989.

Zepezauer, Mark and Arthur Naiman. *Take the Rich off Welfare.* Tuscon, AZ: Odonian Press, 1996.

Zunz, Oliver. *Making America Corporate, 1870–1920*. Chicago: University of Chicago Press, 1990.

JOURNALS AND OTHER MATERIALS

Aceves, William J. "Lost Sovereignty? The Implications of the Uruguay Round Agreements." *Fordham International Law Journal* 19 (1995): 427–474.

Altman, Roger C. "The Force Is with Us." *Seattle-Post Intelligencer* (March 8, 1998): E1.

Aluetta, Ken. "The Next Corporate Order American Keiretsu." *New Yorker* (October 20, 1997): 225–227.

Arlen, Jennifer and Reinier Kraakman. "Controlling Corporate Misconduct: An Analysis of Corporate Liability Regimes." *New York University Law Review* 72 (October 1997): 687–779.

Baker, Mark B. "Private Codes of Corporate Conduct: Should the Fox Guard the Hen House?" *University of Miami InterAmerican Law Review* 24 (1993): 399–433.

Ball, George W. "Cosmocorp: The Importance of Being Stateless." *Columbia Journal of World Business* (1967): 25–30.

Barclays Bank PLC v. Franchise Tax Board of California, 114 S. Ct. 2268 (1994).

Barnet, Harold C. "Can Confrontation, Negotiation, or Socialization Solve the Superfund Enforcement Dilemma?" In *Corporate Crime: Contemporary Debates*, edited by Frank Pearce and Laureen Snider. Toronto, Canada: University of Toronto Press, 1995.

Barnet, Richard J. "Lords of the Global Economy." *The Nation* (December 19, 1994): 754–757.

Barshefsky, Charlene. The United States Trade Representative. Commencement Address, Washington College of Law, American University, Washington, DC, May 24, 1998.

Bell, Daniel. "Downfall of the Business Giants." *Dissent* (Summer 1993): 316–323.

Bentley, Eric, Jr. "Toward an International Fourth Amendment: Rethinking Search and Seizure Abroad after Verdugo-Urquidez." *Vanderbilt Journal of Transnational Law* 27 (1994): 329–417.

Blustein, Paul. "Japan Fines Coke, Alleges That It Understated Income." *Washington Post* (March 26, 1994): G2.

———. "Putting 'Us' in Focus: New Arguments on Going Global." *Washington Post* (January 1, 1997).

Brewer, Thomas L. "International Investment Dispute Settlement Procedures: The Evolving Regime for Foreign Direct Investment." *Law and Policy in International Business* 26 (1995): 633–671.

Brower, Charles N. "Notes from the President—The Society's Program Priority: Compliance with International Law." *American Society of International Law* (January–February 1997).

Campbell, C. J. "Running Out of Gas, This Time the Wolf *Is* Coming." *The National Interest* 51 (Spring 1998): 47–55.

Carpency, Gerald J. "The Valdez Principle: A Corporate Counselor's Perspective." *Wake Forest Law Review* 26 (1991): 11–37.

Carter-Stem, Kathleen. "In Search of Justice: Foreign Victims of Silicone Breast Implants and the Doctrine of Forum Non Conveniens." *Suffolk Transnational Law Review* 18 (1995): 167–195.

Cates, Cynthia L. "Splitting the Atom of Sovereignty: *Term Limits, Inc.'s* Conflicting Views of Popular Autonomy in a Federal Republic." *Publius* 26 (Summer 1996): 127–140.

Charney, Jonathan I. "Transnational Corporations and Developing Public International Law." *Duke Law Journal* (1983): 748–787.

Chinen, Mark A. "Jurisdiction: Foreign Plaintiffs, Forum Non Conveniens, and Litigation Against Multinational Corporations (Union Carbide Corp. Gas Plant Disaster, Bhopal December 1984)." *Harvard International Law Journal* 28 (1987): 202–209.

Chopra, Sudhir K. "Multinational Corporations in the Aftermath of Bhopal: The Need for a New Regime for Transnational Corporate Activity." *Valparaiso University Law Review* 29 (1994): 236–284.

Coffee, John C., Jr. "Beyond the Shut-Eyed Sentry: Toward a Theoretical View of Corporate Misconduct and an Effective Legal Response." *Virginia Law Review* 63 (1977): 1099–1278.

———. "Corporate Crime and Punishment: A Non-Chicago View of the Economics of Criminal Sanctions." *American Criminal Law Review* 17 (1980): 419–476.

———. "Corporate Criminal Responsibility." *Encyclopedia of Crime and Justice*. New York: The Free Press, 1983.

———. "No Soul to Damn; No Body to Kick: An Unscandalized Inquiry Into the Problem of Corporate Punishment." *Michigan Law Review* 79 (1981) 386–450.

———. "Paradigms Lost: The Blurring of the Criminal and Civil Law Models—And What Can Be Done About It." *Yale Law Journal* 101 (1992): 1875–1893.

Cohn, Jonathan. "Decisive Moments." *Mother Jones* (January/February 1997): 50.

Collins, Norman R. and Lee E. Preston. "The Size Structure of the Largest Industrial Firms, 1909–1958." *American Economic Review* 51 (1961): 986–1011.

Curran, John. "GE Capital: Jack Welch's Secret Weapon." *Fortune* (November 10, 1997): 116–132.

Cushman, John H., Jr. "Adversaries Back Pollution Rules Now on the Books." *New York Times* (February 12, 1996): A1.

Davlin, James A. "The Uncertainty of Foreign Blocked Income: Trying to Reconcile the 1994 § 482 Regulations with Procter & Gamble." *Duke Journal of Comparative and International Law* 5 (1994): 117–143.

Del Ponte, Karen G. "Formulating Customary International Law: An Examination of the WHO International Code of Marketing of Breast Milk Substitutes." *Boston College International and Comparative Law Review* 2 (1982): 377–403.

Economist. "The Fall of Big Business." Editorial (April 17–23, 1993): 13–14.

Elliott, Jamie. "Developments in Transfer Pricing." *British Tax Review* 4 (1995): 348–357.

Fahim-Nader, Mahnaz and William J. Zeile. "Foreign Direct Investment in the United States." *Survey of Current Business* (May 1995): 57–81.

Farhi, Paul. "Murdoch Empire Finds Business Not So Strong." *Washington Post* (December 7, 1997).

Fialka, John J. "Senate GOP Leaders Offer Bill to Limit Liabilities of Some Super Fund Suits." *Wall Street Journal* (January 23, 1997): B6.

Fortune. "Gentlemen, Start Your Engines: Daimler-Benz's Schrempp and Chrysler's

Eaton Discuss Their Deal and the Auto Industry's Future.'' (June 8, 1998): 138–146.

Fortune. "Global 500." (August 5, 1996).

Fowler, Robert J. "International Environmental Standards for Transnational Corporations." *Environmental Law* 25 (1995): 1–30.

Fox, Eleanor M. "Toward World Antitrust and Market Access." *American Journal of International Law* 91 (January 1997): 1–25.

Frankel, Glenn. "In Ex-Soviet Markets, U.S. Brands Took on Role of Capitalist Liberator." *Washington Post* (November 19, 1996).

———. "Thailand Resists U.S. Brand Assault." *Washington Post* (November 18, 1996).

———. "U.S. Aided Cigarette Firms on Conquests Across Asia." *Washington Post* (November 17, 1996).

———. "Vast China Market Key to Smoking Disputes." *Washington Post* (November 20, 1996).

Friedland, Jonathan and Raphael Pura. "Troubled at Home, Asian Timber Firms Set Sights on the Amazon." *Wall Street Journal* (November 11, 1996): A1, A10.

Friedman, Milton. "Milton Friedman on Hong Kong's Future." *Wall Street Journal* (February 12, 1997): A16.

Friedman, Thomas L. "Revolt of the Wannabes." *New York Times* (February 7, 1996): A19.

Friedman, Wolfgang G. "Corporate Power, Government by Private Groups and the Law." *Columbia Law Review* 57 (1957): 155–186.

Fromm, Eva M. "Commanding Respect: Criminal Sanctions for Environmental Crimes." *St. Mary's Law Journal* 21 (1990): 821–864.

Geist, Michael A. "Toward a General Agreement on the Regulation of Foreign Direct Investment." *Law and Policy in International Business* 26 (1995): 673–717.

Gray, Cheryl W. and William W. Jarosz. "Law and Regulation of Foreign Direct Investment: The Experience of Central and Eastern Europe." *Columbia Journal of Transnational Law* 33 (1995): 1–40.

Greider, William. "Global Warning, Curbing the Free-Trade Free Fall." *The Nation* (January 13–20, 1997): 11–17.

———. "Saving the Global Economy." *The Nation* (December 15, 1997): 11–16.

———. "Why the Mighty General Electric Can't Strike Out." *Rolling Stone* (April 21, 1994): 36.

Grossman, Claudio and Daniel D. Bradlow. "Are We Being Propelled Towards a People-Centered Transnational Legal Order?" *American University Journal of International Law and Policy* 9 (1993): 1–25.

Grossman, Richard L. "Revoking the Corporation." *Journal of Environmental Law and Litigation* 11 (1996): 141–152.

Grossman, Richard L. and Frank T. Adams. *Taking Care of Business: Citizenship and the Charter of Incorporation.* Cambridge, MA: Charter, Ink./CSPP, 1993.

Guzzardi, Walter, Jr. "Business Is Learning to Win in Washington." *Fortune* (March 27, 1978): 53–58.

Hansen, Patricia I. "The Impact of the WTO and NAFTA on U.S. Law." *Journal of Legal Education* 46 (December 1996): 569–578.

Harmon, James D., Jr. "Rico Meets Keiretsu: A Response to Predatory Transfer Pricing." *Vanderbilt Journal of Transnational Law* 25 (1992): 3–36.

Henkoff, Ronald. "My Life as a Mole" (Mark Whitacre Interview). *Fortune* (September 5, 1995).

Hines, James R., Jr. "Tax Policy and the Activities of Multinational Corporations." NBER Working Paper Services. Cambridge, MA: National Bureau of Economic Research, 1996.

Hu, Yao-Su. "Global or Stateless Corporations Are National Firms with International Operations." *California Management Review* (Winter 1992): 107–126.

Huff, Kevin B. "The Role of Corporate Compliance Programs in Determining Corporate Criminal Liability: A Suggested Approach." *Columbia Law Review* 96 (1996): 1252–1298.

Huntington, Samuel P. "The Clash of Civilizations?" *Foreign Affairs* 72 (1993): 22–49.

Husain, Zain E. "Barclays Bank PLC v. Franchise Tax Board of California: Does the Application of Worldwide Unitary Taxation to Non-U.S. Parent Corporate Groups Violate the Commerce Clause?" *Fordham International Law Review* 18 (1995): 1475–1525.

International Labour Office (ILO). *Child Labour: Targeting the Intolerable.* International Labour Office, Geneva, Switzerland, 1996a.

———. *World Employment 1995.* International Labour Office, Geneva, Switzerland, 1995.

———. *World Employment 1996/1997: National Policies in a Global Context.* International Labour Office, Geneva, Switzerland, 1996b.

Johns, Fleur. "The Invisibility of the Transnational Corporation: An Analysis of International Law and Legal Theory. *Melbourne University Law Review* 19 (1994): 893–923.

Kamel, Rachael. *The Global Factory: Analysis and Action for a New Economic Era.* Omega Press, 1990.

Kapstein, Ethan B. "We Are US—The Myth of the Multinational." *The National Interest* (Winter 1991/1992): 55–62.

Karp, Adam. "China Must Not Wait Until the Evening: Resisting Mass Motorization's Assault on Bicycles and Mass Transit." *Pacific Rim Law and Policy Journal* 6, No. 3 (1997): 717–753.

Kaufman, Henry. "Preventing the Next Global Financial Crisis." *Washington Post* (January 28, 1998).

Kelly, Marjorie. "30's Editors Were Sure Economy Needed Government Involvement— Now Have We Developed a Case of Global Amnesia?" *Star Tribune* (February 24, 1997): D3.

Koenig, Peter. "If Europe Is Dead, Why Is GE Investing Billions There?" *Fortune* (September 9, 1996).

Kofele-Kale, Ndiva. "Patrimonicide: The International Economic Crime of Indigenous Spoliation." *Vanderbilt Journal of Transnational Law* 28 (1995): 45–118.

Kotkin, Joel and David Friedman. "As Wall Street Pats Itself on the Back, Trouble Lurks Behind the Boom." *Washington Post* (May 24, 1998): C1.

Kristol, Irving. "On Corporate Capitalism in America." *Public Interest* 41 (Fall 1975): 124–141.

Kuttner, Robert. "The Corporation in America." *Dissent* (Winter 1993): 35–49.

Lehner, Urban C. "Money Hungry." *Wall Street Journal* (September 18, 1997): R1, R28.

Leiken, Robert S. "Controlling the Global Corruption Epidemic." *Foreign Policy* 105 (Winter 1996–97): 55–73.

Lenzer, Robert and Stephen S. Johnson. "Seeing Things As They Really Are" (Interview of Peter F. Drucker). *Forbes* (March 10, 1997): 122–128.

Levinson, Jerome I. "Review of Global Dreams." *Law and Policy in International Business* 27 (1996): 513–539.

Lewis, Kenneth. "Second Thoughts on Free Trade." *New York Times* (July 13, 1997).

Lohr, Steve. "Though Upbeat on the Economy, People Still Fear for Their Jobs." *New York Times* (December 29, 1997): 1, 22.

LoPucki, Lynn M. "The Death of Liability." *Yale Law Journal* 106 (1996): 1–89.

Louis K. Liggett Company v. J. M. Lee, 288 U.S. 517–586 (1932).

Mander, Jerry. "The Dark Side of Globalization." *The Nation* (July 15–22, 1996): 10.

Mann, Judy. "America's Bottom-Line Blues." *Washington Post* (January 12, 1996): E3.

Mann, Kenneth. "Punitive Civil Sanctions: the Middle Ground Between Criminal and Civil Law." *Yale Law Review* 101 (1992): 1796–1871.

Mann, Michael A., Daniel J. Atherton et al. "U.S. International Sales and Purchases of Private Services." *Survey of Current Business* 76 (November 1996): 70–81.

Mason, James R., Jr. "PSSST, Hey Buddy, Wanna Buy a Country? An Economic and Political Policy Analysis of Federal and State Laws Governing Foreign Ownership of United States Real Estate." *Vanderbilt Journal of Transnational Law* 27 (1994): 454–488.

Mataloni, Raymond J., Jr. "A Guide to BEA Statistics on U.S. Multinational Companies." *Survey of Current Business* (March 1995): 38–55, and (June 1995).

Mataloni, Raymond J., Jr. and Mahnaz Fahim-Nader. "Operations of U.S. Multinational Companies: Preliminary Results from the 1994 Benchmark Survey." *Survey of Current Business* 76 (December 1996): 11–37.

Mathews, Jessica T. "Power Shift." *Foreign Affairs* 76 (1997): 50–66.

Miller, Arthur S. "The Corporation as a Private Government in the World Community. *Virginia Law Review* 46 (1960) 1539–1572.

Miller, Bill. "New Sentencing Rules for Corporations: The Politics of Punishment." Unpublished paper. Washington, DC: American University, June 1992.

Mintzberg, Henry. "Managing Government—Governing Management." *Harvard Business Review* (May-June 1996): 75–83.

Morris, Betsy. "Roberto Goizveta and Jack Welch: The Wealth Builders." *Fortune* (December 11, 1995): 80–94.

Mother Jones. "The *Mother Jones* 400." (March/April 1996): 38–59.

Mueller, Gerhard O. W. "*Mens Rea* and the Corporation: A Study of the Model Penal Code Position on Corporate Crime Liability." *University of Pittsburgh Law Review* 19 (1957): 21–50.

Mullen, Eileen M. "Rotating Japanese Managers in American Subsidiaries of Japanese Firms: A Challenge for American Employment Discrimination Law." *Stanford Law Review* 45 (1993): 725–782.

Muller v. Oregon, 208 U.S. 412 (1908).

Multinational Monitor. "Labor vs. Captial." *Multinational Monitor* 18 (March 1997): Entire issue.

Murray, Matt. "GE Sees $100 Billion in 1998 Revenue Due to Quality Control, Asia Investment." *Wall Street Journal* (April 23, 1998): A4.

Neal, Terry M. "Cleanup Measure Passes in MD." *Washington Post* (February 19, 1997): B1–5.

Noah, Timothy. "House Plan Would Cut Firms' Cleanup Liability." *Wall Street Journal* (February 13, 1996): A2.

North, Douglass C. "Economic Performance Through Time." *American Economic Review* (June 1994): 359–368.

O'Connor, Marleen A. "The Human Capital Era: Reconceptualizing Corporate Law to Facilitate Labor-Management Cooperation." *Cornell Law Review* 78 (1993): 899–965.

Organization for Economic Cooperation and Development. "Multilateral Agreement on Investment." (January 13, 1997). Draft.

Oswald, Lynda J. "Strict Liability of Individuals Under CERCLA: A Normative Analysis." *Environmental Affairs* 20 (1993): 579–637.

Parry, Robert. "Dole: What Wouldn't Bob Do for Koch Oil?" *The Nation* (August 26–November 2, 1996): 11–17.

Pasztor, Andy and Stacy Kravetz. "UNOCAL Is Shifting Strategy to International Operations with Tosco Deal: Quintessential California Oil Firm Sees Future Abroad." *Wall Street Journal* (November 20, 1996): B4.

Pauly, Louis W. and Simon Reich. "National Structures and Multinational Corporate Behavior: Enduring Differences in the Age of Globalization." *International Organization* 51, No. 1 (Winter 1997): 1–30.

Perez-Lopez, Jorge F. "Labor and the North American Free Trade Agreement." *Dickinson Journal of International Law* 11 (1993): 565–578.

Pfaff, William. "It Isn't Working—Globalization and the New Capitalism Are Not Delivering the Utopia They Promised." *Notre Dame Magazine* (Autumn 1996): 23–27.

Phillips, Don. "U.S. Officials Troubled by New Airline Alliances." *Washington Post* (April 25, 1998): A1.

Pincus, Laura B., Theodore H. Pincus and Michael Reid. "Legal Issues Involved in Corporate Globalization." *Columbia Business Law Review* 2 (1991): 269–285.

Public Citizen. "Public Citizen's Global Trade Watch, NAFTA's Broken Promises: The Border Betrayed." Washington, DC: Public Citizen Publications, January 1996.

Public Citizen. "Public Citizen's Global Trade Watch, NAFTA's Broken Promises: Failure to Create U.S. Jobs." Washington, DC: Public Citizen Publications, February 1997.

Rappoport, Sloan. "NAFTA and the Petrochemical Industry: A Disastrous Combination for Life at the U.S.–Mexico Border." *Dickinson Journal of International Law* 11 (1993): 579–604.

Reich, Robert B. "Who Is Us?" *Harvard Business Review* 68 (January–February 1990): 53–64.

Roehrdanz, Charles O. "Reducing the U.S.–Japan Trade Deficit by Eliminating Japanese Barriers to Foreign Direct Investment." *Minnesota Journal of Global Trade* 4 (Winter 1995): 305–332.

Rowe, Lawrence J. "NAFTA, The Border Area Environmental Program and Mexico's Border Area: Prescription for Sustainable Development." *Suffolk Transnational Law Review* 18 (1995): 197–235.

Rubin, Seymour J. "Transnational Corporations and International Codes of Conduct: A Study of the Relationship Between International Legal Cooperation and Economic

Development." *American University Journal of International Law and Policy* 10 (1995): 1275–1293.

Safire, William. "Crony Capitalism." *New York Times Magazine* (February 1, 1998): 16.

Scaperlanda, Anthony. "Trade in the 1990's: Is an International Organization for Multinational Enterprises Needed?" *Northern Illinois University Law Review* 14 (1994): 421–438.

Schoenberger, Karl. "Motorola Bets Big on China." *Fortune* (May 27, 1996): 116–124.

Scholl, Russell B. "The International Investment Position of the United States in 1994." *Survey of Current Business* 75 (June 1995): 52–60.

Secor, Glen M. "Runaway Plants, Runaway Tax Policy: The Continuing Debate Over the Taxation of Controlled Foreign Corporations." *Suffolk Transnational Law Review* 16 (1992): 200–227.

Shaikh, Rashid A. "The Dilemmas of Advanced Technology for the Third World." *Technology Review* 89, No. 3 (April 1986).

Shelley, Louise I. "Crime and Corruption in the Digital Age." *Journal of International Affairs* 51, No. 2 (Spring 1998): 605–620.

———. "Criminal Kaleidoscope: The Diversification and Adaptation of Criminal Activities in the Soviet Successor State." *European Journal of Crime, Criminal Law and Criminal Justice* (1996): 243–356.

———. "Eradicating Crime Groups." *Foreign Service Journal* (September 1997): 18–23.

———. "Transnational Organized Crime: An Imminent Threat to the Nation-State?" *Journal of International Affairs* 48, No. 2 (Winter 1995).

Shirouzu, Norihiko. "Ex-Daiwa Trader Alleges 'Double-Cross'." *Wall Street Journal* (January 1, 1997): A18.

Soros, George. "The Capitalist Threat." *Atlantic Monthly* (February 1997): 45–58.

Steiner, Robert. "Japan's Tax Man Leans on Foreign Firms—Coke, Goodyear Charged with Moving Profit Abroad." *Wall Street Journal* (November 25, 1996).

Steinmetz, Greg and Matt Marshall. "How a Chemical Giant Goes About Becoming a Lot Less German." *Wall Street Journal* (February 18, 1997).

Stern, Brigette. "The Changing Role of States." Unpublished Speech, 1996.

Stone, Christopher. "The Place of Enterprise Liability in the Control of Corporate Conduct." *Yale Law Journal* 90 (1980): 1–77.

Sugawara, Sandra. "With Billions in Sales At Stake, Boeing Goes to Bat for China." *Washington Post* (July 11, 1996): H1.

Survey of Current Business. "U.S. International Sales and Purchases of Private Services." November 1996: 70–81.

Survey of Current Business. "Operation of U.S. Multinational Companies: Preliminary Results from the Benchmark Survey." December 1996: 11–37.

Survey of Current Business. "U.S. Multinational Companies: Operations in 1992." June 1994: 42–62.

Swardson, Anne. "Global Investment Accord Put on Hold." *Washington Post* (April 29, 1998): C13.

Taylor, Allyn L. "An International Regulatory Strategy for Global Tobacco Control." *Yale Journal of International Law* 21 (1996): 258–304.

Thompson, Robert B. "Piercing the Corporate Veil: An Empirical Study." *Cornell Law Review* 76 (1991): 1036–1074.

Timberg, Sigmund. "An International Trade Tribunal—A Step Forward Short of Surrender of Sovereignty." *Georgetown Law Journal* 33 (1945): 373.

———. "Corporate Fictions, Logical, Social and International Implications." *Columbia Law Review* 46 (1946): 533–580.

———. "International Combines and National Sovereigns." *University of Pennsylvania Law Review* 95 (1947): 575–620.

———. "The Corporation As a Technique of International Administration." *University of Chicago Law Review* 19 (1952): 739–758.

Torres, Craig. "Foreigners Snap Up Mexican Companies: Impact Is Enormous." *Wall Street Journal* (September 30, 1997).

Troy, G. L. "Money and Politics, The Oldest Connection." *Wilson Quarterly* (Summer 1997): 14–32.

Trubeck, David M., Yves Dezalay, Ruth Buchanan and John R. Davis. "Global Restructuring and the Law: Studies of the Internationalization of Legal Fields and the Creation of Transnational Arenas." *Case Western Reserve Law Review* (1994): 407–498.

Turley, Jonathan. "When in Rome: Multinational Misconduct and the Presumption Against Extraterritoriality." *Northwestern University Law Review* 84 (1990): 598–664.

Uchitelle, Louis. "Global Tug, National Tether: As Companies Look Overseas, Governments Hold the Strings." *New York Times* (April 30, 1998): D-1.

———. "Like Oil and Water: A Tale of Two Economists." *New York Times* (February 16, 1997).

———. "More Downsized Workers Are Returning as Rentals." *New York Times* (December 8, 1996): 1, 34.

United States Congress, Office of Technology Assessment (OTA). "Multinationals and the National Interest: Playing by Different Rules." OTA-ITE-569. Washington, DC: U.S. Government Printing Office, September 1993.

United States Department of Commerce, Bureau of Census. "World Population Profile, 1994." Washington, DC: U.S. Government Printing Office, February 1994.

United States General Accounting Office (U.S. GAO) "Money Laundering." Washington, DC: GAO/GGD-96–105, May 1996.

United States General Accounting Office (U.S. GAO). "Report to Congressional Requestors, International Taxation, Transfer Pricing and Information on Nonpayment of Tax." Washington, DC: GAO/GGD-95–101, April 1995.

United States General Accounting Office (U.S. GAO) "Report to Senator Byron L. Dorgan, Tax Policy and Administration, California Taxes as Multinational Corporations and Related Federal Issues." Washington, DC: GAO/GGD-95–171, July 1995.

United States House of Representatives. 102nd Congress, 2nd Session. "Illegal Military Assistance to Israel." Hearing July 29, 1992. Washington, DC: U.S. Government Printing Office, 1993.

United States Senate, Committee on Governmental Affairs. 98th Congress, 1st Session. "Staff Study of the Crime and Secrecy: The Use of Offshore Banks and Companies." Washington, DC: U.S. Government Printing Office, 1983.

United States Senate, Committee on Governmental Affairs, 103rd Congress, 1st Session. "The Breakdown of IRS Tax Enforcement Regarding Multinational Corporations: Revenue Losses, Excessive Litigation and Unfair Burdens for U.S. Producers."

Hearing March 25, 1993. Washington, DC: U.S. Government Printing Office, 1993.

United States Senate, Committee on Labor and Human Resources, 103rd Congress, 2nd Session. "Child Labor and the New Global Marketplace: Reaping Profits at the Expense of Children?" Hearing September 21, 1994. Washington, DC: U.S. Government Printing Office, 1994.

United States v. GE, 808 F. Supp. 580, 1992.

United States v. Nippon Paper Industries, 103 F. 3d. 1 (USCA 1st Circuit, Boston, March 17, 1997).

Vagts, Detlev F. "The Multinational Enterprise: A New Challenge for Transnational Law." *Harvard Law Review* 83 (1970): 739–792.

Wald, Matthew L. "Oil Imports Are Up: Fretting About It Is Down." *New York Times* (January 26, 1997).

Wall Street Journal. "Commercial Corruption." Editorial. January 2, 1997.

Walsh, Charles J. and Alissa Pyrich. "Corporate Compliance Programs as a Defense to Criminal Liability: Can a Corporation Save Its Soul?" *Rutgers Law Review* 47 (1995): 606–691.

Washington Post. "Misstep on the Environment." Editorial (January 29, 1996): A8.

Weissman, Robert. "Stolen Youth: Brutalized Children, Globalization and the Campaign to End Child Labor."*Multinational Monitor* (February 1997): 10–16.

Werder, Richard I., Jr. "A Critical Assessment of Intracorporate Loss Shifting After Prosecutions Based on Criminal Wrongdoing." *Delaware Journal of Corporate Law* 18 (1993): 35–63.

Werlau, Maria C. "Foreign Investment in Cuba, the Limits of Commercial Engagement." *World Affairs* 160 (1997): 51–69.

Wessel, David and John Harwood. "Capitalism Is Giddy with Triumph: Is It Possible to Overdo It?" *Wall Street Journal* (May 14, 1998): A1.

Whalley, John and Colleen Hamilton. "The Intellectual Underpinnings of North American Economic Integration." *Minnesota Journal of Global Trade* 4 (1995): 43–77.

Woodrow Wilson Conference on International Trade, Washington, DC, April 17, 1998.

World Bank. "Workers in an Integrating World." *World Development Report*. New York: Oxford University Press, 1995.

Wray, Christopher A. "Corporate Probation Under the New Organizational Sentencing Guidelines." *Yale Law Journal* 101 (1992): 2017–2042.

Zachary, G. Pascal. "Estimate of Child-Labor Levels Triples." *Wall Street Journal* (November 12, 1996): A2.

Name Index

Adams, Walter, 38
Albert, Michel, 77
Alexander, Titus, 250
Altman, Roger C., 78
Andreas, Dwayne O., 218, 220
Andreas, Michael D., 218, 220
Annan, Kofi A., 258

Bailey, David, 152, 173–174, 195, 250, 255
Ball, George W., 57
Barlett, Donald L., 227–228
Barlow, Maude, 4
Barsotti, Charles, 145
Barzun, Jacques, 2
Beer, Samuel H., 55, 65–68, 74
Berle, Adolph A., Jr., 37–38
Bhagwati, Jagdish, 184, 187
Bhattacharja, A., 207
Bialos, Jeffrey P., 225
Blankenship, Michael B., 201
Blecker, Robert A., 123
Bluestone, Barry, 21
Blumberg, Phillip I., 61, 180–182, 190, 195, 226
Bowman, Scott R., 12, 68
Boyer, Robert, 153, 249
Braithwaite, John, 201

Brandeis, Louis D., 34–35, 37–38, 40, 95–96
Braudel, Fernand, 80–82, 144
Brickey, Kathlen F., 201
Brock, James W., 38
Buchman, Patrick J., 69, 90
Bull, Hedley, 69–71, 168–169, 195
Bunck, Julie M., 46–47
Bush, George, 44

Calhoun, John C., 65
Campbell, C. J., 111
Carson, Rachel L., 243–245
Caufield, Catherine, 271
Cavanagh, John, 43, 258
Chandler, Alfred D., 41, 45, 100, 254
Chayes, Abraham, 172–173
Chayes, Antonia Handler, 172–173, 195
Clarke, Tony, 121, 251, 277
Cleveland, Harlan, 170–171, 194
Clinard, Marshall B., 39, 201, 204–205
Clinton, William J., 30, 33, 38, 69, 82, 104, 142, 198, 229
Cobden, Richard, 57
Cochrane, James L., 209
Coffee, John C., Jr., 200–201
Cohen, Stephen D., 123

Subject Index

About the Author

DAVID J. SAARI has taught in the School of Public Affairs, American University, Washington, DC, for more than 25 years. He also consults for management in government and industry. Among his many articles and books are *Too Much Liberty? Perspectives on Freedom and the American Dream* (Praeger, 1995), *The Court and Free-Lance Reporter Profession: Improved Management Strategies* (Quorum, 1988), and *American Court Management: Theories and Practices* (Quorum, 1982).